Poetical Works

OF

LORD BYRON.

The Armenian Convent, Venice.

From a photograph by R. Oswald Smith.

Walker & Cockerell, Ph. Sc.

The Works

OF

LORD BYRON.

A NEW, REVISED AND ENLARGED EDITION
WITH ILLUSTRATIONS.

Poetry.   Vol. VII.

EDITED BY

ERNEST HARTLEY COLERIDGE, M.A.,

HON. F.R.S.L.

LONDON:
JOHN MURRAY, ALBEMARLE STREET.
NEW YORK: CHARLES SCRIBNER'S SONS.
1904.

PREFACE TO
THE SEVENTH VOLUME.

<hr/>

OF the seventy-three "Epigrams and Jeux d'Esprit," which are printed at the commencement of this volume, forty-five were included in Murray's one-volume edition of 1837, eighteen have been collected from various publications, and ten are printed and published for the first time.

The "Devil's Drive," which appears in Moore's *Letters and Journals*, and in the sixth volume of the Collected Edition of 1831 as an "Unfinished Fragment" of ninety-seven lines, is now printed and published for the first time in its entirety (248 lines), from a MS. in the possession of the Earl of Ilchester. "A Farewell Petition to J. C. H. Esq.;" "My Boy Hobbie O;" "[Love and Death];" and "Last Words on Greece," are reprinted from the first volume of *Murray's Magazine* (1887).

A few imperfect and worthless poems remain in MS. ;

but with these and one or two other unimportant exceptions, the present edition of the Poetical Works may
be regarded as complete.

In compiling a "Bibliography of the successive Editions
and Translations of Lord Byron's Poetical Works," I have
endeavoured, in the first instance, to give a full and
particular account of the collected editions and separate
issues of the poems and dramas which were open to
my inspection; and, secondly, to extract from general
bibliographies, catalogues of public and private libraries,
and other sources bibliographical records of editions
which I have been unable to examine, and were known
to me only at second-hand.   It will be observed that
the *title-pages* of editions which have passed through my
hands are aligned; the *titles* of all other editions are
italicized.

I cannot pretend that this assortment of bibliographical entries is even approximately exhaustive; but
as "a sample" of a bibliography it will, I trust, with
all its imperfections, be of service to the student of
literature, if not to the amateur or bibliophile.   With
regard to nomenclature and other technicalities, my aim
has been to put the necessary information as clearly
and as concisely as possible, rather than to comply
with the requirements of this or that formula.   But
the path of the bibliographer is beset with difficulties.
"Al Sirat's arch"—"the bridge of breadth narrower
than the thread of a famished spider, and sharper than

the edge of a sword" (see *The Giaour*, line 483, *note* 1)—
affords an easier and a safer foothold.

To the general reader a bibliography says little or
nothing; but, in one respect, a bibliography of Byron
is of popular import. It affords scientific proof of an
almost unexampled fame, of a far-reaching and still
potent influence. Teuton and Latin and Slav have taken
Byron to themselves, and have made him their own.
No other English poet except Shakespeare has been so
widely read and so frequently translated. Of *Manfred*
I reckon one Bohemian translation, two Danish, two
Dutch, three French, nine German, three Hungarian,
three Italian, two Polish, one Romaic, one Roumanian,
four Russian, and three Spanish translations, and, in
all probability, there are others which have escaped my
net. The question, the inevitable question, arises—
What was, what is, the secret of Byron's Continental
vogue? and why has his fame gone out into all lands?
Why did Goethe enshrine him, in the second part of
Faust, "as the representative of the modern era . . .
undoubtedly to be regarded as the greatest genius of
our century?" (*Conversations of Goethe*, 1874, p. 265).

It is said, and with truth, that Byron's revolutionary
politics commended him to oppressed nationalities and
their sympathizers; that he was against "the tramplers"
—Castlereagh, and the Duke of Wellington, and the
Holy Alliance; that he stood for liberty. Another point
in his favour was his freedom from cant, his indifference

to the pieties and proprieties of the Britannic Muse; that he had the courage of his opinions. Doubtless in a time of trouble he was welcomed as the champion of revolt, but deeper reasons must be sought for an almost exclusive preference for the works of one poet and a comparative indifference to the works of his rivals and contemporaries. He fulfilled another, perhaps a greater ideal. An Englishman turns to poetry for the expression in beautiful words of his happier and better feelings, and he is not contented unless poetry tends to make him happier or better—happier because better than he would be otherwise. His favourite poems are psalms, or at least metrical paraphrases, of life. Men of other nations are less concerned about their feelings and their souls. They regard the poet as the creator, the inventor, the maker *par excellence*, and he who can imagine or make the greatest *eidolon* is the greatest poet. *Childe Harold* and *The Corsair*, *Mazeppa* and *Manfred*, *Cain* and *Sardanapalus* were new creations, new types, forms more real than living man, which appealed to their artistic sense, and led their imaginations captive. "It is a mark," says Goethe (*Aus meinem Leben: Dichtung und Wahreit*, 1876, iii. 125), "of true poetry, that, as a secular gospel, it knows how to free us from the earthly burdens which press upon us, by inward serenity, by outward charm. . . . The most lively, as well as the gravest works have the same end—to moderate both pleasure and pain through a happy mental representation."

It is passion translated into action, the pageantry of history, the transfiguration into visible lineaments of living moods and breathing thoughts which are the notes of this "secular gospel," and for one class of minds work out a secular redemption.

It was not only the questionable belief that he was on the side of the people, or his ethical and theological audacities, or his prolonged Continental exile, which won for Byron a greater name abroad than he has retained at home; but the character of his poetry. "The English may think of Byron as they please" (*Conversations of Goethe*, 1874, p. 171), "but this is certain, that they can show no poet who is to be compared to him. He is different from all the others, and, for the most part, greater." The English may think of him as they please! and for them, or some of them, there is "a better œnomel," a *vinum Dæmonum*, which Byron has not in his gift. The evidence of a world-wide fame will not endear a poet to a people and a generation who care less for the matter than the manner of verse, or who *believe* in poetry as the symbol or "*credo*" of the imagination or the spirit; but it should arrest attention and invite inquiry. A bibliography is a dull epilogue to a poet's works, but it speaks with authority, and it speaks last. *Finis coronat opus!*

I must be permitted to renew my thanks to Mr. G. F. Barwick, *Superintendent of the Reading Room*, Mr. Cyril Davenport, and other officials of the British Museum, of all grades and classes, for their generous and courteous assistance in the preparation and completion of the Bibliography. The consultation of many hundreds of volumes of one author, and the permission to retain a vast number in daily use, have entailed exceptional labour on a section of the staff. I have every reason to be grateful.

I am indebted to Mr. A. W. Pollard, of the British Museum, for advice and direction with regard to bibliographical formulæ; to Mr. G. L. Calderon, late of the staff, for the collection and transcription of the title-pages of Polish, Russian, and Servian translations; and to Mr. R. Nisbet Bain for the supervision and correction of the proofs of Slavonic titles.

To Mr. W. P. Courtney, the author of *Bibliotheca Cornubiensis*, I owe many valuable hints and suggestions, and the opportunity of consulting some important works of reference.

I have elsewhere acknowledged the valuable information with regard to certain rare editions and pamphlets which I have received from Mr. H. Buxton Forman, C.B.

My especial thanks for laborious researches undertaken on my behalf, and for information not otherwise attainable, are due to M. J. E. Aynard, of Lyons; Signor F. Bianco; Professor Max von Förster, of Würtzburg; Professor Lajos Gurnesovitz, of Buda Pest; Dr. Holzhausen, of Bonn; Mr. Leonard Mackall, of Berlin; Miss Peacock; Miss K. Schlesinger; M. Voynich, of Soho

Square; Mr. Theodore Bartholomew, of the University Library of Cambridge; Mr. T. D. Stewart, of the Croydon Public Library; and the Librarians of Trinity College, Cambridge, and University College, St. Andrews.

I have also to thank, for special and generous assistance, Mr. J. P. Anderson, late of the British Museum, the author of the "Bibliography of Byron's Works" attached to the *Life of Lord Byron* by the Hon. Roden Noel (1890); Miss Grace Reed, of Philadelphia, for bibliographical entries of early American editions; and Professor Vladimir Hrabar, of the University of Dorpat, for the collection and transcription of numerous Russian translations of Byron's Works.

To Messrs. Clowes, the printers of these volumes, and to their reader, Mr. F. T. Peachey, I am greatly indebted for the transcription of Slavonic titles included in the Summary of the Bibliography, and for interesting and useful information during the progress of the work.

In conclusion, I must once more express my acknowment of the industry and literary ability of my friend Mr. F. E. Taylor, of Chertsey, who has read the proofs of this and the six preceding volumes.

The Index is the work of Mr. C. Eastlake Smith.

ERNEST HARTLEY COLERIDGE.

November, 1903.

CONTENTS OF VOL. VII.

— ◦◦◦ —

LIST OF ILLUSTRATIONS.

—•◦•—

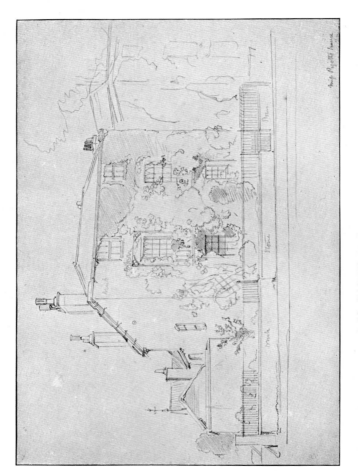

MRS. PIGOTT'S HOUSE, SOUTHWELL.

[To face p. xx.

JEUX D'ESPRIT AND MINOR POEMS, 1798–1824.

EPIGRAM ON AN OLD LADY WHO HAD SOME CURIOUS NOTIONS RESPECTING THE SOUL.

In Nottingham county there lives at Swan Green,[1]
As curst an old Lady as ever was seen;
And when she does die, which I hope will be soon,
She firmly believes she will go to the Moon!

1798.
[First published, *Letters and Journals*, 1830, i. 28.]

EPITAPH ON JOHN ADAMS, OF SOUTHWELL,

A CARRIER, WHO DIED OF DRUNKENNESS.

John Adams lies here, of the parish of Southwell,
A *Carrier* who *carried* his can to his mouth well;

1. ["Swan Green" should be "Swine Green." It lay about a quarter of a mile to the east of St. James's Lane, where Byron lodged in 1799, at the house of a Mr. Gill. The name appears in a directory of 1799, but by 1815 it had been expunged or changed *euphoniæ gratiâ*. (See *A New Plan of the Town of Nottingham, . . .* 1744.)
   Moore took down "these rhymes" from the lips of Byron's nurse, May Gray, who regarded them as a first essay in the direction of poetry. He questioned their originality.]

He carried so much and he carried so fast,
He could carry no more—so was carried at last;
For the liquor he drank being too much for one,
He could not *carry* off;—so he's now *carri-on.*

September, 1807.
[First published, *Letters and Journals*, 1830, i. 106.]

A VERSION OF OSSIAN'S ADDRESS TO THE SUN.

FROM THE POEM "CARTHON."

O Thou! who rollest in yon azure field,
Round as the orb of my forefather's shield,
Whence are thy beams?   From what eternal store
Dost thou, O Sun! thy vast effulgence pour?
In awful grandeur, when thou movest on high,
The stars start back and hide them in the sky;
The pale Moon sickens in thy brightening blaze,
And in the western wave avoids thy gaze.
Alone thou shinest forth—for who can rise
Companion of thy splendour in the skies!
The mountain oaks are seen to fall away—
Mountains themselves by length of years decay—
With ebbs and flows is the rough Ocean tost;
In heaven the Moon is for a season lost,
But thou, amidst the fullness of thy joy,
The same art ever, blazing in the sky!
When tempests wrap the world from pole to pole,
When vivid lightnings flash and thunders roll,
Thou far above their utmost fury borne,
Look'st forth in beauty, laughing them to scorn.
But vainly now on me thy beauties blaze—
Ossian no longer can enraptured gaze!

MRS. BIRDMERE'S HOUSE, SOUTHWELL.

[To face p. 2.

Whether at morn, in lucid lustre gay,
On eastern clouds thy yellow tresses play,
Or else at eve, in radiant glory drest,
Thou tremblest at the portals of the west,
I see no more!   But thou mayest fail at length,
Like Ossian lose thy beauty and thy strength,
Like him—but for a season—in thy sphere
To shine with splendour, then to disappear!
Thy years shall have an end, and thou no more
Bright through the world enlivening radiance pour,
But sleep within thy clouds, and fail to rise,
Heedless when Morning calls thee to the skies!
Then now exult, O Sun! and gaily shine,
While Youth and Strength and Beauty all are thine.
For Age is dark, unlovely, as the light
Shed by the Moon when clouds deform the night,
Glimmering uncertain as they hurry past.
Loud o'er the plain is heard the northern blast,
Mists shroud the hills, and 'neath the growing gloom,
The weary traveller shrinks and sighs for home.

1806.
[First published, *Atlantic Monthly*, December, 1898.] [1]

1. [I am indebted to the courtesy of Mr. Pierre De La Rose for sending me a copy of the foregoing *Version of Ossian's Address to the Sun*, which was "Privately printed at the Press of Oliver B. Graves, Cambridge, Massachusetts, June the Tenth, MDCCCXCVIII.," and was reprinted in the *Atlantic Monthly* in December, 1898. A prefatory note entitled, "From Lord Byron's Notes," is prefixed to the Version: "In Lord Byron's copy of *The Poems of Ossian* (printed by Dewick and Clarke, London, 1806), which, since 1874, has been in the possession of the Library of Harvard University as part of the Sumner Bequest. The notes which follow appear in Byron's hand." (For the *Notes*, see the *Atlantic Monthly*, 1898, vol. lxxxii. pp. 810–814.)

It is strange that Byron should have made two versions (for another "version" from the Newstead MSS., see *Poetical Works*, 1898, i. 229–231) of the "Address to the Sun," which forms the conclusion of "Carthon;" but the Harvard version appears to be genuine. It is to be noted that Byron appended to the earlier

LINES TO MR. HODGSON.

WRITTEN ON BOARD THE LISBON PACKET.

1.

HUZZA! Hodgson,[1] we are going,
   Our embargo 's off at last;
Favourable breezes blowing
   Bend the canvas o'er the mast.
From aloft the signal 's streaming,
   Hark! the farewell gun is fired;
Women screeching, tars blaspheming,
   Tell us that our time 's expired.
      Here 's a rascal
      Come to task all,
   Prying from the Custom-house;
      Trunks unpacking
      Cases cracking,
   Not a corner for a mouse
'Scapes unsearched amid the racket,
Ere we sail on board the Packet.

2.

Now our boatmen quit their mooring,
   And all hands must ply the oar;
Baggage from the quay is lowering,
   We 're impatient, push from shore.
   "Have a care! that case holds liquor—
   Stop the boat—I 'm sick—oh Lord!"

version eighteen lines of his own composition, by way of moral or application.]

  1. [For Francis Hodgson (1781–1852), see *Letters*, 1898, i. 195, *note* 1.]

"Sick, Ma'am, damme, you 'll be sicker,
   Ere you 've been an hour on board."
      Thus are screaming
      Men and women,
   Gemmen, ladies, servants, Jacks ;
      Here entangling,
      All are wrangling,
   Stuck together close as wax.—
Such the general noise and racket,
Ere we reach the Lisbon Packet.

3.

Now we 've reached her, lo ! the Captain,
   Gallant Kidd,[1] commands the crew ;
Passengers their berths are clapt in,
   Some to grumble, some to spew.
"Hey day ! call you that a cabin?
   Why 't is hardly three feet square :
Not enough to stow Queen Mab in—
   Who the deuce can harbour there ?,"
      "Who, sir? plenty—
      Nobles twenty
Did at once my vessel fill."—
      "Did they ? Jesus,
      How you squeeze us !
Would to God they did so still :
Then I 'd 'scape the heat and racket
Of the good ship, Lisbon Packet."

1. [Compare Peter Pindar's *Ode to a Margate Hoy*—

"Go, beauteous Hoy, in safety ev'ry inch !
   That storm should wreck thee, gracious Heav'n forbid !
Whether commanded by brave Captain Finch
   Or equally tremendous Captain Kidd."]

4.

Fletcher! Murray! Bob![1] where are you?
   Stretched along the deck like logs—
Bear a hand, you jolly tar, you!
   Here 's a rope's end for the dogs.
Hobhouse muttering fearful curses,
   As the hatchway down he rolls,
Now his breakfast, now his verses,
   Vomits forth—and damns our souls.
      "Here 's a stanza [2]
      On Braganza—
Help!"—"A couplet?"—"No, a cup
      Of warm water—"
      "What 's the matter?"
"Zounds! my liver 's coming up;
I shall not survive the racket
Of this brutal Lisbon Packet."

5.

Now at length we 're off for Turkey,
   Lord knows when we shall come back!
Breezes foul and tempests murky
   May unship us in a crack.
But, since Life at most a jest is,
   As philosophers allow,
Still to laugh by far the best is,
   Then laugh on—as I do now.
      Laugh at all things,
      Great and small things,

1. [Murray was "Joe" Murray, an ancient retainer of the "Wicked
Lord." Bob was Robert Rushton, the "little page" of "Childe
Harold's Good Night." (See *Poetical Works*, 1899, ii. 26, *note* 1.)]
   2. [For "the stanza," addressed to the "Princely offspring of
Braganza," published in the *Morning Post*, December 30, 1807, see
English Bards, etc., line 142, *note* 1, *Poetical Works*, 1898, i. 308,
309.]

Sick or well, at sea or shore ;
  While we 're quaffing,
  Let 's have laughing—
Who the devil cares for more ?—
Some good wine ! and who would lack it,
Ev'n on board the Lisbon Packet ?

      Falmouth Roads, *June* 30, 1809.
[First published, *Letters and Journals*, 1830, i. 230–232.]

[TO DIVES.[1] A FRAGMENT.]

UNHAPPY Dives ! in an evil hour
 'Gainst Nature's voice seduced to deeds accurst !
Once Fortune's minion now thou feel'st her power ;
Wrath's vial on thy lofty head hath burst.
In Wit, in Genius, as in Wealth the first,
 How wondrous bright thy blooming morn arose !
But thou wert smitten with th' unhallowed thirst
Of Crime unnamed, and thy sad noon must close
In scorn and solitude unsought the worst of woes.

      1809.
[First published, *Lord Byron's Works*, 1833, xvii. 241.]

FAREWELL PETITION TO J. C. H., ESQ^{RE.}

O THOU yclep'd by vulgar sons of Men
Cam Hobhouse ![2] but by wags Byzantian Ben !
Twin sacred titles, which combined appear
To grace thy volume's front, and gild its rear,

  1. [Dives was William Beckford. See *Childe Harold*, Canto I.
stanza xxii. line 6, *Poetical Works*, 1899, ii. 37, *note* 1.]
  2. [For John Cam Hobhouse (1786–1869), afterwards Lord
Broughton de Gyfford, see *Letters*, 1898, i. 163, *note* 1.]

Since now thou put'st thyself and work to Sea
And leav'st all Greece to *Fletcher*[1] and to me,
Oh, hear my single muse our sorrows tell,
One song for *self* and Fletcher quite as well—

First to the *Castle* of that man of woes
Dispatch the letter which *I must* enclose,
And when his lone Penelope shall say
Why, *where*, and *wherefore* doth my William stay?
Spare not to move her pity, or her pride—
By all that Hero suffered, or defied;
The *chicken's toughness*, and the *lack* of *ale*
The *stoney mountain* and the *miry vale*
The *Garlick* steams, which *half* his meals enrich,
The *impending vermin*, and the threatened *Itch*,
That *ever breaking* Bed, beyond repair!
The hat too *old*, the coat too *cold* to wear,
The Hunger, *which repulsed from Sally's door*
Pursues her grumbling half from shore to shore,
Be these the themes to greet his faithful Rib
So may thy pen be smooth, thy tongue be glib!

This duty done, let me in turn demand
Some friendly office in my native land,
Yet let me ponder well, before I ask,
And set thee swearing at the tedious task.

First the Miscellany![2]—to Southwell town
Per coach for Mrs. *Pigot* frank it down,

1. [Fletcher was an indifferent traveller, and sighed for "a' the comforts of the saut-market." See Byron's letters to his mother, November 12, 1809, June 28, 1810.—*Letters*, 1898, i. 256, 281.]

2. [Hobhouse's Miscellany (otherwise known as the *Miss-sell-any*) was published in 1809, under the title of *Imitations and Translations from The Ancient and Modern Classics*. Byron contributed nine original poems. The volume was not a success. "It foundered . . . in the Gulph of Lethe."—Letter to H. Drury, July 17, 1811, *Letters*, 1898, i. 319.]

So may'st thou prosper in the paths of Sale,[1]
And Longman smirk and critics cease to rail.

All hail to Matthews![2] wash his reverend feet,
And in my name the man of Method greet,—
Tell him, my Guide, Philosopher, and Friend,
Who cannot love me, and who will not mend,
Tell him, that not in vain I shall assay
To tread and trace our "old Horatian way,"[3]
And be (with prose supply my dearth of rhymes)
What better men have been in better times.

Here let me cease, for why should I prolong
My notes, and vex a *Singer* with a *Song?*
Oh thou with pen perpetual in thy fist!
Dubbed for thy sins a stark Miscellanist,
So pleased the printer's orders to perform
For Messrs. *Longman, Hurst* and *Rees* and *Orme.*
Go—Get thee hence to Paternoster Row,
Thy patrons wave a duodecimo!
(Best form for *letters* from a distant land,
It fits the pocket, nor fatigues the hand.)
Then go, once more the joyous work commence[4]
With stores of anecdote, and grains of sense,

1. [The word "Sale" may have a double meaning. There may
be an allusion to George Sale, the Orientalist, and translator of the
Koran.]
2. ["In Matthews I have lost my 'guide, philosopher, and
friend.'"—Letter to R. C. Dallas, September 7, 1811, *Letters*, 1898,
ii. 25. (For Charles Skinner Matthews, see *Letters*, 1898, i. 150,
note 3.)]
3. [Compare—
     " In short, the maxim for the amorous tribe is
        Horatian, ' Medio tu tutissimus ibis.' "
            Don Juan, Canto V. stanza xvii. lines 8, 9.
The "doctrine" is Horatian, but the words occur in Ovid,
Metam., lib. ii. line 137.—*Poetical Works*, 1902, vi. 273, *note* 2.]
4. [Hobhouse's *Journey through Albania and other Provinces of
Turkey*, 4to, was published by James Cawthorn, in 1813.]

Oh may Mammas relent, and Sires forgive !
And scribbling Sons grow dutiful and live !

Constantinople, June 7ᵗʰ, 1810.
[First published, *Murray's Magazine*, 1887, vol. i. pp. 290, 291.]

TRANSLATION OF THE NURSE'S DOLE IN THE *MEDEA* OF EURIPIDES.

OH how I wish that an embargo
Had kept in port the good ship Argo !
Who, still unlaunched from Grecian docks,
Had never passed the Azure rocks ;
But now I fear her trip will he a
Damn'd business for my Miss Medea, etc., etc.[1]

June, 1810.
[First published, *Letters and Journals*, 1830, i. 227.]

MY EPITAPH.[2]

YOUTH, Nature, and relenting Jove,
To keep my lamp *in* strongly strove ;

1. ["I am just come from an expedition through the Bosphorus to the Black Sea and the Cyanean Symplegades, up which last I scrambled with as great risk as ever the Argonauts escaped in their hoy. You remember the beginning of the nurse's dole in the *Medea* [lines 1–7], of which I beg you to take the following translation, done on the summit ;—[A 'damned business'] it very nearly was to me ; for, had not this sublime passage been in my head, I should never have dreamed of ascending the said rocks, and bruising my carcass in honour of the ancients."—Letter to Henry Drury, June 17, 1810, *Letters*, 1898, i. 276.
Euripides, *Medea*, lines 1–7—

Εἴθ' ὤφελ' Ἀργοῦς μὴ διαπτάσθαι σκάφος, κ.τ.λ.]

2. ["The English Consul . . . forced a physician upon me, and in three days vomited and glystered me to the last gasp. In this state I made my epitaph—take it."—Letter to Hodgson, October 3, 1810, *Letters*, 1898, i. 298.]

But Romanelli was so stout,
He beat all three—and *blew* it *out.*

October, 1810.
[First published, *Letters and Journals,* 1830, i. 240.]

SUBSTITUTE FOR AN EPITAPH.

KIND Reader! take your choice to cry or laugh;
Here HAROLD lies—but where 's his Epitaph?
If such you seek, try Westminster, and view
Ten thousand just as fit for him as you.

Athens, 1810.
[First published, *Lord Byron's Works,* 1832, ix. 4.]

EPITAPH FOR JOSEPH BLACKET, LATE POET AND SHOEMAKER.[1]

STRANGER! behold, interred together,
The *souls* of learning and of leather.
Poor Joe is gone, but left his *all:*
You 'll find his relics in a *stall.*
His works were neat, and often found
Well stitched, and with *morocco* bound.
Tread lightly—where the bard is laid—
He cannot mend the shoe he made;
Yet is he happy in his hole,
With verse immortal as his *sole.*
But still to business he held fast,
And stuck to Phœbus to the *last.*

1. [For Joseph Blacket (1786–1810), see *Letters,* 1898, i. 314, *note* 2; see, too, *Poetical Works,* 1898, i. 359, *note* 1, and 441–443, *note* 2. The *Epitaph* is of doubtful authenticity.]

Then who shall say so good a fellow
Was only "leather and prunella?"
For character—he did not lack it;
And if he did, 'twere shame to "Black-it."

Malta, *May* 16, 1811.
[First published, *Lord Byron's Works*, 1832, ix. 10.]

ON MOORE'S LAST OPERATIC FARCE, OR FARCICAL OPERA.[1]

GOOD plays are scarce,
So Moore writes *farce:*
The poet's fame grows brittle[i.]—
We knew before
That *Little*'s Moore,
But now 't is Moore that 's *little.*

September 14, 1811.
[First published, *Letters and Journals*, 1830, i. 295 (*note*).]

[R. C. DALLAS.][2]

YES! wisdom shines in all his mien,
Which would so captivate, I ween,
Wisdom's own goddess Pallas;

i. *Is fame like his so brittle?*—[*MS.*]

1. ["On a leaf of one of his paper books I find an epigram, written at this time, which, though not perhaps particularly good, I consider myself bound to insert."—Moore, *Life*, p. 137, *note* 1. The reference is to Moore's *M.P.; or, The Blue Stocking*, which was played for the first time at the Lyceum Theatre, September 9, 1811. For Moore's *nom de plume*, "The late Thomas Little, Esq.," compare Praed's *The Belle of the Ball-Room*—

"If those bright lips had quoted Locke,
I might have thought they murmured Little."]

2. ["A person observing that Mr. Dallas looked very wise on a certain occasion, his Lordship is said to have broke out into the following impromptu."—*Life, Writings, Times, and Opinions of Lord Byron*, 1825, ii. 191.]

That she 'd discard her fav'rite owl,
And take for pet a brother fowl,
 Sagacious R. C. Dallas.

[First published, *Life, Writings, Opinions, etc.*, 1825, ii. 192.]

AN ODE[1] TO THE FRAMERS OF THE FRAME BILL.[2]

I.

OH well done Lord E——n! and better done R——r![3]
 Britannia must prosper with councils like yours;
Hawkesbury, Harrowby, help you to guide her,
 Whose remedy only must *kill* ere it cures:
Those villains; the Weavers, are all grown refractory,
 Asking some succour for Charity's sake—
So hang them in clusters round each Manufactory,
 That will at once put an end to *mistake*.[4]

1. ["LORD BYRON TO EDITOR OF THE *MORNING CHRONICLE*.

"SIR,—I take the liberty of sending an alteration of the two last lines of stanza 2ᵈ, which I wish to run as follows:—

 "'Gibbets on Sherwood will *heighten* the scenery,
 Shewing how commerce, *how* liberty thrives.'

I wish you could insert it tomorrow for a particular reason; but I feel much obliged by your inserting it at all. Of course do *not* put my name to the thing—believe me,
     "Your obliged
    and very obedient servant,
       "BYRON.
"8, St. James's Street,
 Sunday, March 1, 1812."]

2. [For Byron's maiden speech in the House of Lords, February 27, 1812, see *Letters*, 1898, ii. 424–430.]

3. [Richard Ryder (1766–1832), second son of the first Baron Harrowby, was Home Secretary, 1809–12.]

4. Lord E., on Thursday night, said the riots at Nottingham arose from a "*mistake.*"

2.

The rascals, perhaps, may betake them to robbing,
   The dogs to be sure have got nothing to eat—
So if we can hang them for breaking a bobbin,
   'T will save all the Government's money and meat:
Men are more easily made than machinery—
   Stockings fetch better prices than lives—
Gibbets on Sherwood will heighten the scenery,
   Shewing how Commerce, how Liberty thrives!

3.

Justice is now in pursuit of the wretches,
   Grenadiers, Volunteers, Bow-street Police,
Twenty-two Regiments, a score of Jack Ketches,
   Three of the Quorum and two of the Peace;
Some Lords, to be sure, would have summoned the Judges,
   To take their opinion, but that they ne'er shall,
For LIVERPOOL such a concession begrudges,
   So now they 're condemned by *no Judges* at all.

4.

Some folks for certain have thought it was shocking,
   When Famine appeals and when Poverty groans,
That Life should be valued at less than a stocking,
   And breaking of frames lead to breaking of bones.
If it should prove so, I trust, by this token,
   (And who will refuse to partake in the hope?)
That the frames of the fools may be first to be *broken*,
   Who, when asked for a *remedy*, sent down a *rope*.

[First published, *Morning Chronicle, Monday, March* 2, 1812.]
   [See a *Political Ode by Lord Byron, hitherto unknown as
      his production.*   London, John Pearson, 46, Pall
      Mall, 1880, 8°.   See, too, Mr. Pearson's prefatory
      Note, pp. 5, etc.]

TO THE HON^{BLE} M^{RS} GEORGE LAMB.[1]

1.

THE sacred song that on mine ear
   Yet vibrates from that voice of thine,
I heard, before, from one so dear—
   'T is strange it still appears divine.

2.

But, oh ! so sweet that *look* and *tone*
   To her and thee alike is given ;
It seemed as if for me alone
   That *both* had been recalled from Heaven !

3.

And though I never can redeem
   The vision thus endeared to me ;
I scarcely can regret my dream,
   When realised again by thee.

1812.

[First published in *The Two Duchesses*, by Vere Foster,
1898, p. 374.]

[LA REVANCHE.]

1.

THERE is no more for me to hope,
   There is no more for thee to fear ;
And, if I give my Sorrow scope,
   That Sorrow thou shalt never hear.

1. [Caroline Rosalie Adelaide St. Jules (1786–1862) married, in
1809, the Hon. George Lamb (see *English Bards, etc.*, line 55,
Poetical Works, 1898, i. 300, *note* 1), fourth son of the first Viscount
Melbourne.]

Why did I hold thy love so dear?
Why shed for such a heart one tear?
Let deep and dreary silence be
My only memory of thee!

2.

When all are fled who flatter now,
　Save thoughts which will not flatter then;
And thou recall'st the broken vow
　To him who must not love again—
　Each hour of now forgotten years
　Thou, then, shalt number with thy tears;
And every drop of grief shall be
A vain remembrancer of me!

Undated, ? 1812.
[From an autograph MS. in the possession of Mr. Murray,
now for the first time printed.]

TO THOMAS MOORE.

WRITTEN THE EVENING BEFORE HIS VISIT TO MR. LEIGH
HUNT IN HORSEMONGER LANE GAOL, MAY 19, 1813.

OH you, who in all names can tickle the town,
Anacreon, Tom Little, Tom Moore, or Tom Brown,—[1]
For hang me if I know of which you may most brag,
Your Quarto two-pounds, or your Two-penny Post Bag;

*　　*　　*　　*　　*　　*

But now to my letter—to *yours* 't is an answer—
To-morrow be with me, as soon as you can, sir,

1. [Moore's "*Intercepted Letters; or, The Twopenny Post-Bag*,
By Thomas Brown, the Younger," was published in 1813.]

Walker & Cockerell Ph. Sc.

Sir George Sinclair, Bart, M.P.
as a boy.
From a painting after Raeburn, in the possession of
Sir Tollemache Sinclair.

All ready and dressed for proceeding to spunge on
(According to compact) the wit in the dungeon—[1]
Pray Phœbus at length our political malice
May not get us lodgings within the same palace !
I suppose that to-night you 're engaged with some codgers,
And for Sotheby's Blues [2] have deserted Sam Rogers ;
And I, though with cold I have nearly my death got,
Must put on my breeches, and wait on the Heathcote ; [3]
But to-morrow, at four, we will both play the *Scurra*,
And you 'll be Catullus, the Regent Mamurra.[4]

[First published, *Letters and Journals*, 1830, i. 401.]

ON LORD THURLOW'S POEMS.[5]

I.

WHEN Thurlow this damned nonsense sent,
(I hope I am not violent)
Nor men nor gods knew what he meant.

1. [James Henry Leigh Hunt (1784–1859) was imprisoned February, 1813, to February, 1815, for a libel on the Prince Regent, published in the *Examiner*, March 12, 1812.—*Letters*, 1898, ii. 205–208, *note* 1.]

2. [For "Sotheby's Blues," see Introduction to *The Blues*, *Poetical Works*, 1901, iv. 570, *et ibid.*, 579, 580.]

3. [Katherine Sophia Manners was married in 1793 to Sir Gilbert Heathcote. See *Letters*, 1898, ii. 402, 406.]

4. [See *Catullus*, xxix. 1–4—

> " Quis hoc potest videre? quis potest pati,
> Nisi impudicus et vorax et aleo,
> Mamurram habere, quod Comata Gallia
> Habebat uncti et ultima Britannia ? " etc.]

5. [One evening, in the late spring or early summer of 1813, Byron and Moore supped on bread and cheese with Rogers. Their host had just received from Lord Thurlow [Edward Hovell Thurlow, 1781–1829] a copy of his *Poems on Several Occasions* (1813), and Byron lighted upon some lines to Rogers, " On the Poem of Mr.

VOL. VII.   D

2.

And since not even our Rogers' praise
To common sense his thoughts could raise—
Why *would* they let him print his lays?

3.

*   *   *   *

4.

*   *   *   *

Rogers, entitled 'An Epistle to a Friend.'" The first stanza ran thus—

> "When Rogers o'er this labour bent,
> Their purest fire the Muses lent,
> T' illustrate this sweet argument."

"Byron," says Moore, "undertook to read it aloud;—but he found it impossible to get beyond the first two words. Our laughter had now increased to such a pitch that nothing could restrain it. Two or three times he began; but no sooner had the words 'When Rogers' passed his lips, than our fit burst forth afresh,—till even Mr. Rogers himself . . . found it impossible not to join us. A day or two after, Lord Byron sent me the following:—'My dear Moore, "When Rogers" must not see the enclosed, which I send for your perusal.'"—*Life*, p. 181; *Letters*, 1898, ii. 211–213, *note* 1.]

Thurlow's poems are by no means contemptible. A sonnet, "To a Bird, that haunted the Water of Lacken, in the Winter," which Charles Lamb transcribed in one of Coleridge's note-books, should be set over against the absurd lines, "On the Poems of Mr. Rogers."

> "O melancholy bird, a winter's day
>   Thou standest by the margin of the pool;
>   And, taught by God, dost thy whole being school
> To Patience, which all evil can allay:
> God has appointed thee the fish thy prey;
>   And giv'n thyself a lesson to the fool
>   Unthrifty, to submit to moral rule,
> And his unthinking course by thee to weigh.
>   There need not schools nor the professor's chair,
> Though these be good, true wisdom to impart;
>   He, who has not enough for these to spare
> Of time, or gold, may yet amend his heart,
>   And teach his soul by brooks and rivers fair,
> Nature is always wise in every part."

Select Poems, 1821, p. 90.
[See " Fragments of Criticism," *Works of Charles Lamb*,
1903, iii. 284.]

5.

To me, divine Apollo, grant—O!
Hermilda's[1] first and second canto,
I 'm fitting up a new portmanteau;

6.

And thus to furnish decent lining,
My own and others' bays I 'm twining,—
So, gentle Thurlow, throw me thine in.

June 2, 1813.
[First published, *Letters and Journals*, 1830, i. 396.]

TO LORD THURLOW.[2]

1.

" *I lay my branch of laurel down.*"
" THOU lay thy branch of *laurel* down!"
  Why, what thou 'st stole is not enow;
And, were it lawfully thine own,
  Does Rogers want it most, or thou?
Keep to thyself thy withered bough,
Or send it back to Doctor Donne:[3]

1. [*Hermilda in Palestine* was published in 1812, in quarto, and twice reissued in 1813, as part of *Poems on Various Occasions* (8vo). The Lines upon Rogers' *Epistle to a Friend* appeared first in the *Gentleman's Magazine* for April, 1813, vol. 83, p. 357, and were reprinted in the second edition of *Poems, etc.*, 1813, pp. 162, 163. The lines in italics, which precede each stanza, are taken from the last stanza of Lord Thurlow's poem.]

2. [" On the same day I received from him the following additional scraps ['To Lord Thurlow']. The lines in Italics are from the eulogy that provoked his waggish comments."—*Life*, p. 181. The last stanza of Thurlow's poem supplied the text—

"Then, thus, to form Apollo's crown,
  (Let ev'ry other bring his own,)
  I lay my branch of laurel down."]

3. [Lord Thurlow affected an archaic style in his Sonnets and

Were justice done to both, I trow,
    He 'd have but little, and thou—none.

2.

"*Then, thus, to form Apollo's crown.*"

A crown! why, twist it how you will,
Thy chaplet must be foolscap still.
When next you visit Delphi's town,
    Enquire amongst your fellow-lodgers,
They 'll tell you Phœbus gave his crown,
    Some years before your birth, to Rogers.

3.

"*Let every other bring his own.*"

When coals to Newcastle are carried,
    And owls sent to Athens, as wonders,
From his spouse when the Regent's unmarried,
    Or Liverpool weeps o'er his blunders;
When Tories and Whigs cease to quarrel,
    When Castlereagh's wife has an heir,
Then Rogers shall ask us for laurel,
    And thou shalt have plenty to spare.

[First published, *Letters and Journals*, 1830, i. 397.]

other verses. In the Preface to the second edition of *Poems, etc.*,
he writes, "I think that our Poetry has been continually declining since the days of Milton and Cowley . . . and that the
golden age of our language is in the reign of Queen Elizabeth."]

THE DEVIL'S DRIVE.[i, 1]

1.

THE Devil returned to Hell by two,
    And he stayed at home till five ;
When he dined on some homicides done in *ragoût*,
    And a rebel or so in an *Irish* stew,
And sausages made of a self-slain Jew,
And bethought himself what next to do,
    " And," quoth he, " I 'll take a drive.
I walked in the morning, I 'll ride to-night ;
In darkness my children take most delight,
    And I 'll see how my favourites thrive.   10

2.

" And what shall I ride in ? " quoth Lucifer, then——
    " If I followed my taste, indeed,
I should mount in a waggon of wounded men,
    And smile to see them bleed.
But these will be furnished again and again,
    And at present my purpose is speed ;

i. The Devil's Drive.   *A Sequel to Porson's* Devil's Walk.—
                        [*MS. H.*]

1. [" I have lately written a wild, rambling, unfinished rhapsody, called ' The Devil's Drive,' the notion of which I took from Porson's *Devil's Walk*."—*Journal*, December 17, 18, 1813, *Letters*, 1898, ii. 378. " Though with a good deal of vigour and imagination, it is," says Moore, "for the most part rather clumsily executed, wanting the point and condensation of those clever verses of Coleridge and Southey, which Lord Byron, adopting a notion long prevalent, has attributed to Porson." The *Devil's Walk* was published in the *Morning Post*, September 6, 1799. It has been published under Porson's name (1830, ed. H. Montague, illustrated by Cruikshank). (See *Poetical Works*, 1898, i. 30, *note* 1.)]

To see my manor as much as I may,
And watch that no souls shall be poached away.

3.

" I have a state-coach at Carlton House,
   A chariot in Seymour-place; [1]   20
But they 're lent to two friends, who make me amends
   By driving my favourite pace :
And they handle their reins with such a grace,
I have something for both at the end of the race.

4.

" So now for the earth to take my chance."
   Then up to the earth sprung he ;
And making a jump from Moscow to France,
   He stepped across the sea,
And rested his hoof on a turnpike road,
No very great way from a Bishop's abode. [2]   30

5.

But first as he flew, I forgot to say,
That he hovered a moment upon his way,
   To look upon Leipsic plain ;

1. [Lord Yarmouth, nicknamed " Red Herrings," the eldest son of the Regent's elderly favourite, the Marchioness of Hertford (the " Marchesa" of the *Twopenny Post-Bag*), lived at No, 7, Seamore Place, Mayfair. Compare Moore's " Epigram :" " 'I want the Court Guide,' said my lady, 'to look If the House, Seymour Place, be at 30 or 20,'" etc.—*Poetical Works*, 1850, p. 165.]

2. [The allusion may be to a case which was before the courts, the Attorney-General *v.* William Carver and Brownlow Bishop of Winchester (see *Morning Chronicle*, November 17, 1813). Carver held certain premises under the Bishop of Winchester, at the entrance of Portsmouth Harbour, which obstructed the efflux and reflux of the tide. " The fact," said Mr. Serjeant Lens, in opening the case for the Crown, " was of great magnitude to the entire nation, since it effected the security, and even the existence of one of the principal harbours of Great Britain."]

And so sweet to his eye was its sulphury glare,
And so soft to his ear was the cry of despair,
  That he perched on a mountain of slain;
And he gazed with delight from its growing height,
Nor often on earth had he seen such a sight,
  Nor his work done half as well:
For the field ran so red with the blood of the dead,   40
  That it blushed like the waves of Hell!
Then loudly, and wildly, and long laughed he:
" Methinks they have little need here of *me!* "

6.

Long he looked down on the hosts of each clime,
  While the warriors hand to hand were—
Gaul—Austrian and Muscovite heroes sublime,
And—(Muse of Fitzgerald arise with a rhyme!)
  A quantity of *Landwehr!*[1]
    Gladness was there,
For the men of all might and the monarchs of earth,   50
There met for the wolf and the worm to make mirth,
  And a feast for the fowls of the Air!

7.

But he turned aside and looked from the ridge
  Of hills along the river,
And the best thing he saw was a broken bridge,[2]
  Which a Corporal chose to shiver;

  1. [The Russian and Austrian troops at the battle of Leipsic,
October 16, 1813, were, for the most part, veterans, while the
Prussian contingent included a large body of militia.]
  2. [For the incident of the " broken bridge " Byron was indebted
to the pages of the *Morning Chronicle* of November 8, 1813, " Paris
Papers, October 30 "—
  " The Emperor had ordered the engineers to form fougades under
the grand bridge which is between Leipsic and Lindenau, in order
to blow it up at the latest moment, and thus to retard the march
of the enemy and give time to our baggage to file off. General

Though an Emperor's taste was displeased with his haste,
　The Devil he thought it clever;
And he laughed again in a lighter strain,
　O'er the torrent swoln and rainy,　　　　　　60
When he saw "on a fiery steed" Prince Pon,
In taking care of Number *One*—
　Get drowned with a great *many!*

8.

But the softest note that soothed his ear
　Was the sound of a widow sighing;
And the sweetest sight was the icy tear,
Which Horror froze in the blue eye clear
　Of a maid by her lover lying—
As round her fell her long fair hair,
And she looked to Heaven with that frenzied air　　70
Which seemed to ask if a God were there!
And stretched by the wall of a ruined hut,
With its hollow cheek, and eyes half shut,
　A child of Famine dying:

Dulaulov had entrusted the operation to Colonel Montford. The Colonel, instead of remaining on the spot to direct it, and to give the signal, ordered a corporal and four sappers to blow up the bridge the instant the enemy should appear. The corporal, an ignorant fellow, and ill comprehending the nature of the duty with which he was charged, upon hearing the first shot discharged from the ramparts of the city, set fire to the fougades and blew up the bridge. A part of the army was still on the other side, with a park of 80 pieces of artillery and some hundreds of waggons. The advance of this part of the army, who were approaching the bridge, seeing it blow up, conceived it was in the power of the enemy. A cry of dismay spread from rank to rank. 'The enemy are close upon our rear, and the bridges are destroyed!' The unfortunate soldiers dispersed, and endeavoured to effect their escape as well as they could. The Duke of Tarentum swam across the river. Prince Poniatowsky, mounted on a spirited horse, darted into the water and appeared no more. The Emperor was not informed of this disaster until it was too late to remedy it. . . . Colonel Montfort and the corporal of the sappers have been handed over to a court-martial."]

And the carnage *begun*, when *resistance* is done,
  And the fall of the vainly flying!

9.

Then he gazed on a town by besiegers taken,
  Nor cared he who were winning;
But he saw an old maid, for years forsaken,
  Get up and leave her spinning;   80
And she looked in her glass, and to one that did pass,
  She said—"pray are the rapes beginning?" [1]

10.

But the Devil has reached our cliffs so white,
  And what did he there, I pray?
If his eyes were good, he but saw by night
  What we see every day;
But he made a tour and kept a journal
Of all the wondrous sights nocturnal,
And he sold it in shares to the *Men* of the *Row*,
Who bid pretty well—but they *cheated* him, though!   90

11.

The Devil first saw, as he thought, the *Mail*,
  Its coachman and his coat;
So instead of a pistol he cocked his tail,
  And seized him by the throat;

1. [Compare *Don Juan*, Canto VIII. stanza cxxxii. line 4. Sir Walter Scott (*Journal*, October 30, 1826 [1890, i. 288], tells the same story of "an old woman who, when Carlisle was taken by the Highlanders in 1745, chose to be particularly apprehensive of personal violence, and shut herself up in a closet, in order that she might escape ravishment. But no one came to disturb her solitude, and . . . by and by she popped her head out of her place of refuge with the pretty question, 'Good folks, can you tell me when the ravishing is going to begin?'" In 1813 Byron did not know Scott, and must have stolen the jest from some older writer. It is, probably, of untold antiquity.]

"Aha!" quoth he, "what have we here?
'T is a new barouche, and an ancient peer!" [1]

12.

So he sat him on his box again,
   And bade him have no fear,
But be true to his club, and staunch to his rein,
   His brothel and his beer;   100
"Next to seeing a Lord at the Council board,
I would rather see him here."

13.

Satan hired a horse and gig
   With promises to pay;
And he pawned his horns for a spruce new wig,
   To redeem as he came away:
And he whistled some tune, a waltz or a jig,
   And drove off at the close of day.

14.

The first place he stopped at—he heard the Psalm
   That rung from a Methodist Chapel: 110

1. [The "Four-Horse" Club, founded in 1808, was incorrectly styled the Four-in-Hand Club, and the Barouche Club. According to the Club rules, the barouches were "yellow-bodied, with 'dickies,' the horses bay, with rosettes at their heads, and the harness silver-mounted. The members wore a drab coat reaching to the ankles, with three tiers of pockets, and mother-o'-pearl buttons as large as five-shilling pieces. The waistcoat was blue, with yellow stripes an inch wide; breeches of plush, with strings and rosettes to each knee; and it was *de rigueur* that the hat should be 3½ inches deep in the crown." (See *Driving*, by the Duke of Beaufort, K.G., 1894, pp. 251-258.)

The "ancient peer" may possibly be intended for the President of the Club, Philip Henry, fifth Earl of Chesterfield (1755-1815), who was a member of the Privy Council, and had been Postmaster-General and Master of the Horse.]

" 'T is the best sound I 've heard," quoth he, " since my
    palm
  Presented Eve her apple !
When *Faith* is all, 't is an excellent sign,
That the *Works* and Workmen both are mine."

15.

He passed Tommy Tyrwhitt,[1] that standing jest,
  To princely wit a Martyr :
But the last joke of all was by far the best,
  When he sailed away with " the Garter " !
"And "—quoth Satan—" this Embassy 's worthy my sight,
Should I see nothing else to amuse me to night.   120
With no one to bear it, but Thomas à Tyrwhitt,
This ribband belongs to an ' Order of Merit ' ! "

16.

He stopped at an Inn and stepped within
  The Bar and read the " Times ; "

1. [Sir Thomas Tyrwhitt (*circ.* 1762-1833) was the son of the
Rev. Edmund Tyrwhitt, Rector of Wickham Bishops, etc., and
nephew of Thomas Tyrwhitt, the editor of the *Canterbury Tales.* He
was Private Secretary to the Prince of Wales, auditor of the Duchy
of Cornwall (1796), and Lord Warden of the Stannaries (1805).
He was knighted May 8, 1812. He was sent in the following year
in charge of the Garter mission to the Czar, and on that occasion
was made a Knight of the Imperial Order of St. Anne, First Class.
He held the office of Gentleman Usher of the Black Rod, 1812–
1832. "Tommy Tyrwhitt" was an important personage at Carlton
House, and shared with Colonel McMahon the doubtful privilege
of being a confidential servant of the Prince Regent. Compare
Letter III. of Moore's *Twopenny Post-Bag,* 1813, p. 12. "From
G. R. to the E. of Y——th."

"I write this in bed while my whiskers are airing,
  And M—c has a sly dose of jalap preparing
  For poor T—mm—y T—rr—t at breakfast to quaff—
As I feel I want something to give me a laugh,
  And there's nothing so good as old T—mm—y kept close
  To his Cornwall accounts, after taking a dose !"
  See *Gentleman's Magazine,* March, 1833, vol. 103, pt. i. pp.
275, 276.]

And never such a treat, as—the epistle of one " Vetus," [1]
 Had he found save in downright crimes :
" Though I doubt if this drivelling encomiast of War
Ever saw a field fought, or felt a scar,
Yet his fame shall go farther than he can guess,
For I 'll keep him a place in my *hottest Press ;*   130
And his works shall be bound in Morocco *d'Enfer*,
And lettered behind with his *Nom de Guerre.*"

17.

The Devil gat next to Westminster,
 And he turned to " the room " of the Commons ;
But he heard as he purposed to enter in there,
 That " the Lords " had received a summons ;
And he thought, as " a *quondam* Aristocrat,"
He might peep at the Peers, though to *hear* them were flat ;
And he walked up the House so like one of his own,
That they say that he stood pretty near the throne.   140

18.

He saw the Lord Liverpool seemingly wise,
 The Lord Westmoreland certainly silly,
And Jockey of Norfolk—a man of some size—
 And Chatham, so like his friend Billy ; [2]

1. [" Vetus " [Edward Sterling] contributed a series of letters to
the *Times*, 1812, 1813. They were afterwards republished. Vetus
was not a Little Englander, and his political sentiments recall the
obiter dicta of contemporary patriots ; *e.g.* " the only legitimate
basis for a treaty, if not on the part of the Continental Allies, at least
for England herself [is] that she should conquer all she can, and
keep all she conquers. This is not by way of retaliation, however
just, upon so obdurate and rapacious an enemy—but as an indis-
pensable condition of her own safety and existence." The letters
were reviewed under the heading of "Illustrations of Vetus," in the
Morning Chronicle, December 2, 10, 16, 18 ; 1813. The reviewer
and Byron did not take the patriotic view of the situation.]
  2. [Robert Banks Jenkinson (1770–1828), second Earl of Liverpool, on the assassination of Perceval, became Prime Minister, June

And he saw the tears in Lord Eldon's eyes,
  Because the Catholics would *not* rise,
  In spite of his prayers and his prophecies ;
And he heard—which set Satan himself a staring—
A certain Chief Justice say something like *swearing*.[1]
And the Devil was shocked—and quoth he, " I must go,
For I find we have much better manners below.   151
If thus he harangues when he passes my border,
I shall hint to friend Moloch to call him to order."

19.

Then the Devil went down to the humbler House,
  Where he readily found his way
As natural to him as its hole to a Mouse,
  He had been there many a day ;
And many a vote and soul and job he
  Had bid for and carried away from the Lobby :

7, 1812 ; John Fane (1759–1841), tenth Earl of Westmoreland, was Lord Privy Seal, 1798–1827 ; Charles Howard (1746–1815), eleventh Duke of Norfolk, known as " Jockey of Norfolk," was a Protestant and a Liberal, and at one time a friend of the Prince of Wales. Wraxall, *Posthumous Memoirs*, 1836, i. 29, says that " he might have been mistaken for a grazier or a butcher by his dress and appearance." He figures *largely* in Gillray, see *e.g.* " Meeting of the Moneyed Interest," December, 1798. John Pitt (1756–1835), second Earl of Chatham, the hero of the abortive Walcheren expedition, had been made a general in the army January 1, 1812. He " inherited," says Wraxall, *ibid.*, iii. 129, " his illustrious father's form and figure ; but not his mind."]

1. [Edward Law (1750–1818), first Baron Ellenborough, Lord Chief Justice of the King's Bench, 1802–18, was given to the use of strong language. His temper (see Moore's " Sale of the Tools ") was " none of the best." On one occasion, speaking in the House of Lords (March 22, 1813) with regard to the " delicate investigation," he asserted that the accusation [" that the persons intrusted had thought fit to fabricate an unauthorized document "] " was as false as hell ; " and by way of protest against the tedious harangues of old Lord Darnley, " I am answerable to God for my time, and what account can I give at the day of judgment if I stay here longer ? "]

But there now was a " call " and accomplished debaters
Appeared in the glory of hats, boots and gaiters—   161
Some paid rather more—but *all* worse dressed than
  Waiters !

20.

There was Canning for War, and Whitbread for peace,
    And others as suited their fancies ;
But all were agreed that our debts should increase
    Excepting the Demagogue Francis.
That rogue ! how could Westminster chuse him again
    To leaven the virtue of these honest men !
But the Devil remained till the Break of Day
    Blushed upon Sleep and Lord Castlereagh :[1]   170
Then up half the house got, and Satan got up
    With the drowsy to snore—or the hungry to sup :—
But so torpid the power of some speakers, 't is said,
That they sent even him to his brimstone bed.

21.

He had seen George Rose—but George was grown
    dumb,
    And only lied in thought ![2]
And the Devil has all the pleasure to come
    Of hearing him talk as he ought.

1. [Compare Moore's " Insurrection of the Papers "—
        " Last night I toss'd and turn'd in bed,
          But could not sleep—at length I said,
          'I'll think of Viscount C—stl—r—gh,
          And of his speeches—that's the way."]

2. [George Rose (1744–1818) was at this time Treasurer of the
Navy. Wraxall, who quotes the " Probationary Odes " with regard
to his alleged duplicity, testifies that he " knew him well in his official
capacity, during at least twelve years, and never found him deficient
in honour or sincerity " (*Posthumous Memoirs*, 1836, i. 148). Moore
(" Parody of a Celebrated Letter ") makes the Regent conceive how
shocked the king would be to wake up sane and find " that R—se
was grown honest, or W—stm—rel—nd wiser."]

With the falsest of tongues, the sincerest of men—
   His veracity were but deceit—   180
And Nature must first have unmade him again,
Ere his breast or his face, or his tongue, or his pen,
Conceived—uttered—looked—or wrote down letters ten,
   Which Truth would acknowledge complete.

22.

Satan next took the army list in hand,
   Where he found a new " Field Marshal ; "
And when he saw this high command
   Conferred on his Highness of Cumberland,[1]
" Oh ! were I prone to cavil—or were I not the Devil,
   I should say this was somewhat partial ;   190
Since the only wounds that this Warrior gat,
Were from God knows whom—and the Devil knows
      what ! "

23.

He then popped his head in a royal Ball,
   And saw all the Haram so hoary ;

1. [Ernest Augustus (1771–1851), Duke of Cumberland and King of Hanover, fifth son of George III., was gazetted as Field-Marshal November 27, 1813. His "wounds," which, according to the Duke's sworn testimony, were seventeen in number, were inflicted during an encounter with his valet, Joseph Sellis (? Sélis), a Piedmontese, who had attempted to assassinate the Prince (June 1, 1810), and, shortly afterwards, was found with his throat cut. A jury of Westminster tradesmen brought in a verdict of *felo de se* against Sellis. The event itself and the trial before the coroner provoked controversy and the grossest scandal. The question is discussed and the Duke exonerated of the charges brought against him, by J. H. Jesse, *Memoirs, etc., of George III.*, 1864, iii. 545, 546, and by George Rose, *Diaries, etc.*, 1860, ii. 437–446. The scandal was revived in 1832 by the publication of a work entitled *The Authentic Memoirs of the Court of England for the last Seventy Years*. The printer and publisher of the work was found guilty. (See *The Tria of Josiah Phillips for a Libel on the Duke of Cumberland*, 1833.)]

And who there besides but Corinna de Staël![1]
   Turned Methodist and Tory!
" Aye—Aye "—quoth he—"'t is the way with them all,
   When Wits grow tired of Glory:
But thanks to the weakness, that thus could pervert her,
Since the dearest of prizes to me 's a deserter: 200
Mem—whenever a sudden conversion I want,
To send to the school of Philosopher Kant;
And whenever I need a critic who can gloss over
All faults—to send for Mackintosh to write up the
      Philosopher."[2]

24.

The Devil waxed faint at the sight of this Saint,
   And he thought himself of eating;
And began to cram from a plate of ham
   Wherewith a Page was retreating—
Having nothing else to do (for "the friends" each so
      near
   Had sold all their souls long before),   210

1. [" At half-past nine [Wednesday, December 8, 1813] there was
a grand dress party at Carlton House, at which her Majesty and the
Prince Regent most graciously received the following distinguished
characters from the Russian Court, viz. the Count and Countess
Leiven, Mad. La Barrone (*sic*) de Staël, Monsieur de Staël," etc.—
Morning Chronicle, December 10, 1813.]

2. [In the review of Madame de Staël's *De L'Allemagne* (*Edinburgh Review*, October, 1813, vol. 22, pp. 198–238), Sir James
Mackintosh enlarged upon and upheld the " opinions of Kant " as
creative and seminal in the world of thought. In the same article
he passes in review the systems of Hobbes, Paley, Bentham,
Reid, etc., and finds words of praise and admiration for each in
turn. See, too, a passage (p. 226) in which he alludes to Coleridge
as a living writer, whose " singular character and unintelligible
style " might, in any other country but England, have won for him
attention if not approval. His own " conversion " from the extreme
liberalism of the *Vindiciæ Gallicæ* of 1791 to the philosophic con-
servatism of the *Introductory Discourse* (1798) to his lecture on
The Law of Nature and Nations, was regarded with suspicion by
Wordsworth and Coleridge, who, afterwards, were still more
effectually " converted " themselves.]

As he swallowed down the bacon he wished himself a
    Jew
  For the sake of another crime more :
For Sinning itself is but half a recreation,
Unless it ensures most infallible Damnation.

25.

But he turned him about, for he heard a sound
  Which even his ear found faults in ;
For whirling above—underneath—and around—
  Were his fairest Disciples Waltzing ! [1]
And quoth he—"though this be—the *premier pas* to me,
  Against it I would warn all—   220
Should I introduce these revels among my younger
    devils,
  They would all turn perfectly carnal :
And though fond of the flesh—yet I never could bear it
Should quite in my kingdom get the upper hand of Spirit."

26.

The Devil (but 't was over) had been vastly glad
  To see the new Drury Lane,
And yet he might have been rather mad
  To see it rebuilt in vain ;
And had he beheld their " Nourjahad," [2]
  Would never have gone again :   230

1. [See Introduction to *The Waltz, Poetical Works*, 1898, i. 475.]
2. [*Illusion, or the Trances of Nourjahad*, a melodrama founded
on *The History of Nourjahad*, By the Editor of Sidney Bidulph
(Mrs. Frances Sheridan, *née* Chamberlaine, 1724–1766), was played
for the first time at Drury Lane Theatre, November 25, 1813.
Byron was exceedingly indignant at being credited with the author-
ship or adaptation. (See Letter to Murray, November 27, 1813,
Letters, 1898, ii. 288, *note* 1.) Miss Sophia Lee, who wrote some of
the *Canterbury Tales*, "made a very elegant musical drama of it"
(*Memoirs of Mrs. F. Sheridan*, by Alicia Lefanu, 1824, p. 296) ;
but this was not the *Nourjahad* of Drury Lane.]

And Satan had taken it much amiss,
They should fasten such a piece on a friend of his—
Though he knew that his works were somewhat sad,
He never had found them *quite* so bad :
For this was "the book" which, of yore, Job, sorely
    smitten,
Said, " Oh that *mine* enemy, *mine* enemy had written " !

27.

Then he found sixty scribblers in separate cells,[1]
    And marvelled what they were doing,
For they looked like little fiends in their own little hells,
    Damnation for others brewing—   240
Though their paper seemed to shrink, from the heat of
    their ink,
    They were only *coolly* reviewing !
And as one of them wrote down the pronoun " *We*,"
    " That Plural "—says Satan—" means *him* and *me*,
With the Editor added to make up the three
Of an Athanasian Trinity,
And render the believers in our ' Articles ' sensible,
How many must combine to form *one* Incomprehensible " !

December 9, 1813.
[Stanzas 1, 2, 3, 4, 5, 8, 10, 11, 12, 17, 18, first published,
    Letters and Journals, 1830, i. 471–474 : stanzas 6, 7,
    9, 13, 14, 15, 16, 19–27, now published for the first
    time from an autograph MS. in the possession of the
    Earl of Ilchester.]

1. [Millbank Penitentiary, which was built in the form of a
pentagon, was finally taken in hand in the spring of 1813.   Solitary
confinement in the "cells" was, at first, reserved as a punishment
for misconduct.—*Memorials of Millbank*, by Arthur Griffiths, 1875,
i. 57.]

WINDSOR POETICS.

LINES COMPOSED ON THE OCCASION OF HIS ROYAL
HIGHNESS THE PRINCE REGENT BEING SEEN STAND-
ING BETWEEN THE COFFINS OF HENRY VIII. AND
CHARLES I., IN THE ROYAL VAULT AT WINDSOR.

FAMED for contemptuous breach of sacred ties,
By headless Charles see heartless Henry lies ;
Between them stands another sceptred thing—
It moves, it reigns—in all but name, a king :

Charles to his people, Henry to his wife,
—In him the double tyrant starts to life :
Justice and Death have mixed their dust in vain,
Each royal Vampire wakes to life again.
Ah, what can tombs avail !—since these disgorge
The blood and dust of both—to mould a George.[1]

[First published, *Poetical Works*, Paris, 1819, vi. 125.]

1. ["I cannot conceive how the *Vault* has got about ; but so it is. It is too *farouche* ; but truth to say, my satires are not very playful."—Letter to Moore, March 12, 1814, *Letters*, 1899, iii. 57-58. Moore had written to him, "Your lines about the bodies of Charles and Henry are, I find, circulated with wonderful avidity ; even some clods in this neighbourhood have had a copy sent to them by some 'young ladies in town.'"—*Ibid.*, p. 57, *note* 3.

The discovery "that King Charles I. was buried in the vault of King Henry VIII.," was made on completing the mausoleum which George III. caused to be built in the tomb-house. The Prince Regent was informed of the circumstance, and on April 1, 1813, the day after the funeral of his mother-in-law, the Duchess of Bruns-wick, he superintended in person the opening of the leaden coffin, which bore the inscription, "King Charles, 1648" (*sic*). See *An Account af what appeared on Opening the Coffin of King Charles the First*, by Sir H. Halford, Bart., 1813, pp. 6, 7. Cornelia Knight, in her *Autobiography* (1861, i. 227), notes that the frolic prince, the "Adonis of fifty," who was in a good humour, and "had given to Princess Charlotte the centre sapphire of Charles's crown," acted "the manner of decapitation on my shoulders." He had "forgotten" Cromwell, who, as Lord Auchinleck reminded Dr. Johnson, had "gart kings ken that they had a *lith* in their neck !"]

[ANOTHER VERSION.]

ON A ROYAL VISIT TO THE VAULTS.[1]

[OR CÆSAR'S DISCOVERY OF C. I. AND H. 8. IN YE SAME
VAULT.]

FAMED for their civil and domestic quarrels
See heartless Henry lies by headless Charles;
Between them stands another sceptred thing,
It lives, it reigns—"aye, every inch a king."
Charles to his people, Henry to his wife,
In him the double tyrant starts to life:
Justice and Death have mixed their dust in vain.
The royal Vampires join and rise again.
What now can tombs avail, since these disgorge
The blood and dirt [2] of both to mould a George!

ICH DIEN.

FROM this emblem what variance your motto evinces,
For the *Man* is his country's—the Arms are the Prince's!

? 1814.
[From an autograph MS. in the possession of Mr. A. H.
Hallam Murray, now for the first time printed.]

1. [From an autograph MS. in the possession of the Hon. Mrs.
Norbury.
The first wrapper has written upon it, "The original Impromptu
within is in the handwriting of the noble author Lord Byron, given
to Mr. Norbury [private secretary to Lord Granville] by Mr. Dallas,
his Lordship's valued relative."
Second wrapper, "Autograph of Lord Byron—*tres précieux.*"
Third (outside) wrapper, "Autographe célèbre de Lord Byron."]

2.   [Πηλὸν αἵματι πεφυραμένον.
"Clay kneaded with blood."
Suetonius, in *Tiberium*, cap. 57.]

CONDOLATORY ADDRESS

TO. SARAH COUNTESS OF JERSEY, ON THE PRINCE
REGENT'S RETURNING HER PICTURE TO MRS. MEE.[1]

WHEN the vain triumph of the imperial lord,
Whom servile Rome obeyed, and yet abhorred,
Gave to the vulgar gaze each glorious bust,
That left a likeness of the brave, or just;
What most admired each scrutinising eye
Of all that decked that passing pageantry?
What spread from face to face that wondering air?
The thought of Brutus[2]—for his was not there!
That absence proved his worth,—that absence fixed
His memory on the longing mind, unmixed;   10
And more decreed his glory to endure,
Than all a gold Colossus could secure.

   If thus, fair Jersey, our desiring gaze
Search for thy form, in vain and mute amaze,
Amidst those pictured charms, whose loveliness,
Bright though they be, thine own had rendered less:
If he, that VAIN OLD MAN, whom truth admits
Heir of his father's crown, and of his wits,
If his corrupted eye, and withered heart,
Could with thy gentle image bear to part;   20

   1. [" The gentlemen of the *Champion*, and Perry, have got hold
(I know not how) of the condolatory Address to Lady Jersey on
the picture-abduction by our Regent, and have published them—
with my name, too, smack—without even asking leave, or inquiring
whether or no! Damn their impudence, and damn every thing. It
has put me out of patience, and so, I shall say no more about it."—
Letter to Moore, August 3, 1814, *Letters*, 1899, iii. 118. For
Byron's letter to Lady Jersey, of May 29, 1814, and a note from her
with reference to a lost (?) copy of the verses, *vide ibid.*, p. 85. Mrs.
Anne Mee (1775?–1851) was a miniature-painter, who was employed
by the Prince Regent to take the portraits of fashionable beauties.]
   2. [Compare *Childe Harold*, Canto IV. stanza lix. line 3, *Poetical
Works*, 1899, ii. 374, *note* 2.]

That tasteless shame be *his*, and ours the grief,
To gaze on Beauty's band without its chief:
Yet Comfort still one selfish thought imparts,
We lose the portrait, but preserve our hearts.

What can his vaulted gallery now disclose?
A *garden* with all flowers—except the rose;—
A *fount* that only wants its living stream;
A *night*, with every star, save Dian's beam.
Lost to our eyes the present forms shall be,
That turn from tracing them to dream of thee;   30
And more on that recalled resemblance pause,
Than all he *shall* not force on our applause.

Long may thy yet meridian lustre shine,
With all that Virtue asks of Homage thine:
The symmetry of youth—the grace of mien—
The eye that gladdens—and the brow serene;
The glossy darkness of that clustering hair,[1]
Which shades, yet shows that forehead more than fair!
Each glance that wins us, and the life that throws
A spell which will not let our looks repose,   40
But turn to gaze again, and find anew
Some charm that well rewards another view.
These are not lessened, these are still as bright,
Albeit too dazzling *for a dotard's sight;*
And those must wait till ev'ry charm is gone,
To please the paltry heart that pleases none;—
That dull cold sensualist, whose sickly eye
In envious dimness passed thy portrait by;
Who racked his little spirit to combine
Its hate of *Freedom's* loveliness, and *thine.*   50

May 29, 1814.
[First published in *The Champion*, July 31, 1814]

1. [See *Conversations . . . with the Countess of Blessington*, 1834, p. 50.]

ANNESLEY HALL.

[*To face p.* 38.

FRAGMENT OF AN EPISTLE TO THOMAS MOORE.

" WHAT say *I?* "—not a syllable further in prose;
I 'm your man " of all measures," dear Tom,—so here
    goes !
Here goes, for a swim on the stream of old Time,
On those buoyant supporters, the bladders of rhyme.
If our weight breaks them down, and we sink in the
    flood,
We are smothered, at least, in respectable mud,
Where the divers of Bathos lie drowned in a heap,
And Southey's last Pæan has pillowed his sleep;
That *Felo de se* who, half drunk with his Malmsey,
Walked out of his depth and was lost in a calm sea,   10
Singing " Glory to God " in a spick and span stanza,
The like (since Tom Sternhold was choked) never man
    saw.[1]

The papers have told you, no doubt, of the fusses,
The fêtes, and the gapings to get at these Russes,[2]—
Of his Majesty's suite, up from coachman to Hetman,—
And what dignity decks the flat face of the great man.

   1. [The two first stanzas of Southey's " *Carmen Triumphale,* for
the Commencement of the Year 1814," end with the line—

     " Glory to God—Deliverance for Mankind ! "]

   2. [" The newspapers will tell you all that is to be told of
emperors, etc. They have dined, and supped, and shown their flat
faces in all thoroughfares and several saloons."—Letter to Moore,
June 14, 1814, *Letters,* 1899, iii. 93, 94.
   From June 6 to June 27, 1814, the Emperor of Russia, and the
King of Prussia were in England. Huge crowds watched all day
and night outside the Pulteney Hotel (105, Piccadilly), where the
Emperor of Russia stayed. Among the foreigners in London were
Nesselrode, Metternich, Blücher, and Platoff, Hetman of the Cossacks.
The two latter were the heroes of the mob. *Ibid.,* p. 93, *note* 1.]

I saw him, last week, at two balls and a party,—
For a Prince, his demeanour was rather too hearty.
You know, *we* are used to quite different graces,

*   *   *   *   *

The Czar's look, I own, was much brighter and brisker,
But then he is sadly deficient in whisker;   21
And wore but a starless blue coat, and in kersey-
mere breeches whisked round, in a waltz with the Jersey,[1]
Who, lovely as ever, seemed just as delighted
With Majesty's presence as those she invited.

*   *   *   *   *

*   *   *   *   *

June, 1814.

[First published, *Letters and Journals,* 1830, i. 561, 562 (*note*).]

ANSWER TO ——'S PROFESSIONS OF AFFECTION.

In hearts like thine ne'er may I hold a place
Till I renounce all sense, all shame, all grace—
That seat,—like seats, the bane of Freedom's realm,
But dear to those presiding at the helm—
Is basely purchased, not with gold alone;
Add Conscience, too, this bargain is your own—
'T is thine to offer with corrupting art
The *rotten borough*[2] of the human heart.

? 1814.

[From an autograph MS., now for the first time printed.]

1. ["The Emperor," says Lady Vernon (*Journal of Mary Frampton,* pp. 225, 226), "is fond of dancing. . . . He waltzed with Lady Jersey, whom he admires, to the great discomposure of the Regent, who has quarrelled with her."]

2. [The phrase, "rotten borough," was used by Sir F. Burdett, *Examiner,* October 12, 1812.]

ON NAPOLEON'S ESCAPE FROM ELBA.[1]

ONCE fairly set out on his party of pleasure,
Taking towns at his liking, and crowns at his leisure,
From Elba to Lyons and Paris he goes,
Making *balls for* the ladies, and *bows to* his foes.

March 27, 1815.
[First published, *Letters and Journals*, 1830, i. 611.]

ENDORSEMENT TO THE DEED OF SEPARATION, IN THE APRIL OF 1816.

A YEAR ago you swore, fond she!
" To love, to honour," and so forth :
Such was the vow you pledged to me,
And here 's exactly what 't is worth.

[First published, *Poetical Works*, 1831, vi. 454.]

[TO GEORGE ANSON BYRON (?) [2]]

I.

AND, dost thou ask the reason of my sadness?
Well, I will tell it thee, unfeeling boy !

1. [It may be taken for granted that the " source " of this epigram was a paragraph in the *Morning Chronicle* of March 27, 1815 : " In the *Moniteur* of Thursday we find the Emperor's own account of his *jaunt* from the Island of Elba to the palace of the Thuilleries. It seems certainly more like a jaunt of pleasure than the progress of an invader through a country to be gained."]
2. [" A short time before Lord Byron quitted England, in 1816, he addressed these lines to an individual by whom he deemed himself injured ; they are but little known."—*Nicnac*, March 25, 1823.]

'T was ill report that urged my brain to madness,
'T was thy tongue's venom poisoned all my joy.

2.

The sadness which thou seest is not sorrow ;
  My wounds are far too deep for simple grief ;
The heart thus withered, seeks in vain to borrow
  From calm reflection, comfort or relief.

3.

The arrow 's flown, and dearly shalt thou rue it ;
  No mortal hand can rid me of my pain :
My heart is pierced, but thou canst not subdue it—
  Revenge is left, and is not left in vain.

? 1816.

[First published, *Nicnac*, March 25, 1823.]

SONG FOR THE LUDDITES.[1]

1.

As the Liberty lads o'er the sea
Bought their freedom, and cheaply, with blood,
    So we, boys, we
  Will *die* fighting, or *live* free,
And down with all kings but King Ludd !

1. [The term "Luddites" dates from 1811, and was applied first to frame-breakers, and then to the disaffected in general. It was derived from a half-witted lad named Ned Lud, who entered a house in a fit of passion, and destroyed a couple of stocking-frames. The song was an impromptu, enclosed in a letter to Moore of December 24, 1816. "I have written it principally," he says, "to shock your neighbour [Hodgson ?] who is all clergy and loyalty— mirth and innocence—milk and water." See *Letters*, 1900, iv. 30 ; and for General Lud and "Luddites," see *Letters*, 1898, ii. 97, *note* 1.]

2.

When the web that we weave is complete,
And the shuttle exchanged for the sword,
 We will fling the winding sheet
 O'er the despot at our feet,
And dye it deep in the gore he has poured.

3.

Though black as his heart its hue,
Since his veins are corrupted to mud,
  Yet this is the dew
  Which the tree shall renew
Of Liberty, planted by Ludd !

December 24, 1816.
[First published, *Letters and Journals*, 1830, ii. 58.]

TO THOMAS MOORE.

WHAT are you doing now,
 Oh Thomas Moore?
What are you doing now,
 Oh Thomas Moore?
Sighing or suing now,
Rhyming or wooing now,
Billing or cooing now,
 Which, Thomas Moore?

But the Carnival 's coming,
 Oh Thomas Moore !
The Carnival 's coming,
 Oh Thomas Moore !

Masking and humming,
Fifing and drumming,
Guitarring and strumming,
Oh Thomas Moore !

December 24, 1816.
[First published, *Letters and Journals*, 1830, ii. 58, 59.]

TO MR. MURRAY.

To hook the Reader, you, John Murray,
   Have published " Anjou's Margaret," [1]
Which won't be sold off in a hurry
   (At least, it has not been as yet) ;
And then, still further to bewilder him,
   Without remorse, you set up " Ilderim ; " [2]
   So mind you don't get into debt,—
Because—as how—if you should fail,
These books would be but baddish bail.
And mind you do *not* let escape
   These rhymes to *Morning Post* or Perry,
Which would be *very* treacherous—*very*,
And get me into such a scrape !
   For, firstly, I should have to sally,
   All in my little boat, against a *Galley* ;
And, should I chance to slay the Assyrian wight,
Have next to combat with the female Knight :
And pricked to death expire upon her needle,
A sort of end which I should take indeed ill !

March 25, 1817.
[First published, *Letters and Journals*, 1830, ii. 91.]

1. [*Margaret of Anjou*, by Margaret Holford, 1816.]
2. [*Ilderim, a Syrian Tale*, by H. Gally Knight, 1816.]

VERSICLES.

I READ the " Christabel ;" [1]
  Very well :
I read the " Missionary ; " [2]
  Pretty—very :
I tried at " Ilderim ; "
  Ahem !
I read a sheet of " Marg'ret of *Anjou ;* "
  Can you ?
I turned a page of Webster's " Waterloo ;" [3]
  Pooh ! pooh !
I looked at Wordsworth's milk-white " Rylstone Doe ;" [4]
  Hillo !
I read " Glenarvon," too, by Caro Lamb ; [5]
  God damn !

       March 25, 1817.
  [First published, *Letters and Journals*, 1830, ii. 87.]

QUEM DEUS VULT PERDERE PRIUS DEMENTAT. [6]

GOD maddens him whom 't is his will to lose,
And gives the choice of death or phrenzy—choose.

    [First published, *Letters*, 1900, iv. 93.]

1. [*Christabel, etc.*, by S. T. Coleridge, 1816.]
2. [*The Missionary of the Andes, a Poem*, by W. L. Bowles, 1815.]
3. [*Waterloo and other Poems*, by J. Wedderburn Webster, 1816.]
4. [*The White Doe of Rylstone, or the Fate of the Nortons, a Poem*, by W. Wordsworth, 1815.]
5. [*Glenarvon, a Novel* [by Lady Caroline Lamb], 1816.]
6. [*A propos* of Maturin's tragedy, *Manuel* (*vide post*, p. 48, *note* 1), Byron "does into English" the Latin proverb by way of contrast to the text, " Whom the Lord loveth He chasteneth ; blessed be the Name of the Lord" (Letter to Murray, April 2, 1817).]

TO THOMAS MOORE.

1.

My boat is on the shore,
    And my bark is on the sea;
But, before I go, Tom Moore,
    Here's a double health to thee!

2.

Here's a sigh to those who love me,
    And a smile to those who hate;
And, whatever sky's above me,
    Here's a heart for every fate.

3.

Though the Ocean roar around me,
    Yet it still shall bear me on;
Though a desert shall surround me,
    It hath springs that may be won.

4.

Were 't the last drop in the well,
    As I gasped upon the brink,
Ere my fainting spirit fell,
    'T is to thee that I would drink.

5.

With that water, as this wine,
    The libation I would pour
Should be—peace with thine and mine,
    And a health to thee, Tom Moore.[1]

July, 1817.

[First published, *Waltz,* London, W. Benbow, 1821, p. 29.]

1. ["This should have been written fifteen months ago; the first stanza was."—Letter to Moore, July 10, 1817.]

EPISTLE FROM MR. MURRAY TO DR. POLIDORI.[1]

DEAR Doctor, I have read your play,
Which is a good one in its way,—
Purges the eyes, and moves the bowels,
And drenches handkerchiefs like towels
With tears, that, in a flux of grief,
Afford hysterical relief
To shattered nerves and quickened pulses,
Which your catastrophe convulses.

   I like your moral and machinery;
Your plot, too, has such scope for Scenery!   10
Your dialogue is apt and smart;
The play's concoction full of art;
Your hero raves, your heroine cries,
All stab, and every body dies.
In short, your tragedy would be
The very thing to hear and see:
And for a piece of publication,
If I decline on this occasion,
It is not that I am not sensible
To merits in themselves ostensible,   20
But—and I grieve to speak it—plays
Are drugs—mere drugs, Sir—now-a-days.

1. ["By the way," writes Murray, Aug. 5, 1817 (*Memoir, etc.*, i. 386), "Polidori has sent me his tragedy! Do me the kindness to send by return of post a *delicate* declension of it, which I engage faithfully to copy."
"I never," said Byron, "was much more disgusted with any human production than with the eternal nonsense, and *tracasseries*, and emptiness, and ill-humour, and vanity of this young person; but he has some talent, and is a man of honour, and has dispositions of amendment. Therefore use your interest for him, for he is improved and improvable;" and, in a letter to Murray, Aug. 21, 1817, "You want a 'civil and delicate declension' for the medical tragedy? Take it."—For J. W. Polidori (1795-1821), see *Letters*, 1899, iii. 284 *note* 1.]

I had a heavy loss by *Manuel*—[1]
Too lucky if it prove not annual,—
And Sotheby, with his *Orestes*,[2]
(Which, by the way, the old Bore's best is,
Has lain so very long on hand,
That I despair of all demand ;
I 've advertised, but see my books,
Or only watch my Shopman's looks ;—   30
Still *Ivan, Ina*,[3] and such lumber,
My back-shop glut, my shelves encumber.

    There 's Byron too, who once did better,
Has sent me, folded in a letter,
A sort of—it 's no more a drama
Than *Darnley, Ivan*, or *Kehama* ;
So altered since last year his pen is,
I think he 's lost his wits at Venice.

    *   *   *   *   *

    *   *   *   *   *

In short, Sir, what with one and t' other,
I dare not venture on another.   40
I write in haste ; excuse each blunder ;
The Coaches through the street so thunder !
My room 's so full—we 've Gifford here
Reading MS., with Hookham Frere,

    1. [Maturin's second tragedy, *Manuel*, produced at Drury Lane, March 8, 1817, with Kean as "Manuel Count Valdis, failed, and after five nights was withdrawn." It was published in 1817. "It is," says Byron (letter to Murray, June 14, 1817), "the absurd work of a clever man."—*Letters*, 1900, iv. 134, and *note* 1.]

    2. [Sotheby published, in 1814, *Five Tragedies*, viz. "The Confession," "Orestes," "Ivan," "The Death of Darnley," and "Zamorin and Zama."]

    3. [*Ina, A Tragedy*, by Mrs. Wilmot [Barberina Ogle (1768–1854), daughter of Sir Chaloner Ogle], afterwards Lady Dacre, was produced at Drury Lane, April 22, 1815. Her "tragedy," writes Byron to Moore, April 23, 1815, "was last night damned." See *Letters*, 1898, ii. 332, *note* 3, *etc.* ; *ibid.*, 1899, iii. 195, *note* 1.]

Pronouncing on the nouns and particles,
Of some of our forthcoming Articles.

    The *Quarterly*—Ah, Sir, if you
Had but the Genius to review !—
A smart Critique upon St. Helena,
Or if you only would but tell in a   50
Short compass what——but to resume ;
As I was saying, Sir, the Room—
The Room 's so full of wits and bards,
Crabbes, Campbells, Crokers, Freres, and Wards
And others, neither bards nor wits :
My humble tenement admits
All persons in the dress of Gent.,
From Mr. Hammond to Dog Dent.[1]

    A party dines with me to-day,
All clever men, who make their way :   60
Crabbe, Malcolm,[2] Hamilton,[3] and Chantrey,
Are all partakers of my pantry.
They 're at this moment in discussion
On poor De Staël's late dissolution.
Her book,[4] they say, was in advance——

1. [George Hammond (1763–1853) was a distinguished diplomatist, who twice (1795–1806 and 1807–1809) held the office of Under-Secretary of State for Foreign Affairs. He is associated with the foundation of the *Anti-Jacobin* and the *Quarterly Review*. In the drawing-room of Albemarle Street, he was Murray's "chief 4-o'clock man," until his official duties compelled him to settle at Paris.—*Letters*, 1900, iv. 160, *note* 1.

John Dent, M.P., a banker, was nicknamed "Dog Dent" because he was concerned in the introduction of the Dog-tax Bill in 1796. In 1802 he introduced a Bill to abolish bull-baiting.—*Ibid.*]

2. [Sir John Malcolm (1769–1833), soldier, administrator, and diplomatist, published (January, 1815) his *History of Persia*.—*Letters*, 1899, iii. 113, *note* 1.]

3. [For "Dark Hamilton," W. R. Hamilton (1777–1859), see *Childe Harold*, Canto II. stanza xiii. *var.* 1, *Poetical Works*, 1899, ii. 108, *note* 1. Lines 61, 62 were added October 12, 1817.]

4. [Madame de Staël's *Considérations sur la Révolution Française* was offered to Murray in June, 1816 (*Memoir, etc.*, 1891, i. 316),

Pray Heaven, she tell the truth of France !
'T is said she certainly was married
To Rocca, and had twice miscarried,
No—not miscarried, I opine,—
But brought to bed at forty-nine.   70
Some say she died a Papist ; some
Are of opinion that 's a Hum ;
I don't know that—the fellows Schlegel,[1]
Are very likely to inveigle
A dying person in compunction
To try th' extremity of Unction.
But peace be with her ! for a woman
Her talents surely were uncommon,
Her Publisher (and Public too)
The hour of her demise may rue——   80
For never more within his shop he—
Pray—was not she interred at Coppet?
Thus run our time and tongues away ;—
But, to return, Sir, to your play :
Sorry, Sir, but I cannot deal,
Unless 't were acted by O'Neill.
My hands are full—my head so busy,
I 'm almost dead—and always dizzy ;
And so, with endless truth and hurry,
Dear Doctor, I am yours,   90
                    JOHN MURRAY.

August 21, 1817.
[First published, *Letters and Journals*, 1830, ii. 139-141.
Lines 67–82 first published, *Letters*, 1900, iv. 161.]

and the sum of £4000 asked for the work. During the negotiations,
Madame de Staël died (July 14, 1817), and the book was eventually
published by Messrs. Baldwin and Cradock.—*Letters*, 1900, iv. 94,
note.]

1. [Byron and the elder Schlegel met at Copet, in 1816, but they
did not take to each other. Byron " would not flatter him,"
perhaps because he did not appreciate or flatter Byron.]

EPISTLE TO MR. MURRAY.

I.

MY dear Mr. Murray,
You 're in a damned hurry
  To set up this ultimate Canto;[1]
But (if they don't rob us)
You 'll see Mr. Hobhouse
  Will bring it safe in his portmanteau.

2.

For the Journal you hint of,[2]
As ready to print off,
  No doubt you do right to commend it;
But as yet I have writ off
The devil a bit of
  Our " Beppo : "—when copied, I 'll send it.

3.

In the mean time you 've " Galley "[3]
Whose verses all tally,
  Perhaps you may say he 's a Ninny,
But if you abashed are
Because of *Alashtar*,
  He 'll piddle another *Phrosine*.[4]

1. [The Fourth Canto of *Childe Harold*.]
2. [Murray bought a half-share in *Blackwood's Edinburgh Monthly Magazine* in August, 1818, and remained its joint proprietor till December, 1819, when it became the property of William Blackwood. But perhaps the reference is to Byron's Swiss Journal of September, 1816.]
3. [Henry Gally Knight (1786–1846), who was a contemporary of Byron at Trinity College, Cambridge, was a poetaster, and, afterwards, a writer of works on architecture. His Oriental verses supplied Byron with a subject for more than one indifferent *jeu d'esprit*.]
4. [*Phrosyne*, a Grecian tale, and *Alashtar*, an Arabian tale, were

4.

Then you 've Sotheby's Tour,—[1]
No great things, to be sure,—
   You could hardly begin with a less work ;
For the pompous rascallion,
Who don't speak Italian
   Nor French, must have scribbled by guess-work.

5.

No doubt he 's a rare man
Without knowing German
   Translating his way up Parnassus,
And now still absurder
He meditates Murder
   As you 'll see in the trash he calls *Tasso*'s.

6.

But you 've others his betters
The real men of letters
   Your Orators—Critics—and Wits—
And I 'll bet that your Journal
(Pray is it diurnal ?)
   Will pay with your luckiest hits.

7.

You can make any loss up
With "Spence"[2] and his gossip,
   A work which must surely succeed ;

published in 1817. In a letter to Murray, September 4, 1817,
Byron writes, " I have received safely, though tardily, the magnesia
and tooth-powder, *Phrosine* and *Alashtar*. I shall clean my teeth
with one, and wipe my shoes with the other."—*Letters*, 1901, iv.]
  1. [Sotheby's *Farewell to Italy* and *Occasional Poems* were published in 1818, as the record of a tour which he had taken in 1816–17
with his family, Professor Elmsley, and Dr. Playfair. For Byron's
unfinished skit on Sotheby's Tour, see *Letters*, 1900, iv. Appendix V.
pp. 452, 453.]
  2. [*Observations, Anecdotes, and Characters of Books and Men*, by

Then Queen Mary's Epistle-craft,[1]
With the new " Fytte" of " Whistlecraft,"
   Must make people purchase and read.

8.

Then you 've General Gordon,[2]
Who girded his sword on,
   To serve with a Muscovite Master,
And help him to polish
A nation so owlish,
   They thought shaving their beards a disaster.

9.

For the man, " *poor and shrewd*," [3]
With whom you 'd conclude
   A compact without more delay,
Perhaps some such pen is
Still extant in Venice ;
   But please, Sir, to mention *your pay*.

10.

Now tell me some news
Of your friends and the Muse,
   Of the Bar, or the Gown, or the House,

the Rev. Joseph Spence, arranged, with notes, by the late Edmund
Malone, Esq., 1 vol. 8vo, 1820.]
   1. [*The Life of Mary Queen of Scots*, by George Chalmers, 2 vols.
4to, 1819.]
   2. [Thomas Gordon (1788–1841) entered the Scots Greys in
1808. Two years later he visited Ali Pasha (see *Letters*, 1898, i.
246, *note* 1) in Albania, and travelled in Persia and Turkey in the
East. From 1813 to 1815 he served in the Russian Army. He
wrote a *History of the Greek Revolution*, 1832, 2 vols., but it does
not appear that he was negotiating with Murray for the publication
of any work at this period.]
   3. *Vide* your letter.

From Canning, the tall wit,
To Wilmot,[1] the small wit,
   Ward's creeping Companion and *Louse*,

11.

Who 's so damnably bit
With fashion and Wit,
   That he crawls on the surface like Vermin,
But an Insect in both,—
By his Intellect's growth,
   Of what size you may quickly determine.

Venice, *January* 8, 1818.
[First published, *Letters and Journals*, 1830, ii. 156, 157;
stanzas 3, 5, 6, 10, 11, first published, *Letters*, 1900,
iv. 191–193.]

ON THE BIRTH OF JOHN WILLIAM RIZZO HOPPNER.[3]

His father's sense, his mother's grace,
   In him, I hope, will always fit so;
With—still to keep him in good case—
   The health and appetite of Rizzo.

February 20, 1818.
[First published, *Letters and Journals*, 1830, ii. 134.]

1. [Probably Sir Robert John Wilmot (1784–1841) (afterwards
Wilmot Horton), Byron's first cousin, who took a prominent part in
the destruction of the "Memoirs," May 17, 1824. (For Lady
Wilmot Horton, the original of "She walks in beauty," see *Poetical
Works*, 1900, iii. 381, *note* 1.)]
2. [Stanzas 12, 13, 14 cannot be published.]
3. [Richard Belgrave Hoppner (1786–1872), second son of John
Hoppner, R.A., was appointed English Consul at Venice, October,
1814. (See *Letters*, 1900, iv. 83, *note* 1.) The quatrain was translated (see the following poem) into eleven different languages—
Greek, Latin, Italian (also the Venetian dialect), German, French,

[E NIHILO NIHIL;

OR

AN EPIGRAM BEWITCHED.]

OF rhymes I printed seven volumes— [1]
The list concludes John Murray's columns:
Of these there have been few translations [2]
For Gallic or Italian nations;
And one or two perhaps in German—
But in this last I can't determine.
But then I only sung of passions
That do not suit with modern fashions;
Of Incest and such like diversions
Permitted only to the Persians,
Or Greeks to bring upon their stages—
But that was in the earlier ages
Besides my style is the romantic,
Which some call fine, and some call frantic;
While others are or would seem *as* sick
Of repetitions nicknamed Classic.
For my part all men must allow
Whatever I was, I 'm classic now.

Spanish, Illyrian, Hebrew, Armenian, and Samaritan, and printed
"in a small neat volume in the seminary of Padua." For nine of
these translations see *Works*, 1832, xi. pp. 324–326, and 1891,
p. 571. Rizzo was a Venetian surname. See W. Stewart Rose's
verses to Byron, "Grinanis, Mocenijas, Baltis, Rizzi, Compassionate
our cruel case," etc., *Letters*, iv. 212.]

1. [Byron must have added the Fourth Canto of *Childe Harold*
to the complete edition of the *Poetical Works* in six volumes. See
Murray's list, dated "Albemarle Street, London, January, 1818."
The seventh volume of the Collected Works was not issued till 1819.]

2. [A French translation of the *Bride of Abydos* appeared in
1816, an Italian translation of the *Lament of Tasso* in 1817.
Goethe (see *Letters*, 1901, v. 503–521) translated fragments of
Manfred in 1817, 1818, but the earliest German translation of the
entire text of *Manfred* was issued in 1819.]

I saw and left my fault in time,
And chose a topic all sublime—
Wondrous as antient war or hero—
Then played and sung away like Nero,
Who sang of Rome, and I of Rizzo :
The subject has improved my wit so,
The first four lines the poet sees
Start forth in fourteen languages !
Though of seven volumes none before
Could ever reach the fame of four,
Henceforth I sacrifice all Glory
To the Rinaldo of my Story :
I 've sung his health and appetite
(The last word 's not translated right—
He 's turned it, God knows how, to vigour) [1]
I 'll sing them in a book that 's bigger.
Oh ! Muse prepare for thy Ascension !
And generous Rizzo ! thou my pension.

February, 1818.

[From an autograph MS. in the possession of Mr. Murray,
now for the first time printed.]

TO MR. MURRAY.

I.

STRAHAN, Tonson, Lintot of the times,[2]
Patron and publisher of rhymes,
For thee the bard up Pindus climbs,
    My Murray.

1. [See the last line of the Italian translation of the quatrain.]
2. [William Strahan (1715–1785) published Johnson's *Dictionary*,
Gibbon's *Decline and Fall*, Cook's *Voyages*, *etc.* He was great-
grandfather of the mathematician William Spottiswoode (1825–
1883).

2.

To thee, with hope and terror dumb,
The unfledged MS. authors come ;
Thou printest all—and sellest some—
                My Murray.

3.

Upon thy table's baize so green
The last new Quarterly is seen,—
But where is thy new Magazine,[1]
                My Murray ?

4.

Along thy sprucest bookshelves shine
The works thou deemest most divine —
The Art of Cookery,[2] and mine,
                My Murray.

5.

Tours, Travels, Essays, too, I wist,
And Sermons, to thy mill bring grist ;
And then thou hast the *Navy List*,
                My Murray.

Jacob Tonson (1656?–1736) published for Otway, Dryden, Addison,. etc. He was secretary of the Kit-Cat Club, 1700. He was the publisher (1712, etc.) of the *Spectator*.

Barnaby Bernard Lintot (1675–1736) was at one time (1718) in partnership with Tonson. He published Pope's *Iliad* in 1715, and the *Odyssey*, 1725–26.]

1. [See note 2, p. 51.]

2. [Mrs. Rundell's *Domestic Cookery*, published in 1806, was one of Murray's most successful books. In 1822 he purchased the copyright from Mrs. Rundell for £2000 (see *Letters*, 1898, ii. 375 ; and *Memoir of John Murray*, 1891, ii. 124).]

6.

And Heaven forbid I should conclude,
Without " the Board of Longitude," [1]
Although this narrow paper would,
     My Murray.

Venice, April 11, 1818.

[First published, Letters and Journals, 1830, ii. 171.]

BALLAD.

TO THE TUNE OF " SALLEY IN OUR ALLEY."

1.

OF all the twice ten thousand bards
    That ever penned a canto,
Whom Pudding or whom Praise rewards
    For lining a portmanteau ;
Of all the poets ever known,
    From Grub-street to Fop's Alley,[2]
The Muse may boast—the World must own
    There 's none like pretty Gally ! [3]

2.

He writes as well as any Miss,
    Has published many a poem ;

1. [The sixth edition of Childe Harold's Pilgrimage (1813) was "printed by T. Davison, Whitefriars, for John Murray, Bookseller to the Admiralty, and the Board of Longitude." Medwin (Conversations, 1824, p. 259) attributes to Byron a statement that Murray had to choose between continuing to be his publisher and printing the "Navy Lists," and "that there was no hesitation which way he should decide : the Admiralty carried the day." In his "Notes" to the Conversations (November 2, 1824) Murray characterized "the passage about the Admiralty" as "unfounded in fact, and no otherwise deserving of notice than to mark its absurdity."]
2. [For Fop's Alley, see Poetical Works, 1898, i. 410, note 2.]
3. [H. Gally Knight (1786–1846) was at Cambridge with Byron.]

The shame is yours, the gain is his,
  In case you should not know 'em :
He has ten thousand pounds a year—
  I do not mean to vally—
His songs at sixpence would be dear,
  So give them gratis, Gally !

3.

And if this statement should seem queer,
  Or set down in a hurry,
Go, ask (if he will be sincere)
  His bookseller—John Murray.
Come, say, how many have been sold,
  And don't stand shilly-shally,
Of bound and lettered, red and gold,
  Well printed works of Gally.

4.

For Astley's circus Upton[1] writes,
  And also for the Surry ; (sic)
Fitzgerald weekly still recites,
  Though grinning Critics worry :
Miss Holford's Peg, and Sotheby's Saul,
  In fame exactly tally ;
From Stationer's Hall to Grocer's Stall
  They go—and so does Gally.

1. [William Upton was the author of *Poems on Several Occasions*, 1788, and of the *Words of the most Favourite Songs, Duets, etc.*, sung at the Royal Amphitheatre, Westminster Bridge, etc. In the dedication to Mrs. Astley he speaks of himself as the author of the *Black Castle*, *Fair Rosamond*, etc. He has also been credited with the words of James Hook's famous song, *A Lass of Richmond Hill*, but this has been disputed. (See *Notes and Queries*, 1878, Series V. vol. ix. p. 495.)]

5.

He rode upon a Camel's hump [1]
　Through Araby the sandy,
Which surely must have hurt the rump
　Of this poetic dandy.
His rhymes are of the costive kind,
　And barren as each valley
In deserts which he left behind
　Has been the Muse of Gally.

6.

He has a Seat in Parliament,
　Is fat and passing wealthy ;
And surely he should be content
　With these and being healthy :
But Great Ambition will misrule
　Men at all risks to sally,—
Now makes a poet—now a fool,
　And *we* know *which*—of Gally.

7.

Some in the playhouse like to row,
　Some with the Watch to battle,
Exchanging many a midnight blow
　To Music of the Rattle.
Some folks like rowing on the Thames,
　Some rowing in an Alley,
But all the Row my fancy claims
　Is *rowing* of my *Gally*.

April 11, 1818.[2]

1. [Compare—
　　"Th' unloaded camel, pacing slow,
　Crops the rough herbage or the tamarisk spray."
Alashtar (by H. G. Knight), 1817, Canto I. stanza viii. lines 5, 6.]
2. [From an autograph MS. in the possession of Mr. Murray,

ANOTHER SIMPLE BALLAT.

1.

Mrs. Wilmot sate scribbling a play,
  Mr. Sotheby sate sweating behind her;
But what are all these to the Lay
  Of Gally i.o. the Grinder?
    Gally i.o. i.o., etc.

2.

I bought me some books tother day,
  And sent them down stairs to the binder;
But the Pastry Cook carried away
  My Gally i.o. the Grinder.
    Gally i.o. i.o., etc.

3.

I wanted to kindle my taper,
  And called to the Maid to remind her;
And what should she bring me for paper
  But Gally i.o. the Grinder.
    Gally i.o. i.o.

4.

Among my researches for Ease
  I went where one 's certain to find her:
The first thing by her throne that one sees
  Is Gally i.o. the Grinder.
    Gally i.o. i.o.

now for the first time printed. For stanzas 3, 4, 6, see *Letters*,
1900, iv. 219, 220. For stanzas 1, 2, 3 of "Another Simple
Ballat. To the tune of Tally i.o. the Grinder" (probably a variant
of Dibdin's song, "The Grinders, or more Grist to the Mill"),
vide ibid., pp. 220, 221.]

5.

Away with old Homer the blind—
    I 'll show you a poet that 's blinder :
You may see him whene'er you 've a mind
    In Gally i.o. the Grinder.
        Gally i.o. i.o., etc.

6.

Blindfold he runs groping for fame,
    And hardly knows where he will find her :
She don't seem to take to the name
    Of Gally i.o. the Grinder.
        Gally i.o. i.o., etc.

7.

Yet the Critics have been very kind,
    And Mamma and his friends have been kinder;
But the greatest of Glory 's behind
    For Gally i.o. the Grinder.
        Gally i.o. i.o.

April 11, 1818.
[From an autograph MS. in the possession of Mr. Murray,
now for the first time printed.]

EPIGRAM.

FROM THE FRENCH OF RULHIÈRES.[1]

IF for silver, or for gold,
    You could melt ten thousand pimples
    Into half a dozen dimples,

---

1. [" Would you like an epigram—a translation ? It was written
on some Frenchwoman, by Rulhières, I believe."—Letter to
Murray, August 12, 1819, *Letters*, 1900, iv. 346.
    Claude Carloman de Rulhière (1718–1791), historian, poet, and
epigrammatist, was the author of *Anecdotes sur la révolution de Russie
en l'année* 1762, *Histoire de l'anarchie de Pologne* (1807), etc.   His

Then your face we might behold,
  Looking, doubtless, much more snugly,
  Yet even *then* 'twould be damned ugly.

August 12, 1819.
[First published, *Letters and Journals*, 1830, ii. 235.]

EPILOGUE.[1]

1.

THERE 's something in a stupid ass,
  And something in a heavy dunce ;
But never since I went to school
  I heard or saw so damned a fool
As William Wordsworth is for once.

2.

And now I 've seen so great a fool
  As William Wordsworth is for once ;
I really wish that Peter Bell
  And he who wrote it were in hell,
For writing nonsense for the nonce.

epigrams are included in "Poésies Diverses," which are appended
to *Les jeux de Mains*, a poem in three cantos, published in 1808, and
were collected in his *Œuvres Posthumes*, 1819 ; but there is no trace
of the original of Byron's translation. Perhaps it is *after* de Rulhière,
who more than once epigrammatizes "Une Vieille Femme."]

1. [The MS. of the "Epilogue" is inscribed on the margin of a
copy of Wordsworth's *Peter Bell*, inserted in a set of Byron's *Works*
presented by George W. Childs to the Drexel Institute. (From
information kindly supplied by Mr. John H. Bewley, of Buffalo,
New York.)

The first edition of *Peter Bell* appeared early in 1819, and a
second edition followed in May, 1819. In Byron's Dedication of
Marino Faliero, "To Baron Goethe," dated October 20, 1820
(*Poetical Works*, 1891, iv. 341), the same allusions to Sir George
Beaumont, to Wordsworth's "place in the Excise," and to his
admission that *Peter Bell* had been withheld "for one and twenty
years," occur in an omitted paragraph first published, *Letters*, 1891,
v. 101. So close a correspondence of an unpublished fragment
with a genuine document leaves little doubt as to the composition of
the "Epilogue."]

3.

It saw the " light in ninety-eight,"
　　Sweet babe of one and twenty years ! [1]
And then he gives it to the nation
　　And deems himself of Shakespeare's peers !

4.

He gives the perfect work to light !
　　Will Wordsworth, if I might advise,
Content you with the praise you get
　　From Sir George Beaumont, Baronet,
And with your place in the Excise !

1819.

[**First** published, *Philadelphia Record, December* 28, 1891.]

ON MY WEDDING-DAY.

HERE 's a happy New Year ! but with reason
　　I beg you 'll permit me to say—
Wish me *many* returns of the *Season,*
　　But as *few* as you please of the *Day.*[2]

January 2, 1820.

[First published, *Letters and Journals,* 1830, ii. 294.]

EPITAPH FOR WILLIAM PITT.

WITH Death doomed to grapple,
　　Beneath this cold slab, he
Who lied in the Chapel
　　Now lies in the Abbey.

January 2, 1820.

[First published, *Letters and Journals,* 1830, ii. 295.]

1. [The missing line may be, " To *permanently* fill a station," see
Preface to *Peter Bell.*]
2. [Medwin (*Conversations,* 1824, p. 156) prints an alternative—
　　" You may wish me returns of the season,
　　　　Let us, prithee, have none of the day ! "]

EPIGRAM.

IN digging up your bones, Tom Paine,
    Will. Cobbett [1] has done well:
You visit him on Earth again,
    He 'll visit you in Hell.

or—

    You come to him on Earth again
    He 'll go with you to Hell!

January 2, 1820.
[First published, *Letters and Journals*, 1830, ii. 295.]

EPITAPH.

POSTERITY will ne'er survey
    A nobler grave than this;
Here lie the bones of Castlereagh:
    Stop traveller,   *   *

January 2, 1820.
[First published, *Lord Byron's Works*, 1833, xvii. 246.]

EPIGRAM.

THE world is a bundle of hay,
    Mankind are the asses who pull;
Each tugs it a different way,—
    And the greatest of all is John Bull!

[First published, *Letters and Journals*, 1830, ii. 494.]

1. [Cobbett, by way of atonement for youthful vituperation (he called him "a ragamuffin deist") of Tom Paine, exhumed his bones from their first resting-place at New Rochelle, and brought them to Liverpool on his return to England in 1819. They were preserved by Cobbett at Normanby, Farnham, till his death in 1835, but were sold in consequence of his son's bankruptcy in 1836, and passed into the keeping of a Mr. Tilly, who was known to be their fortunate possessor as late as 1844. (See *Notes and Queries*, 1868, Series IV. vol. i. pp. 201–203.)]

MY BOY HOBBIE O.[1]

New Song to the tune of

> " *Whare hae ye been a' day,*
> *My boy Tammy O ?*
> *Courting o' a young thing*
> *Just come frae her Mammie O.*"

I.

How came you in Hob's pound to cool,
  My boy Hobbie O ?

1. [John Cam Hobhouse (1786–1869) (see *Letters*, 1898, i. 163, *note* 1) was committed to Newgate in December, 1819, for certain passages in a pamphlet entitled, *A Trifling Mistake in Thomas Lord Erskine's recent Preface*, which were voted (December 10) a breach of privilege. He remained in prison till the dissolution on the king's death, February 20, 1820, when he stood and was returned for Westminster. Byron's Liberalism was intermittent, and he felt, or, as Hobhouse thought, pretended to feel, as a Whig and an aristocrat with regard to the free lances of the Radical party. The sole charge in this "filthy ballad," which annoyed Hobhouse, was that he had founded a Whig Club when he was an undergraduate at Cambridge. He assured Murray (see his letter, November, 1820, *Letters*, vol. iv. Appendix XI. pp. 498–500) that he was not the founder of the club, and that Byron himself was a member. "As for his Lordship's vulgar notions about the *mob*," he adds, "they are very fit for the Poet of the *Morning Post*, and for nobody else." There is no reason to suppose that Byron was in any way responsible for the version as sent to the *Morning Post*.

"MY BOY HOBBY O.

[ANOTHER VERSION.]

"To the Editor of the *Morning Post*.

"SIR,—A copy of verses, to the tune of ' *My boy Tammy*,' are repeated in literary circles, and said to be written by a Noble Lord of the highest poetical fame, upon his quondam friend and annotator. My memory does not enable me to repeat more than the first two verses quite accurately, but the humourous spirit of the Song may be gathered from these :—

I.

"Why were you put in Lob's pond,
  My boy, HOBBY O ? (*bis*)
For telling folks to pull the House
  By the ears into the Lobby O !

Because I bade the people pull
The House into the Lobby O.

2.

" Who are your grand Reformers now,
My boy, HOBBY O ? (*bis*)
There 's me and BURDETT,—gentlemen,
And Blackguards HUNT and COBBY O !

3.

" Have you no other friends but these,
My boy, HOBBY O ? (*bis*)
Yes, Southwark's *Knight*,* the County BYNG,
And in the City, BOBBY O !

4.

" How do you recreate yourselves,
My boy, HOBBY O ? (*bis*)
We spout with tavern Radicals,
And drink with them hob-nobby O !

5.

" What purpose can such folly work,
My boy, HOBBY O ? (*bis*)
It gives our partisans a chance
Watches to twitch from fob-by O !

6.

" Have they no higher game in view,
My boy, HOBBY O ? (*bis*)
Oh yes ; to stir the people up,
And then to head the mob-by O.

7.

" But sure they 'll at their ruin pause,
My boy, HOBBY O ? (*bis*)
No ! they 'd see King and Parliament
Both d—d without a sob-by O !

8.

" But, if they fail, they 'll be hanged up,
My boy, HOBBY O ? (*bis*)
Why, then, they 'll swing, like better men,
And that will end the job-by O !
"PHILO-RADICLE.

"April 15, 1820."

* " Southwark's Knight " was General Sir Robert Thomas Wilson
(1777–1849), who was returned for Southwark in 1818, and again

2.

What did the House upon this call,
  My boy Hobbie O?
They voted me to Newgate all,
  Which is an awkward Jobby O.

3.

Who are now the people's men,
  My boy Hobbie O?
There's I and Burdett—Gentlemen
  And blackguard Hunt and Cobby O.

4.

You hate the house—*why* canvass, then?
  My boy Hobbie O?
Because I would reform the den
  As member for the Mobby O.

5.

Wherefore do you hate the Whigs,
  My boy Hobbie O?
Because they want to run their rigs,
  As under Walpole Bobby O.

6.

But when we at Cambridge were
  My boy Hobbie O,
If my memory dont err
  You founded a Whig Clubbie O.

in 1820; "County Byng" was George Byng, M.P. for Middlesex; and "Bobby" was Sir Robert Waithman (1764–1833), who represented the City of London in 1818, but lost his seat to Sir William Curtis in 1820. All these were advanced Liberals, and, as such, Parliamentary friends of Hobhouse.]

7.

When to the mob you make a speech,
  My boy Hobbie O,
How do you keep without their reach
  The watch within your fobby O?

8.

But never mind such petty things,
  My boy Hobbie O ;
God save the people—damn all Kings,
  So let us Crown the Mobby O !

Yours truly,

(Signed)   *INFIDUS SCURRA.*

March 23*rd*, 1820.
[First published *Murray's Magazine*, March, 1887, vol. i.
pp. 292, 293.]

LINES

ADDRESSED BY LORD BYRON TO MR. HOBHOUSE ON HIS
ELECTION FOR WESTMINSTER.[1]

WOULD you go to the house by the true gate,
  Much faster than ever Whig Charley went;
Let Parliament send you to Newgate,
  And Newgate will send you to Parliament.

April 9, 1820.
[First published, *Miscellaneous Poems*, printed for J. Bumpus,
1824.]

1. ["I send you 'a Song of Triumph,' by W. Botherby, Esqre
price sixpence, on the election of J. C. H., Esqre., for Westminster
(*not* for publication)."—Letter to Murray, April 9, 1820, *Letters*,
1901, v. 6.]

A VOLUME OF NONSENSE.

DEAR MURRAY,—
    You ask for a " *Volume of Nonsense*,"
Have all of your authors exhausted their store?
I thought you had published a good deal not long since.
    And doubtless the Squadron are ready with more.
But on looking again, I perceive that the Species
Of " Nonsense" you want must be purely "*facetious ;* "
And, as that is the case, you had best put to press
    Mr. Sotheby's tragedies now in M.S.,
        Some Syrian Sally
        From common-place Gally,
Or, if you prefer the bookmaking of women,
Take a spick and span "Sketch" of your feminine
    He-Man.[1]

Sept. 28, 1820.
[First published, *Letters*, 1900, v. 83.]

STANZAS.[2]

WHEN a man hath no freedom to fight for at home,
    Let him combat for that of his neighbours ;

1. [For Felicia Dorothea Browne (1793–1835), married in 1812 to Captain Hemans, see *Letters*, iii. 368, *note* 2. In the letter which contains these verses he writes, " I do not despise Mrs. Heman ; but if she knit blue stockings instead of wearing them it would be better." Elsewhere he *does* despise her : " No more *modern* poesy, I pray, neither Mrs. Hewoman's nor any female or male Tadpole of poet Wordsworth's."—*Ibid.*, v. 64.]

2. [The lines were sent in a letter to Moore (November 5, 1820) by way of *Autoepitaphium*, " if ' honour should come unlooked for ' to any of your acquaintance ;" *i.e.* if Byron should fall in the cause of Italian revolution, and Moore should not think him worthy of commemoration, here was a threnody "ready at hand."]

Let him think of the glories of Greece and of Rome,
    And get knocked on the head for his labours.

To do good to Mankind is the chivalrous plan,
    And is always as nobly requited ;
Then battle for Freedom wherever you can,
    And, if not shot or hanged, you 'll get knighted.

November 5, 1820.
[First published, *Letters and Journals*, 1830, ii. 377.]

TO PENELOPE.[1]

JANUARY 2, 1821.

THIS day, of all our days, has done
    The worst for me and you :—
'T is just *six* years since we were *one*,
    And *five* since we were *two*.

November 5, 1820.
[First published, Medwin's *Conversations*, 1824, p. 106.]

THE CHARITY BALL.[2]

WHAT matter the pangs of a husband and father,
    If his sorrows in exile be great or be small,
So the Pharisee's glories around her she gather,
    And the saint patronises her " Charity Ball ! "

1. ["For the anniversary of January 2, 1821, I have a small grateful anticipation, which, in case of accident, I add."—Letter to Moore, November 5, 1820, *Letters*, 1891, v. 112.]

2. [Written on seeing the following paragraph in a newspaper : " Lady Byron is this year the lady patroness at the annual Charity Ball, given at the Town Hall, at Hinckley, Leicestershire. . . ."— *Life*, p. 535. Moore adds that " these verses [of which he only prints two stanzas] are full of strong and indignant feeling,—every stanza concluding pointedly with the words ' Charity Ball.' "]

What matters—a heart which, though faulty, was feeling,
  Be driven to excesses which once could appal—
That the Sinner should suffer is only fair dealing,
  As the Saint keeps her charity back for "the Ball!"

                     December 10, 1820.
    [First published, *Letters and Journals*, 1830, ii. 540.]

EPIGRAM

ON THE BRAZIERS' ADDRESS TO BE PRESENTED IN
ARMOUR BY THE COMPANY TO QUEEN CAROLINE.[1]

IT seems that the Braziers propose soon to pass
An Address and to bear it themselves all in brass;

---

1. [The allusion is explained in Rivington's *Annual Register*,
October 30, 1820 (vol. lxii. pp. 114, 115)—

"ADDRESSES TO THE QUEEN.

". . . The most splendid exhibition of the day was that of the
brass-founders and braziers. The procession was headed by a man
dressed in a suit of burnished plate armour of brass, and mounted
on a handsome black horse, the reins being held by pages . . .
wearing brass helmets. . . . A man in a complete suite of brass
armour . . . was followed by two persons, bearing on a cushion
a most magnificent imitation of the imperial Crown of England.
A small number of the deputation of brass-founders were admitted
to the presence of her Majesty, and one of the persons in armour
advanced to the throne, and bending on one knee, presented the
address, which was enclosed in a brass case of excellent workman-
ship."—See *Letters*, 1901, v. 219, 220, *note* 2.

In a postscript to a letter to Murray, dated January 19, 1821,
he writes, "I sent you a line or two on the Braziers' Company last
week, *not* for publication. The lines were even worthy

    'Of ——dsworth the great metaquizzical poet,
      A man of great merit amongst those who know it,
      Of whose works, as I told Moore last autumn at *Mestri*
      I owe all I know to my passion for *Pastry*.'"

He adds, in a footnote, "*Mestri* and *Fusina* are the ferry trajects
to Venice: I believe, however, that it was at Fusina that Moore

A superfluous pageant, for by the Lord Harry!
They'll *find*, where they 're going, much *more* than they
    carry.
Or—

THE Braziers, it seems, are determined to pass
An Address, and present it themselves all in brass ;—
A superfluous $\begin{cases} \text{pageant} \\ \text{trouble} \end{cases}$ for, by the Lord Harry !
They 'll find, where they 're going, much more than they
    carry.

January 6, 1821.

[First published, *Letters and Journals*, 1830, ii. 442.]

ON MY THIRTY-THIRD BIRTHDAY.

JANUARY 22, 1821.[1]

THROUGH Life's dull road, so dim and dirty,
    I have dragged to three-and-thirty.
    What have these years left to me?
    Nothing—except thirty-three.

[First published, *Letters and Journals*, 1830, ii. 414.]

and I embarked in 1819, when Thomas came to Venice, like Coleridge's Spring, 'slowly up this way.'"

Again, in a letter to Moore, dated January 22, 1821, he encloses slightly different versions of both epigrams, and it is worth noting that the first line of the pendant epigram has been bowdlerized, and runs thus—

" Of Wordsworth the grand metaquizzical poet."

—*Letters*, 1901, v. 226, 230.]

1. [" To-morrow is my birthday—that is to say, at twelve o' the clock, midnight ; *i.e.* in twelve minutes I shall have completed thirty and three years of age!!! and I go to my bed with a heaviness of heart at having lived so long, and to so little purpose. * * * It is three minutes past twelve—''Tis the middle of night by the castle clock,' and I am now thirty-three !—

    ' Eheu, fugaces, Posthume, Posthume,
      Labuntur anni ;'—

MARTIAL, Lib. I. Epig. I.

" Hic est, quem legis, ille, quem requiris,
    Toto notus in orbe Martialis," etc.

He, unto whom thou art so partial,
Oh, reader ! is the well-known Martial,
The Epigrammatist : while living,
Give him the fame thou would'st be giving ;
So shall he hear, and feel, and know it—
Post-obits rarely reach a poet.

[N.D. ? 1821.]
[First published, *Lord Byron's Works*, 1833, xvii. 245.]

BOWLES AND CAMPBELL.

To the air of " How now, Madam Flirt," in the *Beggar's Opera*.[1]

BOWLES.

" Why, how now, saucy Tom ?
    If you thus must ramble,

but I don't regret them so much for what I have done, as for what
I *might* have done."—Extracts from a Diary, January 21, 1821,
Letters, 1901, v. 182.

In a letter to Moore, dated January 22, 1821, he gives another
version—

" Through Life's road, so dim and dirty,
    I have dragged to three-and-thirty.
What *have* these years left to me ?
    Nothing—except thirty-three."

Ibid., p. 229.]

1. [Compare the *Beggar's Opera*, act ii. sc. 2—

        Air, " Good morrow, Gossip Joan."
    " Polly. *Why, how now, Madam Flirt ?*
        If you thus must chatter,

I will publish some
   Remarks on Mister Campbell.
             Saucy Tom!"

CAMPBELL.

"WHY, how now, Billy Bowles?
   Sure the priest is maudlin!
   (*To the public*) How can you, d—n your souls!
   Listen to his twaddling?
           Billy Bowles!"

February 22, 1821.
[First published, *The Liberal*, 1823, No. II. p. 398.]

ELEGY.

BEHOLD the blessings of a lucky lot!
   My play is *damned*, and Lady Noel *not*.

May 25, 1821.
[First published, Medwin's *Conversations*, 1824, p. 121.]

And are for flinging dirt,
   Let's try who best can spatter,
      Madam Flirt!

"*Lucy. Why, how now, saucy jade?*
   Sure the wench is tipsy!
 How can you see me made
   The scoff of such a gipsy?   [To him.]
     Saucy jade!"   [To her.]

Bowles replied to Campbell's Introductory Essay to his *Specimens of the English Poets*, 7 vols., 1819, by *The Invariable Principles of Poetry*, in a letter addressed to Thomas Campbell. For Byron's two essays, the "Letter to . . . . [John Murray]" and "Observations upon Observations," see *Letters*, 1901, v. Appendix III. pp. 536–592.]

JOHN KEATS.[1]

WHO killed John Keats?
  "I," says the Quarterly,
  So savage and Tartarly;
"'T was one of my feats."

Who shot the arrow?
  "The poet-priest Milman
  (So ready to kill man)
"Or Southey, or Barrow."

          July 30, 1821.
[First published, *Letters and Journals*, 1830, ii. 506.]

FROM THE FRENCH.

ÆGLE, beauty and poet, has two little crimes;
She makes her own face, and does not make her rhymes.

          Aug. 2, 1821.
[First published, *The Liberal*, 1823, No. II. p. 396.]

TO MR. MURRAY.

I.

FOR Orford[2] and for Waldegrave[3]
You give much more than me you *gave*;
Which is not fairly to behave,
        My Murray!

1. [For Croker's "article" on Keats's *Endymion* (*Quarterly Review*, April, 1818, vol. xix. pp. 204–208), see *Don Juan*, Canto XI. stanza lx. line 1, *Poetical Works*, 1902, vi. 445, *note* 4.]

2. [Horace Walpole's *Memoirs of the Last Nine Years of the Reign of George II.*]

3. [*Memoirs* by James Earl Waldegrave, Governor of George III. when Prince of Wales.]

2.

Because if a live dog, 't is said,
Be worth a lion fairly sped,
A *live lord* must be worth *two* dead,
                    My Murray!

3.

And if, as the opinion goes,
Verse hath a better sale than prose,—
Certes, I should have more than those,
                    My Murray!

4.

But now this sheet is nearly crammed,
So, if *you will, I* shan't be shammed,
And if you *won't,—you* may be damned,
                    My Murray!¹
                    August 23, 1821.
[First published, *Letters and Journals*, 1830, ii. 517.]

[NAPOLEON'S SNUFF-BOX.]²

LADY, accept the box a hero wore,
    In spite of all this elegiac stuff:
Let not seven stanzas written by a bore,
    Prevent your Ladyship from taking snuff!
                    1821.
[First published, *Conversations of Lord Byron*, 1824, p. 235.]

---

1. ["Can't accept your courteous offer [*i.e.* £2000 for three cantos of *Don Juan, Sardanapalus*, and *The Two Foscari*]. These matters must be arranged with Mr. Douglas Kinnaird. He is my trustee, and a man of honour. To him you can state all your mercantile reasons, which you might not like to state to me personally, such as 'heavy season'—'flat public'—'don't go off'—'lordship writes too much'—'won't take advice'—'declining popularity'—'deductions for the trade'—'make very little'—'generally lose by him'—'pirated edition'—'foreign edition'—'severe criticisms,' etc., with other hints and howls for an oration, which I leave Douglas, who is an orator, to answer."—Letter to Murray, August 23, 1821, *Letters*, 1901, v. 348.]
2. [Napoleon bequeathed to Lady Holland a snuff-box which had

THE NEW VICAR OF BRAY.

I.

Do you know Doctor Nott?[1]
With "a crook in his lot,"
Who seven years since tried to dish up
A neat Codi*cil*
To the Princess's Will,[2]
Which made Dr. Nott *not* a bishop.

been given to him by the Pope for his clemency in sparing Rome. Lord Carlisle wrote eight (not seven) stanzas, urging her, as Byron told Medwin, to decline the gift, "for fear that horror and murder should jump out of the lid every time it is opened."—*Conversations*, 1824, p. 362. The first stanza of Lord Carlyle's verses, which *teste* Medwin, Byron parodied, runs thus—

"Lady, reject the gift! 'tis tinged with gore!
    Those crimson spots a dreadful tale relate;
It has been grasp'd by an infernal Power;
    And by that hand which seal'd young Enghien's fate."

The snuff-box is now in the jewel-room in the British Museum.]

1. [George Frederick Nott (1767–1841), critic and divine, was Rector of Harrietsham and Woodchurch, a Prebendary of Winchester and of Salisbury. He was Bampton Lecturer in 1802, and, soon afterwards, was appointed sub-preceptor to the Princess Charlotte of Wales. He was a connoisseur of architecture and painting, and passed much of his time in Italy and at Rome. When he was at Pisa he preached in a private room in the basement story of the house in Pisa where Shelley was living, and fell under Byron's displeasure for attacking the Satanic school, and denouncing *Cain* as a blasphemous production. "The parsons," he told Moore (letter, February 20, 1820), "preached at it [*Cain*] from Kentish Town to Pisa." Hence the apostrophe to Dr. Nott. (See *Records of Shelley, Byron, and the Author*, by E. T. Trelawny, 1887, pp. 302, 303.)]

2. [According to Lady Anne Hamilton (*Secret History of the Court of England*, 1832, i. 198–207), the Princess Charlotte incurred the suspicion and displeasure of her uncles and her grandmother, the Queen, by displaying an ardent and undue interest in her sub-preceptor. On being reproved by the Queen for "condescending to favour persons in low life with confidence or particular respect, persons likely to take advantage of your simplicity and innocence," and having learnt that "persons" meant Mr. Nott, she replied by threatening to sign a will in favour of her sub-preceptor, and by actually making over to him by a deed her library, jewels, and all

2.

So the Doctor being found
A little unsound
In his doctrine, at least as a teacher,
And kicked from one stool
As a knave or a fool,
He mounted another as preacher.

3.

In that Gown (like the Skin
With no Lion within)
He still for the Bench would be driving;
And roareth away,
A new Vicar of *Bray*,
Except that *his bray* lost his living.

4.

" Gainst Freethinkers," he roars,
" You should all block your doors
Or be named in the Devil's indentures : "
And here I agree,
For *who* e'er would be
A Guest where old Simony enters?

5.

Let the Priest, who beguiled
His own Sovereign's child
To his own dirty views of promotion,
Wear his Sheep's cloathing still
Among flocks to his will,
And dishonour the Cause of devotion.

other private property. Lady Anne Hamilton is not an accurate
or trustworthy authority, but her extremely circumstantial narrative
was, no doubt, an expansion of the contemporary scandal to which
Byron's lampoon gave currency.]

6.

The Altar and Throne
Are in danger alone
From such as himself, who would render
The Altar itself
But a step up to Pelf,
And pray God to pay his defender.

7.

But, Doctor, one word
Which perhaps you have heard
" He should never throw stones who has windows
Of Glass to be broken,
And by this same token
As a sinner, you can't care what Sin does.

8.

But perhaps you do well :
Your own windows, they tell,
Have long ago sufferéd censure ;
Not a fragment remains
Of your character's panes,
Since the Regent refused you a glazier.

9.

Though your visions of lawn
Have all been withdrawn,
And you missed your bold stroke for a mitre ;
In a very snug way
You may still preach and pray,
And from bishop sink into backbiter ! "

[First published, *Works* (Galignani), 1831, p. 116.]

LUCIETTA. A FRAGMENT.

LUCIETTA, my deary,
That fairest of faces !
Is made up of kisses ;
But, in love, oft the case is
Even stranger than this is—
There 's another, that 's slyer,
Who touches me nigher,—
A Witch, an intriguer,
Whose manner and figure
Now piques me, excites me,
Torments and delights me—

Cætera desunt.

[From an autograph MS. in the possession of Mr. Murray,
now for the first time printed.]

EPIGRAMS.

OH, Castlereagh ! thou art a patriot now ;
Cato died for his country, so did'st thou :
He perished rather than see Rome enslaved,
Thou cut'st thy throat that Britain may be saved !

———————

So Castlereagh has cut his throat !—The worst
Of this is,—that his own was not the first.

———————

So *He* has cut his throat at last !—He ! Who ?
The man who cut his country's long ago.

? August, 1822.
[First published, *The Liberal*, No. I., October 18, 1822, p. 164.]

THE CONQUEST.[1]

THE Son of Love and Lord of War I sing;
    Him who bade England bow to Normandy,
And left the name of Conqueror more than King
    To his unconquerable dynasty.
Not fanned alone by Victory's fleeting wing,
    He reared his bold and brilliant throne on high;
The Bastard kept, like lions, his prey fast,
And Britain's bravest Victor was the last.

March 8–9, 1823.
[First published, *Lord Byron's Works*, 1833, xvii. 246.]

IMPROMPTU.[2]

BENEATH Blessington's eyes
    The reclaimed Paradise
Should be free as the former from evil;
    But if the new Eve
    For an Apple should grieve,
What mortal would not play the Devil?

April, 1823.
[First published, *Letters and Journals*, 1830, ii. 635.]

1. [This fragment was found amongst Lord Byron's papers, after his departure from Genoa for Greece.]

2. [With the view of inducing these friends [Lord and Lady Blessington] to prolong their stay at Genoa, he suggested their taking a pretty villa, called "Il Paradiso," in the neighbourhood of his own, and accompanied them to look at it. Upon that occasion it was that, on the lady expressing some intention of residing there, he produced the following impromptu.—*Life,* 577.]

JOURNAL IN CEPHALONIA.

THE dead have been awakened—shall I sleep?
  The World's at war with tyrants—shall I crouch?
The harvest's ripe—and shall I pause to reap?
  I slumber not; the thorn is in my Couch;
Each day a trumpet soundeth in mine ear,
  Its echo in my heart——

June 19, 1823.
[First published, *Letters*, 1901, vi. 238.]

SONG TO THE SULIOTES.

1.

UP to battle! Sons of Suli
Up, and do your duty duly!
There the wall—and there the Moat is :
Bouwah![1] Bouwah! Suliotes!
There is booty—there is Beauty,
Up my boys and do your duty.

2.

By the sally and the rally
Which defied the arms of Ali ;
By your own dear native Highlands,
By your children in the islands,
Up and charge, my Stratiotes,
Bouwah!—Bouwah!—Suliotes!

1. "Bouwah!" is their war-cry.

3.

As our ploughshare is the Sabre :
Here 's the harvest of our labour ;
For behind those battered breaches
Are our foes with all their riches :
There is Glory—there is plunder—
Then away despite of thunder !

[From an autograph MS. in the possession of Mr. Murray,
now for the first time printed.]

[LOVE AND DEATH.]

I.

I WATCHED thee when the foe was at our side,
    Ready to strike at him—or thee and me.
Were safety hopeless—rather than divide
    Aught with one loved save love and liberty.

2.

I watched thee on the breakers, when the rock
    Received our prow and all was storm and fear,
And bade thee cling to me through every shock ;
    This arm would be thy bark, or breast thy bier.

3.

I watched thee when the fever glazed thine eyes,
    Yielding my couch and stretched me on the ground,
When overworn with watching, ne'er to rise
    From thence if thou an early grave hadst found.

4.

The earthquake came, and rocked the quivering wall,
    And men and nature reeled as if with wine.

Whom did I seek around the tottering hall?
  For thee. Whose safety first provide for? Thine.

5.

And when convulsive throes denied my breath
  The faintest utterance to my fading thought,
To thee—to thee—e'en in the gasp of death
  My spirit turned, oh! oftener than it ought.

6.

Thus much and more; and yet thou lov'st me not,
  And never wilt! Love dwells not in our will.
Nor can I blame thee, though it be my lot
  To strongly, wrongly, vainly love thee still.[1]

        [First published, *Murray's Magazine*, February, 1887,
                vol. i. pp. 145, 146.]

LAST WORDS ON GREECE.

WHAT are to me those honours or renown
  Past or to come, a new-born people's cry?
Albeit for such I could despise a crown
  Of aught save laurel, or for such could die.
I am a fool of passion, and a frown
  Of thine to me is as an adder's eye.
To the poor bird whose pinion fluttering down
  Wafts unto death the breast it bore so high;

1. [" The last he ever wrote. From a rough copy found amongst his papers at the back of the 'Song of Suli.' Copied November, 1824.—John C. Hobhouse."
" A note, attached to the verses by Lord Byron, states they were addressed to no one in particular, and were a mere poetical Scherzo. —J. C. H."]

Such is this maddening fascination grown,
So strong thy magic or so weak am I.

[First published, *Murray's Magazine*, February, 1887,
vol. i. p. 146.]

ON THIS DAY I COMPLETE MY THIRTY-SIXTH YEAR.[1]

1.

'T is time this heart should be unmoved,
Since others it hath ceased to move :
Yet, though I cannot be beloved,
Still let me love !

2.

My days are in the yellow leaf ;
The flowers and fruits of Love are gone ;
The worm, the canker, and the grief
Are mine alone !

1. ["This morning Lord Byron came from his bedroom into the apartment where Colonel Stanhope and some friends were assembled, and said with a smile—'You were complaining, the other day, that I never write any poetry now :—this is my birthday, and I have just finished something, which, I think, is better than what I usually write.' He then produced these noble and affecting verses, which were afterwards found written in his journals, with only the following introduction : 'Jan. 22 ; on this day I complete my 36th year.'" —*A Narrative of Lord Byron's Last Journey to Greece*, 1825, p. 125, by Count Gamba. In the *Morning Chronicle*, October 29, 1824, the lines are headed, "Lord Byron's Latest Verses," and are prefaced by the following note : " We have been indebted to a friend for the following immortal verses, the last he ever composed. Four of the lines have already appeared in an article in the *Westminster Review*" (" Lord Byron in Greece," July, 1824, vol. ii. p. 227).]

3.

The fire that on my bosom preys
  Is lone [i.] as some Volcanic isle ;
No torch is kindled at its blaze—
    A funeral pile.

4.

The hope, the fear, the jealous care,
  The exalted portion of the pain
And power of love, I cannot share,
    But wear the chain.

5.

But 't is not *thus*—and 't is not *here*— [ii.]
  Such thoughts should shake my soul, nor *now*
Where Glory decks the hero's bier, [iii.]
    Or binds his brow.

6.

The Sword, the Banner, and the Field, [iv.]
  Glory and Greece, around me see !
The Spartan, borne upon his shield, [1]
    Was not more free.

7.

Awake ! (not Greece—she *is* awake !)
  Awake, my spirit !   Think through *whom*

i. *Is like to* ——.—[*M.C.*]
ii. —— *it is not here.*—[*M.C.*]
iii. —— *seals the hero's bier.*—[*M.C.*]
iv. *The steed—the Banner—and the Field.*—[*MS. B.M.*]

1. [The slain were borne on their shields.   Witness the Spartan mother's speech to her son, delivered with his buckler : " either *with* this *or on* this " (B.M. Addit. MS. 31,038).]

Thy life-blood tracks its parent lake,[i.]
And then strike home !

8.

Tread those reviving passions down,[ii.]
Unworthy manhood !—unto thee
Indifferent should the smile or frown
Of Beauty be.

9.

If thou regret'st thy youth, *why live ?*
The land of honourable death
Is here :—up to the Field, and give
Away thy breath !

10.

Seek out—less often sought than found—
A soldier's grave, for thee the best ;
Then look around, and choose thy ground,
And take thy Rest.

Missolonghi, *Jan.* 22, 1824.
[First published, *Morning Chronicle*, October 29, 1824.]

i. *My life-blood tastes* ——.—[*M.C.*]
ii. *I tread reviving* ——.—[*M.C.*]

A
BIBLIOGRAPHY
OF THE

SUCCESSIVE EDITIONS AND TRANSLATIONS
OF
LORD BYRON'S *POETICAL WORKS.*

———◆◆◆———

COLLECTED EDITIONS.

I.

The/ Poetical Works/ of/ Lord Byron./ In Two Volumes./
Vol. I./ [Vol. II.] From the last London Edition./ Phila-
delphia :/ Published by Moses Thomas,/ N.º 52, Chesnut
Street./ William Fry, Printer./ 1813./ [16º
[A bound copy : smooth blue calf, lettered "LORD
BYRON."]

Collation—
  Vol. I. : pp. *1–203*—Title, one leaf ; Cont. ; Half-title ;
Dedication ; and Text, pp. *1–203.*
  Vol. II. : pp. xii. + *261*—Title, one leaf ; Cont. ; Half-title ;
Preface, etc., pp. i.–xii. ; Text, pp. *1–261.*

Contents—

Vol. I. :—Poems, Original and Translated . . . p. **1**	Canto II. (lxxxviii. stanzas) p. 9
English Bards, etc. p. **137**	Notes . . . . . p. 99
	Poems (xx.) . . . p. 156
Vol. II. :—Childe Harold's Pilgrimage, Canto I. (xciii. stanzas) . . . . . p. **13**	The Giaour (**1215** lines) p. 205
	Note . . . . . p. 261

  Note (Vol. I.).—On fly-leaf : "To the R.ᵗ Honourable Lord
Byron from his ob.ᵗ servant Geo Ticknor, June 20. 1815."

"This book was given to me by Lord Byron, April 20, 1816, on his leaving England.   Scrope Davies."

ΑΠΟ : ΙΩ :

Κεφ. θ.

Καὶ ἐν ταῖς ἡμέραις ἐκείναις ζητήσουσιν οἱ ἄνθρωποι τὸν θάνατον καὶ οὐχ εὑρήσουσιν αὐτὸν· καὶ ἐπιθυμήσουσιν ἀποθανεῖν, καὶ φεύξεται ὁ θάνατος ἀπ᾿ αὐτῶν.

On second fly-leaf: "Semper ego tui memoriam colam ; semper tua imago ante oculos observabitur ; semper idem mihi eras ; qui idem semper eras bonis omnibus."

These volumes which were presented by George Ticknor to Lord Byron,* and, in turn, presented by him to Scrope Davies, passed into the hands of Sir Francis Burdett (1770-1844), and are now in the possession of his grandson, Mr. F. B. Money-Coutts.

* " He [Byron] spoke to me of a copy of the American edition of his poems, which I had sent him, and expressed his satisfaction at seeing it in a small form, because in that way, he said, nobody would be prevented from purchasing it" ("Journal," June 21, 1815).—*Life, Letters, and Journals* of George Ticknor, Boston, 1876, i. 62.

II.

The/ Poetical Works/ of/ Lord Byron./   From   the last London Edition./ In Two Volumes./ Volume I./ [Vol. II.]   Boston :/   Published by Cummings & Hilliard,/ N.º 1, Cornhill./ Joseph T. Buckingham, Printer,/ 1814./   [12.º

Collation—
    Vol. I. : pp. xi. + 308—Title, one leaf, pp. i., ii. ; Cont., pp. iii., iv. ; *Lord Byron* [excerpt from the *Analectic Magazine*], pp. v.-xi. ; Text, pp. *1*-308.
    Vol. II. : pp. iv. + 251—Title, one leaf, pp. i, ii ; Cont., pp. iii, iv ; Text, pp. *1*-251.

Contents—

Vol. I. :—Poems, Original and Translated . . . p. 1	The Giaour (Fifth Edition) p. 47
English Bards, etc. (Third Edition) (1050 lines), with Postscript . . . . p. 123	The Bride of Abydos (Seventh Edition) . . . . p. 103
Childe Harold's Pilgrimage, Cantos I., II. (First Edition), with Notes, etc. . . p. 179	The Corsair (Sixth Edition) p. 159
Vol. II. :—Poems [Twenty-six, *i.e.* poems issued with Sec. Ed. of *Childe Harold*, and six (not tabulated) issued with the *Corsair*] . . . . . p. 1	Prize Prologue (Oct. 1812) (Second Edition) . p. 241
	Ode to Napoleon Buonaparte (Second Edition: sixteen stanzas) p. 245

III.

The/ Works/ of/ The Right Honorable/ Lord Byron./ In Four Volumes./ Vol. I./ [Vol. II., etc.] Childe Harold./ London :/ Printed for John Murray, Albemarle-Street./ 1815./ [8°

Collation—

Vol. I. : pp. xviii. + 218—Gen. Half-title, one leaf, pp. i., ii. ; Title (R. *T. Davison, Lombard-Street,| White-Friars, London.*), pp. iii., iv. ; General Contents to the Four Volumes, pp. v.-x.* ; Half-title (R. Motto—*Le Cosmopolite*), *n.p.* ; Prefaces, pp. xi.-xviii. ; Cont. to Vol. I., one leaf, *n.p.* ; Text, pp. *1–218.* The Imprint is at the foot of p. 218.

Note.—In the earlier copies of Vol. I. of this edition, the misplaced " Advertisement " to *The Giaour* is on pp. i., ii., and pp. ix.*, x.*, giving Cont. of *Hebrew Melodies,* are not inserted.

Vol. II. : pp. *1–202*—Gen. Half-title, one leaf ; Title (R. Imprint) ; Cont. to Vol. II. ; Half-title ; Dedication ; Text, pp. *1–202.* The Imprint is in the centre of the last page, p. [204].

Vol. III. : pp. viii. + *9–228*—Gen. Half-title, one leaf ; Title (R. Imprint) ; Cont. to Vol. III. ; Half-title, pp. i., ii. ; Dedication to Thomas Moore, Esq., pp. iii.-viii. ; Text, pp. *9–228.* The Imprint is at the foot of p. 228.

Vol. IV. : pp. viii. [ix.*, x.*] + *203*—Gen. Half-title, one leaf ; Title (R. Imprint), pp. i.-iv. ; Cont. to Vol. IV., pp. v.-x.* ; Text, pp. *1–203.*

Contents—

Vol. I. :—To Ianthe, Childe Harold's Pilgrimage, Cantos I., II., (N. App.) . . . p. 3

Romaic Books and Authors, etc. . . . . . p. 188

Vol. II. :—The Giaour (N.) p. 1

The Bride of Abydos, Cantos I., II. (N.) . . . p. 103

Vol. III. : — The Corsair, Cantos I.—III. (N.) . p. i.

Lara, Cantos I., II. (N.) p. 133

Vol. IV. :—Ode to Napoleon Buonaparte (N.). . . p. 1

Poems (N.) . . . p. 17 [xxxvi., consisting of xxix. pub. in the Seventh Ed. of *Childe Harold,* vi. pub. in the Second Ed. of the *Corsair,* and Verses on Sir P. Parker.]

Hebrew Melodies (24) p. 143

Note.—In later issues of Vol. III., 1815, the note on the " Pirates of Barrataria " is inserted and paginated 133*-137*.

IV.

The/ Works/ of The/ Right Hon. Lord Byron./ In Two Volumes./ Vol. I./ [Vol. II.] London :/ Printed for John Murray, Albemarle-Street./ 1815./ [8°

Contents—

 Vol. I. : The Title, as above, is prefixed to *Childe Harold's Pilgrimage*, Cantos I., II. (Fourth Ed.), 1812, pp. iii.–xii. + 300, and *Hebrew Melodies* (First Ed.), 1815, pp. *1–53*.

 Vol. II. : The Title, as above, is prefixed to *Childe Harold's Pilgrimage*, Canto III., pp. *1–79* ; *Childe Harold*, etc., Canto the Fourth ; *Romance Muy Doloroso*, Translation, etc., pp. xiv. + 257 ; *The Lament of Tasso* (Sixth Ed.), 1818, pp. *1–18* ; *Poems* (N.) (Second Ed.), 1816, pp. *1–[40]* ; *Monody*, etc. (New Ed.), 1810, pp. *1–[12]* ; *Ode to Napoleon* (Second Ed.), 1814, pp. *1–14*.

 Note.—These general titles were advertised, in July, 1815, for the purpose of binding, in two volumes, poems which were uniformly printed but had been separately issued. It is evident that they were still to be procured after the collected editions of 1815, 1817, 1818 had been published. In other copies the Contents are arranged in a different order.

V.

The Poetical Works, etc. From the last London Edition. In Three Volumes. New York : Published by David Huntington. 1815.

  [E. Kölbing, *Prisoner of Chillon*, 1896.]

VI.

The Works, etc. Including several poems now first collected. Together with an Original Biography. Embellished with a portrait, title-page, and six other engravings. In Three Vols. Philadelphia : Published by Moses Thomas, J. Maxwell, Printer. 1816.   [12°

        [Kölbing.]

VII.

The/ Works/ of/ The Right Honourable/ Lord Byron./ In Five Volumes./ Vol. I./ [Vol. II., etc.] Childe Harold./ London :/ John Murray, Albemarle-Street./ 1817./   [8°

Collation—

 Vol. I. : pp. xiv. + 218—Title, one leaf, pp. iii., iv. ; Half-title (R. Motto), pp. v., vi. ; Pref., pp. vii.–xiv. ; Cont., *n.p.* ; Text, pp. *1–218*. The Imprint (*T. Davison, Lombard Street,/ Whitefriars, London/*), is in the centre of the last page, p. [220].

 Vol. II. : pp. *1–202*—Title, one leaf ; Cont. to Vol. II. ; Half-title ; Dedication ; Advertisement ; Text, pp. *1–202*. The Imprint is in the centre of the last page, p. [204].

 Vol. III. : pp. viii. + *9–222* : Title, one leaf ; Cont. to Vol.

III. ; Half-title, pp. i. ii. ; Dedication to Thomas Moore, Esq., pp. iii.–viii. ; Text, pp. *9*–222. The Imprint is in the centre of the last page, p. [224].

Vol. IV. : pp. viii. + 203—Title, one leaf; pp. iii., iv. ; Cont. to Vol. IV., pp. v.–viii. ; Text, pp. *1*-203. The Imprint is in the centre of the last page, p. [204].

Vol. V. : pp. vi. + 184—Title, one leaf; Dedication, pp. i., ii. ; Advertisement, pp. iii., iv. ; Cont. to Vol. V., pp. v., vi. ; Half-title ; Text, pp. *1*-184. The Imprint is at the foot of p. 184.

Note.—The Cont. of Vols. I.–IV., 1817, are identical with the Cont. of Vols. I.–IV., 1815.

Contents—

Vol. V. :—Siege of Corinth (N.) . . . . . . p. 1	Poems (eleven, as pub. in *Poems*, 1816) . . . p. 127
Parisina (N.) . . p. 79	Monody, etc. (N.) . p. 171

VIII.

Poems./ By Lord Byron./ New-York:/ Published by Thomas Kirk and Thomas R. Mercein,/ Moses Thomas, M. Carey and Son, Philadelphia ;/ Wells and Lilly, Boston ;/ and Coale and Maxwell, Baltimore./ T. and W. Mercein, Printers, 93, Gold Street./ 1817./ [12?

Collation—

Pp. 1–64 (title-page unnumbered).

IX.

The/ Works/ of/ The Right Honourable/ Lord Byron./ Vol. I./ [Vol. II., etc.] Childe Harold./ London :/ John Murray, Albemarle-Street./ 1818./ [8?

Collation—

Vol. I. : pp. xiv. + 218—Half-title (R. *T. Davison, Lombard Street,/ Whitefriars, London./*), etc. (*Vide supra*, Vol. I., 1817).

Vol. II. : pp. *1*–202—Half-title (R. Imprint), etc. (*Vide supra*, Vol. II., 1817).

Vol. III. : pp. viii. + *9*-222 (*Vide supra*, Vol. III., 1817).

Vol. IV. : pp. viii. + 203—Half-title (R. Imprint) (*Vide supra*, Vol. IV., 1817).

Vol. V. :/ pp. *1*-184—Half-title, *The Siege*, etc., one leaf ; Title [The/ Works/ etc./ The Siege of Corinth—Parisina—Poems./ London :/ John Murray, Albemarle-Street,/ 1818./] ; Cont. of Vol. V. ; Advertisement ; Dedication, "To John Hobhouse, Esq. ;" Text, pp. *1*-104 ; The Imprint, *T. Davison, Lombard-street,/* Whitefriars, London,/ is at the foot of p. 184.

Vol. VI. : pp. 1–187—Gen. Half-title (R. *T. Davison, Lombard Street, Whitefriars, London*) ; Title, one leaf [The/ Works,/ etc. *In Six Volumes/* (in some copies "In six," etc., does not appear] ; Cont. to Vol. VI. ; Half-title ; Text, pp. *1*-187, +

Publisher's List, pp. 189–192. The Imprint is at the foot of p. 192.

Vol. VII. : pp. 1–273—Title [The/ Works, etc./ 1819.] (R. *London :/ Printed by T. Davison, Whitefriars/*) ; Cont. to Vol. VII. ; Text, pp. *1–273* + Publisher's Advertisement of Historical Illustrations (R. *London :/ Printed by Thomas Davison, Whitefriars/*).

Vol. VIII. : pp. 1–165—Gen. Half-title (R. Imprint) ; Title [The/ Works, etc./ 1820] ; Cont. to Vol. VIII. ; Text, pp. *1–165* + Publisher's List (ten pages, with Imprint at the foot of p. [10]).

Note.—For Contents for Vols. I.–V., *vide supra*, Ed. 1817.

Contents—

Vol. VI. :—Sonnet p. 1	Vol. VIII. :—Beppo (N.)
The Prisoner of Chillon (N.)	p. 1
(and six poems, N.). p. 3	Mazeppa . . . . p. 57
To Manfred (N.) . p. 67	Ode . . . . . p. 113
Lament of Tasso p. 169	A Fragment . . . p. 127
Vol. VII. :—Childe Harold's Pilgrimage, Canto III.	Romance Muy Doloroso
(N.) . . . . . . p. 1	(Transl.) . . . . p. 145
Canto IV. (N.) . p. 81	Sonetto di Vittorelli (Transl) p. 162

Note.—Vols. I.–IV. of the Edition of 1818 are illustrated by "Twelve Plates engraved by Charles Heath, and other Artists, from the original Designs of [Tho.] Stothard." The "original Designs," water-colour drawings, were presented by Lord Byron to the third Lord Holland, and are now in the possession of the Earl of Ilchester.

X.

The Works of the right honourable Lord Byron. Comprehending all his suppressed poems. Embellished with a portrait, and a Sketch of his Lordship's life. Vols. I.–VI. Paris : Published by Galignani, at the French, English, Italian, German and Spanish library, N.º 18, Rue Vivienne, 1818, in 12.º

[*Bibliographie de la France*, June 13, 1818.]

XI.

The Works of Lord Byron. In Thirteen Volumes. Published by Gerard Fleischer. Leipzic. 1818–1822. [8.º

[Kayser, *Index Verborum.* 1834. See, too, *Jahrbücher der Literatur.* Vienna, 1821. Vol. xv. pp. 105–145.]

XII.

The/ Works/ of/ Lord Byron./ Vol. I./ [Vol. II., etc.] London :/ John Murray, Albemarle-Street./ 1819./ [8.º

Collation—

Vol. I. : pp. xv. + 479—Title, one leaf, pp. iii., iv. ; Cont. to Vol. I., pp. v., vi. ; Half-title, with Motto, pp. vii., viii. ; Preface, etc., pp. ix.-xv. ; Text, pp. *1*-479. The Imprint (*London :| Printed by Thomas Davison, Whitefriars.|*) is in the centre of the last page, p. [480].

Vol. II. : pp. *1*-491—Gen. Half-title (R. Imprint) ; Title, one leaf ; Cont. to Vol. II. ; Text, pp. *1*-491 ; Notes to *Beppo*, p. [493], one leaf.

Vol. III. : pp. viii. + 330—Gen. Half-title (R. Imprint), pp. i., ii. ; Title, one leaf, pp. iii., iv. ; Cont. to Vol. III., pp. v.-viii. ; Text, pp. *1*-330. The Imprint is at the foot of the last page, p. 330.

Note.—In Vol. I. the text and notes of Cantos I., II. of *Childe Harold* are identical with the Eleventh Edition of 1819, the text with the Tenth Edition of 1815. The text of Cantos III. and IV. is all but identical with the text of the editions of 1816, 1818, but the notes have been reset.

Contents—

Vol. I. : Childe Harold's, etc., Cantos I., II. (N.) p. 1
Canto III. (N.) . p. 195
Canto IV. (N.) . p. 273
Vol. II. :—The Giaour (N.) p. 1
The Bride of Abydos (N.) p. 79
The Corsair (N.) p. 149
Lara (N.) . . . p. 251
The Siege of Corinth (N.) p. 317
Parisina (N.) . . p. 373
The Prisoner of Chillon (N.) p. 411
Beppo (N.) . . . p. 439
Vol. III. :—Manfred (N.) p. 1
Hebrew Melodies (23) p. 81
Ode to Napoleon Buonaparte (N.) . . . . . p. 121
Monody, etc. (N.) . p. 137
Lament of Tasso . p. 147
Poems (N.) . . . p. 163

Note.—The *Poems* include thirty pub. with *Childe Harold*, Ed. 10, 1815 ; six pub. with the *Corsair*, Ed. 2, 1814 ; eleven pub. in *Poems*, 1816 ; *A Sketch*, etc. (now first included) ; six pub. with *The Prisoner of Chillon*, 1816, and the translation from the Spanish Ballad (*Romance*, etc.) and the Italian Sonnet pub. with *Childe Harold*, Canto IV., 1818—fifty-six pieces in all.

XIII.

The/ Works/ of/ The Right Honourable/ Lord Byron./ Comprehending all his Suppressed Poems,/ Embellished with a Portrait and a Sketch of His/ Lordship's Life./ Vol. I./ [Vol. II., etc.] Childe Harold's Pilgrimage,/ Cantos I. and II.—The Giaour./ Second Edition./ Paris./ Published by Galignani,/ At the French, English, Italian, German and Spanish/ Library, N.º 18, Rue Vivienne./ 1819./   [12.º

Collation—
Vol. I. : pp. viii. + viii. + 276—Title, one leaf ; Advertise-
ment, one leaf ; Memoir of the R. H. Lord Byron, pp. i.-viii. ;
Text, pp. i.-viii., *9*-284. Frontispiece : Portrait of Lord Byron
by G. Harlow, Lith. de G. Engelmann.
Vol. II. : pp. *1*-244—Gen. Half-title (R. *Printed by A. Belin*) ;
Title, one leaf ; Text, pp. *1*-244.
Vol. III. : pp. *1*-230—Gen. Half-title, etc., as above ; Text,
pp. *1*-230.
Vol. IV. : pp. *1*-211—Gen. Half-title, etc., as above ; Text,
pp. *1*-211.
Vol. V. : pp. *1* + 225—Gen. Half-title, as above ; Dedication,
pp. iii.-x. ; Text, pp. *11*-235.
Vol. VI. : pp. *1*-130—Gen. Half-title, etc., as above ; Text,
pp. *1*-130 + six pages of General Index.

Contents—

Vol. I. :—Childe Harold's, etc., Cantos I., II. (N.) p. 9
The Giaour (N.)   p. 207
Vol. II. :—The Bride, etc. (N.) .   .   .   .   .   p. 1
The Corsair (N.) .   p. 71
Lara (N.) .   .   .   p. 179
Vol. III. :—Ode to N. B. (N.) .   .   .   .   .   p. 1
Poems (xxxvi.) (N.) p. 13
Hebrew Melodies   p. 79
The Siege, etc. (N.) p. 107
Parisina (N.) .   .   p. 163
Poems, 1816 .   .   p. 195
Monody, etc. (N.) p. 222
Vol. IV. :—The Prisoner of Chillon, etc. (N.) .   .   p. 1
Manfred (N.) .   . p. 51
The Lament of Tasso   p. 125

Childe Harold's, etc., Canto III. (N.) .   .   .   .   p. 139
Vol. V.—Childe Harold's, etc., Canto IV. (N.) .   .   . p. i
Publisher's Advt. . p. [220]
Romance Muy Doloroso (Transl.) .   .   .   . p. 221
Sonetto di Vittorelli (Transl.)   p. 234
Vol. VI. :—Beppo .   p. 1
Suppressed Poems :
English Bards, etc. p. 47
Ode ("Oh, shame to thee," etc.) .   .   .   . p. 121
Windsor Poetics .   p. 125
A Sketch .   .   . p. 126
Mazeppa .   .   .   . p. 5
Ode (To Venice) . p. 47
A Fragment .   .   . p. 57

Note.—Bound up with, and, possibly, an integral part of Vol.
VI., is *Mazeppa. Collation :* pp. 1-69. 12? Half-title (R. *Printed
by A. Belin*) ; pp. 1, 2 ; Title, one leaf (Mazeppa,/ A Poem. :
By Lord Byron./ Second Edition./ Paris :/ Published by
Galignani,/ At the French, English, Italian, German and
Spanish/ Library, N? 18, Rue Vivienne./ 1819./), pp. 3, 4 ;
Second half-title, pp. 5, 6 ; Advertisement, pp. 7, 8 ; and Text,
pp. 9-69. (For Contents, *vide supra.*)

XIV.

The Works of the R. H. Lord Byron. In Six Volumes.
Zwickau. Printed for Brothers Schumann, 1819.
[*Jahrbücher der Lit.*, xv. 105.]

XV.

The Works, etc. In Seven Volumes. Brussels: published at the English Repository of Arts, 1819.
[Kölbing.]

XVI.

Works of Lord Byron. New York. 1820. Four Volumes.
[18°
[Cat. of Library of *Boston Athenæum.*]

Contents—
Vol. I. :—Childe Harold's, etc.
Vol. II. :—Bride, etc.—Corsair—Lara—The Giaour.
Vol. III. :—Siege, etc.—Prisoner of Chillon—Parisina—Beppo
—English Bards, etc.—Mazeppa—Ode—Fragment—Don Juan.
Vol. IV. :—Hebrew Melodies—Ode to N. B.—Monody, etc.
—Lament of Tasso—Manfred—Poems.

XVII.

The/ Works/ of/ Lord Byron./ Vol. I./ [Vol. II., etc.]
London :/ John Murray, Albemarle-Street./ 1821./ [8°

Collation—
Vol. I. : pp. xvi. + 216—Gen. Half-title (R. (*a*) *Thomas
Davison, Whitefriars.*), pp. i., ii. ; Title, one leaf, pp. iii., iv. ;
Cont. to Vol. I., pp. v., vi. ; Preface, etc., pp. vii.–xi. ; Text,
pp. *1–216.* The Imprint (*b*) (*London :*/ *Printed by Thomas Davison, Whitefriars.*) is at the foot of p. 216.
Vol. II. : pp. *1–272*—Gen. Half-title (R. Imprint (*a*)) ; Title,
one leaf ; Cont. to Vol. II. ; Text, pp. *1–272.* The Imprint (*b*)
is at the foot of p. 272.
Vol. III. : pp. *1–237*—Gen. Half-title (R. Imprint (*a*)) ; Title,
one leaf ; Cont. to Vol. III. ; Text, pp. *1–237.* The Imprint (*b*)
is in the centre of p. [240].
Vol. IV. : pp. *1–274*—Gen. Half-title (R. Imprint (*a*)) ; Title,
one leaf ; Cont. to Vol. IV. ; Text, pp. *1–274.* The Imprint (*b*)
is in the centre of p. [276].
Vol. V. : pp. viii. + 284—Gen. Half-title (R. Imprint (*a*)),
pp. i., ii. ; Title, one leaf, pp. iii., iv. ; Cont. to Vol. V., pp. [v.]–
viii. ; Text, pp. *1–284.* The Imprint (*b*) is at the foot of p. 284.

Contents—

Vol. I. :—Childe Harold's, etc., Cantos I., II. (N. App.) p. i.	Vol. III. :—The Giaour (N.) p. 1
Vol. II. :—Childe Harold's, etc., Canto III. (N.) . p. 1	The Bride, etc. (N.) p. 75
	The Corsair (N.) . p. 143
Canto IV. (N.) . . p. 77	Vol. IV. :—Lara (N.) p. 1
	The Siege (N.) . . p. 63

VOL. VII.   O

Parisina . . . . p. 117
The Prisoner (N.) . p. 153
Beppo (N.) . . . p. 179
Mazeppa . . . p. 235
Vol. V. :—Manfred (N.)
                        p. 1

Hebrew Melodies . p. 73
Ode to N. B. (N.). p. 104
Monody, etc. . . p. 121
Lament of Tasso . p. 127
Poems (N.) . . . p. 141

Note.—The Poems (fifty-seven in all) include the *Ode to Venice*.

XVIII.

Lord Byron's/ Works./ Volume the First./ [Volume the Second, etc.] Containing :/ The Bride of Abydos—The Corsair—Lara—/Parisina, etc./ Paris/ Sold by François Louis,/ At his French and English Library,/ Rue Hautefeuille, N⁰ 10 ;/ And Baudry,/ At the Foreign Library,/ Rue du Coq Saint Honoré, N⁰ 9./ 1821./ [12⁰

Collation—

Vol. I. : pp. xii. + 216—Title, one leaf, pp. iii., iv. ; " Memoir of Lord Byron," pp. v.-xii. ; Text, pp. *1*-216.
Vol. II. : pp. *1*-240—Title, one leaf ; Text, pp. *1*-240.
Vol. III. : pp. *1*-[224]—Title, one leaf ; Text, pp. *1*-223 + 1 *n.p.*
Vol. IV.: pp. *1*-[228]—Title, one leaf; Text, pp. *1*-224+4 *n.p.*
Vol. V. : pp. *1*-244—Title, one leaf ; Text, pp. *1*-244.

Contents—

Vol. I. :—The Bride, etc., Cantos I., II. (N.) . p. 1
The Corsair, Cantos I.-III. (N.) . . . . . . p. 55
Lara, Cantos I., II. (N.) p. 131
Parisina . . . . p. 179
Ode to N. B. . . p. 203
Ode to Venice . . p. 211
Vol. II. :—English Bards, etc. . . . . p. 1
Don Juan, Cantos I., II. (N.) . . . . . p. 55
The Giaour (N.) . p. 167
Vol. III. :—Childe Harold, Cantos I.-IV. (N.) . . p. 1
Beppo . . . . p. 187
Fare Thee Well . p. 219
Darkness . . . p. 221
Stanzas for Music (" There be none," etc.). . . p. [224]
Vol. IV. :—Siege, etc. (N.) p. 1

Manfred (N.) . . p. 43
Mazeppa . . . p. 107
Prisoner of Chillon, a Fable, Sonnet, etc. (N.) . p. 139
Sonnet (" Rousseau," etc.) p. 160
Lament of Tasso . p. 161
Various Poems : *
A Sketch, etc. (and 34 others) . . . . p. 173
Vol. V. :—Hours of Idleness (*i.e.* Poems Original and Translated), " The Second English Edition," On Leaving Newstead Abbey, etc. . . . . . p. 1
Critique, etc. . . p. 116
Fugitive Pieces (including *Windsor Poetics*, p. 130, first pub. by Murray 1831, and the spurious *Ode*, " Oh, shame to thee," etc.) . . . p. 163
The Curse of Minerva (full text) . . . . . p. 177

* [Six " Hebrew Melodies " are included in Various Poems.]

Avis ("Le Vampire, fausse-
ment attribué à Lord Byron, est
de *Polidori*, jeune médecin qui
a vécu quelque temps à Genève
avec le poëte anglais," etc.)
p. 191
The Vampyre, A Tale p. 192

Extract of a Letter from
Geneva . . . . p. 194
Introduction . . p. 201
The Vampyre . . p. 207
A Fragment (June 17, 1816)
p. 237

XIX.

The/ Works/ of/ Lord Byron,/ comprehending the/ Sup-
pressed Poems./ Embellished with a Portrait, And a
Sketch of His Life./ Vol. I./ [Vol. II., etc.] Paris :/
Published by A. and W. Galignani,/ At the French,
English, Italian, German and Spanish Library,/ N.º 18,
Rue Vivienne./ 1822./ [8º

Collation—

Vol. I. : pp. 106 + 264—Gen. Half-title (R. *Printed by A.
Belin*); Title, one leaf, pp. 1, 2 ; Contents to Vol. I., pp. 3, 4 ;
The Life of Lord Byron [By J. W. Lake], pp. 5-106 ; Text, pp.
1-264.

Vol. XVI. : pp. 204—Gen. Half-title (R. Imprint) ; Title, one
leaf ; Text, pp. *1-204.*

Contents—

Vol. I. :—Hours of Idleness
p. 1
Translations and Imitations
p. 63
Fugitive Pieces . . p. 97
Critique [*E. R.* Jan. 1808]
p. 153
English Bards, etc. p. 161
Lines written by Mr. Fitz-
gerald in a copy of *English
Bards*, etc., with his Lordship's
Reply . . . . . p. 234

The Curse of Minerva
p. 235
An Ode ("Oh, shame to thee,"
etc.) . . . . . p. 255
Windsor Poetics . p. 259
A Sketch, etc. . p. 260
Vol. XVI. :—The Deformed
Transformed . . . . p. 1
Transl. of Morgante Maggiore
p. 105
Lord Byron's Speeches
p. 157

Note.—The frontispiece of Vol. I. is an engraving of the
Portrait by G. Sanders.

Don Juan was included in successive volumes in accordance
with the date of publication : Cantos I., II. in Vol. VII. ; Cantos
III., IV., V. in Vol. VIII.; Cantos VI.–XI. in Vol. XIV.; and
Cantos XII.–XVI. in Vol. XV.

Volumes XIII.–XV. of this Edition were issued in 1823, and
Vol. XVI. in 1824.

XX.

The/ Works/ of/ Lord Byron./ In Four Volumes./ Vol. I./
[Vol. II., etc.] London :/ John Murray, Albemarle Street./
1823./ [8º

Collation—

Vol. I. : pp. xi. + 303—Title, one leaf, pp. iii., iv. ; Gen. Cont., pp. v., xi. ; Cont. of Vol. I. ; Text, pp. *1-303*. The Imprint (*London :| Printed by Thomas Davison, Whitefriars|*) is in the centre of the last page, p. [304].

Vol. II. : pp. *1-359*—Title, one leaf ; Cont. of Vol. II. ; Text, pp. *1-359*. The Imprint is in the centre of the last page, p. [360].

Vol. III. : pp. *1-345*—Title, one leaf ; Cont. of Vol. III. ; Text, pp. *1-345* ; Notes to *Beppo*, one leaf, p. [347]. The Imprint is in the centre of the last page, p. [348].

Vol. IV. : pp. viii. + 372—Title, one leaf, pp. iii., iv. ; Cont. of Vol. IV., pp. v.–viii. ; Text, pp. *1-372*. The Imprint is at the foot of p. 372.

Contents—

Vol. I. :—Childe Harold's, etc., Cantos I., II. (N. App.) p. 1	The Siege, etc. (N.) p. 169
	Parisina (N.) . . p. 225
Canto III. (N.) . p. 223	The Prisoner of Chillon, Sonnet (N.) . . . p. 265
Vol. II. :—Childe Harold's, etc., Canto IV. (N.) . p. 1	Beppo (N.) . . . p. 293
The Giaour (N.) . p. 207	Vol. IV. :—Mazeppa p. 1
The Bride, etc., Cantos I., II. (N.) . . . . . p. 287	Manfred (N.) . . p. 43
	Hebrew Melodies (23) p. 121
Vol. III. :—The Corsair, Cantos I.–III. (N.) . p. 1	Ode to N. B. (N.) p. 159
Lara, Cantos I., II. (N.) p. 105	Monody, etc. (N.) p. 175
	Lament of Tasso . p. 185
	Poems (57) (N.) . p. 203

Note.—This edition of 1823, 4 vols. 8°, differs from the 3 vols. 8° of 1819, by the addition of *Mazeppa* and the *Ode to Venice.* The Front. of Vol. I. is "Lord Byron," by T. Phillips, R.A., engr. by C. Warren.

XXI.

The Works of Lord Byron. In Twelve Vols. Paris : Printed for Baudry, etc. 1822–1824. [12°

Note.—The *Life and Genius of Lord Byron*, by Sir Cosmo Gordon, is affixed to the twelfth volume. See *La France Littéraire*, by J. M. Quérard. **1827**.

XXII.

The Works of Lord Byron, comprehending the suppressed Poems. Embellished with a portrait, and a sketch of his life. In Twelve Volumes. Printed by A. Belin. Published by Galignani. 1823. [12°

[*B. de la F.*, May 24, 1823.]

XXIII.

The/ Works/ of/ Lord Byron./ Vol. V./ Containing/
Hours of Idleness—Fugitive Pieces—English/ Bards and
Scotch Reviewers—Waltz—/Miscellaneous Poems, etc./
London :/ Knight and Lacey, Paternoster-Row./ 1824./
[8°

Collation—
Vol. V.: pp. xiii. + 154 + 9 + vi. + 57 + vii. + 61 — Gen.
Half-title ; Title (R. *T. C. Hansard, Paternoster-Row Press*) ;
Preface ; Cont., pp. [i.]-xiii. ; Second Half-title ; Text, pp. 2-
154, etc.
Note.—The Imprint (*T. C. Hansard/ Paternoster-Row/*) is at
the foot of the last page (p. 62). Four pages (*n.p.*) of publishers'
list of Sherwood, Jones & Co., etc., dated London, June, 1824,
are bound up with Vol. V.
Vol. VI.: pp. vi. + 308 + 2 pages (*n.p.*)—Gen. Half-title ;
Title [The/ etc. In Seven Volumes./ Vol. VI./ London :/
Printed for John and Henry L. Hunt,/ Tavistock Street./ 1824./]
(R. *London :/ Printed By C. H. Reynell, Broad-Street, Golden-
Square/*) ; Second Half-title ; Dedication ; Preface, pp. i.-vi. ;
Dramatis Personæ, p. [viii.] (*B.A.*) ; Text, pp. 9-308 ; Note to
the Translation of the *Morgante Maggiore*, one leaf, pp. [309, 310].
Vol. VII. : pp. *1*-286—Gen. Half-title ; Title [The, etc./ Tavi-
stock-Street./ 1825./], (R. Imprint as above) ; Text, pp. *1*-286.

Contents—

Vol. V. :—Hours of Idleness	Lines to Mr. Hobhouse
p. 1	p. 60
Review, etc. . . . p. 1	Enigma [H.] . . p. 61
English Bards, etc. . p. i.	Vol. VI. :—Werner p. i.
Waltz [N] . . . . p. i.	Heaven and Earth p. 197
Ode (" Oh, shame to thee,"	Transl. of Morgante Maggiore
etc.) . . . . . p. 19	(Advt.) . . . . p. 259
Adieu to Malta . . p. 23	Vol. VII. :—The Age of
Madame Lavalette . p. 26	Bronze . . . . p. 1
The Curse of Minerva (111	The Island . . . p. 37
lines) . . . . . p. 28	Appendix (Extract from the
Farewell to England p. 35	Voyage of Capt. Bligh)
To my Daughter, etc.	p. 109
p. 46	The Vision of Judgment
Ode to . . . St. Helena	p. 125
p. 50	Appendix (Court of King's
To the Lily of France	Bench, Thursday, January 15,
p. 53	1824. The King *v.* John Hunt)
To Jessy . . . p. 56	p. 187
To T. Moore, Esq. (" My	The Deformed Transformed
Boat," etc.). . . . p. 58	p. 191

Note (1).—In Vol. V. the pagination of the " Postscript " of
English Bards, etc., pp. 45-47, is incorrect.

Note (2).—In Vol. VII. (pp. 125, *sq.*) in the edition of the *Vision of Judgment,* issued after the verdict in the case of the King *v.* John Hunt, January 15, 1824, stanzas viii., ix. (lines 1, 2), xliii. (lines 1–6), xliv., xlv. (lines 1–6), xlvii. (lines 4, 8), are omitted in the text, but are quoted in the report of the trial.

Note (3).—The following slip, headed "Notice to the Binder," is inserted between a fly-leaf and the general half-title of Vols. VI., VII.: "*In order that each purchaser of the two concluding volumes of Lord Byron's Works may be enabled with them to complete his particular set, whatever edition he possesses, an extra Title-page is given with each—there being several editions in print, comprising the same works in different numbers of volumes. In binding these two last volumes, therefore, the binder should be instructed which of the Title-pages to retain.*" Four pages (*n.p.*) consisting of General Half-title (*B.R.*) and Title-page as above [In Eight volumes./ Vol. VII., Vol. VIII./] with Imprint as above, at foot of Reverse, are bound up with Vols. VI., VII. Volume VIII. was not issued.

XXIV.

The Works, etc. In Eight Volumes. London : John Murray, etc., 1825. [Small] 8°.

XXV.

The/ Works /of/ Lord Byron./ In Six Volumes./ Vol. V./ London :/ John Murray, Albemarle Street./ 1825./ [8°

Collation—
Vol. V.: pp. *1*–404—Title, one leaf ; Cont. of Vol. V. ; Text, pp. *1*–404. The Imprint (*London :/ Printed by Thomas Davison, Whitefriars/*) is at the foot of p. 404.
Vol. VI. : pp. viii. + 319—Title, one leaf ; Cont. of Vol. VI. ; Text, pp. *1*–319. The Imprint is in the centre of the last page, p. [320].

Contents—

Vol. V. :—Marino Faliero (N. App.) . . . . p. 1	Vol. VI. :—Sardanapalus (N.) p. 1
Prophecy of Dante, Cantos I.–IV. (N.) . . . p. 243	The Two Foscari (App.) p. 171
Cain . . . . . . p. 291	

XXVI.

The/ Complete Works/ of/ Lord Byron/ With/ A Biographical and Critical notice/ By J. W. Lake, Esq./ Vol. I. [Vol. II., etc.] Childe Harold's Pilgrimage./ [Monogram.] Paris/ From the Press of Jules Didot senior,/ vi, Rue Du Pont-de-Lodi./ Published by

Baudry, Rue du Coq-Saint-Honoré,/ And Amyot, Rue De La Paix./ 1825./ [8°

Collation—

Vol. I.: pp. c. + 353—Title, one leaf; Cont. of the First Vol.; A Biographical, etc., pp. i.–c.; Text, pp. *1*–353.

Vol. II.: pp. *1*–432—Title, one leaf; Cont. of the Second Vol.; Text, pp. *1*–432.

Vol. III.: pp. *1*–466—Title, one leaf; Cont. of the Third Vol.; Text, pp. *1*–466.

Vol. IV.: pp. *1*–426—Title, one leaf; Cont. of the Fourth Vol.; Text, pp. *1*–426.

Vol. V.: pp. *1*–435—Title, one leaf; Cont. of the Fifth Vol.; Text, pp. *1*–435; Note to Cain, one leaf, p. [437].

Vol. VI.: pp. vii. + 529—Title, one leaf, pp. iii., iv.; Cont. of the Sixth Vol., pp. v.–viii.; Text, pp. *1*–529.

Vol. VII.: pp. viii. + 528—Title, one leaf, pp. iii., iv.; Cont. of the Seventh Vol., pp. v.–viii.; Text, pp. *1*–528.

Note.—The Frontispiece of Vol. I. is an engraving of the Portrait of Lord Byron by G. Sanders.

Contents—

Vol. I.:—A Biographical, etc. p. i.

Childe Harold's, etc., Cantos I.–III. (N.) . . . . p. I

Dedication . . . p. 205

Canto IV. (N.) . p. 213

Vol. II.:—Don Juan, Cantos I.–V. (N.) . . . . p. I

Preface to Cantos VI., VII., VIII. . . . . . p. 301

Cantos VI.–VIII. (N.) p. 307

Vol. III.:—Don Juan, etc., etc.

Canto IX. (N.) . . p. I

Canto XVI. (N.) . p. 247

Beppo (N.) . . . p. 295

The Vision of Judgment (N.) p. 333

The Giaour (N.) . p. 373

Parisina . . . . p. 435

Vol. IV.:—Manfred (N.) p. I

Marino Faliero (N.), Preface, etc. . . . . . p. 65

Sardanapalus (N.), Preface, etc. . . . . . p. 267

Vol. V.:—The Two Foscari (N.) . . . . . . p. I

Appendix . . . p. 123

Werner (N.) . . p. 143

Cain (N.) . . . p. 331

Vol. VI.:—Heaven and Earth (N.) . . . . . p. I

The Deformed, etc. (N.) p. 53

The Bride, etc. (N.) p. 133

The Corsair (N.) . p. 193

Lara (N.) . . . p. 279

The Siege, etc. (N.) p. 331

The Prisoner of Chillon (N.), Sonnet, etc. . . . p. 377

Mazeppa (N.), Advt., etc. p. 399

The Island (N.), Advt., etc. p. 435

The Lament of Tasso, Advt. p. 517

Vol. VII.:—The Prophecy of Dante (N.), Dedication, etc. p. I

The Age of Bronze (N.) p. 45

The Curse of Minerva (N.) p. 77

Hours of Idleness . p. 95

Critique, etc. . . p. 211

English Bards, etc., Preface p. 221

Hebrew Melodies . p. 277

Miscellaneous Poems, and The Dream, etc. . . . . p. 301
Morgante Maggiore (N.), Advt. . . . . . . p. 439

Letter to * * * . p. 475
Parliamentary Speeches, Debate on the Framework Bill p. 505

Note.—The Miscellaneous Poems (67) include the following forgeries: Ode ("Oh, shame to thee," etc.), p. 345 ; Madame Lavalette, p. 349 ; Farewell to England, p. 356 ; To my Daughter, p. 366.

XXVII.

Works of Lord Byron. Philadelphia. 1825. Eight Vols. [8°

Contents—
Vol. I. :—Childe Harold's Pilgrimage.
Vol. II. :—Giaour—Two Foscari—Werner.
Vol. III. :—Bride, etc.—Corsair—Cain, a Mystery—Sardanapalus.
Vol. IV. :—Lara—English Bards, and Scotch Reviewers—Marino Faliero—Siege, etc.—Prisoner of Chillon—Song.
Vol. V. : — Manfred — Parisina — Deformed Transformed — Vision of Judgment—Beppo—Age of Bronze—Heaven and Earth —Curse of Minerva, etc.
Vol. VI. :—Mazeppa—The Dream—The Island—Prophecy of Dante—Lament of Tasso—Ode to Buonaparte—Monody, etc.— Hebrew Melodies—Miscellaneous Poems.
Vols. VII., VIII. :—Don Juan.
[Catalogue of the Boston Athenæum Library, 1874.]

XXVIII.

The Works of the R. H. Lord Byron. In Eight Vols. New York: published by Wm Borrodaile, at his wholesale Book Store, 114, Fulton Street. 1825.
[Kölbing.]

XXIX.

The Works of Lord Byron. Complete in Thirty-two Volumes. Published by the Brothers Schumann, Zwickau. 1825–1827. [16°

Note.—Vol. XXXIII. was issued in 1838. [Kayser, 1841.]

XXX.

The Works of Lord Byron, comprising the suppressed poems. In Thirteen Volumes. Paris. Printed by Didot aîné.

Published by A. and W. Galignani, N.º 18, Rue Vivienne 1826.
[*B. de la F.*, June 3, 1826.] [32.º

XXXI.

The/ Works/ of/ Lord Byron/ Including/ The Suppressed Poems./ Complete in one volume/. Paris :/ Published by A. and W. Galignani,/ N.º 18,'Rue Vivienne./ 1826./ [8.

Collation—

Pp. xliii. + 716—Gen. Half-title (R. *Printed by Jules Didot, Senior,| Printer to his Majesty, Rue du Pont de Lodi, N.º 6.|*) ; Title-page, one leaf, pp. i., ii. ; Cont., pp. iii., iv. ; The Life of Lord Byron [by J. W. Lake], pp. v.–xliii. ; Text, pp. *1–716*.

The Front. is a Portrait of Lord Byron by F. Sieurac, engr. by J. T. Wedgwood. The Title-vignette is a harp, etc., resting on foliage (bays and oak leaves).

The Facsimile of the Letter from Lord Byron to M. Galignani, dated Venice, April 27, 1819, is inserted between the "Contents" and the "Life," etc.

Note (1).—Among MISCELLANEOUS POEMS are *The Irish Avatar*, p. 515; *Ode* ("Oh, shame to thee," etc.), p. 539; *Windsor Poetics*, p. 540; and *Carmina Byronis in C. Elgin*, p. 541. The Volume concludes (pp. 711–716) with POEMS ATTRIBUTED TO LORD BYRON, viz.—

Childish Recollections (32 lines) . . . . . p. 711
Lord Byron to his Lady ("How strangely," etc.) *ib.*
Ode to the Island of St. Helena . . . . . *ib.*
To the Lily of France p. 712
Madame Lavalette . *ib.*
Adieu to Malta . . *ib.*
Enigma ("'Twas whispered," etc.) . . . . . p. 713
The Triumph of the Whale *ib.*
To Jessy . . . . *ib.*
To my Daughter . p. 714

To Lady Caroline Lamb p. 715
The Farewell ("When man compelled," etc.) . . *ib.*
Lines ("Would you get to the House," etc.) . . . . *ib.*
Verses ("All hail, Mont Blanc," etc.) . . . . *ib.*
To a Lady ("And wilt thou weep," etc.) 716
*Stanzas ("I heard thy fate," etc.) . . . . . . *ib.*
Lines found in the Travellers' Book at Chamouni . *ib.*
† Lines found in Lord Byron's Bible . . . . . . *ib.*

Note (2).—This edition was reissued, in 1827, on different paper. An impression of the portrait by F. Sieurac, in an unfinished state, precedes the Frontispiece.

---

* "Stanzas" were published *Poetical Works*, 1899, iii. 425, 426, with the title, "On the Death of the Duke of Dorset." Note (1) on p. 425 is incorrect.

† "Lines Found in Lord Byron's Bible" are by Sir Walter Scott (see *Monastery*, chap. xii.).

XXXII.

The Works, etc. Complete.   One Vol.   Frankfort o. M.
Printed by and for H. L. Brœnner. 1826. 4°, pp. xvi. + 776.
[Kölbing.]

Note.—A Second Edition, pp. xlvi. + 804, including *Morgante
Maggiore* and *Parliamentary Speeches*, was issued in 1829, *vide
post*, No. xl. ; and a third, pp. xxx. + 784, including *Francesca di Rimini, Hints from Horace*, and *The Blues*, etc., in
1837.   According to Kayser, the First Edition appeared in 1827,
a second in 1829, and a third, "considerably augmented," in
1837.

XXXIII.

The Works, etc.   In Six Volumes.   London : John Murray
etc.   1827.   [Small 8°
[Kölbing.]

XXXIV.

The/ Works/ of/ Lord Byron./ In Four Volumes./   Vol. I./
[Vol. II., etc.] London :/ John Murray, Albemarle-Street./
1828./   [12°

Collation—
Vol. I. : pp. ix. + 362—Gen. Half-title, Works/ of/ Lord/
Byron./ (R. *London : Printed by Thomas Davison Whitefriars/*),
pp. i., ii. ; Title, one leaf, pp. iii., iv. ; Gen. Cont., pp. v.–ix. ;
Cont. of Vol. I. (*n.p.*) ; Text, pp. *1–362*.
The Front., "Lord Byron," is engr. by E. Finden from a
portrait by G. (*sic*) Phillips, R.A.
Vol. II. : pp. *1–424*—Gen. Half-title (R. Imprint) ; Cont. of
Vol. II. ; Text, pp. *1–424*.   The Imprint is at the foot of p. 424.
The Front., "Medora" (*Corsair*, i. 379), is engr. by E.
Finden from a drawing by H. Corbould.
Vol. III. : pp. vii. + 383—Half-title (R. Imprint), pp. i., ii. ;
Title, one leaf, pp. iii., iv. ; Cont. of Vol. III., pp. v.–vii. ;
Text, pp. *1–383*.   The Imprint is in the centre of the last page,
p. [384].
The Front., "Lord Byron" (" When late I saw thy . . .
child "), is engr. by E. Finden from a drawing by H. Corbould.
Vol. IV. : pp. *1–429*—Gen. Half-title (R. Imprint) ; Title, one
leaf ; Cont. of Vol. IV. ; Text, pp. *1–429*.   The Imprint is in
the centre of the last page, p. [430].
The Front., "Sardanapalus" (act iv. sc. 1, line 1), is engr.
by E. Finden from a drawing by H. Corbould.

Contents—

Vol. I. :—Childe Harold's, etc., Cantos I.–IV. (N.) p. 1	Vol. II. :—The Giaour (N.) p. 1

The Corsair, Cantos I.–III. (N.) . . . . . . p. 61
Lara, Cantos I., II. (N.) p. 143
The Bride, etc., Cantos I., II. (N.) . . . . p. 195
Siege, etc. (N.) . . p. 253
Parisina (N.) . . . p. 299
The Prisoner of Chillon, Sonnet, etc. (N.) . . p. 331
Beppo (N.) . . . . p. 353
Mazeppa . . . . . p. 391
Vol. III. :—Manfred (N.) p. 1
Hebrew Melodies : " She walks in beauty" (and 22 others) p. 61

Ode to N. B. (N.) . p. 89
Monody, etc. . . p. 99
Lament of Tasso . p. 105
Poems :
Written in an Album (and 55 others) . . p. 119
Ode [to Venice] . p. 249
Notes to the Poems p. 255
Prophecy of Dante, Cantos I.–IV. (N.) . . . p. 259
Cain . . . . . p. 299
Vol. IV. :—Marino Faliero (App.) . . . . . . p. 1
Sardanapalus (N.) p. 175
The Two Foscari (App.) p. 303

XXXV.

The/ Works/ of/ Lord Byron/ Including/ The Suppressed Poems./ Complete in One Volume./ Paris :/ Published by A. and W. Galignani,/ No. 18, Rue Vivienne./ 1828./
[8°

Collation—

Pp. xl. + 718.

Note.—This edition closely corresponds with that issued by A. and W. Galignani in 1826-7, *q.v. ante*, No. xxxi. The " Life of Lord Byron," by J. W. Lake, is abbreviated and corrected. Among ATTRIBUTED POEMS are the following additions: *A Drinking Song* ("Fill the goblet," etc.), p. 716 ; *Remember Thee, ibid. ; To Mary* ("Remind me not," etc.), p. 717 ; Verses ("There was a time," etc.), *ibid. ; On Leaving England, ibid. ;* and the following omissions : Verses (" All hail, Mont Blanc," etc.), 1826, p. 715 ; and *Lines Found in Lord Byron's Bible,* 1826, p. 716.

XXXVI.

The Works of Lord Byron. Complete in One Volume. Title-Vignette. Published by Brœnner, Frankfort. 1828.
[8°

Note.—A Second Edition was issued in 1829, and a third, " considerably augmented," in 1837. [Kayser.]

XXXVII.

The/ Works/ of/ Lord Byron./ In Six Volumes./ Vol. I./ [Vol. II., etc.] London :/ John Murray, Albemarle-Street./ 1829./
[8°

Collation—

Vol. I. : pp. ix. + 235—Gen. Half-title, "Byron" (R. *London:*
Printed by Thomas Davison, Whitefriars), pp. i., ii. ; Title, one
leaf, pp. iii., iv. ; General Cont., pp. v.–ix. ; Cont. of Vol. I.,
n.p. ; Text, pp. *1*-235.   The Imprint is in the centre of the last
page, p. [236].

Vol. II. : Gen. Half-title (R. Imprint) ; Title, one leaf ; Cont.
of Vol. II. ; Text, pp. *1*-297.   The Imprint is in the centre of
the last page, p. [300].

Vol. III. : Gen. Half-title, etc., as in Vol. II. ; Text, pp.
1-282.   The Imprint is in the centre of the last page, p. [284].

Vol. IV. : pp. vii. + 275—Half-title (R. Imprint), pp. i., ii. ;
Title, one leaf, pp. iii., iv. ; Cont. of Vol. IV., pp. v.–vii. ;
Text, pp. *1*-275.   The Imprint is in the centre of the last page,
p. [276].

Vol. V. : Half-title, etc., as in Vol. II. ; Text, pp. *1*-264.   The
Imprint is at the foot of p. 264.

Vol. VI. : pp. viii. + 266—Half-title (R. Imprint), pp. i., ii. ;
Title, one leaf, pp. iii., iv. ; Cont. of Vol. VI. (*B.R.*), pp. v., vi. ;
Preface, pp. vii., viii. ; Text, pp. *1*-266.   The Imprint is in the
centre of the last page, p. [268].

Contents—

Vol. I. :—Childe Harold's, etc.,
Cantos I.–III. (Pref. N.) p. 1

Vol. II. :—Childe Harold's,
etc., Canto IV. (N.) . p. 1

The Giaour (N.) . p. 157

The Corsair, Cantos I.–III.
(N.) . . . . . p. 217

Vol. III. :—Lara, Cantos I.,
II. (N.) . . . . p. 1

The Bride, etc., Cantos I., II.
(N.) . . . . . p. 53

Siege, etc. (N.) . p. 111

Parisina (N.) . . p. 157

The Prisoner, etc. (Sonnet,
N.) . . . . . p. 189

Beppo (N.) . . p. 211

Mazeppa . . . p. 249

Vol. IV. :—Manfred (N.)
p. 1

Hebrew Melodies : "She
walks," etc. (and 21 others)
p. 61

Ode to N. B. (N.) p. 85

Monody, etc. . . p. 95

Lament of Tasso . p. 101

Poems : Written in an Album
(and 56 others) (N.) . p. 115

Prophecy of Dante, Cantos
I.–IV. (N.) . . . p. 235

Vol. V. :—Marino Faliero
(App.) . . . . p. 1

Cain . . . . p. 179

Vol. VI. :—Sardanapalus (N.)
p. 1

The Two Foscari (App.)
p. 135

Notes to Captain Medwin's,
etc. . . . . . p. 253

XXXVIII.

The/ Works/ of/ Lord Byron./ In Four Volumes./ Vol. I./
[Vol. II., etc.] London :/ John Murray, Albemarle-Street./
1829./   [12°

Collation—

Vol. I. : pp. x. + 357—Gen. Half-title, "Byron" (R. (*a*)
Printed by Thomas Davison, Whitefriars), pp. i., ii. ; Title, one

leaf, pp. iii., iv. ; Gen. Cont., pp. v.-x. ; Cont. of Vol. I., *n.p.* ; Text, pp. *1-357*. The Imprint (*b*) (*London :| Printed by Thomas Davison, Whitefriars/*), is in the centre of the last page, p. [360].

Vol. II. : pp. *1-424*—Gen. Half-title (R. Imprint (*a*) ; Title, one leaf ; Cont. of Vol. II. ; Text, pp. *1-424*. The Imprint (*b*) is at the foot of p. 424.

Vol. III. : pp. viii. + 383—Gen. Half-title (R. Imprint (*a*)), pp. i., ii. ; Title, one leaf, pp. iii., iv. ; Cont. of Vol. III., pp. v.- viii. ; Text, pp. *1-383*. The Imprint (*b*) is at the foot of the last page, p. [384].

Vol. IV. : pp. *1-412*—Half-title (R. Imprint (*a*)) ; Title, one leaf ; Cont. of Vol. IV. ; Text, pp. *1-412*. The Imprint (*b*) is at the foot of p. 412.

Contents—

The Cont. of Vols. I., II., III. of the Edition of 1829 are identical with the Cont. of Vols. I., II., III. of the Edition of 1828. The pagination of the Text 1829 follows the pagination of the Text 1828, but the type of 1829 is not the type of 1828.

Vol. IV. (1829):—Marino Faliero . . . . p. 1	Appendix . . . . . p. 381
Appendix . . . . p. 147	Notes on Captain Medwin's
Sardanapalus (N.) . p. 161	"Conversations of Lord Byron"
The Two Foscari . p. 289	p. 401

Note.—The original Italian and French Versions of the *Cronica di Sanuto*, and the extracts from the works of P. Daru and P. L. Ginguené, which appeared in 1828, are omitted in 1829, and the notes (by John Murray) on Captain Medwin's *Conversations, etc.* (1824), pp. 401-412, are inserted.

XXXIX.

The Poetic Works, etc., including his *Don Juan*—all his minor poems, and the suppressed pieces of *Cain*, and the *V. of Judgment*, all complete. In Two Vols. Second Edition. Philadelphia : Published by the Washington Press. 1829. [4º and 6º

XL.

The/ Works/ of/ Lord Byron./ Complete/ In One Volume./ [Title-vignette, "Ship in Storm," engraved on steel by C. Tremonet.] The Second Edition, considerably aug- mented./ Francfort O.M./ Printed by and for H. L. Brœnner./ 1829./ [8º

Collation—

Pp. xlvi. + Cont., one leaf + 804—Title, one leaf ; *Life*, etc., by J. W. Lake, pp. i.-xli. + A Character of Lord Byron, by Sir W. Scott, pp. xlii., xliii. + "Goethe und Byron" (including

the stanzas " Ein freundlich Wort," etc.) + " Lord Byron's Last
Lines," pp. xliv.-xlvi. + Cont., one leaf, *n.p.* + Text, pp. *1*–804.
    Note.—The Miscellaneous Poems include Ode " Oh, shame to
thee," etc., p. 630, and On Sir John Moore's Burial, p. 650.
The ATTRIBUTED POEMS are identical with those published
in Paris, 1826 (No. xxxi.), except that they include To Miss
Chaworth (" Remind me not," etc.), and exclude Lines Found
in Lord Byron's Bible. The Notes to *Childe Harold's, etc.*, and
other poems are printed continuously, pp. *715*–792. *The Waltz*,
together with the *Notes*, is on pp. 795–798.

XLI.

The/ Works/ of/ Lord Byron./   In Four Volumes./   Vol. I./
[Vol. II., etc.]   London :/ John Murray, Albemarle-Street./
1830./   [16°

Collation—
    Vol. I.: pp. ix.+359—Title (R. (*a*) *Thomas Davison, London.*),
pp. i., ii. ; General Cont., pp. iii.-ix. ; Cont. of Vol. I., p. x. ;
Text, pp. 1-359.   The Imprint (*b*) (*London :/ Printed by Thomas
Davison, Whitefriars/*) is in the centre of the last page, p. [360].
    The Frontispiece, " Lord Byron," is engraved by E. Finden from
a portrait by T. Phillips, R.A.
    Vol. II.: pp. iv. + 424—Title (R. Imprint), pp. i., ii. ; Cont.
of Vol. II., pp. iii., iv. ; Text, pp. *1*-424.   The Imprint (*b*) is at
the foot of p. 424.
    Vol. III.: pp. vi. + 383—Title (R. Imprint), pp. i., ii. ; Cont.
of Vol. III., pp. iii.-vi. ; Text, pp. *1*-383.   The Imprint (*b*) is in
the centre of the last page, p. [384].
    Vol. IV.: pp. *1*-415—Title (R. Imprint) ; Cont. of Vol. IV.,
one leaf ; Text, pp. *1*-415.   The Imprint (*b*) is in the centre of
the last page, p. [416].
    The Front. of Vol. II. is that of Vol. II., ed. 1828 ; the Front.
of Vol. III. that of Vol. IV., 1828 ; and the Front. of Vol. IV.
that of Vol. III., 1828.
    Note.—The Cont. of Vols. I.-IV., 1830, are identical with the
Cont. of Vols. I.-IV., 1829.   The Notes have been partly re-set.

XLII.

The Complete Works, etc., including his lordship's suppressed poems with others never before published. (With
portrait and *fac-simile*.)   Paris, Galignani, 1830.   [12°
                                                    [Quérard, 1846.]

XLIII.

The/ Works/ of/ Lord Byron./   In Six Volumes./   Vol. I./
[Vol. II., etc.]   London :/   John Murray, Albemarle-
Street./   1831./   [16°

Collation—

Vols. I.–IV. of Ed. **1831** are identical with Vols. I.–IV. of Ed. **1830**. The Frontispieces of Vols. III., IV., which were transposed in Ed. **1830**, are restored to their original position, as in Ed. **1828**.

Vol. V.: pp. xii. + 475—Gen. Half-title (R. (*a*) *Thomas Davison, London*), pp. i., ii. ; Title, one leaf, pp. iii., iv. ; Editor's Advt. to *Hours of Idleness*, pp. v.–vii. ; Cont. of Vol. V., pp. ix., xii. ; Text, pp. *1–475* ; Publisher's Advt. of the Life of Lord Byron (2 Vols. 4to). . . . by Thomas Moore, Esq., p. [477]. The Imprint (*b*) (*London :| Printed by Thomas Davison, Whitefriars.|*) is in the centre of p. 476.

The Frontispiece, "Heaven and Earth," is engr. by E. Finden from a drawing by H. Richter.

Vol. VI. : pp. viii. + 459—Gen. Half-title (R. Imprint), pp. i., ii. ; Title, one leaf, pp. iii., iv. ; Cont. to Vol. VI., pp. v.–viii. ; Text, pp. *1–459*. The Imprint (*b*) is in the centre of the last page, p. [460].

The Frontispiece, "The Island," is engr. by E. Finden from a drawing by H. Richter.

Contents—

Note.—List of publications by John Murray, January 4, 1831— "A fifth and sixth vol. of Lord Byron's Works: containing E. B., etc., *Heaven & E.*, *The Def. Transf.*, *The Island*, etc., etc., forming the portion of the Works recently purchased by Mr. Murray, and rendering them the first and only complete edition (*Don Juan* being alone excepted). 2 vols, 12°

" .· Printed for the first time, to match with the Edition of Lord Byron's Works in 4 vols. 18.° "

XLIV.

The/ Complete works/ of/ Lord Byron,/ Including/ his Lordship's Suppressed Poems,/ With others never before published./ In one Volume./ Paris./ Published by A. and W. Galignani,/ No. 18, Rue Vivienne./ 1831./ [8.°

Collation—

Pp. xxiv. + 730—Half-title (R. *Printed by J. Smith, Rue Montmorency, Paris.*/) ; Title, one leaf ; Cont., pp. i.–iv. ; The Life of Lord Byron [abridged from the *Life* by J. W. Lake] pp. v.–xxiv. ; Text, pp. *1–730.*

The Frontispiece, a portrait of Lord Byron, engr. by J. T. Wedgwood from a painting by W. E. West, in arabesque frame, rests on miniatures of Newstead Abbey and Missolunghi (*sic*) designed by F. Sieurac. The Title-vignette is tomb, harp, willows, etc. A lithograph of letter, April 27, 1819, to the Editor of *Galignani's Messenger,* is inserted between the *Life* and the Text.

Contents—

This edition includes Hours of Idleness (Sec. Ed.), *English Bards*, etc., *The Curse of Minerva, The Waltz,* all poems published by John Murray before **1831**, a selection of poems included in Moore's *Notices of the Life,* etc., poems published by John Hunt, Letter to . . . . on Bowles' Strictures on Pope, Fragment, Parliamentary Speeches, and the following spurious and additional poems :—

Madame Lavalette p. 699	Francesca . . . . . *ib.*
Ode (" Oh, shame to thee," etc.). . . . . . p. 705	Faith, Wisdom, Love and Power . . . . . . *ib.*
Carmina Byronis in C. Elgin p. 707	Thermopylæ . . p. 714
Ode to the Island of St. Helena . . . . . . *ib.*	Song, " Do you know Dr. Nott ? " . . . . p. 716
Enigma on the letter H p. 708	To Mr. Hobhouse, " What made you," etc. (20 lines) p. 717
To Jessy . . . . . *ib.*	Enigma on the letter I. p. 720
To my Daughter . p. 709	
Lines to Mr. Hobhouse p. 710	To Memory (" Oh, memory," etc.) . . . . . p. 721
Lines found in the Travellers' book at Chamouni . . *ib.*	To my dear Mary Anne *ib.*
Stanzas to her who can best understand them . . p. 712	On an Old Lady (" In Nottingham," etc.) . . p. 722
In the Valley of Waters p. 713	

Note.—Among the ATTRIBUTED POEMS are To the Lily of

France, p. 729 ; The Triumph of the Whale, *ib.* ; To Lady C. Lamb, *ib.* ; Stanzas ("I heard thy fate," etc.), p. 730.

XLV.

The Works, etc., including the suppressed poems. Also a Sketch of his Life. By J. W. Lake. Complete in one Vol. Philadelphia. Published by Henry Adams and sold by John Griggs. 1831.   [4°

Collation—
   Pp. xxxix. + 176.

XLVI.

The/ Works/ of/ Lord Byron :/ With/ His Letters and Journals,/ And His Life,/ By Thomas Moore, Esq./ In Fourteen Volumes./ Vol. I. [Vol. II., etc.] London :/ John Murray, Albemarle Street./ 1832./   [8°

Collation—
   Vol. I. : pp. xv. + 359—Title (R. Imprint, *London :| Printed by A. Spottiswoode,| New-Street-Square.|*), pp. i., ii. ; Cont. of Vol. I., pp. iii., iv. ; Half-title, pp. v., vi. ; Dedication to Sir W. Scott, pp. vii., viii. ; Preface to the First Vol. of First Ed., pp. ix., x. ; Preface to the Sec. Vol., pp. xi.–xv. ; Text (*Notices of the Life of Lord Byron*), pp. 1–359.
   The Frontispiece, "Lord Byron at the Age of 19," is engr. by W. Finden from the portrait by G. Sanders: the Title-vignette, "Cadiz," is engr. by E. Finden from a drawing by C. Stansfield.
   Vol. II. : pp. 1–341—The Frontispiece "Tepaleen," is engr. by E. Finden from a drawing by W. Purser ; the Title-vignette, "Constantinople," is engr. by E. Finden from a drawing by C. Stansfield.
   Vol. III. : pp. 1–376—The Front., "Marathon," and the Title-vignette, "A Street in Athens," are engr. by E. Finden from drawings by C. Stansfield.
   Vol. IV. : pp. 1–359—The Front., "The Wengen Alps," and the Title-vignette, "The Coliseum from the Orto Farnese," are engr. by E. Finden from drawings by J. D. Harding.
   Vol. V. : pp. 1–376—The Front., "Sᵗᵃ Maria Dalla Spina," is engr. by E. Finden from a drawing by J. M. W. Turner, R.A.; the Title-vignette, the "Hellespont," is engr. by E. Finden from a drawing by J. D. Harding.
   Vol. VI. : pp. 1–416—The Front., "Newstead Abbey" [from the Monk's Garden], and the Title-vignette, "The Fountain at Newstead Abbey," are engr. by E. Finden from drawings by W. Westall, A.R.A.
   Vol. VII. : pp. xv. + 319—Gen. Half-title (R. Imprint), pp. i., ii. ; Title, one leaf, pp. iii., iv. ; Advt. (editorial, June, 1832), pp. v.–vii. ; Cont. of Vol. VII., pp. ix.–xv. ; Text, pp. 1–319. The Imprint is in the centre of the last page, p. [320].

The Front., "The Gate of Theseus," and the Title-vignette, "The Plains of Troy," are engr. by E. Finden from drawings by J. M. W. Turner, R.A. A facsimile of the two first stanzas of To D—— faces p. 12.

Vol. VIII.: pp. x. + 328—Gen. Half-title (R. Imprint), pp. i., ii.; Title, one leaf, pp. iii., iv.; Advt. (editorial, July 20, 1832), pp. v.-x.; Cont. of Vol. VIII., *n.p.*; Text, pp. *1*-328. The Imprint is at the foot of p. 328.

The Front., "Bacharach," and the Title-vignette, "The Castle of St. Angelo," are engr. by E. Finden from drawings by J. M. W. Turner, R.A. A facsimile of *Childe Harold's, etc.*, Canto III. stanza xci. faces p. 174. In earlier copies the facsimile faced p. [viii.] of Vol. IX. See Note on reverse of p. vii. of that volume.

Vol. IX.: pp. vii. + 360—Title (R. Imprint), pp. i., ii.; Advt. (editorial, July 20, 1832), pp. iii., iv.; Cont. of Vol. IX., pp. v.-vii.; Text, pp. *1*-360. The Imprint is at the foot of p. 360.

The Front., "Petrarch's Tomb," is engr. by E. Finden from a drawing by J. M. W. Turner, R.A.; the Title-vignette, "Seville," is engr. by E. Finden.

Vol. X.: pp. xix. + 316—Gen. Half-title (R. Imprint), pp. i., ii.; Title, one leaf, pp. iii., iv.; Advt. (editorial, September 16, 1832), pp. v.-xiii.; Cont. of Vol. X., pp. xv.-xix.; Text, pp. *1*-316. The Imprint is at the foot of p. 316.

The Front., "Corinth," is engr. by E. Finden from drawings by J. M. W. Turner, R.A., and W. Page; the Title-vignette, "Athens and the Island of Egina," is engr. by E. Finden from drawings by C. Stansfield and W. Page.

Vol. XI.: pp. viii. + 326—Gen. Half-title (R. Imprint), pp. i., ii.; Title, one leaf, pp. iii., iv.; Advt. (editorial, October 10, 1832), pp. v., vi.; Cont. of Vol. XI., pp. vii., viii.; Text, pp. *1*-326. The Imprint is at the foot of p. 326.

The Front., "The Bridge of Sighs," and the Title-vignette, "The Bernese Alps," are engr. by E. Finden, from drawings by J. M. W. Turner, R.A.

Vol. XII.: pp. vi. + 324—Gen. Half-title (R. Imprint), pp. i., ii.; Title, one leaf, pp. iii., iv.; Advt. (editorial, November 10, 1832), pp. v., vi.; Cont. of Vol. XII., *n.p.*; Text, pp. *1*-324. The Imprint is at the foot of p. 324.

The Front., "Florence," is engr. by E. Finden from drawings by J. D. Harding and G. Moran, junr.; the Title-vignette, "San Georgio Maggiore," is engr. by E. Finden from a drawing by C. Stansfield, A.R.A.

Vol. XIII.: pp. vi. + 369—Half-title (R. Imprint), pp. i., ii.; Title, one leaf, pp. iii., iv.; Advt. (editorial, December 12, 1832), pp. v., vi.; Cont. of Vol. XIII., *n.p.*; Text, pp. *1*-369. The Imprint is in the centre of the last page, p. [370].

The Front., "The Arch of Titus," is engr. by E. Finden, from drawings by C. Stansfield and W. Page; the Title-vignette, "The Walls of Rome," is engr. by E. Finden from a drawing by J. M. W. Turner, R.A.

Vol. XIV. : pp. *1*–360—Gen. Half-title (R. Imprint), pp. [i., ii.] ; Title, one leaf, pp. [iii., iv.] ; Advt. (editorial, January 10, 1833), pp. [v., vi.] ; Text, pp. *1*–360. The Imprint is at the foot of p. 360.

The Front., "Parnassus," and the Title-vignette, "The Field of Waterloo," are engr. by E. Finden from drawings by J. M. W. Turner, R.A.

Vol. XV. : pp. vi. + 334—Half-title (R. Imprint), pp. i., ii. ; Title, one leaf, pp. iii., iv. ; Advt. (editorial, February 15, 1833), pp. v., vi. ; Cont. of Vol. XV., *n.p.* ; Text, pp. *1*–334. The Imprint is at the foot of p. 334.

The Front., "Scio," and the Title-vignette, "Genoa," are engr. by E. Finden from drawings by J. M. W. Turner, R.A.

Vol. XVI. : pp. vi. + 335—Half-title (R. Imprint), pp. i., ii. ; Title, one leaf, pp. iii., iv. ; Advt. (editorial, March 15, 1833), pp. v., vi. ; Cont. of Vol. XVI., *n.p.* ; Text, pp. *1*–335. The Imprint is in the centre of the last page, p. [336].

The Front., "Cologne," and the Title-vignette, "St. Sophia," are engr. by E. Finden from drawings by J. M. W. Turner, R.A.

Vol. XVII. : pp. viii. + 304—Half-title (R. Imprint), pp. i., ii. ; Title, one leaf, pp. iii., iv. ; Advt. (editorial, May 15, 1833), pp. v., vi. ; Cont. of Vol. XVII., pp. vii., viii. ; Text, pp. *1*–248 ; Index, pp. 249–304. The Imprint is at the foot of p. 304.

The Front., "The School of Homer," and the Title-vignette, "The Castellated Rhine," are engr. by E. Finden from drawings by J. M. W. Turner, R.A.

Contents—

Vols. I.–V. :—Notices of the Life of Lord Byron.

Vol. VI. :—The Life, etc., from February, 1823–April, 1824 . . . . . p. 1

App. : cont. two epistles from the Armenian, etc. . p. 269

Miscellaneous Pieces in Prose :
Review of Wordsworth's Poems, 1807 . p. 293
Review of Gell's Geography of Ithaca, etc., 1811 p. 296
Parliamentary Speeches, etc. . . . . p. 314
A Fragment. [The Vampyre.] 1816. p. 339
Letter to John Murray, Esq., etc. . p. 346
Observations upon "Observations," etc. [*Now first published*.] . p. 382

Vol. VII. :—Hours of Idleness : a Series of Poems, Original and Translated :
Dedication . . . p. 1
Preface . . . . p. 5
On the Death of a Young Lady (and 69 others) p. 9
Article from the *Edin. Rev.* p. 188
Occasional Pieces : written in 1807–8 :
The Adieu (and 15 others) p. 195
English Bards and Scotch Reviewers . . . p. 219
Occasional Pieces : written in 1808–1810 :
Well, thou art happy (and 15 others) . . p. 291

Vol. VIII. :—Childe Harold's Pilgrimage : Preface to the First and Second Cantos . . p. 3
To Ianthe . . . . . p. 9

Vol. XVII. : — Don Juan (Cantos XI.–XVI.) . p. 1 Appendix : Farewell to Malta (and nine additional occasional pieces) . . . . . p. 239   Concluding Page of Lord Byron's "Observations upon an Article," etc. . . . p. 247 Index . . . . p. 249

Note (1).—The Title-pages of Vols. XIII., XIV., XV., XVI., issued in 1833, do not specify the total number of volumes. The Title-pages of Vol. I. issued in 1835, Vol. II. in 1833, and Vol. IX. in 1834, print the words, "In Seventeen Volumes." There were probably other variations. There is an illustrated Title-page ornamented with a Title-vignette (*vide supra et ante*) to each volume.

Note (2).—The editor of these volumes was John Wright (1770?–1844), the editor of Cobbett's *Parliamentary History*, and the ninth and tenth volumes of Boswell's *Life of Johnson* (1836), and of Sir Henry Cavendish's *Debates of the House of Commons during the Thirteenth Parliament of Great Britain*, etc., two vols. 1841–3.

XLVII.

The Complete Works, etc., including his suppressed poems and others never before published. In Four Volumes. Paris, Baudry. 1832. [8°

[*Katalog der Bücher*, von Eduard Grisebach, 1894, p. 127.]

Note.—The Front. is "Lord Byron," from a portrait by Hopwood. Quérard, 1846, gives the names of the publishers of this edition as Baudry, Barrois, Amyot.

XLVIII.

The Works, etc., In Verse and Prose. Including his Letters, Journals, etc. With a sketch of his Life. New York : George Dearborn, Publisher. 1833. 4° pp. xxviii., 203, 619. [". . . The first complete edition of the Poetical and Prose Works of Lord Byron."—*Publisher's Advt.*]

Note.—The Catalogue of the Library of Congress, 1880, describes this or a Second Edition as consisting of two vols. in one, 8°

XLIX.

The/ Complete Works/ of Lord Byron,/ Reprinted from the last London Edition,/ with considerable additions, now first published ;/ Containing/ Notes and Illustrations/ By/ Moore, Walter Scott, Campbell, Jeffrey, Egerton Brydges, Wilson, Hobhouse,/ Dallas, Hunt, Milman, Lockhart, Bowles, Heber, Medwin, Gamba, Croby, Ugo Foscolo,

Ellis,/ Kennedy, Parry, Stanhope, Galt, Nathan, Lady Blessington, Mrs. Shelley, etc./ And/ A Complete Index ;/ To which is prefixed/ A Life,/ By Henry Lytton Bulwer, Esq., M.P.,/ In one Volume./ Paris/ Published by A. and W. Galignani and Co./ 1835./ [8°

Collation—

Pp. xxxiii. + 935—Half-title (R. *Printed by H. and A. Firmin Didot, rue Jacob, No. 24.*), pp. i., ii. ; Title, pp. iii., iv. ; (Publisher's) Advt., pp. v., vi. ; Cont., pp. vii.–x. ; The Life of Lord Byron, pp. xi.–xxxiii. ; Text, pp. *1*–908 ; Index, pp. 909-935.

The Frontispiece is a portrait of Lord Byron, engr. by J. T. Wedgwood from a painting by W. E. West. The portrait in arabesque frame rests on picture of Newstead Abbey and Missolunghi (*sic*), designed by F. Sieurac. There is a lithographed vignette of tomb, harp, wreath, etc., on the title-page, and on p. xxxiii. a lithograph of the memorial tablet in the chancel of Hucknall Torkard. A facsimile of the letter dated Venice, April 27, 1819, precedes the text, and facsimiles of original MS. of "To D—," and of *Childe Harold*, Canto IV. stanza xcii., face pp. 3, 122.

Miscellaneous Poems—

On an Old Lady ("In Nottingham," etc.) . p. 842

On Lord Elgin ("Noseless himself," etc.) . . p. 864

Stanzas to her who can best understand them . . p. 887

Epigram from Martial ("The Laureate's House," etc.) p. 888

To Mr. Hobhouse ("Would you get," etc.) . . . *ib.*

To Mr. Hobhouse ("What made you," etc.) . . . *ib.*

On Queen Caroline . p. 901

Elegy on the Recovery of Lady *** . . . . . p. 903

Song, "Do you know Doctor Nott?" . . . . . . *ib.*

To — ("But once I dared," etc.) . . . . . p. 904

On Sam Rogers ("Nose and Chin," etc.) . . . . *ib.*

On Lady Milbank's Dog Trim p. 905

Lines to Lady Holland ("Lady, accept," etc.) . *ib.*

Attributed Poems :

To Jessy ("There is a mystic," etc.) p. 906

Lines found in the Travellers' Book at Chamouni . . . *ib.*

To Lady Caroline Lamb p. 907

To the Prince of Whales *ib.*

On the letter I . p. 908

To my dear Mary Anne *ib.*

Stanzas ("I heard thy fate," etc.) . . . . *ib.*

Note.—This edition includes the contents of "the last [edition] published in London in seventeen volumes," together with the poems published in the Appendix to the *Works of Lord Byron* (1832–1833, xvii. 238–248), and the following pieces not recognized or collected by John Murray.

L.

The Complete Works, etc.   In Four Volumes.   Paris,
Baudry, Amyot, Truchy.   1835.   [8°
                                        [Quérard, 1846.]

 Note.—This edition was reissued in 1840.

LI.

The/ Works/ of/ Lord Byron./   Complete In One Volume./
With Notes By/

  Thomas Moore, Esq., Professor Wilson,
  Lord Jeffrey,   J. G. Lockhart, Esq.,
  Sir Walter Scott,   George Ellis, Esq.,
  Bishop Heber,   Thomas Campbell, Esq.,
  Samuel Rogers, Esq., Rev. H. H. Milman,
      etc. etc. etc.

London :/ John Murray, Albemarle Street./ 1837./   [8°

Collation—
 Pp. viii. + 827—Title (R. *London :*| *Printed by A. Spottis-*
woode,| *New-Street-Square.*|), pp. i., ii. ; Contents, pp. iii.–vi. ;
Chronology of Lord Byron's Life and Works, pp. vii., viii. ;
Text, pp. 1–812 ; Index, pp. 813–827.   The Imprint, as above, is
at the foot of p. 827.
 The Frontispiece, "Lord Byron at the age of 19," is engr. by
E. Finden from the portrait by G. Sanders.   The illustrated Title
is embellished with a vignette of "Newstead Abbey," engr. by
E. Finden from a painting by T. Creswick.
 The Dedication is enclosed in an arabesque of oak branches
issuing from a shield bearing the arms and motto (*Industria*) of
Sir Robert Peel.   It runs as follows : To/ The Right Honorable/
Sir Robert Peel, Bart./ etc. etc. etc./ This/ Collective Edition/
of The Works of His/ "School and Form Fellow,"/ Is/
Respectfully Inscribed/ By His/ Faithful and Obedient Servant/
John Murray,/ February Fifth./   MDCCCXXXVII./
 Facsimiles of Lord Byron's Handwriting at Various Periods of
His Life, viz. : I. *At Harrow in* 1803.   II. *From the Giaour,*
1813.   *First draft.*   III. *Marriage Signatures of Lord and Lady*
Byron, January 2, 1815.   IV. *From Lord Byron's Diary,* 1821.
V. *From Lord Byron's last letter to Mr. Murray, dated Missa-*
longhi, February 2, 1824 (four pages, *n.p.*) are inserted between
the "Chronology," etc., and the Text.
 The first edition was bound in brown cloth.   Lord Byron's
Coat of Arms, with Coronet, Supporters and Motto, is stamped in
gold on the cover.
 Note.—This Edition, which is printed in double columns enclosed
by a double line, has been reissued at brief intervals from 1838
to 1902.
 The contents of this volume includes the contents of Vols

VII.–XVII. of the Ed. 1832, 1833, together with the following
additions already printed (except No. 4) in Vols. I.–VI. :—

Contents—

1. Translation of . . . Nurse's Dole ("Oh, how I wish," etc.) . . . . p. 546
2. My Epitaph ("Youth, Nature," etc.). . . . *ib.*
3. Remember thee ! Remember thee ! . . p. 554
4. John Keats . . p. 574
5. Impromptu ("Beneath Blessington's eyes") . p. 577

6. To the Countess of Blessington . . . . . . *ib.*

Appendix :
Conversations of Lord Byron as related by Thomas Medwin, Esq., compared with a Portion of His Lordship's Correspondence. Published, Ed. 1828, iv. 419-429 . . . . . . p. 809

LII.

The/ Complete Works/ of/ Lord Byron/ From the last London
Edition,/ Now first collected and arranged, and Illustrated/
With all the notes/ By Sir Walter Scott [and 24 others—
five lines] To which is prefixed the Life of the Author/ By
John Galt, Esq./ In one Volume./ Paris :/ Baudry's
European Library,/ Rue Du Coq, near the Louvre./ A.
and W. Galignani and Co., 18, Rue Vivienne./ Sold also
by Amyot, Rue de la Paix ; Truchy, Boulevard des
Italiens ; Théophile Barrois, Jun.,/ Rue Richelieu ; at the
Librairie des Étrangers, 55, Rue Neuve-Saint-Augustin ;/
And by all the Principal Booksellers on the Continent./
1837./   [8°

Collation—

Pp. 11 + cxxii. + 954—Half-title (R. *Printed by Casimir,* 12,
Rue de la Vieille-Monnaie) ; Title, one leaf ; Publisher's Advt.,
pp. 1-6 ; Contents, pp. 7-11 ; *The Life of Lord Byron.* By John
Galt, Esq., pp. *i.*-cxxii. ; Text, pp. *1*-941 ; Index, pp. 943-954.
The Imprint, as above, is at the foot of p. 954.

The Frontispiece, "Lord Byron at the age of 17 " (*sic*), is engr.
by Blanchard from the painting by G. Sanders. The Title-page
is embellished with a vignette of a shipwreck.

Facsimiles of Lord Byron's Handwriting, etc. (as in No. li.),
four pages (*n.p.*), are inserted between the "Life," p. cxxii., and
the Text, p. *1.*

Note.—This volume "contains all the works of Lord Byron
carefully reprinted from the [last eleven volumes of the] London
edition published by Mr. Murray in 1833." The prose pieces
published in Vol. VI. of the same edition are included. The
additional poems printed in the Appendix of Vol. XVII., 1833,
"occupy respectively their proper places."

Galt's *Life of Lord Byron* was first published in 1830 as N° 1 of
G. A. Gleig's "National Library."

VOL. VII.   R

LIII.

The Works, etc., Complete in one Vol.   With Notes by
   Th. Moore, Lord Jeffrey, etc. Authorized Foreign Edition.
   London and Leipzig : Black and Armstrong. 1837.

> *Note.*—Kayser (1841) records the issue of *The Works* in seven-
> teen volumes, and *The Complete Works* in ten volumes (pocket
> edition), by the same publisher. (See, too, *The Prisoner of
> Chillon*, by E. Kölbing, 1896, p. 76.)

LIV.

Lord Byron's Complete Works.   In Seven Vols. Mannheim.
   Henry Hoff. 1837.   [16°
                                      [Kayser, 1841.]

LV.

The Complete Works, etc. Including the Suppressed
   Poems and Supplementary pieces selected from his papers
   after his Death. In one Vol. Paris. Published by Garnier,
   Palais-Royal. 1839.   [4°
                                             [Kölbing.]

Collation—
   Pp. xlv. + 724.

LVI.

The/ Poetical Works/ of/ Lord Byron./   In Eight Volumes./
   Vol. I.—Part I./   London :/   John Murray, Albemarle
   Street. 1839./   [4°

> *Note.*—This edition (printed by A. Spottiswoode, New-Street-
> Square), together with *Letters and Journals of Lord Byron, etc.*,
> *by T. Moore.* 2 v. 1830. 4° (" to which have been added the
> Letter to [John Murray] on the Rev. W. L. Bowles' Strictures
> on the life and writings of Pope. . . . Second Edition, and a few
> other printed papers, also numerous views, portraits, autograph
> letters," etc.) bound in 44 vols. with the gen. Title (The/ Poetical
> Works,/ Letters and Journals,/ of/ Lord Byron :/ with/ Notices
> of His Life./ By/ Thomas Moore, Esq./ Vol. I. [Vol. II.]
> London : 1844./), printed expressly for the purpose and prefixed to
> each volume, which is known as the "Watts" Collection (B.M. C.
> 44, e–h), was arranged by the late William Watts, Esq., Member
> of the Philharmonic Society, who died at Jersey, December 28,
> 1859, aged 81. (See Kölbing's *P. of Chillon*, 1896, pp. 90–92.)

LVII.

The Works, etc. Complete in Five Vols. Leipzig : Bernhard
   Tauchnitz. 1842.   [8°
                                             [Kölbing.]

> *Note.*—A Second Edition was issued in 1886.

LVIII.

The Works, etc. A New Edition. Edited by Thomas Moore, Esq. Complete in four volumes. With Engravings. Philadelphia. Carey and Hart. 1843.

[Kölbing.]

LIX.

The Complete Works, etc. . . . A Life by Thomas Moore, Esq. In One Volume. With a Portrait. Second Edition. Frankfort o. M. Published by Joseph Baer. 1846. [8°

Collation—

Pp. xlviii. + 1004.

Note.—Another edition appeared in 1852 (*vide post*, No. lxv.).

[Kölbing.]

LX.

The/ Works of Lord Byron ;/ In Verse and Prose./ Including/ His Letters, Journals, etc./ With/ A Sketch of His Life./ Hartford :/ Published by Silas Andrus and Son./ 1847./ [8°

Collation—

Pp. xxviii. + 319 + 627—Illustrated Title as above (*n.d.*), pp. iii., iv. ; Title (R. Publishers' Advt., New York, Jan. 1834), pp. v., vi. ; Cont., pp. vii.–xiv. ; *The Life of Lord Byron* [By Fitz Green Halleck], pp. xv.–xxviii. ; Text (i.) *Letters* (635), Extracts from a Journal, and Prose Pieces, pp. *1*–319 ; Text (ii.) *Poems*, etc., pp. *1*–627.

The Front., "Lady Noel Byron," is engr. by A. Dick from a painting by W. J. Newton. The vignette or illust. title is Lord Byron, engr. by A. Dick from a painting by W. E. West. To face p. 1 of the *Poems* is "Diodati," engr. by M. Osborne from a sketch by W. Purser ; to face p. 156, "*Mazeppa*," engr. by Illman and Pilbrow from a painting by H. Verner ; facsimiles of Lord Byron's handwriting face pp. 25, 384.

The volume was issued in roan binding, with portrait of Byron stamped in gold on the covers.

Among "Poems not included in any Collection of Lord Byron's Works until after his Death," pp. 467–488, are the following pieces not included in the London editions of 1831, 1832, and of 1833.

To my dear Mary Anne p. 472	"In the Valley of Waters," etc. . . . . . p. 482
To Miss Chaworth ("Oh, memory," etc.) . . . *ib.*	Stanzas to her who can best understand them . p. 486
To Lady Caroline Lamb p. 480	

LXI.

The/ Works/ of/ Lord Byron :/ With a/ Life and Illustrative
Notes,/ By/ William Anderson, Esq.,/ Author of Landscape
Lyrics, Scottish Popular Biography, etc./ In Two
Volumes./ Vol. I./ [Vol. II.] A Fullarton & Co. :/
Stead's Place, Leith Walk, Edinburgh ;/ and 106, Newgate
Street, London./ *n.d.* [1850.] [8°

Collation—
  Vol. I. : pp. ccxxiv. + 270—Title (R. Edinburgh :/ *Fullarton
and Macnab, Printers, Leith Walk*), pp. i., ii. ; Preface, pp. iii.,
iv. ; Cont. of Vol. I. pp. v., vi. ; *Life of Lord Byron*, pp. vii.–
ccxxiv. ; Text, pp. *1–270*. The Imprint, as above, is at the foot
of p. 270.
  The Front. [" Lord Byron at the age of 19"] is engr. by E.
Finden from the painting by G. Sanders. The illustrated Title-
page [The/ Works/ of/ Lord Byron/ With Notes and Illustrations./
Vol. I./ Edinburgh :/ A Fullarton & Co./ Stead's Place, Leith
Walk./] is embellished with a vignette of "Lausanne," engr. by
W. Finden from a drawing by C. Stansfield, A.R.A.
  Vol. II. : pp. 1–465—Title (R. Imprint as above) ; Cont. of
Vol. II. ; Text, pp. *1–465*. The Imprint, as above, is at the
foot of p. 465.
  The Front., "Newstead Abbey," is engr. by E. Finden from
a drawing by W. Westall, A.R.A. The illustrated Title-page is
embellished with a vignette, "Villeneuve," engr. by E. Finden
from a drawing by C. Stansfield, A.R.A.
  Note.—These volumes contain all that " the existing laws of
copyright [1850] allows to be free ;" *e.g.* all the dramas except
Manfred and *Cain, The Island, The Age of Bronze*, etc., are
omitted. In Vol. I. the Life and Text are illust. by 56 Plates ;
in Vol. II. the Text is illust. by 41 Plates. Two pages (B.R.)
headed, " Directions for placing the Plates," and " Directions
for placing Plates in Supplement," are bound up with Vol. II.

LXII.

The/ Poetical Works/ of/ Lord Byron./ Complete in One
Volume./ Collected and Arranged, with Illustrative
Notes,/ By/ Thomas Moore/ [and 9 others]. With a
Portrait, and View of Newstead Abbey./ Philadelphia./
1850./ [8°

Collation—
  Pp. 829.
  Note.—Reissued by the same firm with different addresses in
1854, 1869, 1878, etc. This edition is a reproduction of Murray's
one-volume edition of 1837.

LXIII.

The/ Poetical Works/ of/ Lord Byron./ Containing/ The Giaour,/ [and 17 others]. Also/ Several Attributed and Suppressed Poems not/ Included in Other Editions./ With a Memoir,/ By/ Henry Lytton Bulwer, Esq./ London :/ Henry G. Bohn, York Street, Covent Garden./ 1851./ [12?]

Collation—
Pp. xlviii. + 641.

Attributed Poems—	
Ode (" Oh, shame to thee ") p. 624	To the Lily of France p. 638
Madame Lavalette p. 626	To Jessy . . . p. 640
Farewell to England p. 627	Lines addressed to Mr. Hobhouse . . . . . p. 641
To my Daughter, etc. p. 634	Enigma (H.) . . . *ib.*
Ode to the Island of St. Helena . . . . . p. 636	

Note.—The Front. is " Lord Byron," by Harlow, Sanders, and Phillips (three vignettes), with arabesque border surmounted by arms and coronet. The Title-vignette (on illustrated Title-page, dated 1847) is " Newstead Abbey."

LXIV.

The Poetical Works, etc. Complete in One Volume. Philadelphia : Lippincott, Grambo and Co., successors to Grigg, Elliot and Co., N? 14, North Fourth Street. 1851. [6?]

Note.—A reissue, entitled *The Globe Edition*, Philadelphia, Claxton, Remsen, and Haffelfinger, appeared in 1870.

LXV.

The/ Complete Works/ of/ Lord Byron./ Reprinted from the Last London Edition ;/ Containing Besides the/ Notes and Illustrations/ By/ Moore, (and 24 others = 4 lines). Considerable Additions and Original Notes ;/ To which is Prefixed/ a Life/ By Thomas Moore, Esq./ [Abbreviated.] In One Volume, with a Portrait./ Second Edition./ Frankfort o. M./ Published by Joseph Baer, Bookseller./ 1852./ [8?]

Collation—
Pp. xlviii. + 1004.
The Front., " Lord Byron at the age of 19," is engr. by C. Deucker from the painting by G. Sander (*sic*).

The "Miscellaneous Poems" are identical with the Miscel-
laneous Poems of No. xlviii., save for the omission of the lines,
"In Nottingham County," etc., and twelve lines from the ballad
"On Mr. Hobhouse."

LXVI.

The/ Illustrated/ Byron/ with upwards of/ Two Hundred
Engravings/ From Original Drawings/ By/ Kenny
Meadows/ Birket Foster/ Hablot K. Browne/ Gustave
Janet/ and/ Edward Morin./ Henry Vizetelly London.
Gough Sq., Fleet St./ [1854, 1855.]   [8º

Collation—
Pp. viii. + 632.

LXVII.

Poetical Works, with a memoir of his life. (2 vols.) Philadelphia. 1853.   [8º
                              [Detroit Public Library.]

LXVIII.

Poetical Works, etc.   With life and notes by Allan Cunning-
ham. Family ed. London, Charles Daly, 17 Greville
Street, Hatton Gardens. [1854.]   [12º
                    [Cat. of Lib. of Congress, 1880.]

Collation—
Pp. xxii. + 544.   10 pl.

LXIX.

The Works, etc., embracing his suppressed poems, and a
sketch of his life. Illustrated. New edition, complete in
one volume. Boston : Phillips, Sampson, and Company,
110 Washington Street. 1854.   [4º
                              [Kölbing.]

Collation—
Pp. vi. + 1071.

LXX.

The/ Poetical Works/ of/ Lord Byron./ In Six Volumes—
Vol. I./ [Vol. II., etc.] A New Edition./ With Portrait./
London :/ John Murray, Albemarle Street./ 1855./ [8º

Note.—Front., Portrait of Lord Byron, by T. Phillips, R.A.,
engr. by E. Finden. [Murray's "Library Edition," reissued in
1857 and in 1867.]

LXXI.

(In this Edition Objectionable Pieces have been excluded.)/
The/ Poetical Works/ of/ Lord Byron./ With Life./
Eight engravings on Steel./ Edinburgh :/ Gall and
Inglis, 6 George Street ;/ London : Houlston and
Wright./ [1857.]   [8º

Collation—
     Pp. xix. + 524.
     Note.—The Ed. omits Canto IV. of *Childe Harold*, all the
dramas except *Manfred*, and gives "extracts" from *Don Juan*,
" a poem unfit to be printed in this collection entire." Another
edition, including the Fourth Canto of *Childe Harold's*, *etc.*,
Mazeppa, and the *Ode on Venice*, enclosed in coloured vignette
borders, was issued in 1881.

LXXII.

The Poetical Works, etc. Complete in One Vol. Illustrated. New York. Leavitt and Allen. 1857.   [4º
                                             [Kölbing.]

Collation—
     Pp. xxxiii. + 935.

LXXIII.

The/ Poetical Works/ of/ Lord Byron./ Complete./ New
Edition, The Text Carefully Revised./ With Portrait./
London : John Murray, Albemarle Street./ 1857./ [8º

Collation—
     Pp. viii. + 685. The Front., " Statue of Byron by Thor-
waldsen," is engr. by W. Holl.
     Note.—The arrangement of the poems differs from the edition of
1837. [*Hours of Idleness ;* Occasional Pieces ; *Hebrew Melodies ;*
Domestic Pieces ; Later " Occasional Pieces ;" The Satires ;
Childe Harold ; The Tales ; The Dramas ; *Beppo ; Don Juan ;*
Notes ; Index.] This edition is known as the " Pearl " Edition.
There was a reissue in 1867, with a new Title-page and without
the line-border.

LXXIV.

The Poetical Works, etc. Collected and arranged with
notes by Sir Walter Scott, Lord Jeffrey, Professor Wilson,
Thomas Moore, etc. New and Complete Edition. With
Portrait and Illustrated Engravings. London : John
Murray, etc. 1859.   [8º

Collation—
Pp. x. + 827.
Note.—This edition was reissued in 1866, 1873, 1876, and 1883.

LXXV.

The Poetical Works, etc. With copious illustrative notes, and a memoir of his life. Complete in One Vol. Illust. with elegant steel engravings. Philadelphia : James B. Smith & Co., No. 27, South Seventh Street. 1859. [8.°
[Kölbing.]

Collation—
Pp. 715.

LXXVI.

The Poetical Works, etc. Collected and arranged with notes by Sir Walter Scott, Lord Jeffrey, etc. New and Complete Edition. With Portrait. London : 1860. Leipzig. B. Tauchnitz.   [8.°
Collation—
Pp. x. + 828.
Note.—An edition of *The Works, etc.,* forming part of the "Collection of British Authors" (16.°), was issued by B. Tauchnitz, at Leipzig, 1865–1870. [Kayser, 1865, 1871.]

LXXVII.

The Poetical Works, etc. In Three Vols. F. A. Brockhaus. Leipzig. 1860.   [8.°
Note.—Part of the "Library of British Poets." A Second Edition was issued in 1867. [Kayser, 1866.]

LXXVIII.

The/ Poetical Works/ of/ Lord Byron./ With Illustrations/ By Keeley Halswelle./ Edinburgh : William P. Nimmo, 2 St. David Street./ London : Simpkin, Marshall & Co./ 1861.   [8.°
Collation—
Pp. xxii + 673.
Note.—*The Life of Lord Byron,* pp. v.–xv., is by Alexander Leighton. The dramas are represented by *Manfred, Heaven and Earth,* and *Cain ;* the Satires by *English Bards,* etc., *The Waltz,* and *Vision of Judgment,* . . . *Don Juan* by numerous extracts. Red line-borders.

LXXIX.

The/ Poetical Works/ of/ Lord Byron./ In Ten Volumes./ Vol. I. [Vol. II., etc.] Boston :/ Little, Brown and Company./ New York : Phinney, Blakeman and Mason./ Cincinnati : Rickey, Mallory and Co./ 1861./ [8°

Note (1).—Vol. I. contains *Life of Lord Byron* [Excerpt from the *Encycl. Brit.*, by J. H. Lister], pp. xi.-xxxv. ; *Hours of Idleness* (71), and all the "Occasional Pieces," 1807–1824. Vol. II., The Satires ; Ode to *N. B.* ; *Heb. Melodies* ; "Domestic Pieces ;" *Ode on Venice* ; *Monody, etc.* ; *Lament of Tasso*, etc. Vol. III., *Beppo* ; *Proph. of Dante* ; *Francesca, etc.* ; the Poems published in *The Liberal* ; *The Age of Bronze*. Vol. IV., *Childe Harold's*, *etc*. Vol. V., "The Tales." Vols. VI., VII., VIII., The Dramas. Vols. IX., X., *Don Juan*. The Front. of Vol. I. is "Byron," by T. Phillips, R.A.

Note (2).—This edition professes to be an amended reprint of the London Edition of 1856 in Six Volumes. Doubtful and "attributed" poems are not included.

LXXX.

The Poetical Works, etc. With Life of the Author, and Copious Notes. Beautifully illustrated. Family Edition. Halifax : Milner and Sowerby. 1863. [8°

Collation—
  Pp. xv. + 702.
  Note.—Two other editions of the same work were issued in 1865 by the firm, imprinted *London : Milner and Sowerby, Paternoster Row*. [Kölbing.]

LXXXI.

The Poetical Works/ of Lord Byron./ With Illustrations./ [Life by A. Leighton.] New Edition Carefully Revised./ Edinburgh :/ William P. Nimmo./ [1868.] [8°

Collation—
  Pp. 437.
  Note.—This edition includes three dramas, *Manfred, Cain, Heaven and Earth ; Childe Harold*, and *Don Juan*, but omits *Hints from Horace, The Age of Bronze, The Island, The Blues*, etc., and occasional Pieces first included in the ed. of 1831.

LXXXII.

The Poetical Works/ of Lord Byron./ Reprinted from the Original Editions./ With explanatory notes, etc./ London :/ Frederick Warne and Company,/ Bedford

VOL. VII. S

Street, Covent Garden./   New York : Scribner, Welford
and Co./   [1868.]   [16?

Collation—
 Pp. vii. + 638.
 Note.—Part of the " Chandos Classics."
 Kölbing notes another edition, pp. viii. + 668.
 A Third Edition : London and New York.
 A Fourth Edition : Portrait and Original Illustrations. Part of
" The Lansdowne Poets."

LXXXIII.

The/ Poetical Works/ of/ Lord Byron :/ With/ Life and
 Portrait,/ and/ Sixteen Illustrations./ By F. Gilbert./
 London :/ John Dicks, 313, Strand./ [1869.]   [8?

Collation—
 Pp. xv. + 457.   Double columns.

LXXXIV.

The Poetical Works, etc. New Edition. In Eight Volumes.
 London : John Murray, Albemarle Street.   1870.   [8?
                                                [Kölbing.]

LXXXV.

The/ Poetical Works/ of/ Lord Byron./   Edited, with a
 Critical Memoir,/ By/ William Michael Rossetti./ Illus-
 trated by/ Ford Madox Brown./   London :/ E. Moxon,
 Son, & Co., Dover Street./   1870./   [8?

Collation—
 Pp. xx. + 604.
 Note.—Hints from Horace, Translation of *Francesca of Rimini*,
 and Occasional Pieces, first included in the edition of 1831, are
 omitted.   This edition was reissued in 1872.

LXXXVI.

The Complete/ Poetical Works/ of/ Lord Byron/ with an
 Introductory Memoir/ by/ William B. Scott/ With Illus-
 trations/   London/ George Routledge and Sons/ The
 Broadway, Ludgate/   New York : 416, Broome Street/
 [1874]   [8?

Collation—
 Pp. 750.
 Note.—Double columns bordered with red lines.

LXXXVII.

The Poetical Works/ of/ Lord Byron/ Illustrated Edition/ London/ Virtue and Co., City Road and Ivy Lane/ [1874] [8?

Collation—
Pp. cliv. + 614.
The Front., "Byron," is engr. by W. J. Edwards from the portrait by T. Phillips, R.A. The Title-vignette is "The Corsairs' Isle," and there are fifty other line engravings.
Note.—This edition includes six "*Attributed Poems*," but omits *Hints from Horace,* Transl. of *Francesca of Rimini,* and the Occasional Pieces first collected in the editions of 1831 and 1832–1833. This edition was reissued in 1879.

LXXXVIII.

Poetical Works, etc., embracing his suppressed poems, and a sketch of his life. New Edition. . . . (Portrait . . . 8 plates.) Boston : Lee & Shepard. 1874. [8?
[*Cat. of Lib. of Congress,* 1880.]

LXXXIX.

The/ Poetical Works/ of/ Lord Byron./ London :/ Ward, Lock, and Co., Warwick House,/ Dorset Buildings, Salisbury Square, E.C./ [1878.] [8?
Collation—
Pp. vii. + 604. [Double column.]

XC.

The Poetical Works, etc., complete in one Vol. Collected and arranged, with illustrative notes by Thomas Moore, etc., . . . Boston : Lee and Shepard, 1878. [8?
Collation—
Pp. 829.
Note.—A reproduction of Murray's Edition of 1855. [Kölbing.]

XCI.

The/ Poetical Works/ of/ Lord Byron./ Edited, With a Critical Memoir,/ By/ William Michael Rossetti./ Illustrated by/ Thomas Seccombe./ London :/ Ward, Lock, & Co., Warwick House,/ Dorset Buildings, Salisbury Square, E.C./ [1880.] [8?
Collation—
Pp. xx. + 604.

Note.—Part of "Moxon's Popular Poets." This edition does not contain *Hints from Horace, Francesca of Rimini,* or the Occasional Pieces first collected in the editions of 1831, 1832–1833. The Prefatory Note is by W. M. Rossetti. Double columns bordered with red lines. The same edition, bordered with different red lines and printed on large paper, was issued in 1881.

XCII.

The Poetical Works/ of/ Lord Byron./ Reprinted from the Original Editions,/ With Life, Explanatory Notes, etc./ London :/ Frederick Warne and Co.,/ Bedford Street, Strand./ [1881.]   [8?

Collation—
Pp. xvi. + 720.
Note.—"This edition (known as 'The Albion Edition') contains the whole of Byron's Poems and Dramas, with his Original Notes."—*Publisher's Preface.* The Albion Edition was reissued by Warne and Co. in 1897.

XCIII.

The Complete/ Poetical Works/ of/ Lord Byron/ With an Introductory Memoir/ By/ William B. Scott/ London/ George Routledge and Sons/ Broadway, Ludgate Hill/ New York : 9, Lafayette Place/ 1883/   [8?

Collation—
Pp. 750.
The Front. is the portrait of Lord Byron by G. Sanders; the vignette on Title-page is "Newstead Abbey."
Note.—This edition (double column), which includes all poems published in the one-volume edition of 1837 (No. li.), was reissued in three volumes, 1883, 1886, 1887. Each volume concludes with an Index of First Lines.

XCIV.

The/ Poetical Works/ of/ Lord Byron./ With Life./ Engravings on Steel./ Gall & Inglis./ Edinburgh :/ Bernard Terrace./ London :/ 25 Paternoster Sq[r] / [1881.] [8?

Collation—
Pp. xviii. + 576.
Note.—This edition, which repeats the order and contents of that issued by Gall and Inglis in 1857 (No. lxxi.), adds the Fourth Canto of *Childe Harold's, etc., Mazeppa,* and the *Ode on Venice.* Coloured vignette-borders.

XCV.

The/ Poetical Works/ of/ Lord Byron./   With Original and
Additional Notes./ In Twelve Volumes./ Vol. I./ [Vol. II.,
etc.] Hours of Idleness./ English Bards and Scotch
Reviewers./ London :/ Suttaby and Co., Amen Corner./
New York :/ Scribner and Welford./ 1885./   [8º

Note.—This edition includes all poems contained in the edition
of 1837, but omits the prose pieces.

XCVI.

The Poetical Works, etc. Complete in one vol. Col-
lected and arranged with illustrative notes by Thomas
Moore, etc. New York : P. F. Collier. [1886 ?]
[Folio.

Collation—
   Pp. viii. + 820. [Kölbing.]

XCVII.

The Poetical Works/ of/ Lord Byron./   Edited by/ Mathilde
Blind./ Miscellaneous Poems./   London :/ Walter Scott,
24, Warwick Lane, E.C./ and Newcastle-on-Tyne./ 1886./
[16º

Collation—
   Pp. xxviii. + 280.
   Note.—Part of the " Canterbury Poets." This volume contains
Introductory Notice by Mathilde Blind, pp. vii.–xxviii. ; "Mis-
cellaneous Poems" (including *Vision of Judgment, Manfred, Cain,*
etc.), pp. *1–280.*

XCVIII.

The Poetical Works/ etc. Edited by/ Mathilde Blind./
Childe Harold./ Don Juan./ London, etc./ 1886./
[16º

Collation—
   Pp. *1–369.*
   Note.—These volumes (Nos. xcvii., xcviii.) were issued
separately. Red line-borders.

XCIX.

The Life and Works of, etc., With Notes and Illustrations.
[" Centenary Edition."] In Two Volumes. Thomas C.
Jack, London, Edinb. and Glasgow. 1888.
[Kölbing.]

C.

The Complete/ Poetical Works/ of/ Lord Byron/ With an Introductory Memoir/ By/ William B. Scott/ London/ George Routledge and Sons, Limited/ Broadway, Ludgate Hill/ Glasgow, Manchester, and New York./ 1890/ [8°

Collation—
Pp. 750. Double columns.
Note.—Part of " Routledge's Popular Library." The Front. is an illust. of *Childe Harold*, Canto III. stanza xxi., and the Title-vignette, "Newstead Abbey."

CI.

The Poetical Works, etc. New York : John W. Lovell, Company, 50, Worth Street, Corner Mission Place. 1890? [8°

Collation—
Pp. ii. + 544. [Kölbing.]

CII.

The/ Poetical Works/ of/ Lord Byron./ With Original and Additional Notes./ In Twelve Volumes./ Vol. I. [Vol. II., etc.] Hours of Idleness./ English Bards and Scotch Reviewers./ Griffith Farran Okeden & Welsh/ Newbery House, Charing Cross Road/ London, and Sydney./ [1891.] [8°

Note.—This edition (The " Bijou Byron") is a reissue of *The Poetical Works*, etc., published by Suttaby and Co. (No. xcv.) in 1885.

CIII.

The Poetical Works, etc., Complete Edition. In Three Vols. William W. Gibbings. London. 1892.

Note.—A reprint of the Leipzig edition of 1880, published by F. A. Brockhaus.

CIV.

Works. " Bijou Ed." 12 Vols. Philadelphia, J. B. Lippincott Co. 1892. [Pocket size.
[*Amer. Cat.*, 1892.]

CV.

Dramatic and Poetical Works. "Newstead Ed." Philadelphia, D. McKay. 1895. [8°
[*Amer. Cat.*, 1895.]

Collation—
Pp. 720.

CVI.

Oxford Miniature Byron/ The/ Poetical Works/ of/ Lord
Byron/ In Four Volumes—Vol. I./ London/ Henry
Frowde/ Oxford University Press Warehouse/ Amen
Corner, E.C./ New York: 91 and 93, Fifth Avenue/
1896/ [16°
Note.—"We are indebted to the courtesy of Mr. John Murray,
publisher of the edition of 1867, for permission to use any copy-
right matter contained in that issue."—*Publisher's Advt.*

CVII.

The Poetical/ Works of/ Lord/ Byron/ London/ Bliss/
Sands & Co/ XII. Burl-/ Eigh St./ Strand/ W.C./
[1897] [4°
Collation—
Pp. xvi + 727.
Note.—This edition forms part of " The Apollo Poets." The
Front., "Lord Byron," is a *Lamerciergravure*, printed in Paris,
of the portrait by T. Phillips, R.A.

CVIII.

Poetical Works, etc. New Edition, carefully revised. With
illustrations. W. P. Nimmo. 1897. [8°
[*English Catalogue*, 1898.]
Note.—Part of the "Edinburgh Library of Standard Authors."

CIX.

Poetical Works. (Ed. by T. Moore.) In four volumes.
Philadelphia, J. B. Lippincott Co. 1897. [12°
[*Amer. Cat.*, 1898.]

CX.

The Poetical Works, etc. With Notes, and a memoir of
the author. Pictorial Edition. London : George Henny
& Co., Bartholomew Close. [*n.d.*]
[Kölbing.]

Collation—
Pp. cliv. + 344.

CXI.

The Poetical Works, etc. With explanatory notes and a life of the author, by Thomas Moore. Illustrated with numerous fine steel engravings, embracing the principal female characters, landscape and historical subjects. First quarto edition complete in [? one] volume. New York: Johnson, Fry and Company, 27 Beekman Street. *n.d.* [4°

[Kölbing.]

Collation—
Pp. ii. + 740 + xxviii.

CXII.

The Poetical Works, etc. Complete in one volume. Collected and arranged with illustrative notes by Thomas Moore, etc. New York: P. F. Collier. [1889?] [Fol.

[Kölbing.]

Collation—
Pp. viii. + 820.

CXIII.

The Poetical Works, etc. New York: Hurst & Co., Publishers, 122 Nassau Street. [*n.d.*]

[Kölbing.]

Collation—
Pp. vi. + 608.

TRANSLATIONS OF COLLECTED EDITIONS.

French.

I.

Œuvres/ Complètes/ de Lord Byron,/ Traduites de l'Anglais/ Par MM. A.—P. et E.—D. S. ; [Amédée Pichot et Eusèbe de Salle]/ Troisième édition,/ Entièrement revue et corrigée./ Tome premier./ Paris,/ Ladvocat, Libraire, Palais-Royal,/ Galerie de Bois, N° 195./ 1821./ [12°

Note.—Vols. I.–VIII. were issued in 1821 ; Vols. IX. and X. (in two parts) in 1822. Vol. I. (pp. i.–xlv.) is preceded by *Notice sur Lord Byron, et ses Écrits,* par Amédée Pichot. Vols. XI.–XV. (Œuvres, etc./ Traduites de l'Anglais/ Par A. P.

. . . T./) with Gen. half-title, Œuvres/ de/ Lord Byron./ Inédites,/ were issued in 1824.

In the Museum copy of this edition an unnumbered volume entitled Essai/ Sur le Génie et le Caractère/ de Lord Byron,/ Par A. P. . . . T.,/ Précédé/ d'une Notice Préliminaire/ Par M. Charles Nodier./ Extracts de la Quatrième Édition des Œuvres/ Complètes de Lord Byron,/ (six volumes in-8 ornés de vignettes.) Paris./ Ladvocat, etc./ 1824,/ which includes an essay *Sur la Mort de Byron*, and a transl. of *Heaven and Earth*, pp. 195–252, is bound up with Vol. XV.

Note (1).—"Œuvres de lord Byron. Quatrième édition, entièrement revue et corrigée par A. P. . . . T. ; précédée d'une notice sur lord Byron, par M. Charles Nodier ; ornée de vignettes . . . *A Paris, chez Ladvocat, libraire, Palais-Royal, galerie de bois*, Nᵒ 195 (Impr. Firmin Didot), MDCCCXXII.-MDCCCXXV. (1822-1825), 8 vols. in-8, couv. impr. *Tome I*: [Tome II., etc. (in 8 vols.)], 2 ff. (faux-titre et titre) ; xvi. pp. (notice préliminaire de Ch. Nodier) ; clii. pp. (Essai sur lord Byron) ; 4 pp. (Table générale des matières pour les tomes I. à VI.) ; 249 pp. ; et 1 f. n. ch. (annonce d'ouvrages).

"Frontispiece gravé par Godefroy ; portrait de lord Byron, gravé par Dequevauvilliers ; et 5 figures gravées d'après Richard Westall, par Godefroy, Mougeot, Dequevauvilliers, etc.

"*Tome II.*, etc., etc.

"Les tomes II., III., IV., V., portent la date de 1822 ; les tomes I. et VI., celle de 1823 ; le tome VII., celle de 1824 ; et le tome VIII., la date de 1825." [*Manuel de l'Amateur de Livres du XIXᵉ siècle*. Par Georges Vicaire. Paris, 1894. Fascic. 3 (1ʳᵉ Partie), pp. 989, 990).]

Note (2).—"La prem. édit. de cette trad. parut de 1819 à 1820, et formait 10 vol. in-12 ; la seconde édit. fut. publ. de 1820 à 1822, et formait 5 vol. in-8." [Quérard, *La France Littéraire*, 1827, i. 581.]

"Œuvres complètes, VIᵉ édit. . . . Paris, Ladvocat, Delangle, 1829 et ann. suiv., 20 vol. gr. in-18, fig.—Autre édit. Paris, Furne, 1830-35, 6 vol. in-8, et avec 6 vignettes ajoutées.

XIᵉ édit., avec une notice historique sur lord Byron, des notes et des pièces inédites. Paris, Furne, Ch. Gosselin, 1842, grand in-8 à deux colonnes, avec 15 vignettes." [Quérard, *La Littérature Française Contemporaine*. 1827-1844. 1846, ii. 486.]

II.

Œuvres complètes/ de/ Lord Byron,/ avec notes et commentaires,/ Comprenant/ Ses Mémoires publiés par Thomas Moore,/ et ornées d'un beau portrait de l'auteur./ Traduction nouvelle/ Par M. Paulin Paris,/ de la Bibliothèque du roi./ Tome premier./ Paris./ Dondey-Dupré Père et Fils, impr.—libr., éditeurs,/ Rue Saint-Louis, Nᵒ 46,/ et rue Richelieu, Nᵒ 47 *bis*./ 1830./ [8ᵒ

Note (1).—The Front. of Vol. I., " Noel Byron," is engr. by
Adèle Ethiou, after the portrait by T. Phillips, R.A. The
engraver has added a wreath of bay leaves.
Vols. I.–X. were issued in 1830; Vols. XI., XII., XIII., in
1831.
Note (2).—" Il y a une seconde édition, Paris, etc., Dondey-
Dupré, 1836, in-8, 13 vol." [Quérard, 1846, ii. 486.]

III.

Œuvres complètes/ de/ Lord Byron,/ Traduction nouvelle,/
d'après la dernière édition de Londres,/ Par/ Benjamin
Laroche,/ Traducteur des Œuvres de J. Bentham, Cooper,
etc. ;/ avec les notes et commentaires de Sir Walter
Scott, etc. [Three Lines]. Précédées de/ l'histoire de
la vie et des ouvrages de Lord Byron,/ Par John
Galt./ Tome premier./ Paris./ Charpentier, Libraire-
éditeur,/ Rue de Seine, N° 31./ 1836./ [8°

Note.—The Front. of Vol. I. is " Byron," after the portrait by
T. Phillips, R.A. Vol. I. was issued in 1836, Vols. II.–IV. in
1837. The translator (*Post-Scriptum*, Vol. IV. p. [827]) claims
to have accomplished his work from beginning to end without
collaboration or assistance : " cette traduction a été commencée,
poursuivie et achevée par MOI SEUL."

" IIe édit. . . . précédée de l'histoire de la vie . . . de lord
Byron par *H. Romand*, Paris . . . 1837, grand in 8, avec une
gravure.
" IIIe édit., précédée d'une Notice sur la vie de lord Byron,
par M. Émile Souvestre, Paris, 1838, in-8, avec portrait et
fac-simile.
" IVe édit. Paris, 1840, 1841. 4 vol. in 12.
" V^e édit. ornée d'un *fac-simile*, et précédée d'une Notice sur
lord Byron . . . par M. Villemain. Paris, 1843. Grand in-8."
[Quérard, 1846, ii. 487.]
" La Ire édition de cette traduction a été publiée en 1836,
4 vol. . . . Depuis elle a été réimprimée environ 10 fois,
d'abord par M. Charpentier et puis par M. Lecou, et en dernier
lieu par MM. Hachette et Cie." [Lorenz. *Cat. Gén.* 1867, i. 407.]

IV.

Œuvres, *traduites en vers français* par Orby Hunter, 2 vols.
(Paris, Chapelle. 1841–1842.) [8°
[Lorenz, *Cat. Gén.*, 1867, i. 407.]

V.

Œuvres/ de/ Lord Byron/ Traduites en vers français/ Par/
Orby Hunter & Pascal Ramé/ Tome. I./ Manfred,—

Beppo,—Le Corsair,—Lara/ et Poésies diverses/   Paris/ Daussin,/ Libraire/ Place et rue Favart,/ 8 bis/   1845/
[8°

Vols. I.–III. were issued in 1845.
Note.—Vol. II. contains *Marino Faliero* ; *La Fiancée*, etc. ; *Parisina* ; "Inscription sur le Monument d'un chien," etc. ; *A Venise* ; "Ode sur l'étoile," etc. ; "Adieu !—Elégié." Vol. III. contains *Don Juan*, Chants I.–VI. ; *Notes.*

VI.

Œuvres complètes de lord Byron.   Traduction nouvelle de Louis Barré, illustrée par Ch. Mettais, E. Bocourt, Ed. Frère, Edition Bry aîné Paris, *en vente à la librairie centrale des publications à* 20 *centimes*, 5, *rue du Pont-de-Lodi*, 5 (Typ. Gaittet et Cie.), 1856, gr. in 4.

Collation—
2 ff. (faux-titre et titre) ; et 400 pp.
Texte imprimé sur deux colonnes.
[*Manuel de l'Amateur*, etc., 1894.   Fasc. 3 (I^e Partie), p. 990.]

VII.

Œuvres/ de/ Lord Byron/ Traduction nouvelle/ Précédée d'un/ Essai sur Lord Byron/   Par/ Daniel Le Sueur/ Heures d'oisiveté—Childe Harold/ Paris/ Alphonse Le-merre, éditeur/ 23-31, passage Choiseul, 23-31./   1891./
[12°

Note.—The Front., " Lord Byron," is engr. by Frédéric Massé after the portrait by G. Sanders.   The Title-vignette bears a motto, *Fac et Spera*, and the initials A. L.   A second volume (unnumbered), containing *Le Giaour ; La Fiancée*, etc. ; *Le Corsair ; Lara*, etc., was issued in 1892.   This translation, advertised as *Œuvres Complètes*, and described by Lorenz as " Traduction couronnée par l'Académie française," has not been continued.

German.

I.

Lord Byron's Poesien.   In 31 volumes.   Brothers Schumann, Zwickau.   1821–1828.   [16°

Note.—Among the several translators were Julius Körner, Wilhelm Reinhold, Heinrich Doering, August Schumann, Christian Karl Meissner, etc.   Vols. I.–VI. appeared in 1821 ; Vols. VII.–XII. in 1822 ; Vols. XIII., XIV. in 1824 ; Vols.

XV.-XX. in 1825 ; Vol. XXI. in 1826 ; Vols. XXII.-XXVIII.
in 1827 ; and Vols. XXIX.-XXXI. in 1828.
  [*Lord Byron in Deutschland,* von Dr. Cäsar Flaischlen, *Centralblatt für Bibliothekswesen,* 1890, vii. 462-464.]

II.

Lord Byron's/ sämmtliche Werke./   Herausgegeben/ von/
Dr. Adrian,/ ordentlichem öffentlichem Professor der
neueren Litteratur an der/ Universität zu Giessen./   Erster
Theil./   Lord Byron's Leben./   Mit dem Bildniss, einem
Facsimile der Handschrift und der/ Abbildung des Stamm-
sitzes Lord Byron's./   Frankfurt am Main./   Gedruckt
und verlegt von Johann David Sauerländer./   1830./
                                                    [12°

  Note.—Vols. X. and XII. were issued in 1831. The several
translators were G. H. Bärmann, O. L. B. Wolff, K. L.
Kannegiesser, A. Hungari, P. von Haugwitz, Ph. A. G. von
Meyer (the author of *Byron's Leben,* i. 3–326), and The Editor.
This edition was reissued in twelve vols. (12°) in 1837. [Kayser,
1841.]

III.

Dichtungen von Lord Byron.   Deutsch v. Gustav Pfizer.
4 Sammlungen.   Stuttgart, Liesching.   1836–1839. [8°

  Note.—There was a reissue of this work in 1851.
              [*Centralblatt, etc.,* 1890, vii. 468, 469.]

IV.

Lord Byron's sämmtliche Werke.   Deutsch v. Adolf Böttger
[1 vol., with life and portrait.]   Leipzig, Otto Wigand.
1839–40.   [8°
                            [Kayser, 1841.].

  Note.—This edition was reissued at Leipzig by Otto Wigand
in 1 vol. 8° in 1841, 1844, 1845 ; in 12 vols. 16° in 1841, 1842,
and 1847 ; in diamond edition, in 12 vols. 16°, in 1850, 1852,
1856, 1860, 1861 ; and in 8 vols. 8° in 1854, 1863, 1864.   For
the latest edition, *vide post,* No. xiii. [Kayser, 1848, 1853,
1860, 1865. See, too, *Centralblatt, etc.,* 1890, vii. 457.]

V.

Lord Byron's/ sämmtliche Werke./   Nach den/ Anforde-
rungen unserer Zeit/ neu übersetzt von/ Mehreren./
Zweite unveränderte Ausgabe./ Erster Band./ Pforzheim./
Verlag von Dennig Finck & Co./   [Ten Vols.]   1842./
                                                    [16°

Note (1).—The several translators were E. Ortlepp, Dr. Kotten-kamp, H. Kurtz, Professor Duttenhofer, Bardili, Bernd von Guseck.

Note (2).—This edition was first issued in small octavo by Hoff-mann at Stutgard, in 1839, and reissued (16º) by Scheible, Rieger, and Sattler, 1845, 1846 ; and in 12 vols. (16º) by Rieger at Stutgard, in 1856. [*Centralblatt, etc.*, 1890, vii. 466.]

VI.

Lord Byron's sämmtliche Werke. [8 Bde.] Deutsch von A. Neidhardt. Berlin, Hofmann. 1865.   [8º
[Kayser, 1871.]

VII.

Dichtungen/ von/ Lord Byron./   Deutsch/ von/ Wilhelm Schäffer./   Die Belagerung von Korinth./   Der Gefangene von Chillon.   Die Insel./   Hildburghausen./   Verlag des Bibliographischen Instituts.   1865./   [8º

Note.—This collected edition of translations forms part of the *Bibliothek ausländischer Klassiker, etc.*

Don Juan, Cantos I.-VI., transl. by W. Schäffer, was issued in two vols. in 1867 ; *Childe Harold's, etc.*, transl. by A. H. Janert, in 1868 ; *Corsair, Mazeppa, Beppo*, by W. Schäffer, in 1870 ; *Manfred, Cain, Heaven and Earth, Sardanapalus*, by W. Grüz-macher, in 1872 ; Lyrical Pieces, by Heinrich Stadelmann, in 1872 ; *The Giaour, Bride of Abydos, Lara, Parisina*, by Adolf Strodtmann, in 1872.

VIII.

Lord Byron's ausgewählte Werke, uebersetzt von Mehreren [4 bde.], herausg. von A. Strodtmann. Leipzig, Bibl. Inst. 1865-1872.   [8º
[*Centralblatt, etc.*, 1890, vii. 466.]

IX.

Lord Byron's/ sämmtliche Werke/ in drei Bänden./   Frei überzetzt/ von/ Adolf Seubert./   Erster Band./   Leipzig./ Druck und Verlag von Philipp Reclam jun./   [1874.]
[8º

X.

Lord Byron's Werke.   Deutsch v. Dr Adalbert Schroeter. [6 Bde.] Uebersetzt, mit Einleitung und Anmerkungen versehen.   Stuttgart.   In ; Coll. Spemann.   1885-1890.
[8º

[*Centralblatt, etc.*, 1890, vii. 470.]

XI.

Lord Byron's poetische Werke. In älteren Uebertragungen ;
eingeleitet durch e. Studie v. Henry T. Tuckermann.
Stuttgart. Cotta'sche Bibl. der Weltlitteratur, 1886. [In
eight vols.]   [8°

[Kayser, 1887.]

XII.

Lord Byron's Werke./ Uebersetz/ von/ Otto Gildemeister./
In sechs Bänden./ Erster Band./ Vierte Auflage./
Berlin./ Druck und Verlag von Georg Reimer./ 1888./
[8°

Note.—A First Edition appeared in 1864, a second in 1866,
and a third in 1877. [Kayser, 1865, 1871, 1883.]

XIII.

Byron's/ sämmtliche Werke./ Von/ Adolf Böttger./ Achte
Auflage./ Erster Band./ Leipzig,/ Verlag von Otto
Wigand./ 1901./ [8 Bde.]   [8°

Modern Greek.

Τα Απαντα/ του/ Βυρωνος/ Τομος Πρωτος/ Εν Αθηναις/ Εκ του τυπο-
γραφειου των καταστηματων/ Ανεστη κωνστατινιδου/ 1895/
[Three Vols.]   [8°

Note.—This translation includes *Mazeppa, Parisina, Childe
Harold, The Siege of Corinth, The Bride of Abydos, The Corsair,
The Curse of Minerva, Don Juan, The Giaour.*
The paper wrapper and the title-page are embellished with a
lithograph of the portrait by T. Phillips, R.A.

Italian.

I.

Opere complete/ di/ Lord Byron/ voltate dall' originale
inglese in prosa italiana/ Da/ Carlo Rusconi/ Con note
ed illustrazioni del volgarizzatore/ nonchè dei signori/
Moore (and 33 others = 6 lines)/ a cui si aggiungono/
I dialoghi di Lord Byron compilati da M. Medwin/ Un
saggio sul di lui genio—una prefazione—E un' appendice/
parte desunti da altri scritti, parte tradotti,/ parte originali./ Padova/ coi tipi della Minerva/ 1842/   [8°

Note.—This edition, which forms one volume, pp. xxxix. +

1561, was issued in two parts. A dedication ("A Sua Eccellenza/ Lord Holland/ Ministro Plenipotenziario D'Inghilterra/ alla Corte di Toscana"/) is prefixed to Part I., pp. [ix.]–[xi.].

II.

Opere/ di/ Giorgio Lord Byron/ Precedute/ da alcune avvertenze critiche/ Sulle stesse/ e da un discorso/ di/ Cesare Cantù/ prima edizione napolitana adorna di figure incise/ Napoli/ Francesco Rossi-Romano editore/ Trinità Maggiore, 6/ 1853/   [8°

Note.—The Front. is a lithograph of "Lord Byron nell' età di 17 anni," after the portrait by G. Sanders.

The several translators were Giuseppe Gazzino, Giuseppe Nicolini, Pietro Isola, Pellegrino Rossi, Andrea Maffei, Marcello Mazzoni, and P. G. B. Cereseto.

The translation includes *Childe Harold*, eight tales, and four dramas.

III.

Opere di Lord Byron tradotte ed annotate da Gabr. De Stefano. Napoli, 1857.   [8°

[Pagliaini, 1901.]

Collation—
    Pp. 625.

IV.

Opere/ di/ Lord Giorgio Byron/ Precedute/ da un saggio intorno al genio e al carattere/ Del medesimo/ Volume unico/ Napoli/ Presso Pasquale Perrone libraio-/Editore/ via Costantinopoli, 107./ 1886/   [8°

Note.—The translations include *Childe Harold*, *Don Juan*, eight tales, and seven dramas. A reissue with a portrait, and, apparently, wanting pp. 669–[711] of the appendix, appeared in 1891 (Ferdinando Bideri, editore/ Via Costantinopoli, 89).

Polish.

I.

Poezye/ Lorda Byrona/ w tłumaczeniu Polskiém. Wydane staraniem/ Bolesława Maurycego Wolffa./ Tom. i./ Wędrówki Czajlda-Harolda./ Petersburg./ Nakładem i Drukiem B. M. Wolffa./ 1857./   [12°

Note.—No more published.

II.

Poezye Lorda Byrona w przekładzie polskich poetów. Zbio-
rowe wydanie, pod red. Piotra Chmielowskiego. ("Biblioteka Najcelnijszych Utworów.")   [8°
Warszawa, 1885, *etc.*

Russian.

I.

Сочиненія Лорда Байрона въ переводахъ русскихъ
Поэтовъ, изданныхъ подъ редакціею Н. В. Гербеля.
5 том. *С.-Петербургъ*, 1864–66.   [16°.
Second edition of Gerbel. *С.-Петербургъ*, 1874–77.
In 4 vols.
Third edition. *С.-Петербургъ*, 1883–84. In 3 vols.

II.

Байронъ. "Европейскіе Классики въ русскомъ пере-
водѣ" П. Вейнберга. *С.-Петербургъ*, 1876.

Note.—The translations include *Hebrew Melodies, Sardanapalus,
Manfred, Childe Harold's, etc.,* and *Don Juan.*

Spanish.

Biblioteca Universal./ Coleccion/ de los/ Mejores autores/
Antiguos y modernos,/ Nationales y extranjeros./ Tomo
LXIII./ Lord Byron/ Madrid./ Direccion y administra-
cion/ calle de Leganitos, 18, 2?/ 1880./   [16?

This translation includes *The Corsair, Lara, Darkness,* and
Hebrew Melodies (6), *The Lament of Tasso.* The *Prologo* is by
Rafael Ginard de La Rosa.

Swedish.

Byron's Poetiska Berättelser. Öfversättning af Talis Qualis
[C. W. A. Strandberg]. 1. Mazeppa.—2. Belägringen af
Korinth.—3. Fången på Chillon.—4. Parisina—5. Beppo.
—6. Giaurn.—7. Bruden från Abydos.—8. On Eller
Christian осн Hans Ställbröder. [8 vols.] Stockholm,
J. L. Brudins Förlag. 1854–1856.   [12?

SELECTIONS.

I.

The Beauties of Byron, with a sketch of his life and a disser-
tation on his genius and writings. By Thomas Parry.
London : J. Sudbury. 1823.

[Kölbing.]

II.

The Beauties of Byron. Extracts from the works of the Right Hon. Lord Byron. Embellished with engravings on steel. London : J. Limbird. 1827.

[Kölbing.]

III.

Life/ and/ Select Poems/ of/ Lord Byron,/ Arranged, etc./ By C. Hulbert,/ Author of Literary Beauties, Poetical Bouquet, Museum of the World, etc./ London : Sold by all the Booksellers./ [1828.] [12°

Collation—
Pp. 84.

IV.

The Beauties of Lord Byron, selected by B. F. French 10th ed. [Pp. xi. + 204, 3 pl.] Philadelphia. 1828. [24°
[*Cat. of Library of Congress,* 1880.]

V.

The/ Beauties/ of/ Byron,/ Consisting of/ Selections From His Works./ By J. W. Lake./ [L. B. in Gothic letters, enclosed in bay and oak leaves.] Paris,/ Baudry, at the English, Italian,/ Spanish, German, and Portuguese Library,/ Rue du Coq Saint-Honoré, N°. 9./ Bobée and Hingray, rue de Richelieu, N°. 14./ 1829./ [16°

Collation—
Pp. viii. + 230.

VI.

Lord Byron's Select Works. Vols. I.–III. Frankfort a. M. Brönner. 1831, 1832. [12°
[Kayser, 1834.]

VII.

Childe Harold's Pilgrimage; The Giaour ; The Siege, etc. ; Parisina ; The Island ; The Prisoner, etc. ; Beppo ; Mazeppa ; The Prophecy, etc. ; The Waltz ; The Lament, etc. ; Hebrew Melodies ; Misc. in Prose. By Lord Byron. Paris. 1832. (1 vol.) [8°
[" Le Moniteur de la librairie." *Courrier de l'amateur de livres.* Paris, Barrois. 4e Annèe, 1845, p. 122. (Bibl. Nat. 9, 5610.)]

VIII.

Lord Byron's Select Poetical Works, containing the *Corsair, Lara,* the *Giaour,* the *Siege,* etc., the *Bride,* etc., *Parisina, Mazeppa,* the *Prisoner,* etc.   Paris and Lyons.   1835.
[12°

[Kayser, 1841.]

IX.

Lord Byron's Select Works.   Consisting of *Cain, a Mystery; Hours of Idleness; English Bards,* etc., with Occ. Pieces and Life of the Author.   Asher, London and Berlin.   1837.
[32°

[Kayser, 1841.]

X.

The/ Beauties/ of/ Byron :/ Consisting of/ Selections from the Popular Works of/ This most admired Writer./   By Alfred Howard, Esq./   A new Edition./   London :/ Printed for Thomas Tegg and Son, 73, Cheapside ;/ R. Griffin and Co., Glasgow./   T. T. and H. Tegg, Dublin :/ also, J. and S. A. Tegg, Sydney and Hobart Town./ 1837./   [12°
Collation—
    Pp. 192.

XI.

The/ Beauties/ of/ Byron,/ consisting of/ selections from his Works./   By Alfred Howard, Esq./   London :/ Printed by T. Davison,/ For Thomas Tegg, No. 73, Cheapside ;/ R. Griffin and Co. Glasgow ;/ and/ J. Cummings, Dublin./ [*n.d.*]   [12°
Collation—
    Pp. **212.**
    Note.—The following advertisement is printed on the R. of the Gen. Half-title : " To the few persons who have not read Lord Byron's poems, but who, after perusing these specimens, will un-doubtedly wish to read the whole of them, we beg leave to say that the only correct editions are published by Mr. Murray, of Albemarle Street, and Messrs. J. & H. L. Hunt, of Tavistock Street.   The first eight volumes are to be had from the former publisher ; the last two from the latter.   All other editions are piracies, and inflict even more injury on the sense and poetry of the noble bard than they do on the property of the proprietors."

XII.

Byron's Select Works, containing the Corsair ; Lara ;
Giaour ; the Bride, etc. ; the Siege, etc. ; the Prisoner,
etc. ; Select Poems, etc., etc. ; to which is prefixed a
biographical notice of Lord B. by J. W. Lake. Paris,
Truchy. 1843. [12?
[*Le Moniteur*, etc., 1845, p. 122. See, too, *Bibl.
de la France*, Aug. 12, 1843, vol. xxxii. p. 413.]

XIII.

A Selection from Lord Byron's Poetical Works, containing,
etc. Intended for the use of young people, and provided
with explanatory German notes by Charles Graeser.
Marienwerder, Edward Levysohn. 1846.
[Kölbing.]

XIV.

Select Poetical Works of Lord Byron. Containing, etc.
With a memoir by Henry Lytton Bulwer, Esq. London,
Adam Scott. 1848.
[Kölbing.]

XV.

Lord Byron's Select Works, with an Appendix, containing
songs and ballads for the use of schools, edited by F.
Breier. Oldenburg, Schulze. 1848. [8?
[Kayser, 1853.]

XVI.

Selections/ From The/ Writings of Lord Byron./ Poetry./
By a Clergyman./ London :/ John Murray, Albemarle
Street./ 1854./ [8?
Collation—
Pp. viii. + 175.
Note.—The Selection (two vols.—Prose, Poetry) is one of a
series called " Murray's Railway Reading." The editor was the
Rev. Whitwell Elwin, sometime editor of the *Q. R.*

XVII.

Moxon's Miniature Poets./ A/ Selection From/ The Works/
of/ Lord Byron./ Edited and Prefaced by Algernon Chas.
Swinburne./ London :/ Edward Moxon & Co., Dover
Street./ 1866./ [8?

Collation—
  Pp. xxxii. + 244.
  Note.—The Selection was reissued by Ward, Lock, and Co. in
1885.

XVIII.

Songs by/ Lord Byron/ [Crest, motto *Crede Byron.*]/
London/ Virtue & Co., Publishers/ 26 Ivy Lane, Paternoster Row/ 1872/   [16°

Collation—
  Pp. 270.
  Note.—There is an index of "Songs set to Music," pp. 268–
270.

XIX.

Selections from the Writings of Lord Byron.   New Edition.
With Portrait.   London, John Murray.   1874.
                                              [Kölbing.]

XX.

Beautés de Byron : Childe Harold, le Corsaire, Lara, le
Giaour, le Siège, etc., Don Juan.   Extraits (texte anglais)
avec préface et notes en français, par A. Biard.   Paris,
Delagrave.   1876.   [12°
                                   [Lorenz, 1886.]

XXI.

Favourite Poems./ By/ Lord Byron./ Illustrated./ Boston :/
James R. Osgood and Company./ Late Ticknor & Fields,
and Fields, Osgood & Co./ . 1877./   [16°

Collation—
  Pp. 127.

XXII.

The Beauties of Byron.   An Original Selection.   Stuttgart,
Paul Neff.
                                              [Kölbing.]

XXIII.

Poetry of Byron/ Chosen and Arranged by/ Matthew
Arnold/ London/ Macmillan and Co./ 1881/   [8°

Collation—
  Pp. xxxvi. + 276.

Note.—The title-page is illustrated by an engraving, by G. J. Stodart, of Thorwaldsen's statue of Lord Byron. The preface (pp. vii.–xxxi.) is by Matthew Arnold.

XXIV.

Routledge's World Library/ "Syllables govern the World." John Selden/ Gems from Byron/ With an Introduction/ By the/ Rev. Hugh Reginald Haweis, M.A./ London/ George Routledge and Sons/ Broadway, Ludgate Hill/ New York : 9 Lafayette Place/ 1886/ [16°

Collation—
Pp. 158.

XXV.

Selections/ From The Poetry of/ Lord Byron/ Edited with/ An Introduction and Notes/ By/ Frederic Ives Carpenter, Ph.D./ Instructor in English, the University of Chicago/ Dir in klar und trüben Tagen/ Lied und Mut war schön und gross./ II. 'Faust,' iii. l. 1426./ New York/ Henry Holt and Company/ 1900/ [8°

Collation—
Pp. lviii. + 412.

XXVI.

Poems/ of/ Lord Byron/ Selected and arranged for use in Schools/ By/ C. Linklater Thomson/ Head-Mistress of the Solihull School for Girls, [etc., three lines]./ London/ Adam and Charles Black/ 1901/ [8°

Collation—
Pp. ix. + 67.

TRANSLATIONS OF SELECTIONS.

Armenian.

Lord Byron's/ Armenian Exercises/ and Poetry./ Venice/ In the Island of S. Lazzaro./ 1886/ [8°

Collation—
Pp. 167 + Index, pp. [169]–[172].
Note.—The Title-page is dated 1886, the paper wrapper (yellow) 1870. Among the exercises are *Pieces of Armenian History, The Epistle of Paul to the Corinthians*, etc. ; and among the translations are " The Destruction of Sennacherib," " On Waterloo," " To the Duke of Dorset," etc.

French.

I.

Choix de Poésies de Byron, de W. Scott et Th. Moore;
trad. libre de l'angl. Genève et Paris, Paschoud. 1820.
[Two Vols.]   [8°
                    [Quérard, 1827.]

II.

Les Beautés de lord Byron, galerie de quinze tableaux tirés
de ses œuvres, accompagnée d'un texte traduit par
Amédée Pichot. Paris, Aubert, Giraldon. 1838. [4°
                    [Quérard, 1846.]

III.

Écrin poétique/ de/ littérature anglaise./   Traduction en
vers français,/ Avec notes historiques,/ De poèmes,
épisodes et fragments choisis/ de Lord Byron,/ Thomas
Moore, Gray, Graham, etc./ Ornée du portrait de lord
Byron/ et de jolies vignettes de Thompson./ Par D.
Bonnefin./ Chevalier de la légion d'honneur./ A Paris,/
Chez L. Hachette,/ Libraire de l'Université Royale de
France,/ rue Pierre-Sarrazin, no. 12./ 1841./   [8°
Collation—
   Pp. ix. + 473.

IV.

Chefs-d'œuvre de lord Byron. (Le Pèlerinage, etc., Lara, la
Fiancée, etc., Parisina, Mazeppa, le Siége, etc., le Prisonnier, etc.) La traduction française en regard par M. le
comte d'Hautefeuille ; précédés d'un essai sur la vie et les
œuvres de lord Byron et de ses contemporains, renfer-
mant l'histoire de la poésie anglaise au xixe siècle, par D.
O'Sullivan. 1847. *Place de la Madelaine,* 24.   [8°
                    [Lorenz, 1866.]

V.

Rough Hewing/ of/ Lord Byron/ In French,/ With the
English Text./ By Francis D'Autrey./ . . . Obscurus fio./
Horace, Ars Poetica./   London:/ J. W. Kolckmann,/
Foreign Library,/ 1, Princes Street, Cavendish Square, W./
1869./   [8°
Collation—
   Pp. 233.

VI.

Chefs-d'œuvre de lord Byron. Traduits en vers français par
A. Regnault. (Two Vols.) 1874. [8º
[Lorenz, 1876.]

German.

I.

Lord Byron's ausgewählte Dichtungen. Aus d. Engl. übertragen. Leipzig, Wienbrack. 1838. [8º
[Kayser, 1841.]

II.

Byron-Anthologie./ Auserwähltes/ aus/ Lord Byron's Dichtungen,/ übertragen/ von/ Eduard Hobein./ Schwerin./
Stiller'sche Hotbuchhandlung./ (G. Bolhoevener.) 1866.
[8º

Collation—
    Pp. 187.

III.

Auswahl aus Byron: Childe Harold (III. and IV.), *Prisoner,
etc., Mazeppa.* Hrsg. v. J. Hengesbach. 1892. [12º
[Kayser, 1895.]

Collation—
    Pp. viii. + 116.
    Note.—Part of *Textausgaben französischer u. englischer Schrift-
steller f. den Schulgebrauch,* hrsg. v. Osk. Schmager.

Italian.

I.

Poemi/ di/ Lord G. Byron/ Tradotti/ dall' originale
inglese/ da/ Pietro Isola/ Socio corrispondente della R.
Accademia delle scienze ed arti/ di Alessandria/ Torino/
Presso Giuseppe Pomba/ 1827/ [8º
Collation—
    Pp. 204.

II.

Opere scelte, tradotte da M. Mazzoni. Milano. 1852.
[8º
[Pagliaini, 1901.]

III.

A' Mici Amici./ [1873.]　　　　　　　　　　　　[8°

Collation—
　Pp. 27.
　Note.—A translation of a few detached passages, by P. Isola, entitled "In partendo dall' Inghilterra," etc.　There is no Title-page.

MISCELLANEOUS POEMS.

I.

An Ode./　On/ The Star of the Legion of Honour./ Napoleon's Farewell./ Fare Thee Well./ And/ A Sketch, etc./　By Lord Byron./　New-York:/ Published by Van Winkle and Wiley,/ No. 3 Wall-Street./　1816./　　[8°

Collation—
　Title, one leaf, pp. 3, 4 ; Text, pp. 5–24.
　Note.—The Half-title is probably missing.　The "Ode" is the *Ode from the French* ("We do not curse thee, Waterloo !").　The edition contains the five pieces enumerated on the title.

II.

Three Poems,/ not Included in the Works of/ Lord Byron./ Lines to Lady J——./　The Ænigma./　The Curse of Minerva./ [Motto from *Ter. Andria*, five lines.]　London:/ Printed for Effingham Wilson,/ Royal Exchange./　1818./
　　　　　　　　　　　　　　　　　　　　　　[8°

Collation—
　Title (R. *John Hill, Printer, 32, Water Lane, Blackfriars.*), pp. 3, 4 ; Note on the Lines to Lady Jersey, pp. 5, 6 ; Text and Notes, pp. 7–18.　The second poem is Miss Fanshaw's Enigma (Letter H) ; the third, *The Curse of Minerva* (112 lines).

III.

English Bards,/ and/ Scotch Reviewers ;/ A Satire./　Ode to the Land of the Gaul.—Sketch/ From Private Life.— Windsor/ Poetics, etc./　By/ The Right Honorable/ Lord Byron./　Second Edition./　Paris :/ Published by Galig-nani/ At the French, English, Italian, German and Spanish/ Library, N°. 18, Rue Vivienne,/ 1818./　　[12°

Collation—
　Pp. 84.　With half-title, "Suppressed/ Poems."　*English Bards,* etc., a reprint of the Fourth Edition of 1811, numbers 1052 lines.

IV.

The/ Works/ of/ The Right Honourable/ Lord Byron ;/ Containing/ English Bards, and/ Scotch Reviewers ;/ The Curse of Minerva,/ And the Waltz,/ An/ Apostrophic Hymn./ Philadelphia :/ Published By M. Thomas./ 1820./ [8º

Collation—
Pp. viii. + 151.
Note.—The *English Bards, etc.,* is a reprint of the Fourth Edition of 1050 lines. The *Curse of Minerva* is the complete edition of 312 lines. The "Fugitive Pieces" are : (1) To Jessy ; (2) "My Boat is on the Shore ;" (3) Lines addressed to Mr. Hobhouse ; (4) Adieu to Malta ; (5) Enigma [To the Letter H]. It will be observed that, with the exception of No. 5, all these pieces are genuine.

V.

Poems/ By/ The Right Honourable/ Lord Byron ;/ With/ His Memoirs./ London :/ Published by Jones and Company,/ Nº 3, Warwick Square./ 1825./ [8º

Collation—
Pp. 292 + Cont., p. [293].
This edition contains *Hours of Idleness, English Bards, etc.* (3rd ed.), " Poems on His Domestic Circumstances" (twenty-five, including eight forgeries), and the whole of *Don Juan.*

VI.

The/ Miscellaneous Poems/ of/ Lord Byron./ London :/ Benbow, Printer and Publisher, 252, High/ Holborn./ 1825./ [12º

Collation—
Pp. 94.
Note.—The collection numbers fifty-three poems, including the twenty-five published by R. Bumpus in 1824 (No. xi. of " Poems on His Domestic Circumstances "), and twenty-eight others (all genuine), including the *Ode to Napoleon Buonaparte,* and the *Monody on the Death of Sheridan.*

VII.

Don Juan,/ Complete ;/ English Bards and Scotch/ Reviewers ;/ Hours of Idleness ;/ The Waltz ;/ and all the other Minor Poems :/ By/ Lord Byron./ [Emblem (Dove and olive-branch) :—motto (*Perseverantia et Amicis*).] London :/ Printed and Published by J. F. Dove,/ Sᵗ John's Square./ 1827./ [12º

VOL. VII.   X

Collation—
 Pp. iv. + 574.
 Note.—A second Title-page, with Title-vignette. *English Bards, etc.*, numbers 1050 lines. Among the "Minor Poems" are the seven forgeries : (1) Farewell to England ; (2) To my Daughter ; (3) Ode—St. Helena ; (4) To the Lily of France ; (5) Ode ("Oh, shame to thee," etc.) ; (6) Madame Lavalette ; (7) Enigma (Letter H) ; and *The Curse of Minerva* (111 lines).

VIII.

Don Juan ;/ Hours of Idleness ;/ English Bards and Scotch Reviewers ;/ The Waltz ;/ and other Poems./ By Lord Byron./ In Two Volumes./ Vol. I. [Vol. II.] London : J. F. Dove, St John's Square./ 1828./   [12°

Collation—
 Vol. I. : pp. xiv. + 384.
 Vol. II. : pp. iv. + 428.
 Note.—These pirated volumes were occasionally bound up with Murray's four-volume edition of 1828, and numbered Vols. V., VI.

IX.

The/ Miscellaneous Works/ of/ Lord Byron./ Containing/ Werner, a Tragedy ; Heaven and Earth ;/ Morgante Maggiore ; Age of Bronze ; The Island ;/ Vision of Judgment ;/ and The Deformed Transformed./ London :/ Printed for Hunt and Clarke,/ Tavistock Street ;/ and sold by all Booksellers./ 1830./   [8°

Collation—
 Pp. vi. + 7–308 + 286—Title, one leaf ; Half-title (Werner) ; pp. i., ii. ; Dedication, pp. iii., iv. ; Preface, pp. v., vi. ; Dramatis Personæ, p. [8] ; Text (*Werner, Heaven and Earth,* Translation of *Morgante Maggiore*), pp. 9–308 ; Text (*The Age of Bronze, The Island* (App.), *The Vision of Judgment* (App.), *The Deformed Transformed*), pp. 1–286. The Imprint (London :/ *Printed by C. H. Reynell, Broad Street, Golden Square.*/) is at the foot of p. 286.

X.

The Corsair—Lara. Tales by Lord Byron, with a notice and explanatory arguments by Lake. Paris. 1830. [12°
       [*Le Moniteur*, etc., 1845.]

XI.

The Bride of Abydos — The Corsair — Lara — Curse of Minerva — Morg. Magg. — Hours of Idleness — Engl.

Bards, etc.—Miscell. Poems. [In one vol.] By Lord
Byron. Paris. 1832. [8°

[*Le Moniteur*, etc., 1845.]

XII.

Manfred—Marino Faliero—Sardanapalus—The Two Foscari—Cain—Werner—Heaven and Earth—The Deformed
Transf. By Lord Byron. [In one vol.] Paris. 1832.
[8°

[*Le Moniteur*, etc., 1845.]

XIII.

Don Juan—The Age of Bronze—The Vision of Judgment.
By Lord Byron. [In one vol.] Paris. 1832. [8°
[*Le Moniteur*, etc., 1845.]

XIV.

Miscellanies./ By/ Lord Byron./ In Three Volumes./
Vol. I./ [Vol. II., etc.] London :/ John Murray, Albemarle Street./ 1837./ [12°

Collation—
    Vol. I. : pp. vi. + 316.
    Vol. II. : pp. iv. + 305.
    Vol. III. : pp. viii. + 288.
    Note.—Vol. I. contains *Hours of Idleness ; English Bards,
etc. ; Hints from Horace.*
    Vol. II. contains *The Curse of Minerva ; The Waltz ; Ode to
N. B. ; Hebrew Melodies ; The Morgante Maggiore ; The Prophecy
of Dante ; The Blues ; The Vision of Judgment ; The Age of
Bronze.*
    Vol. III. contains "Occasional Pieces," 1807–1824; "Domestic
Pieces," 1816; *Monody, etc. ; The Dream ; Darkness ; The Lament
of Tasso ; Ode on Venice ; Francesca da Rimini ;* and, interspersed
with these, pp. 171–261, other minor pieces and epigrams. The
App. (pp. 265–288) contains "Remarks on the Romaic," etc.

XV.

Tales./ By/ Lord Byron./ In Two Volumes./ Vol. I./
London :/ John Murray, Albemarle Street./ 1837./
[12°

Collation—
    Vol. I. : pp. 263.
    Vol. II. : pp. 260.
    Note.—Vol. I. contains *The Giaour ; The Bride, etc. ; The
Corsair ; Lara.* Vol. II. contains *The Siege, etc. ; Parisina ;
The Prisoner, etc. ; Beppo ; Mazeppa ; The Island.*

XVI.

Lord Byron's/ Tales :/ Consisting of/ The Giaour, The Bride of Abydos,/ The Corsair, Lara ;/ With all the Notes :/ Hebrew Melodies,/ and other Poems./ Halifax :/ Printed and Published by William Milner,/ Cheapside./ 1845./ [16º

Collation—
Pp. viii. + 9–256.
Note.—Among the " Poems " are twelve pieces, " The Illuminated City," " The Wreath," " A Child at Prayer," etc., which are, apparently, attributed to Lord Byron, but are neither his compositions nor capable of being described as forgeries or imitations. They precede six genuine poems.
For an interesting account (by W. Roberts) of other editions (1838, 1865, etc.), published at Halifax, see *Notes and Queries*, 1886, iv. S. v. 225, etc. ; and *The Antiquarian Magazine*, vol. xii., July—November, 1887, pp. 101–106.

XVII.

The Giaour,/ and/ The Bride of Abydos./ By/ Lord Byron./ London :/ H. G. Clarke & Co., 278, Strand./ 1848./ [16º

Collation—
Pp. 154.
Note.—Part of " Clarke's Cabinet Series."

XVIII.

Miscellanies./ By Lord Byron./ In Two Volumes.—Vol. I./ [Vol. II.] London :/ John Murray, Albemarle Street./ 1853./ [16º

Collation—
Vol. I. : pp. vii. + 364.
Vol. II. : pp. viii. + 360.
Note.—Vol. I. contains *Hours of Idleness ; English Bards, etc. ; Hints from Horace ; The Curse of Minerva ; The Waltz ; Ode to Napoleon Buonaparte ; Hebrew Melodies ;* Domestic Pieces ; *Monody, etc. ; The Dream.*
Vol. II. contains *The Lament of Tasso ; Ode on Venice ; The Morgante Maggiore ; The Prophecy of Dante ; Francesca of Rimini ; The Blues ; The Vision of Judgment ; The Age of Bronze ;* Occasional Pieces, 1807–1824.

XIX.

Tales and Poems./ By Lord Byron./ Containing/ The Giaour./ Bride of Abydos./ The Corsair./ Lara./ Siege

of Corinth./ Parisina./ Prisoner of Chillon./ Mazeppa./
The Island./ London : John Murray, Albemarle Street./
1853./   [16º

Collation—
  Pp. vi. + 7–358.

XX.

Beppo and Don Juan./ By Lord Byron./ In Two Volumes.
—Vol. I./ [Vol. II.] London :/ John Murray, Albemarle
Street./ 1853./   [16º

Collation—
  Vol. I. : pp. 353.
  Vol. II. : pp. 367.

XXI.

Poems/ By/ The Right Honourable/ Lord Byron ;/ With/
His Memoirs./ London :/ Thomas Nelson & Sons,/
Paternoster Row./ 1855./   [32º

Collation—
  Pp. xvi. + 174.
  Note.—"Poems on Domestic Circumstances," etc. (pp. 133–
174) are identical with those published by J. F. Dove, 1827, pp.
536–574 (see No. vii.); and the entire contents of the volume
are identical with Poems/ By the/ Right Honourable Lord Byron./,
which form part (Vol. II. pp. *1–46*) of "The Cabinet Edition of
the British Poets." In Four Volumes./ London :/ Henry G.
Bohn, York Street, Covent Garden./ 1851./ [8º]

XXII.

Lord Byron's Tales and Poems. Leipzig, Brockhaus. 1857.
                                                  [8º
                    [Kayser, 1860.]

XXIII.

Poems./ By Lord Byron./ [Motto : "Like an archangel,"
etc., twelve lines, *Anon.*] With Eight Illustrations,/ By
Birket Foster, John Gilbert, etc./ London :/ Routledge,
Warne, and Routledge,/ Farringdon Street ;/ New York :
56, Walker Street./ 1859./   [8º

Collation—
  Pp. xxxii. + 539.

XXIV.

Eastern Tales :/ By/ Lord Byron./ Comprising/ The
Corsair, Lara, The Giaour,/ The Bride of Abydos, and

The Siege of Corinth./   With the Author's original Intro-
ductions and Notes./   Illustrated./   London :/   David
Bogue, 86, Fleet Street./   [1859.]   [8°

Collation—
   Pp. 5-265.

XXV.

Byron's/ Siege of Corinth/ And/ Ode to Napoleon Buonaparte./   With Notes/ For students for the first examina-
tion in Arts,/ University of Madras./   1877./   Madras :/
Addison and Co., 18, Mount Road./   1876./   [8°

Collation—
   Pp. 56.

XXVI.

Poems/   By/ Lord Byron/   London/ George Routledge
and Sons/ Broadway, Ludgate Hill./   New York : 416
Broome Street/   [1880.]   [8°

Collation—
   Pp. xxxii. + 719.
   Note.—Part of the " Excelsior Series."

XXVII.

Poems/ of/ Lord Byron./   Carefully Selected./   In Two
Volumes./   Vol. I./   [Vol. II.]   Cassell & Company,
Limited :/   London, Paris, New York, & Melbourne./
[1886.]   [32°

Collation—
   Vol. I. : pp. 3-316.
   Vol. II. : pp. x. + 11-316.
   Note.—Part of Cassell's " Miniature Library of the Poets."

XXVIII.

Byron's/ Prisoner of Chillon/ und/ Siege of Corinth./   Mit
bibliographischem Material,/ litterarischer Einleitung und
sachlichen/ Anmerkungen für Studierende/ Herausge-
geben/ von/ J. G. C. Schuler./   Halle./   Max Niemeyer./
1886./   [8°

Collation—
   Pp. 92 + " Lesarten aus Byron's MSS.," pp. 93, 94.
   Note.—No. 8 of " Materialen für das Neuenglische Seminar."
Herausg. v. Ernst Regel.

XXIX.

The Corsair. Lara. Illustrated by Gambard and Mittis. With Introduction by M. F. Sweetser. Boston, Joseph Knight & Co. 1893. [32°

[*Amer. Cat.*, 1894.]

Collation—
Pp. 142.
Note.—Part of the " World's Classics."

TRANSLATIONS OF MISCELLANEOUS POEMS.

Bohemian.

Korsár. Laŗa/ Básnické Povídky/ Lorda Byrona/ Přeložil/ Čeněk Ibl./ V Praze/ Tiskem A Nákladem Dra Ed. Grégra/ 1885/ [8°

Collation—
Pp. 128.
Note.—Poesie Světová, Pt xxiii., 1871, etc.

Danish.

I.

Udvalgte/ Dramatiske Digte/ OG/ Fortœllinger/ Af/ Byron./ Oversatte af Edv. Lembcke./ Første Bind./ (Dramatiske Dicte.)/ Kjøbenhavn./ Forlagt af J. H. Schubothes. Boghandel./ Græbes Bogtrykkeri./ 1873./ [8°

Collation—
Vol. I. : pp. 594.
Vol. II. : [1876] pp. 422.
Note.—Vol. I. contains *Sardanapalus ; Manfred ; Cain ; Marino Faliero.*
Vol. II. contains *The Siege, etc. ; Mazeppa ; The Bride, etc. ; Corsair ; Giaour ; Lara ; The Prisoner, etc. ; The Island.*

II.

Byron :/ Manfred,/ Fangen paa Chillon og Mazeppa./ Oversat af/ Alfred Ipsen./ København./ Forlagt af P. Hauberg & Comp. og Jul. Gjellerup./ Trykt hos Martius Truelsen. [1889?] [16°

Collation—
Pp. 136.

III.

Beppo./ Dommedagssynet./ Af/ Lord Byron./ Oversatte/ Af/ Alfred Ipsen./ København,/ Forlagt Af I. H. Schu-bothes Boghandel./ Græbes Bogtrykkeri./ 1891./ [8°

Collation—
Pp. 88.

Dutch.

I.

Navolgingen/ van/ Lord Byron./ Door/ Nicolaas Beets./ De gevangene van Chillon./ Mazeppa. Parisina. Frag-menten. Joodsche zangen./ Verscheiden gedichten./ Nieuwe, Herziene Uitgave./ Vermeederd met een Woord over Byrons Poëzy./ Te Haarlem, By/ De Erven F. Bohn./ 1848./   [8°

Collation—
Pp. xl. + 170.
Note.—The vignette (a bunch of cornflowers) on the illustrated title-page (Gedichten/ van/ Nicolaas Beets./) is engraved by J. W. Kaiser.

II.

Gedichten/ van/ Lord Byron./ Door/ J. J. L. Ten Kate./ Eerste Volledige Uitgave./ Te Leiden, Bij A. W. Sijthoff. [1870?]   [8°

Collation—
Pp. 242.

French.

I.

Le Corsaire, Mazeppa, traduits en vers français suivis de poésies diverses, par Lucien Méchin, 1848. Paris, Paulin. [12°

[Lorenz, 1840–1865.]

II.

Le/ Prisonnier de Chillon/ Lara/ Parisina/ Poémes de Lord Byron,/ Traduits en vers/ et/ Poésies diverses/ Par H. Gomont/ Membre correspondant de l'Académie de Stanislas/ Paris/ Amyot, Libraire/ Rue de la Paix, 6/ [the second column] Nancy./ Mlle Gonet, libraire/ Rue des Dominicains, 14/ 1862/   [12°

Collation—
Pp. viii. + 228.

III.

Le Corsaire, Lara, le Siége de Corinthe. Traduction nouvelle par Paul Lorencin. (*Libraire de la Bibliothéque Nationale*, tom. 117.) 1868.   [32º

[Lorenz, 1876.]

IV.

Chefs-D'œuvre/ de/ Lord Byron/ Traduits en vers français/ par/ A. Regnault/ Bibliothécaire et archiviste honoraire du Conseil D'État/ Membre de l'Académie de Lyon/ Auteur d'une histoire du Conseil D'État,/ D'un Voyage en Orient (Gréce, Turquie, Égypte)/ Et de notices historiques sur Moscou et Saint-Pétersbourg/ Tome premier/ Paris/ Amyot, Librairie-Éditeur/ 8, rue de la Paix, 8/ Et à la librairie, Galignani/ 224, rue de Rivoli, 224/ 1874/ Touts droits réservés/   [8º

Collation—

Vol. I. : pp. xxxii. + 518.
Vol. II. : pp. 511.
Note.—Vol. I. contains *Childe Harold's, etc.* ; *The Bride, etc.* ; *The Giaour* ; *The Siege, etc.* ; *Manfred* [Scènes Détachées].
Vol. II. contains *The Corsair* ; *Lara* ; *Mazeppa* ; *The Prisoner, etc.* ; *Parisina* ; *Beppo* ; Juan and Haidee ; Poésies Diverses.

V.

Lord Byron/ Les/ Deux Foscari/ Tragédie historique/ Beppo/ Poème humoristique/ Traduction en vers (ornée de 15 vignettes)/ Par/ Achille Morisseau/ Paris/ Calmann Lévy, éditeur/ 3, rue Auber, 3/ 1881/   [8º

Collation—

Pp. xiii. + 258.

VI.

Le Corsaire. Lara. Illustrations de Gambard et Mittis. Paris, Dentre. 1892.   [32º

[Fait partie de la " Petite Collection Guillaume," Lorenz, 1900.]

German.

I.

Gefangener von Chillon u. Parisina, nebst e. Anh. seiner lyrischen Gedichte, übers. durch Paul Graf v. Haugwitz. Breslau, W. G. Korn. Übers. 1821.   [8º

[Kayser, 1834.]

II.

Manfred. — Die Finsterniss.—Der Traum. Aus d. Engl. übersetzt von Er. Köpke. Berlin, Schröder. 1835. [8°.
[Kayser, 1841.]

III.

Der Giaur. Hebräische Gesänge. Aus dem Engl. übers. von Friederike Friedmann. Leipzig. 1854. Brockhaus.
[16°.
[Kayser, 1860.]

IV.

Kain./ Ein Mysterium./ Mazeppa./ Von/ Lord Byron./ Aus dem Englischen übersetzt/ von/ Friederike Friedmann./ Leipzig :/ F. A. Brockhaus./ 1855./ [16°.
Collation—
  Pp. 154.

V.

Manfred. Der Gefangene von Chillon, Hebräische Gesänge, u. Lyrische Gedichte. Deutsch von A. R. Niele. Münster, Coppenrath. 1857. [16°.
[Kayser, 1859.]

VI.

Lord Byron's/ Mazeppa, Korsar und Beppo./ In das Deutsche übertragen/ von/ Wilhelm Schäffer./ *Stulta est clementia, quum tot ubique/ Vatibus occurras, periturœ parcere chartœ./* Juvenal./ [Emblem — Griffin with shield bearing motto "F. A. B. 1805."] Leipzig : F. A. Brockhaus./ 1864./ [8°.
Collation—
  Pp. 138.

VII.

Die Braut von Abydos./ Der Traum./ Zwei Gedichte./ von/ Lord Byron./ Im Versmass des Originals übertragen/ von/ Dr Otto Riedel./ Hamburg./ Hermann Grüning./ 1872./ [16°.
Collation—
  Pp. 80.

VIII.

Der Gefangene v. Chillon. *Mazeppa.* Von Lord Byron.
[Kayser, 1877.]

Note.—No. 557 of the "Universal Bibliothek." Leipzig, 1871–1876.

IX.

Der Gefangene v. Chillon. *Parisina.* Zwei poet. Erzählungen, übers. v. Otto Michaeli. Halle. 1887–1890.
[8°

Note.—Part of the " Bibl. der Gesamt= Litteratur des In= u. Auslandes." [Kayser, 1891.]

Hungarian.

Byron Lord'/ Élete's Munkái./ Irta/ Petrichevich Horváth Lázár./ Harmadik Rész./ Pesten./ Nyomtatta Landerer és Heckenast./ 1842./   [12°

Collation—
Pp. 154 + Sajtó-hibák, p. [155].
Note.—The translations include *Mazeppa ; The Dream ;* and sixteen lyrical pieces.

Icelandic.

Bandinginn í Chillon/ og/ Dramurinn,/ Eptir/ Byron Lávard./ Steingrímur Thorsteinson,/ Íslenzkadi./ Kaupmannahöfn./ Útgefandi Páll Sveinsson./ Prentad Hjá Louis Klein./ 1866./   [12°
Collation—
Pp. 70.

Italian.

I.

Poemi/ di/ Lord G. Byron/ Tradotti dall' originale inglese/ Da/ Pietro Isola/ Socio corrispondente/ della R. Accademia delle scienze ed arti di Alessandria./ Primo volume/ Lugano/ coi tipi di Francesco Veladini e Comp./ 1832./   [8°
Collation—
Vol. I. : pp. 221 + Note, Indice, pp. [222]-[224]. N.B.—Pp. 1-19 are not numbered.
Vol. II. : pp. 298 + Indice, p. [299]. Pp. 1-13 are not numbered.

II.

Poemi/ di/ Giorgio Lord Byron/ Recati in italiano/ da/
Giuseppe Nicolini/ con alcuni componimenti originali/
del traduttore./   Milano/ Per Giuseppe Crespi e C./
1834./   [8°

Collation—
  Pp. 433 + Indice, p. [435].
  Note.—The Title-vignette is a portrait of Lord Byron.

III.

Poemi/ di Giorgio Lord Byron/ Recati in italiano/   Da
Giuseppe Nicolini/ Nuova edizione eseguita su quella del
1837/ Riveduta ed aumentata dal traduttore/ Vol. I./
[Vol. II.]   Milano/ Presso la ditta Angelo Bonfanti
1842/   [12°

Collation—
  Vol. I. : pp. 283.
  Vol. II. : pp. 255.

IV.

Poemi e novelle. Milano, Sonzogno. 1882   [16°
                                          [Pagliaini, 1901.]

Collation—
  Pp. 107.

V.

Opere/ Edite e postume/ di Giacinto Casella/ Già Acca-
demico della Crusca/ Con prefazione del Prof. Ales-
sandro d'Ancona,/ Uno scritto critico sul Properzio del
Prof. G. Rigutini/ E una notizia biografica sull' autore/
Scritta da sua moglie./ Due Vol.—Vol. I./ Parte I.—Il
Pellegrinaggio d'Aroldo, la Parisina,/ il Beppo e la sposa
d'Abido, di Lord Byron.—Sopra M. Aurora., di S. Fenzi./
Un frammento dal *Lambros*, di D. Solomos./ Parte II.
—Liriche originali./ Firenze,/ Tipografia di G. Barbéra./
1884./   [8°

Collation—
  Vol. I. : pp. lvi. + 438 + Errata Corrige, p. [439].
  Vol. II. : pp. xviii. + 450 [Text = pp. 3–450] + *Indice*, etc.,
p. [451].
  Note.—The translations of *Childe Harold*, *Parisina*, *Beppo*,
and the *Bride, etc.*, are on pp. 1–311 of the first part of the first
volume.

VI.

Misteri e canti; Caino ; Parisina ; Un sogno. Traduzione
di Andrea Maffei. Milano, Hoepli. 1886. [64°
[Pagliaini, 1901.]

Collation—
Pp. 198.

VII.

Misteri, novelle e liriche. Traduzione di Andrea Maffei.
Firenze, Le Monnier. 1890. [64°
[Pagliaini, 1901.]

Collation—
Pp. xxxviii. + 441.

Polish.

I.

Poemata i powieści...Przez B. hr. K. [Brunona hr. Kiciń-
skiego]. Tom. 1. (Oblężenie Koryntu, Korsarz.)
Warszawa, 1820. [8°.
*Part of "Biblioteka Romansów," etc. Wyd. przez
W. Malecką.*

II.

Powieści, przekład Wandy Maleckiéj. (Mazepa, przek.
H. Dembińskiego, Paryzyna, Giaur, Upiór.) pp. 196.
w druk. J. Wróblewskiego: Warszawa, 1828. [8°.
Wybór Romansów, wyd. W. Maleckiéj. Tom. XIII.

[Another edition.] *Warszawa,* 1831. [8°.

III.

Paryzyna, Kalmar i Orla, dwa poemata...Przekład Ign.
Szydłowskiego. pp. 58.
druk. J. Zawadzkiego: Wilno, 1834. [8°.

IV.

Poezye/ Lorda Byrona/ tłumaczone/ Giaur/ przez/ Adama
Mickiewicza,/ Korsarz/ Przez/ Edwarda Odyńca./ Wydanie Alexandra Jełowickiego./ W. Paryżu./ 1835/ [12°

Collation—
Pp. xiv. + 202.

V.

Tłómaczenia/ Antoniego Edwarda/ Odyńca./ Tom Drugi./ Narzeczona z Abydos./ W Lipsku/ u Breitkopfa i Haertela./ 1838./

Collation—
Pp. 216.
Note.—The translation of the *Bride of Abydos*, with the Notes, is on pp. *1*–83 of this volume.

VI.

Tłomaczenia/ Antoniego Edwarda/ Odyńca./ Tom Trzeci./ Korsarz./ Niebo i Ziemia./ W Lipsku/ u Breitkopfa i Haertela./ 1841./ 　　　　　　　[12°

Collation—
Pp. 201.
Note.—The translation of the *Corsair*, with Notes, is on pp. *1*-112 ; of *Heaven and Earth*, pp. *116*-201.

VII.

Poemata. Z oryginału przełożył Ant. Zawadzki. (Żale Tassa ; Werner ; Narzeczona z Abydos ; Wyspa.) pp. 392. *H. Skimborowicz : Warszawa*, 1846. 　　　　[8°.

VIII.

Pięć Poematów/ Lorda Birona/ Przełożył/ Franciszek Dzierżykraj Morawski./ Nakładem Autora./ Leszno./ Drukiem Ernesta Günthera./ 1853./ 　　　　[8°

Collation—
Pp. 272.
Note.—The translations include *Manfred ; Mazeppa ; The Siege, etc. ; Parisina ;* and *The Prisoner, etc.*

IX.

Kruzer (Karol) Przekłady i rymy własne. 5 tom. *druk. E. Skiwskiego : Warszawa*, 1876. 　　　[8°.
Tom. 3. Parisina. Lara. Kain. Poezje ulotne.
Tom. 4. Poezje ulotne Lorda Byrona.

Portuguese.

Traducções/ Poeticas/ de/ Francisco José Pinheiro Guimarães/ Bacharel em sciencias sociaes e juridicas/ Childe

Harold e Sardanapalo,/ De Lord Byron ;/ O Roubo da Madeixa, de Pope ;/ Hernani, de Victor Hugo/   Rio de Janeiro/ Typographia universal de Laemmert/ Rua dos Invalidos, 61 B./ 1863/   [8°

Collation—
   Pp. 636.
   Note.—The Title-page, a Dedication, and *O Sonho*, an imitation of Byron's *Dream*, are unpaged.   The translations of *Childe Harold*, Cantos I.–IV., and of *Sardanapalus*, are on pp. *1–424*.

Roumanian.

Din Scrierile/ Loui/ Lord Byron/ 3 P^t / Tradduce/ de/ J. Eliad/ Boukouresti/ In Tipographia loui Eliad/   1834/
                                                   [8°

Collation—
   Pp. 74.
   Note.—The Title-page, in old Roumanian character, has been transliterated.   The translations consist of *The Prisoner of Chillon*, *The Lament of Tasso*, and *Beppo*. The volume concludes with a Half-title, *The Vampire.*

Spanish.

I.

Odas/ A Napoleon,/ Por lord Byron./   Traduccion castellana./ [Emblem—eagle flying to the sun.]   Paris,/ Libreria americana,/ Calle del Temple, N° 69./ 1830./
                                                   [12°

Collation—
   Pp. 60.
   Note.—The translations include the *Ode to Napoleon Buonaparte; Napoleon's Farewell; On the Star of " The Legion of Honour ;" From the French; Ode from the French.*

II.

Biblioteca Jané./   Poemas/ de Lord/ Byron,/ Con notas, comentarios y aclaraciones/ Primera version española, en vista de la ultima edicion/ Por Ricardo Canales./ Lara.—El Sitio de Corinto.—Parisina. — Mazeppa./—La Peregrinacion de Childe—Harold.—Las Lamentaciones/ del Tasso. — Beppo./ Barcelona./ Jané Hermanos, Editores./ Ronda de San Antonia, 58./ [? 1876.] [8°
Collation—
   Pp. 352 + *Indice*, p. [353].

III.

Cuatro poemas/ de/ Lord Byron/ Traducidos en verso
castellano/ Por/ Antonio Sellen/ Parisina.—El prisionero
de Chillon.—/ Los lamentos del Tasso.—La novia de
Abydos/ New York./ Imprenta y librería de N. Ponce
Leon, 40 y 42 Broadway/ 1877/   [12°

Collation—
   Pp. xiii. + *15*-111.

IV.

D. Juan/ El Hijo de Doña Inés/ Poema de/ Lord Byron/
seguido de/ Las lamentaciones del Tasso/ del proprio
autor/ Version de/ J. A. R./ Ilustrada con dibujos à la
pluma/ Por R. Escaler/ Barcelona/ Administracion :
Nueva San Francisco, 11 y 13/ 1883/   [8°

Collation—
   Pp. viii. + *9*-414 + *Indice*, p. [415].
   Note.—Part of the " Biblioteca Amena é Instructiva."

COLLECTIONS OF DRAMAS.

I.

Dramas/ By/ Lord Byron./ In Two Volumes./ Vol. I./
London :/ John Murray, Albemarle Street./ 1837./ [12°

Collation—
   Vol. I. : pp. 403.
   Vol. II. : pp. 391.
   Note.—Vol. I. contains *Manfred ; Marino Faliero ; Heaven
and Earth ; Sardanapalus.* Vol. II. contains *The Two Foscari ;
Cain ; The Deformed Transformed ; Werner.* The Title-vignette
on the illustrated Title-page of Vol. I. is "Fall of the Staubach,"
engraved by E. Finden, from a drawing by G. Bulmer from a
sketch by Mrs. Somerville. These volumes, together with the
Miscellanies, Tales, etc., were bound in green cloth, with Lord
Byron's arms with supporters stamped in gold on one side.

II.

Dramas./ By Lord Byron./ In Two Volumes.—Vol. I./
Containing/ Manfred./ Marino Faliero./ Heaven and
Earth./ Sardanapalus./ London :/ John Murray, Albe-
marle Street./ 1853./   [8°

Collation—
   Vol. I. : pp. 325. The Imprint (*Bradbury & Evans, Printers,
Whitefriars.*) is at the foot of p. 325.

Vol. II. : pp. **318.** The Imprint (*London : Bradbury & Evans, Printers, Whitefriars*) is at the foot of p. **318.**
Note.—Vol. II. contains *The Two Foscari, Cain, The Deformed Transformed*, and *Werner*.

TRANSLATIONS OF COLLECTIONS OF DRAMAS.

German.

Lord Byrons/ Dramatische Werke./   Deutsch/ von/ W. Grüzmacher./   Manfred.   Kain.   Himmel und Erde. Sardanapal./   Hildburghausen./   Verlag des Bibliographischen Instituts./ 1870./   [8?

Collation—
 Pp. 323 + Inhalt, p. [324].
 Note.—No. 112 of the " Bibliothek Ausländischer Klassiker."

Italian.

I.

Marino Faliero/ E/ I Due Foscari/ Tragedie/ di/ Lord G. Byron/ Versione dall' originale inglese/ del/ P. G. B. Cereseto/ Delle scuole pie./   Savona 1845./   Presso Luigi Sambolino/ Editore-librajo./   [8?

Collation—
 Pp. 304.

II.

Tragedie/ di/ Giorgio Lord Byron/ Traduzione/ del/ Cav. Andrea Maffei./   Sardanapalo.—Marino Faliero./ I Due Foscari./   Firenze./   Felice Le Monnier./   1862./ [8?

Collation—
 Pp. 493 + Indice, p. [495].

Spanish.

Poemas dramáticos/ De Lord Byron/ Caín.—Sardanápalo. —Manfredo./   Traducidos en verso castellano/ Por D. José Alcalá Galiano/ con una carta prólogo de/ D. Marcellino Menéndez y Pelayo/ Madrid/ Imprenta de A. Pérez Dubrull/ Flor Baja, núm. 22./ 1886./   [8?

Collation—
 Pp. xxxvi. + 382.
 Note.—Vol. 45 of the " Coleccion de Escritores Castellanos."

POEMS, DRAMAS, AND COLLECTIONS OF POEMS.

The Age of Bronze.

The/ Age of Bronze ;/ or,/ Carmen Seculare et Annus Haud
Mirabilis./ "Impar *Congressus* Achilli."/ London, 1823 :/
Printed for John Hunt,/ 22, Old Bond street./   [8⁰

Collation—
    Half-title (R. *London : Printed by C. H. Reynell, Broad
Street, Golden Square./*), pp. 1, 2 ; Title, one leaf, pp. 3, 4 ;
Text, pp. 5–36. The Imprint (*London :/ C. H. Reynell, Printer,
45, Broad-Street, Golden-Square./*) is at the foot of p. 36.
    Note.—The Second and Third Editions are identical with the
First, save that in the Third Edition the Imprint at the foot of p. 36
runs thus : *London :/ Printed by C. H. Reynell, Broad Street, Golden-
Square.* A page of advertisements ("*Works about to be published
by* Mr. John Hunt, 22, *Old Bond Street* ") follows p. 36 in the
Second Edition. The *Age of Bronze* was reissued by John Hunt
in 1825 and in 1830 (the Miscellaneous Works, Part II. pp. *1–35*),
and by (?) W. Dugdale, 1824, together with other poems ; and,
in France, by A. and W. Galignani, Paris, 1823 (12⁰), but was
not included in any of John Murray's Collected Editions till 1831.

Beppo.

I.

Beppo,/ A Venetian Story./ ROSALIND. Farewell, Monsieur Traveller : Look, you lisp, and wear/ Strange suits ;
disable all the benefits of your own country ; be out
of love/ with your Nativity, and almost chide God for
making you that countenance/ you are ; or I will scarce
think that you have swam in a GONDOLA./ AS YOU LIKE
IT, Act iv. Sc. I./ *Annotation of the Commentators./*
That is, been at *Venice*, which was much visited by the
young English/ gentlemen of those times, and was then
what *Paris* is *now*—the seat of all dissoluteness. S. A./
Second Edition./ London :/ John Murray, Albemarle-
Street./ 1818./   [8⁰

Collation—
    Pp. 49. The Imprint (*T. Davison, Lombard-Street, White-
friars, London./*) is at the foot of the Reverse of the Half-title.
    Note (1).—The Text numbers 95 stanzas.
    Note (2).—" Beppo, a Venetian Story. [Quotation.] London :
John Murray, Albemarle Street. 1818. 8vo. Pp. 49 " (the
First Edition), is included in the catalogue of the *Rowfant Library*,
1886, p. 146.

II.

Beppo,/ A Venetian Story./ By Lord Byron./ [Motto, nine lines, as above.] Fifth Edition./ London :/ John Murray, Albemarle-Street./ 1818./ [8°.

Collation—

Pp. 51. The Imprint, as above, is at the foot of p. 51. The Imprint (*T. Davison, Lombard-Street, Whitefriars./*) is at the foot of the Reverse of the Half-title.

Note.—The Text numbers 99 stanzas. Byron sent four additional stanzas, viz. stanzas xxviii., xxxviii., xxxix., lxxx., to Murray *circ.* March 9, 1818. A Second Edition of Beppo, *vide supra,* was published March 12, 1818, and the fifth, May 30, 1818. The intervening editions, third and fourth, were not advertised in the *Morning Chronicle, Morning Post, Courier,* and, in the absence of direct evidence, it may be conjectured that the additional stanzas first appeared in the Fifth Edition. A Sixth Edition, and a Seventh Edition identical with the Fifth Edition, were issued in 1818.

III.

Beppo; a Venetian Story. Boston. 1818. [12°.

Collation—

Pp. 36.

IV.

Beppo, A Venetian Story. Paris, A. and W. Galignani. 1821. [12°.

[Quérard, 1827.]

Translations of Beppo.

Dutch.

Vertalingen/ En/ Navolgingen/ In Poezy/ door/ Mr. J. Van Lennep./ [Motto, seven lines.] Te Amsterdam, bij/ P. Meljer Warnars./ 1834./ [8°.

Collation—

Beppo,/ Eine Venetiansche/ Vertelling./ Naar het Engelsch/ van/ Lord Byron./ pp. 119–159.

Note.—The Title-vignette is the Muse of Poetry with Cupids and scrolls labelled Walter Scott, Moore, Byron, and Shakespeare.

French.

S. Clogenson/ Beppo/ Poëme/ de Byron/ Traduit en vers français, avec texte anglais en regard/ Paris,/ Michel

Lévy frères, libraires éditeurs/ Rue Vivienne, 2 bis, et boulevard des Italiens, 15/ à la librairie-nouvelle./ 1865./ [12°

Collation—
   Pp. 159 + Notes, pp. [161, 162].

Russian.

Беппо...пер. Д. Минаева. [" Современникъ," 1863. No. 8.]

Spanish.

Beppo, novela veneciana, por L. B. traduccion castellana. Paris, 1830. [8°
[*Le Moniteur,* etc., 1845.]

Swedish.

Beppo,/ En Venetiansk Historia/ AF/ Lord Byron./ Af Lord Byron./ Öfversättning/ Af/ Talis Qualis./ Stockholm,/ J. L. Brudins Förlag./ [8°

Collation—
   Pp. 48. (A Preliminary Note, *n.p.,* on fly-leaf.)
   Note.—Part (No. 5) of " Byron's Poetiska Berättelser," 1853, etc.

Bride of Abydos.

I.

The/ Bride of Abydos./ A Turkish Tale./ By Lord Byron./ Had we never loved so kindly,/ Had we never loved so blindly,/ Never met or never parted,/ We had ne'er been broken-hearted./ Burns./ London/ *Printed by T. Davison, Whitefriars,* For John Murray, Albemarle-Street./ 1813./
[8°

Collation—
   Title, one leaf; Dedication, one leaf; Text, pp. *1–60*; Notes, pp. *61–72.* The Imprint (*T. Davison, Lombard Street,| Whitefriars, London|*) is at the foot of p. **72.**
   Note.—Canto I. numbers 483 lines; Canto II., 724 lines (*not,* as numbered, **722** lines, line 492 being numbered 490).

II.

The/ Bride of Abydos./ A Turkish Tale./ By Lord Byron./ [Motto, five lines, as above.] Second Edition./ London :/ *Printed by T. Davison, Whitefriars,/* For John Murray, Albemarle-Street./ 1813./ [8°

Collation—
  Vide supra.
  Note.—Canto II. numbers 730 lines (not, as numbered, 724).
On p. 45, after line 401, six additional lines ("Blest as the
Muezzin's, . . . long-loved voice endears") are inserted; but
line 414 is numbered 410, and the wrong enumeration of the
First Edition is repeated. A Third Edition is identical with
the Second.

III.

The/ Bride of Abydos,/ etc. Fourth Edition,/ etc. 1813./
                                        [8°

Collation—
  Vide supra.
  Note.—Canto II. numbers 732 lines. The additions in the
Fourth Edition are lines 662, 663 (p.157), "Hark —— to the
hurried," etc. The enumeration of the lines is correct. A Fifth
Edition is identical with the Fourth.

IV.

The/ Bride of Abydos,/ etc. Sixth Edition,/ etc. 1814./
                                        [8°

  This edition is identical with the Second and Third Editions.
Lines 622, 623 are omitted. Seventh, Eighth, and Tenth Editions,
issued in 1814, are identical with the Fourth. An Eleventh
Edition was issued in 1815.

V.

The Bride of Abydos./ A Turkish Tale./ By Lord Byron./
Had we never loved so kindly,/ Had we never loved so
blindly,/ Never met or never parted,/ We had ne'er been
broken-hearted./ Burns./ Philadelphia :/ Published by
Moses Thomas,/ No. 52 Chestnut-Street./ William Fry,
Printer./ 1814./   [12°
Collation—
  Pp. 72.

VI.

The Bride of Abydos :/ A Turkish Tale,/ By Lord Byron./
[Motto.] [London, 1844.]
Collation—
  Pp. *1*-39.
  Note.—Part of " Clarke's Home Library."

Translations of Bride of Abydos.

Bohemian.

Lorda Byrona/ Nevěsta z Abydu./ Pověst turecká./ Z ang-
lického přeložil/ Josef V. Frič./ V Praze./ Tisk a náklad
Jaroslava Pospíšila./ 1854./ [16⁰

Collation—
Pp. 66.

Bulgarian.

Абидонска Невѣста, поболгарилъ Н. Д. Катрановъ.
Москва, 1850.

Dutch.

De/ Abydeensche/ Verloofde./ Uit het Engelsch van/ Lord
Bijron/ door/ Mr. J. Van Lennep./ Te Amsterdam, bij/
P. Meijer Warnars./ 1826./ [8⁰

Collation—
Pp. iv. + 67.
Note.—The Title-vignette represents a pillar with skull and
cross-bones struck by lightning. The " ghastly-turbaned head "
(line 1208) hovers above. There is a Half-title, with Motto and
Transl., on the Reverse.

French.

I.

Zuleika et Selim, ou la vierge d'Abydos : par lord Byron :
trad. de l'anglais par Léon Thiessé ; et suivi de notes aug-
mentées du *Fare Thee Well,* et autres morceaux du même
auteur. A Paris, chez Plancher. 1816. [12⁰
[*B. de la France*, Oct. 5, 1816.]

II.

La Fiancée d'Abydos, poëme en II chants, avec des notes ;
imité de l'angl. par Aug. Clavareau, Gand, Houdin. 1823.
[8⁰

[Quérard, 1827.]

German.

I.

Die Braut von Abydos. Deutsch v. Dʳ J. v. Adrian. Frank-
furt-a-M., Sauerländer. 1819. [8⁰
[*Centralblatt*, 1890, vii. 456.]

II.

Die Braut von Abydos, eine türkische Sage.   Getreu in's Deutsche übers. u. seinen Schülern gewidmet von Finck de Bailleul.   Landau.   1843.   [8º

[Kayser, 1848.]

III.

Die Braut von Abydos.   Aus der engl. in freie, deutsche Dichtg. übertrag. von Frdr. Kley.   Halle, Schmidt.   1884.
                                                              [8º
[Kayser, 1887.]

Collation—
  Pp. 62.

Hungarian.

Az abydoszi ara.   [*The Bride of Abydos*, transl. by Tercsi.] Hangok a multból és Byrontol énekek.   pp. 25–66. B'pest.   1884.
  [*Egyetemes Philologiai Közlöny*, 1901, xxv. 227.]

Italian.

La fidanzata d'Abido.   Traduzione di Giov. Giovio.   Milano, Guglielmini.   1854.   [8º

[Pagliaini, 1901.]

Polish.

Dziewica z Abydos, poema.   Prezkł.   Wł. hr. Ostrowskiego. *Warszawa, Glücksberg.*   1818.   [8º
Collation—
  Pp. 94.

Russian.

I.

Абидосская Невѣста. Турецкая повѣсть. М. Каченов-скій. Выборъ изъ сочиненій лорда Байрона. 1821.
  Note.—Bride of Abydos, pp. 177–255.

II.

Невѣста Абидосская. Турецкая повѣсть лорда Байрона. Перевелъ съ англійскаго Иванъ Козловъ.
  pp. i.–x. 1–92.   *С.-Петербургъ,* 1826.   8º.

Second edition.   *С.-Петербургъ,* 1831.   16º.

III.

Абидосская Невѣста...Передѣлана...М. Политков-
ской. *Москва*, 1859.   [8º.
Collation—
    Pp. 1–57.

Swedish.

Bruden Från Abydos,/ En Turkisk Berättelse/ Af/ Lord
Byron./   Ofversättning./   Stockholm,/   J. L. Brudins
Förlag./   [8º
Collation—
    Pp. 72.
    Note.—No. 7 of " Byron's Poetiska Berättelser," 1853, etc.

Cain.

[*Note.*—*Cain, A Mystery* was published by John Murray,
together with *Sardanapalus, A Tragedy,* and *The Two Foscari,
A Tragedy,* Dec. 21, 1821 ; *vide post, Sardanapalus, A Tragedy,*
No. i. (p. 293).]

I.

Cain ;/ A Mystery./   By the author of Don Juan./   " Now
the Serpent was more subtil than any beast of/ the field
which the Lord God had made."/ Gen. iii. 1./   London :/
Printed for the Booksellers,/ By W. Benbow, Castle-Street,
Leicester-Square./   1822./   [12º
Collation—
    Pp. vii. + 8–93.

II.

Cain ;/ A Mystery./   By Lord Byron./   To which is added/
a Letter from the Author/ To/ Mʳ. Murray, the original
Publisher./   " Now the Serpent was more subtil than any
Beast of the Field which the Lord/ God had made."/
Gen. iii. 1./   Second Edition./   London :/ Printed and
Published by R. Carlile, 55, Fleet Street./   1822./   [8º
Collation—
    Pp. iv. + 5–23 + Letter, etc., p. [24].

III.

Cain ;/ A Mystery./   By Lord Byron./   " Now the Serpent
was more subtil than any beast of the/ field which the

Lord God had made."/ Gen. iii. 1./ London :/ Printed
for the Booksellers,/ *By H. Gray, Nº 2, Barbican.*/ 1822./
[12º

Collation—
Pp. vii. + 8-72.

IV.

Cain, A Mystery. New York. 1822. [24º
Collation—
Pp. 100.

V.

Cain, a Mystery. Paris, A. and W. Galignani. 1822. [12º
[Quérard, 1827.]

VI.

Cain,/ A Mystery./ By Lord Byron./ " Now the Serpent
was more subtil than any beast of the/ field which the
Lord God had made."/ Gen. iii. 1./ London :/ Printed
for the Booksellers,/ Published by W. Benbow, 252, High
Holborn./ 1824./ [12º
Collation—
Pp. vii. + 8-85.

VII.

Lord Byron's/ Cain, A Mystery :/ with/ Notes :/ Wherein
the/ Religion of the Bible/ Is considered, in reference to
acknowledged/ Philosophy and Reason./ By Harding
Grant;/ *Author of " Chancery Practice."*/ " Judge Righteous
Judgment,"/ " Prove all things."/ " Justify the ways of
God."/ London :/ William Crofts, 19, Chancery Lane./
1830./ [8º
Collation—
Pp. xvi. + 432.

VIII.

Cain ;/ A Mystery./ By Lord Byron./ " Now the Serpent
was more subtil than any beast of the field/ which the
Lord God had made."—Gen. iii. 1./ To which is added/
A Letter from the Author/ To/ Mr. Murray, the original
Publisher./ London :/ J. Watson, 33, Windmill Street,/
Finsbury./ 1832./ [12º
Collation—
Pp. iv. + 5-47 + Letter, etc., p. [48].

VOL. VII. 2 A

IX.

Cain, a Mystery. Breslau, Kern. 1840.   [16?
                                [Kayser, 1841.]

X.

Cain./ By/ Lord Byron./ " I tread on air, and sink not ;
yet I fear to sink."/ New and Complete Edition.—Price
One Penny./ London : J. Dicks, 313, Strand ; and all
Booksellers./ New York Samuel French & Son, 122,
Nassau Street—Sole Agents./ 1883, etc./   [12?
Collation—
    Pp. 143-160.
    Note.—No. 203 of " Dicks' Standard Plays."

Translations of Cain.
Bohemian.

Kain/ Dramatická Báseň/ Lorda Byrona/ Přeložil/ Jose
Durdík/ V Praze/ Tisk a náklad dra. Ed. Grégra/
1871/   [8?
Collation—
    Pp. 117.

French.

Caïn,/ Mystère dramatique/ En trois actes,/ De Lord
Byron,/ Traduit en vers français,/ Et réfuté dans une
suite de remarques philosophiques/ et critiques ;/ Pré-
cédé/ d'une lettre adressée à Lord Byron, sur les motifs/
et le but de cet ouvrage,/ Par Fabre d'Olivet./ à Paris,/
Chez Servier, libraire,/ rue de L'Oratoire, N? 6./ 1823./
                                               [8?

Collation—
    Pp. 248 + p. [249], Table (R. " Fautes à corriger ").

German.

I.

Cain, ein Mysterium. Deutsch v. G. Parthey. Berlin,
Nicola'ische Buchh. 1831.   [12?
                        [*Centralblatt*, vii. 468.]

II.

Cain. Ein Mysterium. Von Lord Byron. Frei übers. v.
Adf. Seubert. Leipzig. 1871-1876.
                                [Kayser, 1877.]

Collation—
    Pp. 70.
    Note.—No. 779 of *Universal Bibliothek*.

Hebrew.

קַיִן/ שִׁיר־חִזָּיוֹן עַל־פִּי כִתְבֵי הַקֹּדֶשׁ/ מֵאֵת/ לוֹרְד בַּיְרוֹן/ תִּרְגֵּם מֵאַנְגְלִית
לְעִבְרִית/ דּוּד פְרִישְׁמַן/ וַוארשׁא תר״ם

Collation—
Pp. xl. + 44.

Hungarian.

I.

Kain. [*Cain*, transl. by Ilona Györy.] Franklin-Társulat.
1895.
[*Eg. Phil. Köz.,* 1901, xxv. 222.]

II.

Kain. [*Cain*, transl. by Lajos Mikes.] (*Magyar Könyvtár*,
p. 128.) B'pest, Lampel. 1898.
[*Eg. Phil. Köz.,* 1901, xxv. 224.]

International Language.

Kain./ Mistero/ de/ Lord Byron/ (Bajron)./ Tradukis A.
Kofman./ Nurnbergo./ Presejo de W. Tümmel./ 1896./
[8°

Collation—
Pp. ix. + 102.

Italian.

Caino : mistero, tradotto da Andrea Maffei. Milano, Pirola.
1852–6. [8°
[Pagliaini, 1901.]

Polish.

Kain./ Poemat Dramatyczny/ Lorda Bajrona/ W trzech
aktach/ przełożył/ Adam Pajgert./ A waż był chytrzejszy
nad wszystkie/ zwierzęta polne, które uczynił Pan Bóg./
Genezis R. III. w. I./ Lwów/ Nakładem Wydawnictwa
Dziennika Literackiego./ 1868./ [8°

Collation—
Pp. 125.

Russian.

I.

Каинъ...Переводъ Ефрена Барышева.
С.-Петербург, 1881.

II.

Каинъ...Переводъ П. А. Каленова. *Москва*, 1883.

Childe Harolds Pilgrimage.

I.

Childe Harold's Pilgrimage./ A Romaunt./ By/ Lord Byron./ L'univers est une espèce de livre, dont on n'a lu que la première page quand on n'a vu que son pays./ J'en ai feuilleté un assez grand nombre, que j'ai trouvé également mauvaises. Cet examen ne m'a point/ été infructueux. Je haïssais ma patrie. Toutes les impertinences des peuples divers, parmi lesquels j'ai vécu,/ m'ont réconcilié avec elle. Quand je n'aurais tiré d'autre bénéfice de mes voyages que celui-là, je n'en re/gretterais ni les frais, ni les fatigues./ *Le Cosmopolite.*/ London :/ Printed for John Murray, 32, Fleet-Street ;/ William Blackwood, Edinburgh ; and John Cumming, Dublin./ *By Thomas Davison, White-Friars.*/ 1812./　　　　　[4°

Collation—
Title, one page, pp. i., ii. ; Preface, pp. iii.-vi. ; Cont. (*Errata* on Reverse) ; Sec. Half-title, pp. **1, 2** ; Text, pp. **3–226** + two pages of publisher's advertisements, pp. **[227, 228]**. The Imprint (*T. Davison, Lombard Street,/ Whitefriars, London./*) is at the foot of p. [228].

Contents—

Childe Harold's Pilgrimage, Canto I. . . . . . p. 1
Childe Harold's Pilgrimage, Canto II. . . . p. 59
　Notes to Canto I. . p. 111
　Notes to Canto II. . p. 119
Poems—
　I. Written in an Album
　　　　　p. 165
　II. To . . . . : p. 166
　III. Stanzas . . . p. 169
　IV. Stanzas . . . p. 171
　V. Written at Athens
　　　　　p. 177
　VI. Written after Swimming, etc. . . . . . . p. 178
　VII. Song . . . p. 181
　VIII. Translation of a Greek War Song . . . . p. 183

IX. Translation of a Romaic Song . . . . . . p. 186
X. Written Beneath a Picture
　　　　　p. 189
XI. On Parting . p. 190
XII. To Thyrza . p. 192
XIII. Stanzas . . p. 195
XIV. To Thyrza . p. 197
Appendix—
Romaic Books and Authors
　　　　　p. 203
Specimens of the Romaic
　　　　　p. 207
Fac Simile of a Romaic Letter [inserted between Cont. and Half-title]

II.

Childe Harold's Pilgrimage./ A Romaunt./ By/ Lord Byron./ [Motto from *Le Cosmopolite*, seven lines.] The Second Edition./ London :/ Printed for John Murray, Fleet Street ;/ William Blackwood, Edinburgh ; and John Cumming,/ Dublin./ *By Thomas Davison, White-Friars./* 1812./ [8°

Collation—

Half-title ; Title, one leaf ; Preface ; Cont., pp. i.–xii. ; Note on the Errors in the Inscriptions at Orchomenus, *n.p.* ; Text, pp. 1–300. The Imprint (*T. Davison,/ Lombard Street, White-friars, London./*) is at the foot of p. 300.

Contents—

Childe Harold's Pilgrimage, Cantos I. (93 stanzas), II. (88 stanzas) (N.) . . . pp. 3–201
Poems (as in First Ed., Nos. I.–XIV.), . . . pp. 205–237
XV. Euthanasia . p. 241
XVI. Stanzas (" And thou art dead," etc.) . . . p. 244
XVII. Stanzas (" If sometimes," etc.) . . . p. 249
XVIII. On a Cornelian Heart, etc. . . . . p. 252
XIX. To a Youthful Friend p. 253
XX. To . . . (" Well ! thou art happy ") . . . p. 260
Appendix . . . p. 267
Specimens of the Romaic p. 273
Fac Simile of a Romaic Letter [inserted between Half-title and Title]

III.

Childe Harold's Pilgrimage,/ A Romaunt : and/ Other Poems./ By/ Lord Byron./ [Motto from *Le Cosmopolite,* six lines.] Third Edition./ London : *Printed by T. Davison, Whitefriars,/* For John Murray, Fleet Street ;/ W. Blackwood, Edinburgh ; and J. Cumming, Dublin./ 1812./ [8°

Note.—Collation and Cont. are identical with those of the Second Edition. The Note on the Errors in the Inscriptions at Orchomenus is omitted. The Fac Simile of a Romaic Letter is inserted at the end of the volume, after p. 300.

IV.

Childe Harold's Pilgrimage,/ a Romaunt :/ and/ Other Poems./ By Lord Byron./ [Motto from *Le Cosmopolite,* six lines.] Fourth Edition./ London :/ *Printed by T. Davison, Whitefriars,/* For John Murray, Fleet Street ;/ William Blackwood, and J. Ballantyne and Co. Edin-/ burgh ; and J. Cumming, Dublin./ 1812./ [8°

Collation—

Title, one leaf, pp. iii., iv. ; Preface, pp. v.–ix. ; Addition to the Preface, pp. ix.–xii. ; Cont., pp. xi., xii. (*sic*) ; Text, pp. *1–300*. The Imprint is at the foot of p. 300.

Note.—The Cont. are identical with those of the Second Edition. The Fac Simile of the Romaic Letter is inserted at the beginning of the volume (in a bound copy between pp. 184, 185).

V.

Childe Harold's Pilgrimage,/ A Romaunt :/ and/ Other Poems./ By/ Lord Byron./ [Motto from *Le Cosmopolite*, six lines.] Fifth Edition./ London :/ *Printed by T. Davison, Whitefriars,*/ For John Murray, (*removed to*) Albemarle-Street ;/ William Blackwood, Edinburgh ; and J. Cumming,/ Dublin./ 1812./ [8°

Collation—

Half-title, pp. iii., iv. ; Title, one leaf, pp. v., vi. ; Preface, pp. vii.–xi. ; Addition to the Preface, pp. xi.–xiv. ; Cont., pp. xv.–xvi. ; Text, pp. *1–300*. The Imprint is at the foot of p. 300.

Note.—The Cont. are identical with those of the Second Edition ; but the Fac Simile of the Romaic Letter is not mentioned in the Table of Cont. nor inserted in the volume.

VI.

Childe Harold's Pilgrimage,/ A Romaunt :/ and/ Other Poems./ By Lord Byron./ [Motto—*Le Cosmopolite*.] The First American Edition./ Philadelphia :/ Published by Moses Thomas,/ No. 52, Chestnut-Street./ William Fry, Printer. 1812./ [12°

Collation—

Pp. 179.

Note.—"For sale in Philadelphia, by the publisher, M. Carey, and Bradford and Inskip ; in New York, by Inskip and Bradford, and J. Eastburn ; in Boston, by Munroe and Francis, and West and Blake ; and in Baltimore, by F. Lucas, Junr. William Fry, Printer. 1812."

VII.

Childe Harold's Pilgrimage,/ A Romaunt :/ And/ Other Poems./ By/ Lord Byron./ [Motto from *Le Cosmopolite*, six lines.] The Sixth Edition./ London :/ *Printed by T. Davison, Whitefriars,*/ For John Murray, Bookseller to the Admiralty,/ And to the Board of Longitude,/ 50, Albemarle-Street./ 1813./ [8°

Note.—The Collation and Cont. are identical with those of the Fifth Edition ; but in the Table of Cont. the words "Fac Simile of a Romaic Letter" occur as in the Fourth Edition ; but in the copy belonging to the British Museum the letter is not inserted. In the Sixth Edition the words *Childe Harold's Pilgrimage* are printed in Roman type, and the words *A Romaunt* in Gothic type, whereas in all other editions *Childe*, etc., is in Gothic, and *A Romaunt* in Roman type.

VIII.

Childe Harold's Pilgrimage,/ A Romaunt :/ And/ Other Poems./ By/ Lord Byron./ [Motto from *Le Cosmopolite*, six lines.] Seventh Edition./ London :/ *Printed by Thomas Davison, Whitefriars,*/ For John Murray, Albe-marle-Street,/ 1814./ [8º

Collation—

Half-title ; Title, one leaf ; Preface, etc. ; Cont., pp. iii.–xvi. ; Text, pp. *1–296*. The Imprint (*T. Davison, Lombard-Street,/ Whitefriars, London./*) is at the foot of p. 296. The Fac Simile of the Romaic Letter is inserted between pp. 294, 295.

Contents—

To Ianthe . . . p. 3		XXIV. To Time . p. 250
Childe Harold's, etc., Canto I. (93 stanzas) . . . p. 6		XXV. Translation of a Romaic Love Song . p. 252
Childe Harold's, etc., Canto II. (98 stanzas) . . p. 65		XXVI. A Song (" Thou art not false," etc.) . . p. 255
Notes to Canto I. . p. 121		XXVII. Origin of Love p. 257
Notes to Canto II. . p. 125		XXVIII. Remember him
Poems—		p. 257
Nos. I.–XX. as in Eds. II.– VI. . . . . . p. 191		XXIX. Lines inscribed upon a Cup formed from a Skull
XXI. From the Portuguese p. 245		p. 261
XXII. Impromptu in Reply to a Friend . . . p. 246		Romaic Books and Authors p. 264
XXIII. Address to Drury-Lane Theatre . . . p. 246		Specimen of the Romaic p. 271

IX.

Childe Harolds Pilgrimage,/ A Romaunt :/ And/ Other Poems./ By/ Lord Byron./ [Motto from *Le Cosmopolite*, five lines.] Eighth Edition./ London :/ Printed for John Murray, Albemarle-Street :/ *By Thomas Davison, White-friars.*/ 1814./ [8º

Collation—

Title, one leaf, pp. i., ii. ; Preface, pp. iii.–vii. ; Addition to the Preface, pp. vii.–x. ; Cont., pp. xi., xii. ; Text, pp. *1–296*. *Note.*—The Cont. are identical with those of the Seventh Edition.

X.

Childe Harold's Pilgrimage,/ A Romaunt :/ And/ Other
Poems./ By/ Lord Byron./ [Motto from *Le Cosmopolite,*
five lines.] Tenth Edition./   London :/ Printed for John
Murray ; Albemarle-Street,/ 1815./   [8º

Collation—
    Title (R. *T. Davison, Lombard street/ Whitefriars, London./*),
pp. i., ii. ; Preface, pp. iii.–vii. ; Addition to the Preface, pp.
vii.–x. ; Cont., pp. xi., xii. ; Text, pp. 1–302.   The Imprint
(*T. Davison, Lombard-Street, /Whitefriars, London./*) is in the
centre of p. [304].
    Note.—The Cont. are identical with those of the Seventh
Edition, save for the insertion of a thirtieth (No. XXX., p. 263)
poem, "On the Death of Sir Peter Parker."

XI.

Childe Harold's Pilgrimage./   Canto the Third./   By Lord
Byron./ "Afin que cette application vous forçât de penser
à autre chose ; il n'y a/ en vérité de remède que celui-là
et le temps."/   Lettre du Roi de Prusse à D'Alembert,
Sept. 7, 1776./   London :/ Printed for John Murray,
Albemarle-Street./   1816./   [8º

Collation—
    Half-title (R. Published THIS DAY in 8vo. 5*s.* 6*d.*/ THE
PRISONER OF CHILLON ;/ A DREAM ;/ And Other Poems./
By the Right Hon. Lord Byron./   *T. Davison, Lombard Street,/
Whitefriars, London./*) ; Title, one leaf ; Text, pp. **1**–79.
    Note (1).—The Imprint, as above, is at the foot of p. 79 ; and
on the reverse of p. 79, "List of the Poems," etc.
    Note (2).—*Childe Harold's Pilgrimage,* Canto III., was pub-
lished at Boston, 1817, 16º, pp. 72 ; and, together with *The
Prisoner of Chillon* and other Poems, at Philadelphia, 1817, 16º

XII.

Childe Harold's Pilgrimage./   Canto the Fourth./   By Lord
Byron./   Visto ho Toscana, Lombardia, Romagna,/ Quel
Monte che divide, e quel che serra/ Italia, e un mare e
l'altro, che la bagna./   Ariosto, Satira iii./   London :/
John Murray, Albemarle-Street./   1818./   [8º

Collation—
    Title, pp. i., ii. ; Dedication, pp. iii.–xiv. ; Cont., *n.p.* ; Text,
pp. **1**–257. The Imprint (*T. Davison, Lombard-Street, Whitefriars, London.*) is at the foot of p. [259].

Contents—

Childe Harold's, etc., Canto IV. [N.] . . . . . p. 3	Translation . . . p. 241
Poems. *Romance*, etc.	Per Monaca. Sonetto di
p. 240	Vittorelli . . . p. 256
	Translation . . . p. 257

Note (1).—In another copy, Cont., *n.p.*, precedes the Dedication.

Note (2).—*Childe Harold's Pilgrimage*, Canto IV., to which are added *Beppo*, and other Poems, was published at Philadelphia in 1818, 24°, pp. 270.

XIII.

Childe Harold's/ Pilgrimage./ Canto the Fourth./ By Lord Byron./ [Motto—Ariost., Sat. iii., four lines.] New York :/ Published by James Eastburn and Co./ At the Literary Rooms, Broadway./ Clayton & Kingsland, Printers./ 1818./ [12°

Collation—
Pp. 143.

XIV.

Childe Harold's Pilgrimage,/ A Romaunt :/ And/ Other Poems./ By/ Lord Byron./ [Motto from *Le Cosmopolite*, six lines.] Eleventh Edition./ London :/ John Murray, Albemarle-Street./ 1819./ [8°

Note.—The Collation of the preliminary matter is identical with that of the Tenth Edition. The Cont. are also identical, save that on p. 274 a note headed " Conclusion " (on pp. 301, 302 of the Tenth Edition) is omitted. The Imprint (*London :| Printed by Thomas Davison, Whitefriars.|*) is at the foot of p. 274.

XV.

Childe Harold's/ Pilgrimage./ A Romaunt,/ In Four Cantos./ By the Right Honourable/ Lord Byron./ In Two Volumes./ Vol. I./ [Vol. II.] Containing Cantos I., II./ London:/ John Murray,/Albemarle-Street./ 1819./ [8°

Collation—
Vol. I. : Title (R. *London :| Printed by T. Davison, Whitefriars.|*), pp. iii., iv. ; Half-title (R. Motto, *Le Cosmopolite*, eight lines), pp. v., vi. ; Preface, pp. vii.–xiv. ; Cont., one leaf ; Text, pp. *1–218*. The Imprint (*T. Davison, Lombard Street,| Whitefriars, London.|*) is in the centre of p. [220].

Vol. II. : Title (R. Imprint, as above) ; Cont., one leaf ; Text, pp. *1–273*; Advt. of *Historical Illustrations* (R. Imprint, *London :| Printed by Thomas Davison, Whitefriars*), pp. [*275, 276*].

VOL. VII. 2 B

XVI.

Childe Harold's Pilgrimage. [Two vols.] Leipzig, Brockhaus. 1820.   [8°
        [Kayser, 1834.]

XVII.

Childe Harold's/ Pilgrimage./ A Romaunt./ By Lord
Byron./ London :/ Printed and Published by W. Dugdale,/
Russell Court, Drury Lane./ 1825./   [12°
Collation—
 Pp. vi. + 7–182.

XVIII.

Childe Harold's Pilgrimage. [Two vols.] Paris, A. and
W. Galignani. 1825.   [32°

XIX.

Childe Harold's/ Pilgrimage,/ A Romaunt :/ By Lord
Byron./ London :/ Printed and Published by W. Dug-
dale/ 23, Russell Court, Drury Lane./ 1826./ [12°
Collation—
 Pp. vi. + 1–162.

XX.

Childe Harold's/ Pilgrimage ;/ A Romaunt./ In Four
Cantos./ By Lord Byron./ London :/ Printed for Thomas
Colmer,/ 2, Bell-Isle, Battle Bridge./ 1827./ [24°
Collation—
 Pp. vi. + 161.

XXI.

Childe Harold's Pilgrimage, a poem by Lord Byron. [Two
vols.] Paris. 1827.   [16°
    [*Le Moniteur*, etc., 1845.]

XXII.

Childe Harold's Pilgrimage./ A Romaunt./ By the/ Right
Hon. Lord Byron./ London :/ John Duncombe, 19,
Little Queen Street,/ Holborn./ [1831 ?] [12°
Collation—
 Pp. viii. + 9–270.
 Note.—The Front. is "Lord Byron," by T. Phillips, R.A.,
engraved by R. Page.

XXIII.

Childe Harold's/ Pilgrimage./ A Romaunt/ By/ Lord
Byron./ Campe's Edition./ Nuremberg and New York./
Printed and Published by/ Frederick Campe and Cº/
[1831.]   [12º

Collation—
  Pp. 333.

XXIV.

Childe Harold's/ Pilgrimage./ A Romaunt./ By/ Lord
Byron./ London :/ John Murray, Albemarle Street./
1837./   [8º

Collation—
  Pp. 329. The Imprint (*London :| Printed by A. Spottiswoode,|
New-Street-Square.|*) is in the centre of p. [330].
  Note.—The Front., " Byron," is engraved by E. Finden, from
the portrait by E. Sanders. The Vignette, or illustrated Title,
is the " Lake of Geneva," engraved by E. Finden from a drawing
by G. Stainfield, R.A. This edition is bound in green cloth,
stamped with coat-of-arms, uniform with No. xiv. of Miscellaneous Poems.

XXV.

Childe Harold's Pilgrimage. Mannheim, Hoffmann. 1837.
                                                     [12º
                      [Kayser, 1841.]

XXVI.

Childe Harold's Pilgrimage./ A Romaunt./ By Lord
Byron./ London :/ John Murray, Albemarle Street./
1841./   [8º

Collation—
  Half-title (R. Motto from *Le Cosmopolite*, seven lines), pp. i., ii. ;
Title (R. *Bradbury and Evans,| Printers extraordinary to the
Queen,| Whitefriars.|*), pp. iii., iv. ; Preface, and Addition to
Preface, pp. v.–viii. ; List of Embellishments, pp. ix.–xi. ; Half-
title, pp. xiii., xiv. ; To Ianthe, pp. xv., xvi. ; Text, pp. *1*–320.
The Imprint, as above, is at the foot of p. 320.
  Note.—The Front. is a portrait of " Lord Byron, in his Alba-
nian Dress," by T. Phillips, R.A., engraved by W. Finden. The
Title-vignette on illustrated title is the " Monument of Lysicrates,"
drawn by H. Warren, engraved by W. Finden. There are fifty-
nine other " embellishments," and, inserted between pp. [228],
[229], a Map of Lord Byron's Route through Spain, Portugal,
Holland, etc., with " Picturesque Border."

XXVII.

Childe Harold's Pilgrimage, with Notes by Lord Byron, Carton demi rel. Jolie éd. London. 1842.   [12°
[*Le Moniteur*, etc., 1845.]

XXVIII.

Childe Harold's Pilgrimage./   A Romaunt./   By Lord Byron./   London :/ John Murray, Albemarle Street./ 1853./   [8°

Collation—
    Pp. xii. (To Ianthe, pp. xi., xii.) + 311. The Imprint (*London :/ Bradbury and Evans, Printers, Whitefriars./*) is in the centre of p. [312].

XXIX.

Childe Harold herausg. von Aug. Mommsen. Hamburg, Th. Niemeyer. 1853. [Hamburg, 1869.]   [8°
[Kayser, 1860.]

Collation—
    Pp. iv. + 189.

XXX.

Childe Harold's/ Pilgrimage,/ von/ Lord Byron./   [Two Vols.] Erklärt/ von/ Ferd. Brockerhoff./   Erstes Bändchen./   Berlin./   Verlag von Th. Chr. Fr. Enslin./   1854./ [8°

Collation—
    Pp. 163.
    Note.—Bdchn. of *Sammlung englischer Schriffsteller.* Berlin, Th. Enslin. 1853–1855. "Siebentes Bändchen" contains Cantos I., II. ; "Neuntes Bändchen" (pp. 214), published in 1855, contains Cantos III., IV.

XXXI.

Childe Harold's Pilgrimage/   A Romaunt/   By Lord Byron/ Illustrated From Original Sketches/   London :/   John Murray, Albemarle Street./   1859./   [8°

Collation—
    Title (R. Motto, *Le Cosmopolite*, six lines ; Note, two lines) ; Vignette, "Newstead Abbey" (R. The Illustrations drawn on Wood by Percival Skelton./   Engraved by J. W. Whymper and J. Cooper./) ; List of Illustrations, four pages ; Text, pp. *1–329.* The Imprint (*Printed by R. and R. Clark, Edinburgh*) is at the foot of p. 329.
    Note.—This edition was reissued in 1869.

XXXII.

Childe Harold's Pilgrimage./ A Romaunt./ By Lord Byron./ New Edition./ London :/ John Murray, Albemarle Street./ 1860./ [8?

Collation—
Pp. 192. The Imprint (*London : Printed by William Clowes and Sons, Stamford Street*) is at the foot of p. 192.
Note.—Murray's Complete Edition. ·Price One Shilling. The Front. is "The Earliest Portrait of Byron. Taken at the age of 7 years, from an original by Kay, Edinburgh," engraved by E. Finden.

XXXIII.

Childe Harold's Pilgrimage./ A Romaunt./ By Lord Byron./ A New Edition./ London :/ John Murray, Albemarle Street./ 1860./ [8?

Collation—
Pp. 60. The Imprint (*London : Printed by William Clowes and Sons, Stamford Street,| And Charing Cross.|*) is on Reverse of Title.
Note.—" Murray's Complete Edition." Price Sixpence. The Front. is a lithograph of the portrait of Lord Byron, by T. Phillips, R.A.

XXXIV.

Childe Harold's Pilgrimage. A Romaunt. Leipzig, B. Tauchnitz. 1862. [16?
[Kayser, 1865.]

XXXV.

Childe Harold's/ Pilgrimage/ A Romaunt/ By/ Lord Byron/ With a Memoir/ By/ William Spalding, A.M./ Professor of Logic and Rhetoric in the University of Saint Andrews/ Illustrated/ London/ Charles Griffin and Company/ Stationer's Hall Court/ [1866] [8?

Collation—
Pp. 180.
Note.—The Front. is an engraving of the medallion by E. W. Wyon.

XXXVI.

Childe Harold's Pilgrimage. A Romaunt. Mit erläut. Anmerkungen zum Schul= u. Privatunterricht bearb. von P. Weeg. 1867. [8?

Note.—No. V., Sammlung gediegener u. interessanter Werke der englischen Litteratur. Münster, Brunn's Verl. 1868–1870. [Kayser, 1871.]

XXXVII.

Byron's/ Childe Harold's/ Pilgrimage/ A Romaunt/ With Notes/ W. & R. Chambers/ London and Edinburgh/ 1877/   [12º

Collation—
  Pp. 180.

XXXVIII.

Lord Byron/ Childe Harold's/ Pilgrimage/ Édition classique/ Par/ James Darmesteter/ Docteur ès-Lettres/ Directeur-Adjoint à l'École des Hautes Études/ Paris/ librairie Ch. Delagrave/ 15, rue Soufflot, 15/ 1882/
                                                          [8º

Collation—
  Pp. xxxv. + 342.

XXXIX.

Childe Harold's Pilgrimage. Texte anglais, revu et annoté par l'abbé A. Julien. Paris, Poussielque frères. 1883.
                                                          [12º
                          [Lorenz, 1886.]

XL.

Clarendon Press Series/ Byron/ Childe Harold/ Edited/ With Introduction and Notes/ By/ H. F. Tozer, M.A./ Fellow and Tutor of Exeter College, Oxford/ At the Clarendon Press/ 1885/ [*All rights reserved*]/ [8º
Collation—
  Pp. 336.

XLI.

Childe Harold's Pilgrimage. Illustrated. London, Chatto. 1885.   [8º
                          [*Eng. Cat.*, 1891.]

XLII.

Lord Byron,/ Childe Harold's/ Pilgrimage./ A Romaunt./ Erklärt/ von/ August Mommsen./ Berlin./ Weidmannsche Buchhandlung./ 1885./   [8º
Collation—
  Pp. xxxvi. + 367.

XLIII.

Cassell's National Library./ Childe Harold's/ Pilgrimage./ By/ Lord Byron./ Cassell & Company, Limited :/ London, Paris, New York & Melbourne./ 1886./ [16º

Collation—
Pp. 192.

XLIV.

Childe Harold's/ Pilgrimage/ A Romaunt/ By Lord Byron/ Illustrated/ Boston/ Ticknor and Company/ 1886/ [8º

Collation—
Pp. 236.

XLV.

Childe Harold's Pilgrimage : edited with Notes by W. J. Rolfe, Philadelphia. 1886. [16º
[Detroit Public Library.]

XLVI.

Childe Harold's Pilgrimage. Leipzig, Gressner & Schramm. 1886. [16º
[Kayser, 1887.]

XLVII.

Childe Harold's Pilgrimage. By Lord Byron. Im Auszuge m. Anmerkgn. zum Schulgebrauch hrsg. v. Mart. Krummacher. Mit Anmerkgn. unter dem Text.

Note.—No. 13 of "English Authors." Bielefeld, Velhagen, and Klasing. 1885–1886. [Kayser, 1887.]

XLVIII.

Childe Harold's/ Pilgrimage/ A Romaunt/ By/ Lord Byron/ London/ George Routledge and Sons/ Broadway, Ludgate Hill/ Glasgow and New York/ 1888/ [16º

Collation—
Pp. viii. + *9–320.*
Note.—Part of " Routledge's Pocket Library."

XLIX.

Childe Harold's Pilgrimage. Im Auszuge hrsg. v. Mart. Krummacher. 1891. [Reissued in 1893.] [12º

Note.—Part of "English Authors," *vide supra,* No. xlvii.

L.

Sir John Lubbock's Hundred Best Books/ 29/ Childe Harold's/ Pilgrimage/ A Romaunt/ By/ Lord Byron/ London/ George Routledge and Sons, Limited/ Broadway, Ludgate Hill/ Manchester and New York/ 1892/ [8°

Collation—
  Pp. x. + *11*-249.

LI.

Byron's/ Childe Harold/ With Introduction and Notes/ By/ H. G. Keene, Hon. M.A. Oxon.,/ Fellow of Calcutta University, Author of " A Manual of/ French Literature," etc./ London/ George Bell & Sons, York St, Covent Garden/ And New York/ 1893/   [8°

Collation—
  Pp. xx. + 255.

LII.

Byron/ Childe Harold/ Texte Anglais/ Publié avec une Notice, des Arguments/ Et des Notes en Français/ Par Émile Chasles/ Inspecteur général de l'Instruction publique/ Paris/ Librairie Hachette et Cⁱᵉ/ 79, Boulevard Saint-Germain, 79/ 1893/   [8°

Collation—
  Pp. xxvi. + 261.
  Note.—This edition was reissued in 1894.

LIII.

Childe Harold's Pilgrimage: a Romaunt. New York, T. Y. Crowell & Co. 1894.
                              [*Amer. Cat.*, 1895.]

Collation—
  Pp. 9 + 283.

LIV.

Arnold's British Classics for Schools/ General Editor :/ J. Churton Collins, M.A./ Childe Harold's/ Pilgrimage/ Edited by/ The Rev. E. C. Everard Owen, M.A./ Late Fellow of New College, Oxford ; Assistant Master/ In Harrow School./ Edward Arnold/ London/ 37 Bedford Street/ New York/ 70 Fifth Avenue/ [1897]   [8°

Collation—
  Pp. lxii. + 236.

LV.

Childe/ Harold/ A Romaunt/ George/ Gordon/ Lord/
Byron/ 1898 . Published . by . J. M. Dent . / And .
Co. . Aldine . House . London . E.C./ [8°

Collation—
Pp. xii. + 310 + Note (one leaf) by Editor, I. G., October 1,
1898.
Note.—Part of the "Temple Classics," edited by Israel
Gollmer, M.A. The Front. is a photogravure of the portrait of
"George Gordon Lord Byron," by T. Phillips, R.A.

LVI.

Childe Harold's/ Pilgrimage/ A Romaunt by Lord Byron/
Cantos I. and II./ Edited with Notes and an Introduc-
tion by/ Edward E. Morris/ Professor of English in the
University of Melbourne/ London/ Macmillan and Co.,
Limited/ New York : The Macmillan Company/ 1899/
All rights reserved/ [8°

Collation—
Pp. xxxvi. + 115.

LVII.

Childe Harold's/ Pilgrimage/ A Romaunt by Lord Byron/
Cantos III. and IV./ Edited with Notes and an Introduction by/ Edward E. Morris/ Professor of English in
the University of Melbourne/ London/ Macmillan and
Co., Limited/ New York : The Macmillan Company/
1899/ *All rights reserved/* [8°

Collation—
Pp. xxxvi. + 168.
Note.—The Introduction (pp. vii.–xxxvi.) is a repetition of the
Introduction to the preceding volume.

LVIII.

Childe Harold's Pilgrimage : a Romaunt. Cantos 1, 2, 3,
and 4 ; Edited with Notes and Introduction by E. Morris.
New York, The Macmillan Co. [Two vols.] 1899. [8°
[*Amer. Cat.*, 1900.]

Collation—
Vol. I. : pp. 36 + 115.
Vol. II. : pp. 36 + 168.
Note.—Part of "Macmillan's English Classics."

VOL. VII. 2 C

LIX.

Childe Harold's Pilgrimage: a Romaunt. Edited with Introduction and Notes by Andrew J. George. New York., The Macmillan Co. 1899. [16º [*Amer. Cat.*, 1900.]

Collation—
Pp. 34 + 282.
Note.—Part of "Macmillan's Pocket English Classics."

LX.

Childe Harold's Pilgrimage. New York, Cassell. 1900. [*Amer. Cat.*, 1901.]

Collation—
Pp. 192.
Note.—Part of "Cassell's National Library," N.S.

LXI.

Lord Byron/ Childe Harold's/ Pilgrimage/ Canto II./ Edited by/ John Downie, M.A./ Editor of Macaulay's Lives of Johnson and Goldsmith, Etc. Etc./ London/ Blackie and Son, Limited, 50 Old Bailey, E.C./ Glasgow and Dublin/ 1901/ [8º

Collation—
Pp. 47.

LXII.

Lord Byron/ Childe Harold's/ Pilgrimage/ Canto III./ Edited by/ John Downie, M.A./ [etc., *vide supra*, No. lxi.] 1901/ [8º

Collation—
Pp. 47.
Note.—This and the preceding volume form part of "Blackie's English Classics."

Translations of Childe Harold's Pilgrimage.

Armenian.

Lord Byron/ Childe Harold's Pilgrimage/ Italy/ [Canto IV.] Venice/ Printed/ at the Armenian Monastery of S. Lazarus/ 1872/ [16º

Collation—
Pp. 147.

Note.—The Armenian verse, translated by Gheuond Alíshanian, accompanies the English original. The Notes are in the Armenian language.

Bohemian.

Childe Haroldova pouť Přeložila El. Krásnohorská [in Kabinetní Knihovna]. 1890.

Danish.

Junker Harolds Pilgrimsfart./ Et Romantisk Kvad./ Af/ Byron./ Oversat af/ Adolf Hansen/ Kjøbenhavn./ Forlagt af J. H. Schubothes Boghandel./ Græbes Bogtrykkerei. 1880/   [8?

Collation—
    Pp. 237.

French.

I.

Le Pélerinage de Childe Harold, poème romantique de lord Byron, traduit en vers français par l'auteur des *Helléniennes* et des *Mélodies poétiques.* Paris, Dupont. 1828.
                                                           [18?
                        [Quérard, 1846.]

Collation—
    Pp. 288.

II.

Le Pélerinage de Childe Harold, traduit par P. A. Deguer. Paris, Ponthieu. 1828.   [18?
                        [Quérard, 1846.]

Collation—
    Pp. 84.

III.

Le Pélerinage/ de/ Childe Harold/ Traduction en vers français/ Par/ Eugène Quiertant./ [Motto, *Le Cosmopolite,* nine lines.] Paris/ Librairie de Ch. Blériot,/ rue Bonaparte, 25. 1861./   [8?

Collation—
    Pp. viii. + 266 + "Note de L'Éditeur," one leaf.
    Note.—Le premier chant de cette traduction avait déja été publié en 1852. [Lorenz, 1867.]

IV.

Childe Harold/ Poëme de Lord Byron/ Traduit en vers
    français/ Par/ Lucien Davésiès de Pontès./ Tome
    premier./ Paris/ E. Dentu, libraire-éditeur,/ Galerie
    D'Orléans, Palais-Royal./ 1862./ [8º
    Collation—
    Vol. I. : pp. lv. + 232.
    Vol. II. : pp. 334 + " Errata," one leaf, p. [335].

V.

Le Pélerinage de Childe Harold, traduit en vers d'après
    l'édition anglaise de 1812 ; précédé de Marie-Magdaleine,
    poëme, et de diverses poésies, par Victor Robert Jones,
    Saint-Quentin, *imprimerie Moureau.* 1862.   [12º
                                        [Lorenz, 1867.]

VI.

Childe Harold, poëme de lord Byron, traduit en vers français
    par Lucien Davésiès de Pontès, 2e édition revue et cor-
    rigée par le bibliophile Jacob. Paris, *Amyot.* 1870. [12º
                                        [Lorenz, 1876.]

VII.

Childe Harold. Expliqué littéralement, traduit en français
    et annoté par H. Bellet. Paris, *Hachette et Cie.* 1881.
                                                        [12º
                                        [Lorenz, 1886.]

VIII.

Childe Harold's Pilgrimage. Traduction française littérale,
    par l'Abbé A. Julien. Paris, *Poussielque frères.* 1883.
                                                        [12º
                                        [Lorenz, 1886.]

IX.

Childe Harold, Édition classique, précédée d'une notice
    littéraire, par M. A. Elwall. Paris, *Delalain frères.* 1892.
                                                        [12º
                                        [Lorenz, 1900.]

X.

Childe Harold, Édition classique, avec une notice bio-
    graphique et littéraire, un appendice et des notes par
    Douglas Gibb. Paris, *Belin frères.* 1892.   [12º
                                        [Lorenz, 1900.]

German.

I.

Harold, der Verwiesene. Aus. d. Engl. v. Karl Baldamus. Leipzig, Hartmann. 1835. [8º

[Kayser, 1841.]

II.

Ritter Harold's Pilgerfahrt./ Aus dem Englischen/ des/ Lord Byron./ Im Versmass des Originals übersetzt/ von/ Zedlitz./ Stuttgart und Tübingen,/ Verlag der J. G. Cotta'schen Buchhandlung. 1836./ [8º

Collation—
Pp. xvi. + 381 + Berichtungen, p. [382].

III.

Jungherrn Harold's Pilgerfahrt. Aus d. Engl. ins Deutsche übersetzt von Dᵣ Herm. v. Pommer Esche. Stralsund, Löffler'sche Buch. 1839. [8º

[Kayser, 1841.]

IV.

Erster Gesang des Childe Harald. Freie Uebertragung in Reimen v. C. D. Ansbach, Dollfuss. 1845. [12º

[Kayser, 1848.]

V.

Byron's/ Ritter Harold/ von/ Adolf Böttger/ Diamantausgabe./ Leipzig./ Druck und Verlag von Otto Wigand./ 1846./ [16º

Collation—
Pp. 194.
Note.—The Front. is a portrait of " Byron " (by G. Sanders), engraved by A. H. Payne.

VI.

Childe Harold's/ Pilgerfahrt/ von/ Lord George Gordon Byron./ Aus dem Englischen im Versmass des Originals/ übersetzt/ von/ Alexander Büchner./ Frankfurt a/ M./ Verlag von Meidinger Sohn und Cie./ 1853./ [16º

Collation—
Pp. xxiii. + 342.
Note.—The translation was reissued in 1855.

VII.

Harold's/ Pilgerfahrt./ Aus dem Englischen des Lord
Byron./ Uebersetzt von/ Erich von Monbart./ Köln,
1865./ Druck, Franz Greven, Burgmauer-Ecke 113.
[8?

Collation—
Pp. 143.

VIII.

Childe Harold's/ Pilgerfahrt/ von/ Lord Byron./ Deutsch/
von/ A. H. Janert./ Hildburghausen./ Verlag des Bibliographischen Instituts./ 1868./   [8?

Collation—
Pp. 191.
Note.—No. 87 of the " Bibliothek ausländischer Klassiker."

IX.

Jung Harold's/ Pilgerfahrt./ Von Byron./ Aus dem Englischen metrisch übersetzt/ von/ Ferdinand Schmidt./
Berlin./ Verlag von W. O. H. Stempelmann./ 1869./
[12?]

Collation—
Pp. 132 + " Anmerkungen," pp. [133, 134].

X.

Ritter Harold's Pilgerfahrt. Eine Romanze v. Lord Byron.
Frei ubers. v. Adf. Seubert.   [16?
[Kayser, 1877.]

Collation—
Pp. 224.
Note.—Nos. 516, 517 of the " Universal=Bibliothek," Leipzig,
1871–76.

XI.

Childe Harold's Pilgerfahrt. Ein Epos. Ubertr. v. F.
Dobbert. 1893.   [8?
[Kayser, 1894.]

Collation—
Pp. vi. + 192.
Note.—Part of the " Bibliothek der Gesammtlitteratur d. In= u.
Auslandes."

Hungarian.

Childe Harold/ Byron/ után/ anya nyelvéb"ol magyarra forditotta/ Bickersteth Johanka/ Nyomtatta Puky Miklos Genfben/ 1857/ [8º

Collation—
  Pp. 211. [Line-borders.]

Italian.

I.

L'Italia,/ Canto IV./ del pellegrinaggio/ di Childe H*A*Rold,/ Scritto/ da Lord Byron,/ E tradotto/ da Michele Leoni./ Italia,/ 1819./ [8º

Collation—
  Pp. 77.

II.

Il pellegrinaggio del Giovine Aroldo: poema di Lord Byron, tradotto dá Giuseppe Gazzino genovese. Genova, tipografia arcivescovile, 1836. [8º
[*Bibl. Ital.,* Nov.–Dec., 1836.]

III.

L'Italia/ Canto/ di Lord Byron/ Accomodato/ All' indole del verso italiano/ da/ Melchior Missirini/ Publicato per cura/ del professore/ Francesco Longhena./ Milano/ Coi tipi di Vincenzo Guglielmini/ 1848/ [8º

Collation—
  Pp. 95.

IV.

Il pellegrinaggio del giovane Aroldo: poema recato in italiano da Fr. Armenio. Napoli, 1858. [8º
[Pagliaini, 1901.]

V.

Il pellegrinaggio del giovane Aroldo: con la traduzione armena. Ultimo canto. Venezia. t. s. Lazard, 1860.
[8º
[Pagliaini, 1901.]

VI.

Byron/ Pellegrinaggio D'Aroldo/ Traduzione/ di/ Giovanni
Giovio/ [Then something on poetry/] Schak./ Milano/
Giuseppe Bernardoni/ Tipografo-editore/ 1866/   [8°

Collation—
  Pp. xxxiii. + 122 + "Note," pp. [125, 126].

VII.

Italia/ Canto di Giorgio Byron/ Tradotto/ da/ Andrea
Maffei./ Firenze,/ Successori le Monnier./ 1872./
                                                    [8°

Collation—
  Pp. 190.
  Note.—This edition was reissued in 1874 and in 1897.

V·III.

Il pellegrinaggio/ D'Aroldo./ Poema/ di Lord Byron/ Tra-
dotto/ da Carlo Faccioli./ [Emblem, rose and butterfly,
with motto, "*Non Bramo Altr' Esca.*"] Firenze,/ G.
Barbèra, editore./ 1873./   [8°

Collation—
  Pp. xii. + 249 + Indice, p. [251].

Polish.

I.

Poezye w tłumaczeniu polskiém. Tom. I. (przez Michała
Budzyńskiego) : Wędrówki Czaild Harolda. pp. 256.
M. Wolf : Petersburg, 1857.   [8°.

II.

*Pielgrzymka Czajlda Harolda...*z-polszczone przez Wiktora
z Baworowa, *etc. we Lwowie,* 1857.   [12°.

III.

*Wędrówki Czaild-Harolda...*Przełożył Frederyk Krauze.
1865–71.

IV.

*Wędrówki Rycerza Harolda...*Przekład Jana Kasprowicza.
Warszawa, 1895.

V.

*Wędrówki Czaild-Harolda...*Tłómaczony...przez A. A.
K[rajewskiego]. *Kraków,* 1896.

Russian.

I.

Чайльдъ-Гарольдъ . . . пер. Д. Минаева. ["Русское
Слово," 1864.]

II.

Чайльдъ-Гарольдъ...пер. П. А. Козлова. ["Русская
Мысль," 1890. No. 1, 2, 11.]

Swedish.

Childe Harolds/ Pilgrimsfärd/ Af/ Lord Byron./ Öfversatt
Af/ A. F. Skjöldebrand./ Stockholm./ Tryckt Hos
Johan Hörberg,/ 1832./   [8°
Collation—
    Pp. 192.

The Corsair.

I.

The Corsair,/ A Tale./ By Lord Byron./ "——— I suoi
pensieri in lui dormir non ponno."/ Tasso, *Canto decimo,*
Gerusalemme Liberata./ London :/ *Printed by Thomas*
Davison, Whitefriars, For John Murray, Albemarle-
Street./ 1814./   [8°
Collation—
    Half-title, one leaf, pp. i., ii. ; Title, one leaf, pp. iii., iv. ;
Dedication, " To Thomas Moore, Esq.," pp. v.–xi. ; Text (and
Notes), pp. *1*–100.
    Note.—The Text numbers 1863 lines, the half-lines 154, 159,
669 being reckoned as whole lines. Other half-lines are not so
reckoned, and the First Edition actually numbers 1860 lines.

II.

The Corsair,/ A Tale./ By Lord Byron./ "——— I suoi
pensieri in lui dormir non ponno."/ Tasso, *Canto decimo,*
Gerusalemme Liberata./ Second Edition./ London :/
Printed by Thomas Davison, Whitefriars,/ For John
Murray, Albemarle-Street./ 1814./   [8°

Collation—
　　Half-title, etc. (*vide supra*) ; Text, with Notes and Six Poems,
pp. *1*–108.　The Imprint (*T. Davison, Lombard Street,| White-
friars, London.|*) is at the foot of p. 108.

Poems—

To a Lady weeping . p. [101]	Inscription on the Monument
From the Turkish . p. 102	of a Newfoundland Dog
Sonnet, To Genevra (" Thine	p. 106
eyes," etc.) . . . . p. 104	Farewell (" Farewell ! if
Sonnet, To Genevra (" Thy	ever," etc.) . . . . p. 108
cheek," etc.) . . . p. 105	

III.

The Corsair,/ A Tale./ . . . Third Edition./ . . . 1814./
　　　　　　　　　　　　　　　　　　　　　　　　[8º

Collation—
　　Vide supra, No. 1.　The Imprint (*Printed by T. Davison,
Lombard-Street,| Fleet Street.|*) is at the foot of p. 100.
　　Note.—The Poems which were inserted in the Second Edition
pp. [101]–108, were omitted in the Third Edition.

IV.

The Corsair,/ A Tale./ . . . Fourth Edition. . . . 1814/.
　　　　　　　　　　　　　　　　　　　　　　　　[8º

Collation—
　　Vide supra, the Second Edition, No. ii.
　　Note.—The Poems inserted in the Second, and omitted in the
Third, are included in the Fourth Edition.

V.

The Corsair,/ A Tale./　By Lord Byron./　[Motto as above,
No. i.]　Fifth Edition./　London :/　Printed for John
Murray, Albemarle-Street ;/ *By Thomas Davison, White-
friars,|* 1814./　　　　　　　　　　　　　　　　[8º
Collation—
　　Vide supra, the Second Edition, No. ii.

VI.

The Corsair,/ A Tale./ . . . Sixth Edition./ . . . 1814./
　　　　　　　　　　　　　　　　　　　　　　　　[8º

Collation—
　　For Title, *vide supra*, the Fifth Edition, No. v.

VII.

The Corsair,/ A Tale./ . . . Seventh Edition./ . . . 1814./
　　　　　　　　　　　　　　　　　　　　　　　　[8º

Collation—

Vide supra, Second Edition, No. ii.

Note.—In this edition the last four lines of Canto I. stanza xi. ("The first may turn . . . still it stings!") were added, together with the Note, to Canto II., p. 33, line 18, "It has been objected," etc. The poem numbers 1863 lines, the additional lines not being included in the numeration.

VIII.

The Corsair,/ A Tale./ By Lord Byron./ [Motto as above.] From the Fifth London Edition./ New-York :/ Published by Eastburn, Kirk, and Co./ Literary Rooms, Corner of Wall and Nassau Streets./ 1814./   [6?

Collation—

Pp. xi. + 108.

Note.—The Corsair was also published in Philadelphia in 1814, 16?

IX.

The Corsair ;/ A Tale./ By Lord Byron./ [Motto as above.] Ninth Edition./ London :/ Printed for John Murray, Albemarle-Street./ 1815./   [8?

Collation—

Half-title, one leaf, pp. i., ii. ; Title, one leaf, pp. iii., iv. ; Dedication, pp. v.–xi. ; Text, with Notes, pp. 1–112. The Imprint (*T. Davison, Lombard-Street,/ Whitefriars, London./*) is at the foot of p. 112.

Note.—The poem numbers 1864 lines, the four new lines at the end of Canto I. stanza xi. being included in the numeration. Pp. 101–104 contain "Note 17, p. 95, last line," on the Pirates of Barataria, and (secondly) on Archbishop Blackbourne.

X.

The Corsair,/ A Tale./ By Lord Byron./ [Motto as above.] Tenth Edition./ London :/ John Murray, Albemarle-Street./ 1818./   [8?

Collation—

Half-title (R. *London :/ Printed by T. Davison, Whitefriars./*), pp. 1, 2 ; Title, one leaf, pp. 3, 4 ; Dedication, pp. 5–9 ; Text, pp. 11–96 ; Notes, pp. 97–105 ; Poems, pp. [107]–114.

Note.—The poem is (incorrectly) numbered 1873 lines, line 1506 being numbered 1511.

XI.

The Corsair./ A Tale./ By Lord Byron./ [Motto as above.] London : Printed and Published by W. Dugdale,/ *23, Russell Court, Drury Lane./* 1825./   [12°

Collation—

Pp. 72.

XII.

The Corsair./ A Tale./ By Lord Byron./ " —— I suoi
pensieri in lui dormir non ponno "—Tasso./ [London,
1844.]   [8°

Collation—
   Pp. iv. + 5–48.
   Note.—Part of " Clarke's Home Library."

XIII.

The Corsair :/ A Tale./ By/ Lord Byron./ London :
Archd. K. Murray & Co.,/ 30 Queen Square, W.C. :/
Glasgow : 243 Parliamentary Road./ 1867./   [16°

Collation—
   Pp. 122.
   Note.—Part of " Murray's Standard Poets."

Translations of The Corsair.

German.

I.

Der Korsar, eine Erzählung. [Deutsch v.] F. L. von
Tschirsky. Berlin, Maurer. 1816.   [12°
            [*Centralblatt, etc.,* 1890, vol. vii. p. 472.]

II.

Der Korsar, eine Erzählung. [Deutsch von] Elise von
Hohenhausen. Altona, Hammerich. 1820.   [8°
            [*Centralblatt, etc.,* 1890, vii. 461.]

III.

Der Korsar. Erzählung. Aus d. Engl. übers. v. Friederike
Friedmann. Leipzig, Brockhaus. 1852.   [16°
            [Kayser, 1853.]
Collation—
   Pp. 90.

IV.

Der Corsar. Gedicht. Aus d. Engl. von Vict. v. Arents-
schild. Mainz, Iabern. 1852.   [16°
            [Kayser, 1853.]
Collation—
   Pp. 139.

V.

Der Korsar. Eine Erzählg. v. Lord Byron. Frei übers. v. Adf. Seubert. Leipzig, Ph. Reclam, jr. [1871–76.] [16º
[Kayser, 1877.]

Collation—
 Pp. 69.
 Note.—No. 406 of the " Universal-Bibliothek."

Hungarian.

A Kalóz./ Irta/ Lord Byron./ Angolból Forditotta/ Kacziány Géza./ Budapest./ Franklin-Társulat/ Magyar Irod. Intézet és Könyvnyomda./ 1892./ [16º

Collation—
 Pp. 74.

Italian.

I.

Il Corsaro/ Novella/ di/ Lord Byron/ Versione in prosa/ di L. C./ Torino/ Vedova Pomba e figli/ 1819/ [8º

Collation—
 Pp. v. + 131.
 Note.—The Front. is a lithograph of the portrait of "Giorgio Byron," by G. H. Harlow. A translation, "Al Tempo," "Time on whose arbitrary wing," pp. [129], 131, follows the Notes to the *Corsair.* The translation includes the four additional lines at the end of Canto I. stanza xi., but not the Note on the " Pirates of Barataria."

II.

Il Corsaro/ Novella/ di/ Lord Byron/ Versione in prosa/ di L. C./ Seconda edizione riveduta dall' autore./ Milano/ Presso Rodolfo Vismara/ 1820/ [8º

Collation—
 Pp. 4 + 5–123.
 Note.—For Front., *vide supra*, No. i.

III.

Il Corsaro, novella di lord Byron. Traduzione dall' inglese di Giuseppe Nicolini. Milano, tip. di Giovanni Silvestri. 1842. [16º
[*Bibl. Ital.*, June, 1842.]

Collation—
 Pp. xlviii. + 106.

IV.

Il Corsaro, novella Inglese, tradotta da Eritreo Migdonio.
Firenze, 1842, tipografia Piatti.

[*Bibl. Ital.*, July, 1843.]

V.

Il/ Corsaro/ di/ Lord Byron/ Versione del Cavaliere/ Luigi
Serenelli Honorati/ Già Presid. di Corte d'Appello/
Bologna/ Tip. Mareggiani All' Insegna di Dante/ *1797,
Via Malcontenti,* 1797/ 1870/ [8?

Collation—
Pp. 95.

VI.

Il Corsaro/ Novella di Lord Byron/ Versione/ di/ Carlo
Rosnati/ [1879] [8?

Collation—
Pp. 96 + Sonnet, " Santa Rosa," p. [97].

Russian.

Морской разбойникъ. Переводъ В. Олина (въ прозѣ).
С.-Петербургъ, 1827.

Spanish.

I.

El Corsario. Por el Byron, traducido en castellano por
M. . . . Imp. de David à Paris. A Paris, rue du Temple,
N. 69. 1827. [18?
[*Bibl. de le France,* Aug. 22, 1827.]

II.

El/ Corsario/ Por/ Lord Byron./ Valencia :/ Imprenta de
Cabrerizo./ 1832./ [32?

Collation—
Pp. 272.

Swedish.

Corsaren./ Af/ Lord Byron./ [Motto as above.] Stockholm,/
Tryckt Hos Joh. Beckman, 1868./

Collation—
Pp. 96.
Note.—" Ofversattning af Talis Qualis."

The Curse of Minerva.

I.

The Curse of Minerva./ London :/ Printed by T. Davison, Lombard Street, Whitefriars./ 1812./   [4°

Collation—
    Title, one leaf, pp. 1, 2; Text, pp. 3–25. The Imprint (*Printed by T. Davison, Lombard Street,/ Whitefriars, London./*) is in the centre of p. [27].
    Note.—The pages of the Text measure 280 × 220.

II.

The/ Curse of Minerva./ A Poem,/ By the Right Honourable/ Lord Byron/ —— Pallas te hac [*sic*] vulnere, Pallas/ Immolat, et poenam scelerato ex sanguine sumit./ Philadelphia :/ Printed for De-Silver and Co./ 1815./
                                             [8°

Collation—
    Pp. 24.
    Note.—It is probable that this edition, which closely resembles the later separate issues of the *Corsair*, the *Bride of Abydos*, and the *Giaour*, was printed in London.

III.

The/ Curse of Minerva./ A Poem./ By the Right Honourable/ Lord Byron./ —— Pallas te hac [*sic*] vulnere, Pallas/ Immolat, et poenam scelerato ex sanguine sumit./ Third Edition./ Paris./ Published by Galignani/ at the French, English, Italian, German and Spanish/ Library, N° 18, Rue Vivienne./ 1818./   [12°

Collation—
    Half-title, one leaf, pp. 1, 2; Title, one leaf, pp. 3, 4; Text, pp. 5–[21]. The Imprint (*Printed by A. Belin*) is at the foot of p. [21].
    Note (1).—A Fourth Edition, identical with the Third, was issued by Galignani in 1820. Quérard (1827) records the issue of a Second Edition, published by A. and W. Galignani in 1818.
    Note (2).—*The Curse of Minerva* (full text) is included in the fifth volume of the edition of Byron's Works published by Louis and Baudry in 1825 (see W. No. xviii.); in the first volume of the Fifth Edition, in sixteen volumes, published by A. and W. Galignani in 1822 (see W. No. xix.), but was not published, in its entirety, in England till 1831 (see W. No. xliii.).
    For a bibliographical note on *The Curse of Minerva,* first published as *The Malediction of Minerva, or The Athenian Marble Market* (111 lines), in the *New Monthly Magazine,*

April, 1818, vol. iii. p. 240, and often reprinted in a mutilated
form, see *Poetical Works*, 1898, i. 452.

The Deformed Transformed.

I.

The/ Deformed Transformed;/ A Drama. By the/ Right
Hon. Lord Byron./ London, 1824 :/ Printed for J. and
H. L. Hunt,/ Bond Street, and Tavistock Street./   [8°

Collation—
  Half-title (R. *London :/ Printed by C. H. Reynell, Broad Street,
Golden Square./*), pp. 1, 2 ; Title, pp. 3, 4 ; Author's Advt.,
p. 6 ; *Dramatis Personæ*, one leaf, pp. 7, 8 ; Text, pp. 9–88.
The Imprint, as above, is at the foot of p. 88.
  Note.—A Second and Third Editions, identical with the First,
were issued in 1824.

II.

The Deformed Transformed, a drama by the Right hon.
lord Byron. Impr. de A. Belin, à Pàris, chez A. et W.
Galignani, 1824.   [12°
        [*Bibl. de le France*, March 27, 1824.]

  Note.—*La Métamorphose du Bossu* forms part (pp. *1*-103) of
Tome Quinzième of *Œuvres Complètes* de Lord Byron. Paris,
Ladvocat/ 1824./ (See Transl. of Coll. Ed. No. i.)

III.

The/ Deformed Transformed./ By/ Lord Byron./ [Illus-
tration, "What do I see ?"] New and Complete Edition.
—Price one Penny./ London : J. Dicks, 313, Strand ;
all Booksellers./ [1883, etc.]   [12°

Collation—
  Pp. 583–597.
  Note.—The *Deformed Transformed* is No. 113 of "Dicks'
Standard Plays."

Translation of The Deformed Transformed.
Hungarian.

Budapesti/ Árvizkönyv./ etc. Szerkeszti/ B. Eötvös József./
Negyedik Kötet./ Pesten,/ Kiadja Heckenast Gusztáv./
1840./   [8°

Collation—
  Lord Byron'/ Elváltoztatott Idomtalanjából/   Töredék,/
Lukács Móricztól./ pp. 111-140.

Don Juan.

Cantos I., II.

I.

Don Juan./ " Difficile est proprie communia dicere."/ Hor. *Epist. ad Pison.*/ London :/ Printed by Thomas Davison, Whitefriars./ 1819./ [4°

Collation—

Half-title, one leaf ; Title, one leaf ; Second Half-title, pp. 1, 2 ; Text, pp. 3-227. The Imprint (*London :| Printed by Thomas Davison, Whitefriars.|*) is in the centre of p. [228].

Contents—

Canto I. . . . . . p. 3   Canto II. . . . p. [119]
Notes to Canto I. . p. [115]

Note (1).—The following lines and stanzas are omitted : Canto I. stanzas xv., cxxix. lines 7, 8, cxxx. lines 7, 8, cxxxi. The omissions were first included in the Text in the edition of 1833. (See **vol.** xv. p. 40.)

Note (2).—For the " Dedication " in pamphlet form, *vide post*, p. 304.

II.

Don Juan./ " Difficile est proprie communia dicere."/ Hor. *Epist. ad Pison.*/ A New Edition./ London :/ Printed by Thomas Davison, Whitefriars./ 1819./ [8°

Collation—

Half-title, one leaf ; Title, one leaf ; Second Half-title, pp. 1, 2 ; Text, pp. 3-227. The Imprint, as above, is in the centre of p. [228].

Note.—For omitted lines and stanzas, *vide supra*, No. i. " A New Edition," identical with that of 1819, was issued in 1820.

III.

Don Juan./ " Difficile est," etc. Hor. *Epist. ad Pison.*/ An exact Copy from the Quarto Edition./ London./ Published by J. Onwhyn, No. 4, Catherine-Street./ Strand./ Price Four Shillings./ 1819./ [8°

Collation—

Title, pp. 1, 2 ; Half-title, pp. 3, 4 ; Text, pp. 5-117. The Imprint (*E. Thomas, Printer, Denmark-Court, Strand*) is at the foot of p. 117.

IV.

Don Juan./ " Difficile est," etc./ Hor. *Epist. ad Pison.*/
London :/ Printed by Thomas Davison, Whitefriars./
1820./   [8°

Note.—This edition is identical with the " New Edition " of
1820, but is in smaller type, and the size is crown, not post,
octavo.

V.

Don Juan./ " Difficile," etc./ Hor. *Epist. ad Pison.*/ An
exact copy from the Quarto Edition./ London :/ Printed
for Sherwin and Co. Paternoster Row./   Price Four
Shillings./ 1820./   [8°

Collation—
Half-title, one leaf, pp. 1, 2 ; Title, one leaf, pp. 3, 4 ; Text,
pp. 5–117.   The Imprint (*Sherwin and Co. Printers, Paternoster
Row.*) is at the foot of p. 117.

VI.

Don Juan./ " Difficile est proprie communia dicere."/ Hor.
Epist. ad Pison./ A New Edition./ London :/ Printed
by Thomas Davison, Whitefriars./ 1822./   [8°

Collation—
Half-title (R. *London :*/ *Printed by Thomas Davison, Whitefriars.*/) ; Title, one leaf, etc., *vide supra*, No. ii.
Note.—The " New Edition " of 1822, with the exception of the
first Half-title, is identical with the " New Edition " of 1819.

Cantos III., IV., V.

I.

Don Juan,/ Cantos III, IV, and V./ " Difficile est," etc./
Hor. *Epist. ad Pison.*/ London : Printed by Thomas
Davison, Whitefriars./ 1821./   [8°

Collation—
Half-title, one leaf ; Title, one leaf ; Second Half-title, pp. 1, 2 ;
Text, pp. 3–218.   The Imprint, as above, is in the centre of
p. [220].

Contents—

Canto III. . . . . . p. 3	Notes to Canto IV. . p. 131
Notes to Canto III. . p. 65	Canto V. . . . . p. 135
Canto IV. . . . . . p. 71	Notes to Canto V. . p. 215

Note.—Canto V. stanza lxi. is omitted.   This edition of Cantos
III., IV., V. was issued in post and in crown octavo.

II.

Don Juan./ "Difficile est," etc./ Hor. *Epist. ad Pison./*
Cantos III. IV. and V./ London :/ Printed for Sherwin
and Co. Paternoster Row./ Price Four Shillings./ 1821./
[8°

Collation—
Title, pp. 3, 4 ; Text, pp. 5–114. The Imprint (*Printed by
Sherwin and Co./ Paternoster-Row./*) is at the foot of p. 114.

III.

Don Juan./ Cantos III, IV, and V./ "Difficile est," etc.
Hor. *Epist. ad Pison./* Fifth Edition,/ Revised and Corrected./ London :/ Printed by Thomas Davison, Whitefriars./ 1822./
[8°

Collation—
Half-title, one leaf ; Title, one leaf ; Second Half-title, pp.
1, 2 ; Text, pp. 3–222. The Imprint (*London :/ Printed by
Thomas Davison, Whitefriars*) is in the centre of p. [224].
Note.—The additional matter consists of the citations and
corrections of ten of Bacon's apophthegms, and a defence of the
literary merits of Voltaire, pp. 217–222, which was omitted from
the First Edition (see letter to Murray, August 21, 1821, *Letters,*
1901, v. 351).

Cantos I.–V.

I.

Don Juan./ A/ Poem,/ By/ Lord Byron./ London./
Printed & Sold by W. Benbow./ At the Lord Byron's
Head./ 9, Castle Street, Leicester Square./ 1822./
[12°

Collation—
[Cantos I.–V.], pp. 214 + Notes to Canto First, etc., pp.
[215]–[220]. The Imprint (*Sudbury, Printer, High Holborn*) is
at the foot of p. [220].

II.

Don Juan./ "Difficile est," etc./ Hor. *Epist. ad Pison./*
With/ A Preface,/ By a Clergyman./ London :/ Printed
by and for Hodgson & Co.,/ 10, Newgate Street./ 1822./
[12°

Collation—
Half-title, pp. i., ii. ; Title, pp. iii., iv. ; Publisher's Preface,
pp. v.–x. ; Text, pp. 3–226. The Imprint (*Printed by Hodgson
and C°. 10, Newgate Street, London.*) is at the foot of p. 226.

Note.—The Front. is a lithograph of "Lord Byron." This edition was reissued in **1823** with another Front., a lithograph of "Lord Byron," after the portrait by G. Harlow.

III.

Don Juan./ In Five Cantos./ A New Edition, with Notes./ [Title-vignette, ? Newstead Abbey.] And/ Three Engravings after Corbould./ London :/ Printed by and for Peter Griffin,/ Tabernacle Walk,/ and sold by all Booksellers in Town and Country./ [1823.]   [12º

Collation—
Half-title, one leaf ; Title (R. *Arliss. Typ. London*) ; Second Half-title, with motto, "Difficile est," etc./ Hor./ ; Cont. ; Text [Cantos I.–V.], pp. *1*–180.
Note.—A paper cover with ornamental border bears the date MDCCCXXIII.

IV.

Don Juan./ "Difficile est," etc./ Hor. Epist. ad Pison./ A Correct Copy from the original edition./ London :/ Printed by G. Smeeton, S.t Martin's Church Yard,/ Charing Cross./ [1826 ?]   [8º

Collation—
Title, one leaf, pp. **1, 2** ; Text, pp. *3*-**215** + Notes to Canto I., etc., pp. [217]–[228]. The Imprint (*Printed by G. Smeeton, S.t Martin's Church Yard.*) is at the foot of p. [228].
Note.—There is an illustrated Title (Don Juan/ Cantos **1** to **5**/ London./ Printed by G. Smeeton S.t Martins Church Yard./) with Title-vignette, head of Lord Byron encircled with bay leaves, and six coloured illustrations by I. R. Cruikshank.

Cantos VI., VII., VIII.

I.

Don Juan./ Cantos VI.—VII.—And VIII./ "Dost thou think because thou art virtuous, there shall be no more/ Cakes and Ale ?"—" Yes, by S.t Anne ; and Ginger shall be hot i' the/ mouth too !"—*Twelfth Night, or What you Will./* Shakespeare./ London, 1823 :/ Printed for John Hunt,/ 38, Tavistock Street, Covent Garden, And/ 22, Old Bond Street./   [8º

Collation—
Title (R. London :/ *Printed by C. H. Reynell, Broad Street, Golden Square./*), pp. i., ii. ; Preface to Cantos VI.—VII.—and VIII., pp. [iii.]–vii. ; Second Half-title, one leaf ; Text, pp. *1*-184; "Publications by John Hunt . . . July, 1823," pp. [185], [186].

Note.—Notes to Canto VIII. are on pp. [183], **184.** This edition was reissued in 1825—Printed for Hunt and Clarke,/ Tavistock Street, Covent Garden./ The pagination, etc., is identical with that of the edition of 1823. The Imprint (*London :*/ *Printed by C. H. Reynell, Broad Street, Golden Square.*/) is on p. [186].

II.

Don Juan./ Cantos VI.—VII.—VIII./ " Dost thou think," etc. [Motto, four lines]./ London : Printed and Published by W. Dugdale, 19, Tower Street, Seven Dials./ 1823./ [12º

Collation—

Title, one leaf, pp. i., ii. ; Preface, pp. iii., iv. ; Text, pp. *1*–*221* + Notes to Cantos IX. X. XI., pp. [223], [224]. The Imprint (*Benbow, Printer, 9, Castle - Street, Leicester - square, London.*) is at the foot of p. [224].
Note.—This edition includes Cantos IX., X., XI.

III.

Don Juan./ Cantos VI.—VII.—VIII./ " Dost thou think," etc. [Motto, four lines]./ London : 1823./ Printed for John Hunt, 22, Old Bond-Street, and 38, Tavistock-/ Street, Covent Garden./ [12º

Collation—

Title (R. *London :*/ *Printed by C. H. Reynell, Broad Street, Golden Square.*/), pp. i., ii. ; Preface, pp. iii.-vi. ; Text, pp. 7–97. The Imprint, as above, is at the foot of p. 97.

Cantos IX., X., XI.

I.

Don Juan./ Cantos IX.—X.—And XI./ " Dost thou think because thou art virtuous, there shall be no more/ Cakes and Ale ? "—" Yes, by S: Anne ; and Ginger shall be hot i' the/ mouth too ! "—*Twelfth Night*, or What you Will./ Shakspeare./ London, 1823 :/ Printed for John Hunt,/ 38, Tavistock Street, Covent Garden, And/ 22, Old Bond Street./ [8º

Collation—

Title, one leaf, pp. 1, 2 ; Half-title, pp. 3, 4 ; Text, pp. 5–151. The Imprint (*London :*/ *Printed by C. H. Reynell, Broad Street, Golden Square.*/) is in the centre of p. [152].
Note (1).—The Notes to Canto IX. are on pp. [49], 50 ; the Notes to Canto X. on pp. [97]–99 ; and the Notes to Canto XI.

on pp. [149]–151. Canto XI. stanza lvii. lines 5–8 and stanza lviii.
are omitted.

Note (2).—The motto is here given in full; and note "Shakspeare," not "Shakespeare," as before.

II.

Don Juan./ Cantos IX.—X.—XI./ "Dost thou think,"
etc. [Motto, four lines]./ Shakespeare./ London, 1823 :/
Printed for John Hunt, 38, Tavistock Street, Covent/
Garden ; and 22, Old Bond Street./ [12°

Collation—

Title (R. *Printed by G. H. Reynell,| 45, Broad-Street, Golden-
Square.|*), pp. 1, 2 ; Text, pp. 3–72.

Cantos XII., XIII., XIV.

I.

Don Juan./ Cantos XII.—XIII.—And XIV./ [Motto as
above, three lines.] Shakspeare./ London, 1823 :/ Printed
for John Hunt,/ 38, Tavistock Street, Covent Garden, and/
22, Old Bond-Street./ [8°

Collation—

Title (R. *London.| Printed by C. H. Reynell, Broad Street,
Golden Square.|*), pp. 1, 2 ; Half-title, pp. 3, 4 ; Text, pp. 5–
168. The Imprint, as above, is at the foot of p. 168.

Note.—The Notes to Canto XII. are on pp. [51], 52 ; the
Notes to Canto XIII. on pp. [111], 112 ; and the Notes to Canto
XIV. on pp. [167], 168.

II.

Don Juan./ Cantos XII.—XIII.—XIV./ "Dost thou
think," etc. [Motto, four lines]./ London, 1823 :/ Printed
for John Hunt, 38, Tavistock Street, Covent/ Garden :
and 22, Old Bond-Street./ [12°

Collation—

Title (R. *Printed by G. H. Reynell,| 45, Broad-Street, Golden-
Square.|*), pp. 1, 2 ; Text, pp. 3–83 + six pages of " Publications
by John Hunt," dated December, 1823. This edition is bound
in a paper cover with ornamental border—Don Juan./ Cantos/
XII. XIII. XIV./ Price One Shilling./

III.

Don Juan./ Cantos XII.—XIII.—XIV./ "Dost thou
think," etc. [Motto, four lines (Shakspeare)]./ London :/
Printed for the Booksellers./ 1823./ [12°

Collation—
Title (R. *Sudbury, Printer, 252, High Holborn.*), pp. 1, 2 ; Text, pp. 3–83.   The Imprint, as above, is at the foot of p. 83.

IV.

Don Juan,/ Cantos XII, XIII, XIV./ "Dost thou think," etc. [Motto, four lines (Shakespeare)]./ Paris :/ Published by A. and W. Galignani,/ at the French, English, Italian, German, and Spanish Library,/ N.º 18, Rue Vivienne./ 1824./   [12.º

Collation—
Half-title (R. *Paris : Printed by A. Belin.*) ; Title, one leaf ; Half-title, with Motto, pp. 1, 2 ; Text, pp. 3–162 + Notes to Canto XIV., pp. [163], [164].

Cantos XV., XVI.

I.

Don Juan./ Cantos XV. And XVI./ [Motto as above, three lines.] Shakspeare./ London, 1824 :/ Printed for John and H. L. Hunt,/ Tavistock Street, Covent Garden.
                                                    [8.º

Collation—
Title (R. Imprint as above), pp. 1, 2 ; Half-title, pp. 3, 4 ; Text, pp. 5–125 ; [Works] Published by John and H. L. Hunt, . . . March, 1824, pp. [131], [132].   The Imprint, as above, is in the centre of p. [130].
Note.—The Notes to Canto XV. are on pp. [55]–57 ; the Notes to Canto XVI. on pp. [127]–129.   The following note is on p. [126] : ["The errors of the press in this Canto,—if there be any,—are not to be attributed to the Author, as he was deprived of the opportunity of correcting the proof-sheets."]

II.

Don Juan./ Cantos XV. and XVI./ "Dost thou think," etc. [Motto, three lines]. Shakspeare./ London, 1824 :/ Printed for John and H. L. Hunt,/ Tavistock Street, Covent Garden./   [12.º

Collation—
Title (R. *London :/ Printed by C. H. Reynell, Broad Street, Golden Square./*), pp. 1, 2 ; Half-title, one leaf, pp. 3, 4 ; Text, pp. 5–130.   The Imprint, as above, is at the foot of p. 130.

III.

Don Juan./ Cantos XV. and XVI./ "Dost thou think," etc. [Motto, four lines]./ Shakspeare./ London :/ Printed for the Booksellers./ 1824./   [12.º

Collation—
     Title (R. *Sudbury, Printer,* 252, *High Holborn.*), pp. 1, 2 ; Text, pp. 3–62. The Imprint, as above, is at the foot of p. 62.

IV.

Don Juan./   Cantos XV. and XVI./   "Dost thou think," etc. [Motto, three lines]./   Shakspeare./   London, 1824:/ Printed for John Hunt, 38, Tavistock - Street, Covent/ Garden ; and 22, Old Bond-Street./   [12°

Collation—
     Title (R. *Printed by G. H. Reynell,/* 45, *Broad-Street, Golden-Square./*), pp. 1, 2 ; Text, pp. 3–62.
     Note.—The Title-page and setting of the Notes, and the quality of the paper of this edition differ from that of the preceding, but the text appears to have been set up from the same type.

V.

Don Juan,/ Cantos XV, XVI./   "Dost thou think," etc. [Motto, four lines]./   Paris: Published by A. and W. Galignani,/ At the French, English, Italian, German, and Spanish Library,/ N° 18, Rue Vivienne./   1824./   [12°

Collation—
     Half-title (R. *Paris : Printed by A. Belin.*) ; Title, one page ; Second Half-title, with Motto, pp. 1, 2 ; Text, pp. 3–125.

Full Text.

I.

Don Juan./   By/ Lord Byron./   Cantos I. To VI./   "Difficile est proprie communia dicere."/   Hor./   Vol. I./ [Vol. II.]   London : Printed for the Booksellers./ MDCCCXXVI./   [8°

Collation—
     Vol. I. : General Title (The/ Works/ of/ Lord Byron./ Vol. XII./   London :/ Printed for the Booksellers./   1826) ; Title (R. *Thomas White, Printer,/ Johnson's Court./*) ; Text, pp. 1–353. The Imprint, as above, is at the foot of p. [354].
     Vol. II. : General Title (*The/ Works,/* etc.   Vol. XIII./ etc.) ; Title (Don Juan./   By/ Lord Byron./   Cantos VII. To XVI./ "Dost thou think," etc. [Motto, three lines]./   Shakspeare./ Vol. II., etc.) (R. Imprint as above) ; Half-title, pp. 1, 2 ; Text, pp. 3–398.

II.

Don Juan :/ In/ Sixteen Cantos./   By Lord Byron./ "Difficile est proprie communia dicere."/   *Hor. Epist. ad*

Pison./ Complete in one volume./ London :/ Printed for William Clark,/ 60, Paternoster-Row./ 1826./ [16°

Collation—

Title (R. *W. Wilson, Printer,/ 57, Skinner-Street, London./*), pp. i., ii. ; Biographical Notice, pp. iii.-xii. ; Text, pp. *1-432.* The Imprint (*W. Wilson, Printer, 57, Skinner-Street, London.*) is at the foot of p. 452.

III.

Don Juan :/ In/ Sixteen Cantos./ By the/ Right Hon. Lord Byron./ Difficile est proprie communia dicere./ Hor. Epist. ad Pison./ Complete in one volume./ With a short Biographical Memoir of the/ Author./ [Title-vignette, the Royal Arms.] London :/ Printed for T. and J. Allman,/ Great Queen-Street, Lincoln's Inn Fields./ 1827./ [16°

Collation—

Half-title, one leaf ; Title (R. *Doncaster :/ Printed by C. and J. White, Baxter-Gate./*), pp. i., ii. ; Biographical Memoir, pp. iii.-ix. ; Text, pp. *1-537.* The Imprint, as above, is at the foot of p. 537.

Note.—The Front. (dated 1828) is a portrait of Lord Byron by T. Phillips, R.A., engraved by W. Wise.

IV.

Don Juan./ "Difficile est proprie communia dicere."/ Hor. *Epist. ad Pison./* In Two Volumes./ Vol. I./ London :/ Thomas Davison, Whitefriars./ 1828./ [8°

Don Juan./ "Dost thou think, because thou art virtuous, there shall be/ no more cakes and ale?—Yes, by S*t* Anne ; and ginger/ shall be hot i' the mouth too !"—*Twelfth Night; or What/ you Will./* Shakspeare./ In Two Volumes. Vol. II./ London :/ Thomas Davison, White-friars./ 1828./ [8°

Collation—

Vol. I. : Half-title, one leaf ; Title, one leaf ; Text, pp. *1-343.* The Imprint (*London :/ Printed by Thomas Davison, Whitefriars./*) is in the centre of p. [344].

Vol. II. : Half-title, one leaf ; Title, one leaf ; Text, pp. *1-371.* The Imprint, as above, is in the centre of p. [372].

Note.—The Front. to Vol. I. is "Don Juan, C. ii. St. 89," drawn by R. Westall, R.A., and engraved by E. Finden ; the Front. to Vol. II. is "Don Juan, Canto II. St. 144," by the same artist and engraver.

VOL. VII. 2 F

V.

Don Juan./ By/ Lord Byron./ Cantos I. To VI./ " Difficile est proprie communia dicere."/ Hor./ Vol. I./
London :/ Printed for the Booksellers./ 1828./   [8°
Don Juan./ By/ Lord Byron./ Cantos VII. To XVI./
" Dost thou think," etc. [Motto, three lines]./ Shakespeare./ Vol. II./ London : Printed for the Booksellers./
1828./   [8°

Collation—
    Vol. I. : Half-title, one leaf ; Title (R. *Hamblin, Printer*, 63,
Upper Thames Street.) ; Text, pp. *1*-351. The Imprint, as above,
is at the foot of p. [352].
    Vol. II. : Half-title, one leaf ; Title (R. Imprint as above) ;
Second Half-title, one leaf, pp. 1, 2 ; Text, pp. *3*-392. The
Imprint, as above, is at the foot of p. 392.

VI.

Don Juan in 16 Cantos. Campe's Edition. Nuremberg
and New York, Campe and Co. 1832.   [12°
                               [Kayser, 1834.]

VII.

Don Juan,/ In/ Sixteen Cantos,/ With Notes ;/ By Lord
Byron./ " Difficile est," etc./ Horace./ " Dost thou
think," etc. [Motto, three lines. " Shaks."]/ London :
Printed for Scott and Webster,/ 36, Charter-House
Square./ 1833./   [12°

Collation—
    Title, one leaf, pp. 1, 2 ; Text, pp. *3*-359. The Imprint (*C.
Morris, Printer*, 20, *Sydney Grove, Sydney S!*) is at the foot of
p. 359.
    Note.—The Front. is " Don Juan and Julia," by H. Corbould,
engraved by C. Heath. The Title-vignette of the illustrated Title
(Don Juan :/ Complete./ By Lord Byron./ London :/ Engraved
for the English Classics,/ Published by Scott & Webster./) is
from a drawing by H. Corbould, engraved by C. Heath.

VIII.

Don Juan,/ In/ Sixteen Cantos,/ With Notes ;/ By Lord
Byron./ " Difficile est," etc./ Horace./ " Dost thou
think," etc. [Motto, three lines. " Shaks."]./ London/
Printed for the Booksellers. 1835./   [12°

Collation—
    Vide supra, No. vii.
    Note.—The Front. and illustrated Title are omitted.

IX.

Don Juan./ By/ Lord Byron./ In Two Volumes./ Vol. I./ [Vol. II.] London :/ John Murray, Albemarle Street./ 1837./ [8°

Collation—

Vol. I. : pp. 376. The Imprint (*London :/* Printed by *A. Spottiswoode,/ New-Street-Square./*) is at the foot of p. 376.

Vol. II. : pp. 395. The Imprint, as above, is in the centre of p. [396].

Note.—The Title-vignette of illustrated Title of Vol. I. is "Cape Colonna Sunium," engraved by E. Finden from a drawing by T. Helpman. The Title-vignette of illustrated Title of Vol. II. is "The Brig of Balgownie near Aberdeen," engraved by E. Finden from a drawing by G. Bulmer. The vols. are bound in green cloth, with coat-of-arms in gold.

X.

Don Juan. Mannheim, Hofmann. 1838. [16°
[Kayser, 1841.]

XI.

Don Juan :/ In/ Sixteen Cantos./ By/ Lord Byron./ "Difficile est," etc./ *Hor. Epist. ad Pison./* London : H. G. Bohn, York Street, Covent Garden./ 1849./ [12°

Collation—

Title, one leaf, pp. 1, 2 ; Text, pp. 3–438.

Note.—The Front. is "The Siesta of Haidée and Juan." The Title-vignette on illustrated Title (Don Juan,/ etc. London. MDCCCXLVI./ (*sic*)) is Newstead Abbey from the Lake.

XII.

Don Juan/ By Lord Byron/ Complete Edition with Notes/ "Dost thou think," etc. [Motto, three lines]/ London and New York/ George Routledge and Sons/ [1874] [16°

Collation—

Half-title, one leaf, pp. 1, 2 ; Title (R. *Charles Dickens and Evans,/ Crystal Palace Press./*), pp. 3, 4 ; Text, pp. 5–431. The Imprint, as above, is in the centre of p. [432].

XIII.

Don Juan./ By/ Lord Byron./ "Difficile est," etc./ "Dost thou think," etc. [Motto, three lines (Shakespeare)]./ London : Chatto & Windus, Piccadilly./ 1875./ [16°

Collation—
    Half-title, one leaf; Title, one leaf; List of Cantos, pp. 1, 2 ;
Text, pp. 3–359.
    Note.—Part of "The Golden Library."

XIV.

Don Juan/ By/ Lord Byron/ "Difficile est," etc./ Com-
    plete Edition, with Notes/ London/ George Routledge
    and Sons/ Broadway, Ludgate Hill/ New York : 9 Lafa-
    yette Place/ 1886/   [8°

Collation—
    Half-title, one leaf; Title (R. Advt. of Routledge's Large
Type Three-Volume Classics.) ; Text, pp. 1–476. The Imprint
(*R. Clay and Sons, London and Bungay.*) is at the foot of p. 476.
    Note.—The Front. is "Don Juan," from Canto IV. stanza xvii.
The same issue without the Front. forms part of Routledge's
"Excelsior Series."

Translations of Don Juan.
Danish.
I.

Don Juan. . . . Metrisk bearbeidet efter den engelske
    Original af H. Schou. 1. Hefte Fredericia. 1854. [4°

Collation—
    Pp. 16.
    Note.—No more published. Without Title-page ; the above
Title appears on the wrapper.

II.

Byron : Don Juan./ Oversat Paa Dansk/ Af/ Holger
    Drachmann./ Med ¹Indledningsdigt Af Oversætteren./
    Kjøbenhavn./ Forlagt Af J. H. Schubothes Boghandel./
    Grœbes Bogtrykkeri./ 1880./   [8°

    Note.—The translation was issued in parts. The first volume,
containing Cantos I.–VI. pp. 1–437, was completed in 1882. A
second volume (1890–1902) contains Cantos VII.–XVI. pp. 1–465.

French.
I.

Don Juan, pöeme héroï-comique en 16 chants, traduit et
    précédé de la vie de Lord Byron [par A. P.] avec notes
    et commentaires. Tomes i. et ii. Deux Volumes. Impr.

de P. Renouard à Paris. A Paris, rue Poupée, n. 16.
1827. [Tome III. was issued Sept. 15.]   [18°
          [*Bibl. de la France*, June 2, 1827.]

II.

Don Juan. Traduit en vers français. 2 vol. Paris,
    Librairie centrale. 1866.   [12°
                    [Lorenz, 1876.]

III.

Paul Lehodey./ Don Juan/ de/ Lord Byron,/ Traduction
    nouvelle, précédée d'une préface/ de M. Legouvé,/ de
    l'Académie française./ Paris,/ DeGorge-Cadot, libraire-
    éditeur,/ 37, rue Serpente./ [1869.]   [8°
Collation—
    Pp. xi. + 450 + Table des Matières, p. [451].

IV.

Don Juan. Traduit en vers français par Adolphe Fauvel.
    Troisiéme Édition, entièrement revue et corrigée, 1878.
    Paris, Lemerre.   [8°
                    [Lorenz, 1886.]

    Note.—La 1re édition de cette traduction est de 1866, la 2e de
1868.

German.

I.

Don Juan, aus d. Engl. Im Versmass des Originals über-
    setzt von Ad. v. Marées. Essen, Bädeker. 1839. [12°
                    [Kayser, 1841.]

II.

Byron's/ Don Juan/ übersetzt/ von/ Otto Gildemeister./
    "Difficile est proprie communia dicere."/ Horatius./
    "Vermeinst du, weil du tugendhaft," etc. [Motto, six lines]./
    Shakspeare./ Bremen./ Druck und Verlag von Carl
    Schünemann./ 1845./   [8°
Collation—
    Vol. I. : pp. 314.
    Vol. II. : pp. 276.

III.

Byron's/ Don Juan/ von/ Adolf Böttger./　Diamantausgabe./
Leipzig,/ Verlag von Otto Wigand./　1849./　　　　[8°

Collation—
　Pp. 413.
　Note.—The Front. is "Haidie." This edition was reissued in
1858.

IV.

Byron's/ Don Juan./　Deutsch/ von/ Wilhelm Schäffer./
Erster Theil./ Erster und Zweiter Gesang./　Hildburghausen./ Verlag des Bibliographischen Instituts./　1867./
　　　　　　　　　　　　　　　　　　　　　　　　　[8°

Collation—
　Vol. I. : pp. 124.
　Vol. II. (Cantos III.–VI.) : pp. 152.
　Note.—Nos. 47, 48 of the "Bibliothek ausländischer Klassiker."

Italian.

I.

Don Giovanni : poema, tradotto da Ant. Caccia. Torino,
1853.　　　　　　　　　　　　　　　　　　[16°
　　　　　　　　　　　　[Pagliaini, 1901.]

II.

Don Giovanni ridotto in 8ª rima da Antonietta Sacchi,
Milano, Guglielmini, 1865.　　　　　　　　[8°
　　　　　　　　　　　　[Pagliaini, 1901.]

III.

Giorgio Byron/ Aidea/ Episodio del don Giovanni/ Saggio
d'una traduzione completa/ di/ Vittorio Betteloni/
Verona/ Stabilimento tipografico di G. Civelli/　1875/
　　　　　　　　　　　　　　　　　　　　　　　　[8°

Collation—
　Pp. 119.

IV.

Il/ Don Juan/ di/ Lord Byron/ Recato/ In altrettante
stanze italiane/ dal cavaliere/ Enrico Casali/ Milano/
Natale Battezzati editore/　1876/　　　　　　[8°
Collation—
　Pp. 548 + Indice, p. [549].

V.

Don Giovanni. Traduzione di Vitt. Betteloni, Milano, Ottino, 1880. [8°
[Pagliaini, 1901.]

Polish.

I.

Don Żuan./ Lorda Bajrona./ Pieśń/ Pierwsza/ przełożona/ przez/ Wiktora z Baworowa. Tarnopol./ Drukiem Józefa Pawłowskiego./ 1863./ Na dochód Rannych./ [8°
Collation—
Pp. v. + 60.
Note.—This edition was issued during the last Polish insurrection, for the benefit of the wounded.

(Part of Canto II.)

II.

Ustęp z drugiéj pieśni Don Żuana, przełożył Wiktor z Baworowa. pp. 28. *Druk. " Czasu." Kraków,* 1877. [8°

(Canto III.)

III.

Don Żuan, pieśń trzecia, przekład Wiktora z Baworowa. pp. 35. *redak. " Przeglądu Polskiego," Druk. " Czasu." Kraków,* 1877. [8°

(Cantos II., III., IV.—Haida.)

IV.

Don Żuan, pieśń druga, trzecia i czwarta. Opowiadanie o Haidzie; przekład Wiktora z Baworowa. pp. 118. viii. *Tow. Bratniéj Pomocy Słuchaczów Wszechn. Lwowskiéj: Tarnopol,* 1879. [8°

V.

Don Żuan . . . Przekład Edwarda Porębowicza. *Warszawa,* 1885.

Roumanian.

Don Juan/ dela/ Lord Byron./ Poema epica./ Tradusă de I. Eliade./ [Emblem — Cupid and Mask.]/ *Eliade: Bucuresci./* In tipografia lui Eliade./ 1847./ [8°
Collation—
Pp. 183.

Russian.

I.

Донъ-Жуанъ...Переводъ И. Жандра.
    С.-Петербургъ, 1846.   [8°

Collation—
    Pp. 1–91.

II.

Донъ-Жуанъ...Вольный переводъ В. Любичъ-Рома-
    новича. *С.-Петербургъ*, [1847.] 2 vols.   [12°.

III.

Донъ-Жуанъ...Глава первая.   Переводъ Н. А. Мар-
    кевича. *Лейпзигъ*, 1862.   [16°.
Collation—
    Pp. 164.

IV.

Донъ-Жуанъ...Перев. Д. Минаева.
    С.-Петербургъ, 1866, 67.

V.

Донъ-Жуанъ...Переводъ П. Козлова.   Изданіе 2-е, съ
    примѣчаніями П. Вейнберга. *С.-Петербургъ*, 1889.
    2 vols.

VI.

Донъ-Жуанъ...Переводъ А. Козлова.   2 том.
    С.-Петербургъ, 1892.

Servian.

Дон-Жуанъ ... Превод у прози Окице Глушчевића.
    2 свес. *Београд*, 1888.

Spanish.

I.

Don Juan, novela. Por lord Byron.   Deux Volumes.   Impr.
    de Decourchant, à Paris, A Paris rue du Temple, N. 69.
    1829.   [18°
            [*Bibl. de le France*, January 24, 1829.]

II.

Don Juan/ Poema/ de/ Lord Byron./ Traduccion de/ F.
    Villalva/ Difficile est proprie communia dicere./ Horacio.

Epístola á los Pisones./ Tomo 1/ Madrid/ Librería de Leocadio Lopez/ 13—Calle del Cármen—13/ 1876/ [8°

Collation—
Vol. I. : pp. xv. + 384 + Indice, p. [385].
Vol. II. : pp. 420 + Indice, p. [421].

Swedish.

I.

Don Juan/ Af/ Lord Byron./ Första Sången./   Med upply-sande och utwalde Noter./   Öfversatt ifrån Engelska Originalet./ Stockholm,/ Nordströmska Boktryckeriet,/ 1838./   [8°

Collation—
Pp. 80.

II.

Don Juan/ Af/ Lord Byron./   Förra Delen./   Sångerna I–VI./ Stockholm,/ J. L. Brudins Förlag. [1857.] [8°

Collation—
Vol. I. : pp. 349.
Vol. II. : [Sednare Delen. Sångerna VII.–XVI.—1862], pp. 384.
Note.—This edition (" Öfversättning Af Carl. Wilh. Aug. Strandberg ") was issued in paper covers with vignette portrait of Lord Byron.

English Bards, and Scotch Reviewers.

I.

The/ British Bards,/ A Satire./ [1808.]   [4°

Collation—
No Title-page.   Pp. *1, 2, 3, 4, 5, 6, 7, 8, 9, 10, 11, 12, 13, 14, 15, 16* [pp. 17, 18, 19, 20, proof-sheets of 84 lines :—(line 1), " Health to Immortal Jeffrey ! once in name ;"—(line 84), " Her son, and vanish'd in a Scottish mist " + p. 21, proof-sheet uniform with pp. 1–16, of 20 lines :—(line 1), " Illustrious Holland ! hard would be his lot ;"—(line 20), " Reforms each error, and refines the whole "], pp. 19, 20, 21, 22, 23, 24, 25, 26, 27, 28, 29.
Signature C is at the foot of p. 5 ; D, p. 9 ; E, p. 13 ; G, p. 21 ; H, p. 25.
Pp. 1–16 contain 284 lines : (line 1), " Time was, e'er yet in these degenerate days ;" (line 284), " Of Jefferies ! monarch of the Scourge and, chain." (Lines 281–284 are erased.)
Pp. 19–29 contain 200 lines : (line 1), " Now to the drama turn, oh ! motley sight ;" (line 200), " And urge thy bards, to

gain a name like thine." The last line of p. 29 is numbered 520, and the date 1808 is subscribed.

Note.—The page measures 278 × 218. The water-mark on the last page (p. 29) is 1807; the water-mark on the original wrapper, "J. W. & B. B. 1806." A wrapper of the original sheets is inscribed, "This is the original Satire which Ld B. put into my hands. It was printed in the Country, where he had been staying. He added 110 lines before it was published. R. C. D." (*B. M.,* E.G. 2028.)

II.

English Bards,/ And/ Scotch Reviewers./ A Satire./ I had rather be a kitten, and cry, mew!/ Than one of these same metre ballad-mongers./ Shakspeare./ Such shameless Bards we have; and yet 'tis true,/ There are as mad, abandon'd Critics too./ Pope./ London :/ Printed for James Cawthorn, British Library,/ No. 24, Cockspur Street./ [1809.] [12.°

Collation—

Half-title, one leaf, pp. i., ii.; Title (R. *T. Collins, Printer, No.* 1, *Harvey's Buildings, Strand*), pp. iii., iv.; Preface, pp. v., vi.; Text (696 lines), pp. *1-54.* The Imprint (*T. Collins, Printer, Harvey's Buildings, Strand*) is at the foot of p. 54.

Note.—The words "Scotch Reviewers" on the Title are in Gothic characters. Facsimile of the Title-page faces p. xiv. of *Poetical Works,* 1898, vol. i.

III.

English Bards,/ And/ Scotch Reviewers ;/ A Satire./ By/ Lord Byron./ I had rather be a kitten, and cry, mew!/ Than one of these same metre ballad-mongers./ Shakspeare./ Such shameless Bards we have; and yet 'tis true,/ There are as mad, abandon'd Critics too./ Pope./ Second Edition,/ With/ Considerable Additions and Alterations./ London :/ Printed for James Cawthorn, British Library, N.° 24,/ Cockspur Street./ 1809./ [8.°

Collation—

Half-title, one leaf, pp. i., ii.; Title (R. *Printed by Deans & Co. Hart-Streeet, Covent Garden.*/), pp. iii., iv.; Preface to the Second Edition, pp. v.–vii.; Text (1050 lines), pp. *1-82*; Postscript, pp. 83-85. The Imprint, as above, is at the foot of p. 85. The Advt. (*In the Press,*/ *And speedily will be published,*/ HENRY COUNT DE KOLINSKY, a Polish Tale./) is in the centre of p. [86].

Note.—The words "A Satire" on the Title, and the words "Scotch Reviewers" on the Half-title, are in Gothic characters.

IV.

English Bards,/ And/ Scotch Reviewers ;/ A Satire./ By/ Lord Byron./ I had rather be a kitten, and cry, mew !/ Than one of these same metre ballad-mongers./ Shak-speare./ Such shameless Bards we have ; and yet 'tis true,/ There are as mad, abandon'd Critics too./ Pope./ Third Edition./ London :/ Printed for James Cawthorn, British Library, No. 24,/ Cockspur Street./ 1810./ [8º

Collation—

Half-title, one leaf, pp. i., ii. ; Title (R. Printed by *T. Collins, Harvey's Buildings, Strand, London.*), pp. iii., iv. ; Preface to the Third Edition, pp. v.–vii. ; Text (1050 lines), pp. *1–82* ; Post-script, pp. 83–85 + Advt. of "Books Published by James Cawthorn," etc., pp. [86]–[88]. The Imprint (*Printed by T. Collins, Nº. 1, Harvey's Buildings, Strand, London.*) is at the foot of p. [88].

Note.—The Advt. of "The British Circulating Library, 24 Cockspur Street," etc., is dated March 30, 1810. The words "A Satire" and "London" on the Title, and the words "English Bards" on Half-title, are in Gothic characters.

V.

English Bards,/ And/ Scotch Reviewers ;/ A Satire./ By/ Lord Byron./ I had rather be a kitten, and cry, mew !/ Than one of these same metre ballad-mongers./ Shak-speare./ Such shameless Bards we have ; and yet 'tis true,/ There are as mad, abandon'd Critics too./ Pope./ Fourth Edition./ London :/ Printed for James Cawthorn, British Library, No. 24,/ Cockspur Street./ 1810./ [8º

Collation—

Half-title, one leaf, pp. i., ii. ; Title (R. *Printed by T. Collins, Harvey's Buildings, Strand, London.*), pp. iii., iv. ; Preface to the Third Edition, pp. v.–vii. ; Text (1050 lines), pp. *1–82* ; Postscript, pp. 83–85 + "Books Published by James Cawthorn," etc., pp. [86]–[88]. The Imprint (*Printed by T. Collins, No. 1, Harvey's Buildings, Strand, London*) is at the foot of p. [88].

Note.—The Advt. of the "British Circulating Library, 24, Cockspur Street," etc., is dated March 30, 1810. The words "Satire" and "London" on the Title, and the words "English Bards" on the Half-title, are in Gothic characters.

VI.

English Bards,/ And/ Scotch Reviewers ;/ A Satire./ By/ Lord Byron./ I had rather be a kitten, and cry, mew !/ Than one of these same metre ballad-mongers./ *Shake-speare./* Such shameless Bards we have ; and yet 'tis

true,/ There are as mad, abandon'd Critics too./ *Pope.*/
Fourth Edition./ London :/ Printed for James Cawthorn,
British Library, No. 24,/ Cockspur Street ; and Sharpe
and Hailes, Piccadilly./ 1811./   [8º

Collation—

Half-title, one leaf, pp. i., ii. ; Title (R. *Printed by Cox, Son,
and Baylis, Gᵗ Queen Street, London.*), pp. iii., iv. ; Preface,
pp. v.–vii. ; Text (1052 lines), pp. *1–82* ; Postscript, pp. 83–85 +
"Books published by James Cawthorn," etc., pp. [87], [88].
The Imprint (*Printed by Cox, Son, and Baylis, Great Queen
Street,/ Lincoln's-Inn-Fields./*) is at the foot of p. 85.

Note.—On the Title-page of another copy of this edition there
is a period instead of a comma after " James Cawthorn." The
word " Satire " on the Title, and the words " Scotch Reviewers "
on the Half-title, are in Gothic characters.

VII.

[Fifth Edition.]   [8º

[For Title-page, *vide supra*, Fourth Edition, 1811, No. vi.
No special Title-page for a Fifth Edition was printed.]

Collation—

Text, pp. *1–83*. [Signature B, p. [1] ; C, p. 17 ; D, p. 33 ;
E, p. 49 ; F, p. 65 ; G, p. 81.] There is no Imprint on pp. [1],
83, or on p. [84]. The Text numbers 1070 lines.

Note (1).—The Half-title prefixed to the Title-page of the
Fourth Edition of 1811, which precedes the Museum copy of
the Fifth Edition, bears the MS. signature, " R. C. Dallas," and
a blank leaf the following note : " This is one of the very few
copies preserved of the suppressed edition, which would have
been the Fifth. No Title-page was printed—the one prefixed
was taken from the preceding edition."

Note (2).—Mr. S. Leicester Warren (Lord de Tabley) records
the following MS. notes inscribed in a copy of the Fifth Edition,
which had formerly belonged to James Boswell, jun., and was
then in the possession of Mr. J. R. P. Kirby, of Bloomsbury
Street :—

A. A note on the abortive duel between Jeffrey and Moore is
dated November 4, 1811.

B. A note on the fly-leaf in the handwriting of James Boswell,
jun.—

" This copy purports on the title-page to be the fourth edition,
but is in truth the fifth. Having pointed out to Murray, the
bookseller, a variation between the copy of the fifth edition and
this, he borrowed it from me, that he might show it to Lord
Byron to have the circumstance explained ; that his lordship told
him he had printed the fifth edition, but, before its publication,
having repented of the work altogether, he determined to destroy
the whole impression. But the printer, as he observed, must have
retained at least this one copy, and, by putting a false title-page,

had sold it as the fourth edition," etc.—*Notes and Queries*, 1887, Series V. vol. vii. pp. 203, 204.

Mr. Murray's copy of the Fifth Edition contains, on the fly-leaves at the beginning of the volume, MS. versions of **(1)** *The Curse of Minerva*, pp. [i.]–[xi.] ; (2) The Answer to Fitzgerald's Epigram, written at the "Alfred," on *English Bards, etc.*, p. [xv.] ; and on p. xvi. the following MS. Title-page :—

English Bards/ and Scotch Reviewers ; a/ Satire/ By Lord Byron./ I had rather be a kitten, and cry, mew !/ Than one of these same metre ballad-mongers./ Shakspere./ Such shameless Bards we have ; and yet 'tis true,/ There are as mad, abandon'd critics too./ Pope./ Fifth Edition,/ UNpublished ; with considerable additions./ London :/ Printed for James Cawthorne,/ Cockspur Street./ 1812./

At the end of the volume a MS. version of "Lines on the Removing Lady Jersey's Portrait from the Gallery of Beauties," is on pp. [85], [86], and a MS. version of "On a Recent Discovery, 1813," on p. [89].

P. xiv. is headed by the following MS. note : "Lord Byron has two copies of this work, R. C. Dallas, Esq., has likewise two copies, and Mr. Leigh Hunt one."

VIII.

English Bards, etc. ; a Satire. 1st Amer. from 3rd London Ed. Philadelphia. 1811.   [8?
[Cat. of Boston Athenæum Library, 1874.]

IX.

English Bards, and Scotch Reviewers ; A Satire. By Lord Byron. Charleston : Moxford, Willington & Co., 1811.
[8?

X.

English Bards, and Scotch Reviewers. Boston. 1814.
[12?

Collation—
    Pp. 72.

XI.

English Bards/ And/ Scotch Reviewers ;/ A Satire./ By Lord Byron./ From the last London Edition./ I had rather be a kitten, and cry mew !/ Than one of these same metre ballad-mongers./ *Shakspeare./* Such shameless bards we have ; and yet 'tis true/ There are as mad, abandon'd critics too./ *Pope./* New York :/ Published by A. T. Goodrich & Co., 124 Broad-/Way, Corner of Cedar-Street./ *I. Seymour, print./* 1817./   [12?

Collation—
    Title, one leaf, pp. i., ii. ; Preface to the Third Edition, pp.
iii., iv. ; Text, pp. 5–54.
    Note.—The text numbers 1050 lines, but lacks the Postscript.
The misprint "ingenious" for "ingenuous youth," in footnote
(p. 7) to line 56, which belongs to the Fourth Edition of 1811,
and was corrected by Byron for the Fifth Edition, occurs in this
edition.

XII.

English Bards, And/ Scotch Reviewers ;/ A Satire./ Ode
to the Land of the Gaul.—Sketch/ From Private Life.—
Windsor/ Poetics, Etc./ By/ The Right Honorable/ Lord
Byron./ Second Edition./ Paris :/ Published by Galig-
nani/ At the French, English, Italian, German, and
Spanish/ Library, Nᵒ 18, Rue Vivienne./ 1818./ [12ᵒ

Collation—
    Title, one leaf ; Second Half-title, pp. 1, 2 ; Preface, pp. 3–5 ;
Text, pp. 7–70 ; Postscript, pp. 71–73 ; Ode, etc., pp. 75–84.
    Note.—The Text numbers 1052 lines. This edition follows the
Fourth Edition of 1811. The misprint "ingenious" for "ingenuous" is in a footnote, p. 10. A Third Edition, identical
with the Second, was issued in 1819.

XIII.

English Bards,/ And/ Scotch Reviewers ;/ A Satire./ With
Notes and Preface,/ By/ Lord Byron./ Brussels,/ Published at the English Repository of Arts, Nᵒ 602,/ Rue de
L'Impératrice./ Printed by Demanet, Rue des Bogards./
1819./   [8ᵒ

Collation—
    Title, one leaf ; Half-title with Mottoes, pp. 1, 2 ; Preface,
pp. [3]–[5] ; Text, pp. 7–62 ; Postscript, pp. 63, 64.
    Note.—The Front. is "Lord Byron," "*lith. par Toland.*"
The Text numbers 1052 lines. This edition follows the Fourth
Edition of 1811. The misprint "ingenious" is at the foot of
p. 10.

XIV.

English Bards,/ And/ Scotch Reviewers ;/ A Satire./ By/
The Right Honorable/ Lord Byron./ I had rather be a
kitten, and cry, mew !/ Than one of these same metre
ballad - mongers./ *Shakspeare.*/ Such shameless Bards
we have ; and yet 'tis true,/ There are as mad, abandon'd
Critics too./ *Pope.*/ Geneva :/ Published by P. G.
Ledouble,/ No. 24, Rue de la Cité./ 1820./   [12ᵒ

Collation—

Half-title (R. Advt. of Joseph Forsyth's Remarks on Antiquities, etc., and Imprint, *Printed by Sestié Fils*.); Title, one leaf, pp. 1, 2; Preface, pp. 3–5; Text, pp. *1–66*; Postscript, pp. 67, 68.

Note.—The Text numbers 1052 lines. This edition follows the Fourth Edition of 1811.

XV.

English Bards,/ and/ Scotch Reviewers./ A Satire./ By Lord Byron./ I had rather be a kitten, and cry, Mew !/ Than one of these same metre ballad-mongers./ *Shakespeare*./ Such shameless Bards we have; and yet, 'tis true,/ There are as mad, abandon'd Critics too./ *Pope*./ London :/ Benbow, Printer and Publisher, Byron's Head,/ Castle-Street, Leicester-Square./ 1823./ [12?

Collation—

Pp. v. + [7]–61. The Imprint (*W. Benbow, Printer, Castle-st. Leicester-sq*.) is at the foot of p. 61.

Note.—The Text numbers 1050 lines. This edition follows the Third Edition of 1810.

XVI.

English Bards/ And/ Scotch Reviewers ;/ A Satire./ By Lord Byron./ [Mottoes as above, six lines.] A New Edition,/ With a Life of the Author./ To which is added/ Fare Thee Well, A Poem./ Glasgow :/ Printed by James Starke,/ and sold by All the Booksellers./ 1824./ [12?

Collation—

Pp. xiv. + *15*–52 + Fare Thee Well ! pp. [53], [54].

Note.—The Text numbers 1050 lines, as in the Third Edition. The misprint " ingenious " for " ingenuous " occurs in a footnote to p. 16.

XVII.

English Bards/ and/ Scotch Reviewers :/ A Satire./ By Lord Byron./ [Mottoes as above, six lines (" Shakspeare ").] A New Edition,/ With a life of the Author./ To which is added/ Fare Thee Well, A Poem./ Glasgow :/ Printed for M'Intosh & Co./ And sold by All the Booksellers./ 1825./ [12?

Collation—

Pp. xiv. + 34.

Note.—The Text numbers 1050 lines. This edition is differently paginated from the preceding, and the Notes are reset (the misprint " ingenious " is corrected), but the Text, Preface, and the " Life of the Author " seem to have been set up from the same type.

XVIII.

English Bards/ and/ Scotch Reviewers ;/ A Satire,/ By Lord Byron./ London :/ Printed and Published by W. Dugdale,/ 23, *Russell Court, Drury Lane.*/ 1825./ [12.°

Collation—
    Pp. 50.
    Note.—The Text numbers 1050 lines. The Notes are printed after the text, pp. 35–50. In Note 3 the misprint " ingenious " is retained. The *English Bards, and Scotch Reviewers* (Third Edition, of 1050 lines) was included in the *British Satirist,* Glasgow, 1826, 12.°, pp. *1–46,* and formed part (pp. 139–178) of a collection of Satires, Gifford's *Baviad and Mæviad,* etc., published by J. F. Dove, London, 1827, 12.° The misprint " ingenious " has been corrected in both these issues.

XIX.

English Bards,/ And/ Scotch Reviewers,/ A Satire./ By/ Lord Byron./ I had rather be a kitten, and cry, mew,/ Than one of these same metre ballad-mongers./ *Shakspeare.*/ Such shameless bards we have ; and yet, 'tis true,/ There are as mad abandoned critics too. *Pope.*/ A New Edition./ London :/ Printed by T. Kay, at the Egyptian Press, 1, Welbeck Street,/ Cavendish Square, For the Booksellers./ 1827./   [8.°

Collation—
    Half-title, pp. i., ii. ; Title, pp. iii., iv. ; Preface, pp. v.–vii. ; Text, pp. *1–78* ; Postscript (*sic*), pp. [79]–80. The Imprint (*Printed by T. Kay, 1, Welbeck Street, Cavendish Square.*) is at the foot of p. 80.
    Note.—The Text follows the Third Edition of 1810. The misprint " ingenious " occurs in a footnote to p. 4. The words " A Satire," " Shakspeare," and " Pope " on the Title-page are in Gothic characters.

Fare Thee Well.

I.

Fare Thee Well. First Version, consisting of Thirteen Stanzas, dated March 18, 1816.   [249 × 190.

Collation—
    Pp. [1]–[3].

II.

Fare Thee Well! [Printed and distributed, April 4, 1816.]
[4º

Collation—
Pp. [1]–3. P. [4] is blank. A copy of this pamphlet in the British Museum is marked as "Privately printed for Lord Byron," and measures 237 × 173. The watermark is "J. GREEN, 1815."
Note.—The Text numbers 60 lines. Lines 1–24 are on p. [1]; lines 25–56 on p. 2; and lines 57–60 on p. 3. In line 28 "may" is printed "may." *Fare Thee Well* was first published in *The Champion*, Sunday, April 14, 1816.

III.

Fare Thee Well. Second Version, consisting of Sixty Lines, dated Monday, "April 7, 1816." [250 × 190.

Collation—
Pp. 1–3.

IV.

A Sketch from Private Life, consisting of 104 lines, dated March 30th, 1816. [250 × 190.

Collation—
Pp. [1]–4.

V.

A Sketch, etc. Another copy, dated March 30, 1816, and endorsed, "Correct with most particular care, and print off 50 copies, and keep standing. 1816, April 2."

VI.

Fare Thee Well!—A Sketch, etc.—Napoleon's Farewell.—On the Star of the Legion of Honour.—An Ode. By Lord Byron. London : *Printed for Sherwood, Neely and Jones, Paternoster Row*, 1816. [8º

Collation—
Pp. 27.
Note.—"Original blue paper cover."—*Catalogue of Rowfant Library*, 1886, p. 146.

VII.

Fare Thee Well,/ A Poem./ A Sketch/ From Private Life,/ A Poem,/ By Lord Byron./ Bristol :/ Printed for Barry & Son, High-Street./ 1816./ [8º

Collation—
    Half-title, pp. 1, 2 ; Title (R. *Barry & Son, Printers.*), pp.
3, 4 ; Text (*Fare Thee Well*), pp. 5–7 ; (A Sketch, etc.), pp. 8–
12.   The Imprint, as above, is at the foot of p. 12.
    The Text is identical with that of the pamphlet.

VIII.

Fare Thee Well !/ And/ Other Poems./ By Lord Byron./
    Edinburgh :/ Printed for John Robertson,/ 132, High
    Street./   1816./   [8?

Collation—
    Title, one leaf, pp. 1, 2 ; Text, pp. 3–32.   The Imprint
(*Walker and Greig, Printers*) is at the foot of p. 32.

Contents—

Fare Thee Well . . p. 3	Ode from the French p. 18
A Sketch . . . . p. 7	Ode (" Oh, shame to **thee**,"
Napoleon's Farewell p. 13	etc.) . . . . . . p. 25
On the Star of " The Legion	Madame Lavalette . p. 30
of Honour " . . . . p. 15	

    Note.—An editorial note (p. 24) states that the Ode " Oh, shame
to thee " was first published in the *Morning Chronicle*, July 31,
1815, under the signature " Brutus."   " It has been ascribed by
many to the Author of the *Pleasures of Hope*."   A second note
(p. 30) apologizes for the inclusion of " Madame Lavalette " [first
published in the *Examiner*, January 21, 1816], which " has
appeared in some other Editions of these Poems."

The Giaour.

I.

The Giaour,/ A Fragment of/ A Turkish Tale./   By Lord
    Byron./   " One fatal remembrance — one sorrow that
    throws/ " Its bleak shade alike o'er our joys and our
    woes—/ " To which Life nothing brighter nor darker can
    bring,/ " For which joy hath no balm—and affliction no
    sting."/   Moore./   London :/ *Printed by T. Davison,
    Whitefriars,*/ For John Murray, Albemarle-Street./ 1813./
                                                        [8?

Collation—
    Half-title, one leaf ; Title, one leaf ; Dedication, " To Samuel
Rogers, Esq. ;" Text, pp. 1–41.   The Imprint (*T. Davison,
Lombard-Street,*/ *Whitefriars, London.*/) is in the centre of p. [42].
    Note.—The First Edition of the *Giaour* (June 5, 1813) numbers
685 lines.

II.

The Giaour,/ A Fragment of/ A Turkish Tale./   By Lord
    Byron./   " One fatal remembrance — one sorrow that

throws/ " Its bleak shade alike o'er our joys and our woes—/ " O'er which Life nothing brighter nor darker can fling,/ " For which joy hath no balm—and affliction no sting."/ Moore./ A New Edition, with some Additions./ London :/ *Printed by T. Davison, Whitefriars,*/ For John Murray, Albemarle-Street./ 1813./ [8°

Collation—

Half-title, one leaf ; Title, one leaf ; Dedication as above ; Advt., " The tale," etc. ; Text, pp. *1*–47. The Imprint, as above (No. i.), is in the centre of p. [48].

Note.—The Second Edition of the *Giaour*, published at the end of June or the beginning of July, numbers 816 lines. Note the misprints in third line of the motto, " O'er which " for " To which," and " fling " for " bring." The first edition of the Song, *A Selection of the Irish Melodies*, 1807, i. 45, and other editions read " bring."

III.

The Giaour,/ A Fragment of/ A Turkish Tale./ By Lord Byron./ " One fatal remembrance," etc. [Motto, four lines, as in the Second Edition]./ Moore./ Third Edition,/ With Considerable Additions./ London :/ *Printed by T. Davison, Whitefriars,*/ For John Murray, Albemarle-Street./ 1813./ [8°

Collation—

Half-title (R. Advt. of " Madame de Stael's Long Suppressed Work " [*De L'Allemagne*]) ; Title, one leaf ; Dedication ; Advt., pp. 1, 2 ; Text, pp. 3–53 + Advt. of " Books Lately Published by John Murray," pp. [54]–[56]. The Imprint (*T. Davison, Lombard Street,/ Whitefriars, London./*) is at the foot of p. [56].

Note.—The Text numbers 950 lines. The numbers 5, 10, etc., are printed on the margin. The First and Second Editions are not numbered.

IV.

The Giaour,/ A Fragment of/ A Turkish Tale./ By Lord Byron./ " One fatal remembrance—one sorrow that throws/ It's bleak shade alike o'er our joys and our woes—/ O'er which Life nothing brighter nor darker can fling,/ For which joy hath no balm—and affliction no sting."/ Moore./ From the Third London Edition./ Boston :/ Printed by John Eliot,/ No. 5, Court Street./ 1813.

Collation—

Pp. 72.

Note.—The *Giaour* was also published at Philadelphia in 1813, 53 pp. 24°.

V.

The Giaour,/ A Fragment of/ A Turkish Tale./   By Lord
Byron./   "One fatal remembrance," etc. [Motto, four lines,
as in Second Edition]./   Moore./   Fifth Edition,/ With
Considerable Additions./   London :/ *Printed by T.
Davison, Whitefriars,*/ For John Murray, Albemarle-
Street./   1813./   [8°

Collation—
    Half-title, one leaf ; Title, one leaf ; Advt. ; Text, pp. *1–66.*
    Note.—The Text numbers **1215** lines. The concluding note,
"The circumstance," etc., is enlarged (p. 66) by nine lines : " I
do not know "—" Hall of Eblis."   The Dedication is wanting
in the copy of the Fifth Edition in the British Museum.

VI.

The Giaour,/ etc./   Sixth Edition,/ etc./   1813./   [8°

Collation—
    Title, one leaf ; Dedication ; Advt. ; Text, pp. *1–66.*
    Note.—The Text numbers **1215** lines. The Half-title is missing
in the Museum copy.

VII.

The Giaour,/ A Fragment of/ A Turkish Tale./   By Lord
Byron./   "One fatal remembrance," etc. [Motto, four
lines, as in the First Edition, "bring" for "fling," etc.]/
Moore./   Seventh Edition, With some Additions./
London :/ *Printed by Thomas Davison, Whitefriars,*/
For John Murray, Albemarle Street./   1813./   [8°

Collation—
    Half-title, one leaf ; Title, one leaf ; Dedication ; Advt. ;
Text, pp. *1–75.*   The Imprint (*T. Davison, Lombard Street,*/
Whitefriars, London./) is in the centre of p. [76].
    Note.—The Text numbers **1334** lines. The Notes are printed
at the end (pp. *65–75*) of the volume.

VIII.

The Giaour,/ etc./   The Ninth Edition,/ etc./   1814./   [8°

Collation—
    Vide supra, No. vi.
    Note.—The Half-title is missing in the Museum copy.

IX.

The Giaour,/ etc./   The Tenth Edition,/ etc./   1814./   [8°

Collation—
   Vide supra, No. vi.
   Note.—Four pages of "Interesting Works Published in February, 1814, By John Murray, Bookseller of the Admiralty, and Board of Longitude," etc., are bound up with the Tenth Edition.

X.

The Giaour,/ etc./   The Eleventh Edition,/ etc./   1814./
                                                        [8°

Collation—
   Vide supra, No. vi.
   Note.—The Half-title is missing in the Museum copy.

XI.

The Giaour,/ etc./   The Twelfth Edition./   London :/
Printed for John Murray, Albemarle-Street :/ *By Thomas Davison, Whitefriars./*   1814./   [8°
Collation—
   Vide supra, No. vi.

XII.

The Giaour,/ etc./   The Fourteenth Edition./   London :/
Printed for John Murray, Albemarle-Street./   1815./   [8°
Collation—
   Half-title, one leaf ; Title (R. *T. Davison, Lombard-Street,/ Whitefriars, London./*) ; Dedication ; Advt. ; Text, pp. *1–75.* The Imprint, as above, is in the centre of p. [76].
   Note.—Four pages of Advts., dated "Albemarle - Street, London, January, 1818," are bound up with the Fourteenth Edition.

XIII.

The Giaour ;/ A Fragment of/ A Turkish Tale./   [Motto, four lines.] Moore./   London :/ Printed and Published by W. Dugdale,/ *23, Russell Court, Drury Lane./*   1825./
                                                        [12°
Collation—
   Pp. **51.** The Imprint (*W. Dugdale, Printer,* **23,** *Russell Court, Drury Lane*) is at the foot of p. [52].

XIV.

The Giaour :/ A/ Fragment of a Turkish Tale./   By/ Lord Byron./   London : John Murray, Albemarle Street./   Sold

also by/ Tilt and Bogue, Fleet Street :/ Edinburgh,
Oliver and Boyd : Dublin, John Cumming./ 1842./
                                                  [12º

Collation—
   Pp. 67.   The Imprint (*London :/ Printed by A. Spottiswoode,/
New-Street-Square./*) is in the centre of p. [68].

XV.

The Giaour :/ A Fragment of a Turkish Tale,/ By Lord
Byron./ [Motto, four lines.] Moore./ [1844.]   [8º
Collation—
   Pp. 40.   The Imprint (*H. G. Clarke and Co.*, 66, *Old Bailey*)
is at the foot of p. 40.
   Note.—Part of " Clarke's Home Library."

Translations of The Giaour.
French.

Le Giaour, fragments d'un cante turc, poème traduit de
l'anglais de lord Byron, par J. M. H. Bigeon, Paris,
Ponthieu, Ledoyen, 1828.   [18º
                             [Quérard, 1846.]

German.
I.

Der Gauer, Bruchstück einer türkischen Erzählung, nach
der 7. englischen Ausgabe im Deutschen metrisch bear-
beitet. Berlin, F. Dümmler. 1819.   [12º
             [*Centralblatt, etc.*, 1890, vol. vii. p. 456.]

II.

Der Gjaur. In deutsche Verse übersetzt v. Arthur v.
Nordstern. Mit d. engl. Text zur Seite. Leipzig, Göschen.
1820.   [8º
                             [Kayser, 1834.]

III.

Der Gjaur. Bruchstück e. türk. Erzählg. v. Lord Byron.
Frei übers. v. Adf. Seubert. Leipzig. 1871–76.   [16º
                             [Kayser, 1877.]

Collation—
   Pp. 48.
   Note.—No. 669 of the *Universal=Bibliothek.*

Italian.

I.

Il Giaurro, frammento di novella turca ; recato dall' ingl.
in versi ital. da Pellegrino Rossi.   Genova e Parigi,
Paschoud, 1817.   [12°
                    [Quérard, 1827.]

II.

Il Giaurro. Traduzione di Andrea Maffei.   Milano, Hoepli.
1884.   [64°
                    [Pagliaini, 1901.]

Polish.

I.

Giaur, ułomki powieści tureckiéj, poema...Przeldadania
    Władysl. hr. Ostrowskiego.   pp. 83.
    W drukarni bibliotecznéj : Puławy, 1830.   [8°.

II.

Giaur, Ułamki powieści tureckiéj, tłum. Adam Mickiewicz
    Księgarnia Katol. : Paryż, 1834 [*Wrocław*, 1835]. [8°.

Romaic.

I.

Ποιηματα Βυρωνος/ ὁ Γκιαουρ/ τεμαχιον/ τουρκικου Διηγηματος/ Μετα-
φρασις/ Αἰκατερινης κ. Δοσιου/ ’Εκδιδεται το Δευτερον/ ‘Υπο/ ’Αρ. Κ.
Δοσιου/ ’Αθηνησι/ Τυποις ’Ανδρεου Κορομηλα/ 1873/   [4°
Collation—
    Half-title, one leaf ; Title, one leaf ; Translator's Advt. ;
Προλογος, pp. [α']–ι' + Text, pp. *1*–69 + Παροραματα, p. [70].

II.

Σακελλαριου Βιβλιοθηκη του Λαου/ Ποιηματα Βυρωνος/ ὁ Γκιαουρ/
τεμαχιον/ τουρκικου Διηγηματος/ Μεταφρασις/ Αἰκατερινης κ.
Δοσιου/ ’Εν ’Αθηναις/ Τυποις και ’Αναλωμασι Π. Δ. Σακελλαριου/
[1898 ?]   [8°
Collation—
    Pp. 91. The Imprint (Τυπογραφειον Π. Δ. Σακελλαριου ἐν
’Αθηναις) is in the centre of p. [92].

Russian.

I.

Джяуръ. Отрывки изъ одной турецкой повѣсти. "Выборъ изъ сочиненій лорда Байрона" М. Каченовскаго. pp. 107–176. 1821.

II.

Джяуръ. Отрывки турецкой повѣсти. . . . Переводъ Н. Р. pp. 31. *Москва,* 1822. 8°.

III.

Гяуръ. . .Перевелъ Е. Мишель. [In prose.] [8°.
С.-Петербургъ, 1862.
Collation—
   Pp. 49.

IV.

Гяуръ. . .Перев. размѣромъ подлинника В. Петровъ.
С.-Петербургъ, 1873.

V.

Гяуръ Байрона и Крымскіе сонеты Мицкевича. Перевелъ В. А. Петровъ. Изданіе 2-ое.
С.-Петербургъ, 1874.

Servian.

Ђаур лорда Бајрона. Србски од Ац. Поповиħа. pp. 67.
   Д. Хинц: у Новом-Саду, 1860. [12°.

Spanish.

El Giaur ó el infiel, por lord Byron. Traduccion Castellana.
   Paris, 1828: Madrid, lib. Europea. [12°
      [*Dicc. Gen. de Bibl. Esp.* por D. Dion. Hidalgo, 1862.]

Swedish.

Giaurn,/ Ett Stycke Af en Turkish Berättelse,/ Af/ Lord Byron./ Öfversättning./ Stockholm./ J. L. Brudins Förlag./ 1855./ [8°
   Collation—
      Pp. 80.
      Note.—No. 6 of " Byron's Poetiska Berattelser," translated by Talis-Qualis.

Heaven and Earth.

I.

[*Note.*—For the First Edition of *Heaven and Earth*, see *The Liberal*, No. II., pp. 165–206 (London, L. Hunt, 1822).]

Heaven and Earth,/ A Mystery ;/ Founded on the Following Passage in Genesis,/ Chap. vi./ "And it came to pass . . . that the sons of God saw the/ daughters of men that they were fair ; and they took them/ wives of all which they chose."/ "And woman wailing for her Demon lover."/ Coleridge./ London :/ Benbow, Printer and Publisher, 252, High Holborn./ 1824./ [12°

Collation—

Pp. 35 + "Benbow's Catalogue of Books," p. [36]. The Imprint (*Benbow, Printer, 9, Castle Street, Leicester Square, London*) is at the foot of p. [36].

II.

Heaven and Earth, a Mystery, Paris, Galignani, 1823.
[12°
[Quérard, 1827.]

III.

Heaven and Earth, etc. [12°

Collation—
Pp. 36.
Note.—This edition, printed by (?) W. Dugdale in (?) 1825, bears neither Title-page nor Imprint, and is bound up with *The Bride of Abydos*, printed for Thomas Wilson in 1825, and *The Corsair*, printed and published by W. Dugdale in 1825.

Translations of Heaven and Earth.
French.

Essai/ Sur Le Génie et Le Caractère/ de Lord Byron,/ Par A. P. . . . T. ;/ etc./ Paris./ Ladvocat, Libraire, Palais-Royal,/ Galerie de Bois, N°. 195./ 1824./ [12°

Collation—
Half-title, Le Ciel/ Et La Terre./ Mystère/ Fondé sur ce Passage de La Genèse :/ (Chap. VI)/ : "Et il arriva . . . que les fils de Dieu virent que les filles des/ hommes étaient belles ; et ils prirent pour femmes/ celles d'entre elles qu'ils choisirent./ "La femme regrettant son démon bien-aimé."/ (Coleridge.)/ (R. *Personnages.*), pp. [195], [196] + Text, pp. *197–252*.

Italian.

Cielo e terra : mistero, tradotto da Andrea Maffei.   Milano,
    Gnocchi, 1853.   [16?
                                            [Pagliaini, 1901.]

Russian.

Небо и Земля.   Н. В. Гербель, "Полное собраніе
стихотвореній."   Том. I.

Hebrew Melodies.

I.

A Selection of/ Hebrew Melodies/ Ancient and Modern/
with appropriate Symphonies and accompaniments/ By/
I: Braham & I: Nathan/ the Poetry written expressly
for the work/   By the Right Honble/ Lord Byron/ ent^{d}
at Sta^{rs} Hall/ [Title-vignette, angel holding crown] 1st
Number/ Published and Sold by I: Nathan N? 7 Poland
Street Oxford Str^{t}/ and to be had at the principal Music
and Booksellers/ Price one Guinea/ [1815]   [fol.

[The Title-page is enclosed in an ornamental border, and below
the words, "*Drawn by Edward Blore*," is the signature "I.
Braham ;" and below the words, "*Engraved by W. Lowry*," the
signature "I. Nathan."]
Collation—
    Part I. : Illuminated Dedication "To Her Royal Highness
the Princess Charlotte of Wales," one leaf ; Preface, signed
"I. Braham, I. Nathan," and dated "London, April, 1815," one
leaf ; Index to the First Number, one leaf ; Music and Words,
pp. *1–64*.
    Part II. : Title (A Selection of,/ etc. . . . By the Right
Honorable Lord Byron./ [Motto], "The harp the Monarch
Minstrel swept," etc., five lines./ See Page 4./ Lord Byron./
2nd Number, Price I Guinea./ Ent^{d} at Stationers' Hall./ Published and Sold, etc./ *Prickett scrip. et sculp.*/ [The Title-vignette
is King David playing a harp with angel and tripod, engraved by
H. Moses.] The title is signed "I. Nathan."
Collation—
    Title, one leaf ; Dedication, as above, one leaf ; Index to the
Second Number, one leaf ; Music and Words, pp. 65–133.

Contents—Part I.—

She walks, etc.	. . p. 1		On Jordan's Banks	. p. 29
The Harp, etc.	. . p. 5		Jephtha's Daughter	. p. 36
If that high World	. p. 14		Oh, snatch'd away	. p. 41
The wild Gazelle	. p. 19		My Soul is dark	. p. 44
Oh, weep for those	. p. 25		I saw thee weep	. . p. 49

Note.—For a reissue, with additions, of this collection, see *Fugitive Pieces and Reminiscences of Lord Byron*, etc., by I. Nathan, 1829, No. xii., p. 254.

II.

Hebrew Melodies./ By Lord Byron./ London :/ Printed for John Murray, Albemarle-Street./ 1815./   [8º

Collation—
  Half-title (Hebrew Melodies. *T. Davison, Lombard-Street,/ Whitefriars, London./*), one leaf ; Title, one leaf ; Advt. ; Cont. ; Text (*Hebrew Melodies*), pp. *1–53.*
  Note.—The Cont. are identical with the preceding, save that the lines, "Francisca," a variant of *Parisina* (lines 15–28), are omitted ; the lines *From Job* are inserted pp. 49, 50 ; and the stanzas "On the Death of Sir Peter Parker" (pp. 51–53) are printed at the end of the volume.

III.

Hebrew Melodies. Boston. 1815.   [24º

Collation—
  Pp. 2 + 43.

IV.

Hebrew Melodies. Philadelphia. 1815.   [16º

V.

Hebrew Melodies./ By the Right Honourable/ Lord Byron./ London : Printed and Published by W. Dugdale,/ *Green Street, Leicester Square./* 1823./   [12º

Collation—
  Pp. 36. The Imprint (*Printed by W. Dugdale, Great Street, Leicester Square./*) is at the foot of p. 36.
  Note.—The lines "It is the Hour" (*Parisina*, 1–14) and "Francisca" (*ibid.*, lines 15–28) are omitted.

VI.

Hebrew Melodies./ By Lord Byron./ London :/ Printed
and Published by W. Dugdale,/ *23, Russell Court, Drury
Lane./* 1825./   [12º

Collation—
  Pp. **22.** The Imprint (*Printed by W. Dugdale,* 23, *Russell
  Court, Drury Lane.*) is at the foot of p. **22.**
  Note.—For Cont., *vide supra*, No. v.

Translations of Hebrew Melodies.
Bohemian.

Hebrejské melodie. Přeložili Jaroslen Vrchlický a J. V.
Sládek. *v Praze*, 1890.

Danish.

Lord Byron :/ Jødiske sange./ oversatte/ af/ F. Andresen
Halmrast/ Christiania./ Jacob Dybwads forlag./ 1889./

Collation—
  Pp. **41** + Indhold, pp. [43], [44].

German.
I.

Hebräische Gesänge./ Aus dem Englischen/ des Lord
Byron/ von/ Franz Theremin./ Mit beigedrucktem en-
glischen Text./ Berlin./ Verlag von Dunker und
Humblot./ 1820./   [12º

Collation—
  Pp. viii. + *3*–87.

II.

Hebräische Gesänge. Aus d. Engl. übersetzt von Jos. Emn.
Hitscher. Mit gegenüberstehendem Originale. Laibach,
1833.   [8º

                    [Kayser, 1841.]

III.

Germanische/ Melodien./ Theilweise/ frei nach Lord
Byron's hebräischen Melodien/ von/ Hugo Oelbermann./
Bonn./ Rheinische Verlags-Anstalt./ 1862./   [8º

Collation—
  Pp. 49.

IV.

Lord Byron's/ Hebräische Gesänge./ Aus dem Englischen/ übertragen/ und mit sachlichen Einleitungen und Bemerkungen/ versehen/ von/ Eduard Nickles./ Karlsruhe./ Druck und Verlag von Friedrich Gutsch./ 1863./

Collation—
Pp. 105 + Anmerkung, p. 106 + Anhang, pp. 107–112.
Note.—The English text is printed over against the German. The "Anhang" contains translations of "In the valley," etc., and "They say that hope," etc.

V.

Hebräischer Gesänge./ Aus d. Engl. übers. von Heinr. Stadelmann. Memmingen, 1866. Hartwig in Comm.
[16⁰
[Kayser, 1871.]

Hebrew.

Hebrew Melodies/ of/ Lord Byron/ Translated by/ Dr. S. Mandelkern./ Leipzig./ 1890./ [8⁰

Collation—
Pp. 45 + Cont. (Hebrew character) (R. Advt. of Hebrew Poems (with vowel points) of Dr. S. Mandelkern), pp. [47], [48].
Note.—The Hebrew translation is over against the English text. The Title-page, which is in Hebrew and English, is enclosed in an arabesque border.

Italian.

I.

Melodie ebraiche/ di/ Lord G. Byron/ Versione/ di P. P. Parzanese/ Napoli/ dalla tipografia all' insegna di Tasso/ via Concezione a Toledo N⁰ 3./ 1837/

Collation—
Pp. 47.
Note.—Printed on green paper.

II.

Le Melodie ebree, coll' aggiunta di alcuni altri poemetti. Ivrea, 1855. [16⁰
[Pagliaini, 1901.]

Russian.

Еврейскія мелодіи... Переводъ П. Козлова.
С.-Петербургъ, 1860.

Swedish.

Hebreiska Melodier/ af/ Lord Byron./ Öfversatta/ af/ Theodor Lind./ Helsingfors,/ Theodor Sederholms Förlag./ [1862.]　　　　　　　　　　　　　　[8°

Collation—
　　Pp. 41 + Innehåll, p. [43].

Fugitive Pieces and Minor Poems.

I.

Fugitive Pieces By/ George Gordon Lord Byron/　A Fac-Simile Reprint of/ The Suppressed/ Edition of/ 1806/ [Title-vignette, Venus Anadyomene in shell with attendant Cupids.]　London/ Printed for Private Circulation/　1886/
　　　　　　　　　　　　　　　　　　　　　　[4°

Collation—
　　Advt. of issue (No. 22 of 100 numbered copies) of—*Printers,/ Chiswick Press, Tooks Court,/ Chancery Lane, London./* signed (MS.) "Charles Whittingham & Co.," pp. i., ii. ; Half-title (BYRON'S FUGITIVE PIECES), pp. iii., iv. ; Title, one leaf, pp. v., vi. ; Preface (editorial of facsimile), pp. vii.–x. + blank leaf + Half-title (FUGITIVE PIECES), one leaf + Dedication—"To/ Those Friends,/ At/ Whose Request They were printed,/ For whose/ Amusement or Approbation/ They are/ Solely Intended ;/ These TRIFLES are respectfully Dedicated,/ by the/ Author."/ (R. As these POEMS were never intended to meet the public eye, no apology is necessary for the form in which they now appear. They are printed merely for the perusal of a few friends to whom they are dedicated ; who will look upon them with indulgence ; and as most of them were composed between the age of 15 and 17, their defects will be pardoned or forgotten, in the youth and inexperience of the WRITER.) + Text, pp. [1]–66 ; (the Imprint (*Printed by S. and J. Ridge, Newark.*) is at the foot of p. 66) + p. [67] (emblem—heraldic lion with shield and monogram, sub-scribed with the Imprint, *Chiswick Press :—C. Whittingham and Co., Tooks Court,/ Chancery Lane./*).

Contents—

On Leaving N . . st . . d
　　　　　　　　　　p. [1]
To E. . . . . . .　p. 3
On the Death of a Young Lady, Cousin to the Author and very Dear to him　. .　p. 4
To D. . . . . . .　p. 5
To . . . .　p. 6
To Caroline . . .　p. 7
To Maria —— . .　p. 10
Fragments of School Exer-
cises, From The Prometheus Vinctus of Œschylus (*sic*) p. 11
Lines in " Letters of an Italian Nun," etc. . . . . p. 12
Answer to the above, ad-dress'd to Miss —— . p. 13
On a change of Masters, At a Great Public School
　　　　　　　　　　p. 14
Epitaph on a Beloved Friend
　　　　　　　　　　p. 15

Note.—The original volume measures 8¾ ins. × 7½ ins. The wrapper is of plain greenish-grey paper. The full Titles are given in the Table of Cont. or in the heading of the Poems in *Poetical Works*, 1898, vol. i. pp. xviii., etc. In the original issue the pages are numbered on the head of each page, and subscribed with a double rule. "Ornaments" are to be found on pp. [1], 3, 13, 14, 16, 40, 58, 60, 64, 66.

The signatures B (p. [1]) to S (p. 65) are in due sequence. The numbers at the head of the pages are subscribed with a double rule.

II.

Poems/ On/ Various Occasions./ VIRGINIBUS PUERISQUE CANTO./ Hor. Lib. 3. Od. 1./ Newark : Printed by S. & J. Ridge./ MDCCCVII./ [8?

Collation—

Pp. 12 + 144—Half-title, one leaf, pp. [1], [2] ; Title, one leaf, pp. [3], [4] ; Dedication (as above), pp. [5], [6] ; Author's Advt., dated December 23, 1806, pp. [7], [8] ; Cont., pp. [9]-11 ; Text, 1-144. The Imprint (*Printed by S. and J. Ridge, Newark.*) is at the foot of p. 144.

Contents—

Note.—The Title measures 193 × 113. The first signature, C, is on p. 9; M, on p. 81; O (*not* N), on p. 89; Q, on p. 105; U, on p. 137. Signature P is omitted on p. 97.

The "ornaments" of the Quarto reappear on pp. [1], 9, 25, 32. The numbers at the head of the pages are subscribed with a double rule. A facsimile of the Title-page faces p. x. of vol. i. of the *Poetical Works*, 1898.

III.

Hours of Idleness,/ A/ Series of Poems,/ Original/ And/ Translated,/ By George Gordon, Lord Byron,/ A Minor./ Μητ' αρ με μαλ' αινεε μητε τι νεικει./ Homer. Iliad, 10./ Virginibus puerisque Canto ;/ Horace./ He whistled as he went for want of thought./ Dryden./ Newark: Printed and sold by S. and J. Ridge ;/ Sold also by B. Crosby and Co. Stationer's Court ;/ Longman, Hurst, Rees, and Orme, Paternoster-/Row ; F. and C. Rivington, S: Paul's Church-/Yard ; and J. Mawman, In the Poultry,/ London./ 1807./   [8º

Collation—

Half-title (Hours/ of/ Idleness.), one leaf, pp. i., ii. ; Title, one leaf, pp. iii., iv. ; Preface, pp. [v.]–xiii. (R. *Errata*) ; Text, pp. [1]–187. The Imprint (*Printed by S. and J. Ridge, Newark.*) is at the foot of p. 187.

Contents—

Note (1).—A facsimile of the Title-page (2) faces p. xii. of vol. i.
of the *Poetical Works*, 1898. It has been alleged that large-paper
copies of this edition were issued from the Newark press. It is
certain that large copies (a copy in the British Museum, cut for
binding, measures 220 × 122), printed on paper bearing a water-
mark dated 1806, were thrown upon the market at an early
period, but it has not been ascertained at what date or in what
place they were printed. They are undoubtedly deliberate
forgeries. They purport, even in respect of *errata*, to be identical with the genuine issue of 1807 ; but they were not set up
from the same type, and it is inconceivable that a second issue,
set up from different type and with slightly different ornaments,
was printed by Ridge for piratical purposes. To cite a few
obvious differences—in the title of the large-paper copies the
first A of the word "TRANSLATED" is printed Λ, and the
Greek ν in αινεε and νεικει appears as υ (not ν reversed) ; in the
Errata on the reverse of p. xiii., [Page] "153 Note" is incorrectly given as "163 Note," and this slip on the part of the
falsarius is more remarkable, as two other errata in the Errata
are carefully reproduced ; in the Greek motto on p. 22 the letter ρ
twice appears as ϱ ; and, finally, the ornaments on pp. 1 and 187,
though intended to be, are not identical. In the Museum copy a
portrait of "Lord Byron, from a sketch taken on his leaving
England," engraved by I. West, and "Published by W. Hone,
Ludgate Hill, 1819," precedes the title-page, and, together with
the binding, affords good, if not conclusive, proof that this copy
was printed before 1820.

See, for a correspondence on these L. P. copies of 1807, the
Athenæum, June, 1898, pp. 694, 695.

See, too, for further interesting and conclusive evidence that
the ornament on p. 187 of the L. P. copies was not printed from
the Newark block, *Newark as a Publishing Town*, by T. M.
Blagg, 1898, pp. 28-30.

Note (2).—An autograph note, dated May 20th, 1812, signed
"Byron," is inserted on the fly-leaf of a large-paper copy in the
Rowfant Library (*Catalogue*, 1886, p. 144).

IV.

Poems/ Original and Translated,/ By/ George Gordon, Lord
Byron./   Μητ᾽ αρ᾽ με μαλ᾽ αινεε μητε τι νεικει./   Homer.
Iliad, 10./   He whistled as he went for want of thought./
Dryden./   Second Edition./   Newark :/ Printed and sold
by S. and J. Ridge ;/ Sold also by B. Crosby and Co.
Stationer's Court ;/ Longman, Hurst, Rees, and Orme,
Paternoster-/Row ; F. & C. Rivington, St Paul's Church-/
Yard, and J. Mawman, in the/ Poultry, London./   1808./
                                                      [8º

Collation—
   [? a Half-title] ; Title, one leaf, pp. ii., iii. ; Dedication (To

The Right Honourable/ Frederick,/ Earl of Carlisle,/ Knight of the Garter,/ etc., etc./ The Second Edition/ Of/ These Poems is inscribed,/), By/ His Obliged Ward,/ And/ Affectionate Kinsman,/ The Author.), pp. iv., v. ; Cont., pp. [vi.]–viii. (R. *Errata*) ; Text, pp. [1]–174. The Imprint (*Printed by S. and J. Ridge, Newark-upon-Trent*) is at the foot of p. 174.

Contents—

Note.—The Front. is a lithograph of Harrow-on-the-Hill, with quotation—

> "Ida! blest spot, where Science holds her reign!
> How joyous once I join'd thy youthful train!"

A facsimile of the Title-page faces p. xii. of vol. i. of the *Poetical Works,* 1898.

V.

Imitations and Translations/ From the /Ancient and Modern Classics,/ Together with/ Original Poems/ Never Before

Published./   Collected by/ J. C. Hobhouse, B.A./ of
Trinity College, Cambridge./ " Nos hæc novimus esse
nihil."/   London :/ Printed for Longman, Hurst, Rees,
and Orme,/ Paternoster-Row./   1809./   [8º

Collation—
Half-title with Imprint (T. Davison, *Whitefriars,| London.*),
pp. i., ii. ; Title, one leaf, pp. iii., iv. ; Preface, pp. v.–xi. ;
Cont., pp. xiii.–xv. (R. "Errata.") ; Text, pp. *1–255.* The
Imprint, as above, is in the centre of p. [256].
Note.—Lord Byron contributed nine poems (signed L. B. ; see
Preface, p. xi., to this volume) to this volume, viz. : (i.) *To a
Youthful Friend* ("Few years have past," etc.), p. **185** ; (ii.)
Inscription on the Monument of a Favourite Dog, p. **190** ; (iii.)
To —— (" Well ! thou art happy," etc.), p. **192** ; (iv.) *The Fare-
well To a Lady* ("When man expell'd," etc.), p. **195** ; (v.) *A Love
Song to ——* ("Remind me not," etc.), p. **197** ; (vi.) *Stanzas To
the Same* ("There was a time," etc.), p. **200** ; (vii.) *To the Same*
("And wilt thou weep," etc.), p. **202** ; (viii.) *Song* ("Fill the
goblet again," etc.), p. **204** ; (ix.) *Stanzas to —— on leaving
England* (" 'Tis done," etc.), p. **227**.

VI.

Hours of Idleness ;/ A/ Series of Poems,/ Original and
Translated,/ By George Gordon, Lord Byron,/ A Minor./
Μητ' αρ' με μαλ' αινεε μητε τι νεικει./   Homer. Iliad, 10./
He whistled as he went for want of thought./ Dryden./
Second Edition./   Paris :/ Published by Galignani,/ At
the French, English, Italian, German, and Spanish/
Library, Nº 18, Rue Vivienne./   1819./   [12º

Collation—
Half-title, one leaf ; Title, one leaf ; Advt. ; Dedication ;
Cont. ; Text, pp. *1–149* + "Critique . . . *Ed. Rev.*, No. 22,"
etc., pp. [150]–158.
Note.—A reproduction of *Poems Original and Translated*,
Newark, 1808.

VII.

Hours of Idleness :/ A Series of Poems,/ Original and Translated./ By/ Lord Byron./ Μητ' αρ' με μαλ' αινεε μητε τι
νεικει./ Homer. Iliad, 10./   He whistled as he went
for want of thought./ Dryden./ London :/ Printed for
Sherwin and Co. 24, Paternoster Row./ 1820./   [8º

Collation—
Half-title, pp. i., ii. ; Title, pp. iii., iv. ; Dedication, pp. v.,
vi. ; Cont., pp. vii., viii. ; Text, pp. *1–160.* The Imprint
(*Sherwin and Co., Printers,| Paternoster Row.|*) is at the foot of
p. **160**.

Note.—A reproduction of *Poems Original and Translated*, Newark, 1808. The Front. (a sketch of Harrow-on-the-Hill) is engraved by Eastgate from a painting by H. Halsted, Esq. It is a reproduction (re-touched) of the Front. to the Newark Edition of 1808.

There were two issues of this edition (A and B). In A (Printed for Sherwin and Co. 24 Paternoster Row) the Front. is without letters ; the past tenses and participles are printed "bloom'd," "mail-cover'd," etc. ; and on p. 160 the Imprint, as above, is at the foot of p. 160. In B (Printed for W. T. Sherwin, etc.) the Front. is subscribed with the name of painter and engraver ; the past tenses are printed "bloomed," etc., in full ; and the Imprint (*Sherwin, Printer,*/ *Paternoster Row.*/) is at the foot of p. 160.

VIII.

Hours of Idleness ;/ etc./ Third Edition./ Paris : Published by Galignani,/ etc./ 1820./   [12°

Collation—
   This edition is identical with that of 1819, No. vi. p. 252. The Cont. are printed at the end of the volume.

IX.

Hours of Idleness,/ A Series/ Of Poems,/ Original and Translated./ By a Noble Author./ Virginibus puerisque Canto./ Horace./ He whistled as he went for want of thought./ Dryden./ London :/ Benbow, Printer and Publisher, Castle Street,/ Leicester Square. 1822./ [12°

Collation—
   Title, pp. i., ii. ; Preface, pp. iii.–viii. + Cont. + Text, pp. 9–183.
   Note.—A reissue of *Hours of Idleness*, Newark, 1807.

X.

Hours of Idleness :/ A/ Series of Poems,/ Original and Translated./ By George Gordon, Lord Byron./ A Minor./ Paris :/ Published by A. and W. Galignani,/ At the French, English, Italian, German, and Spanish Library, No 18, Rue Vivienne./ 1822./   [12°

Collation—
   Half-title (R. *Printed by A. Belin*), one leaf ; Title, one leaf ; Cont. ; Text (including Second Half-title and Dedication), pp. 1–152 + *Critique*, etc., pp. [153]–168.
   Note.—A reissue of the Newark edition of 1808, but a distinct edition from those published by Galignani in 1819, 1820.

XI.

Hours of Idleness,/ A/ Series of Poems,/ Original and
Translated./ By Lord Byron./ Virginibus puerisque
canto.—Horace./ He whistled as he went, for want of
thought.—Dryden./ A New Edition./ Glasgow.—Printed
by J. Starke./ 1825./   [8°

Collation—
   Title, one leaf; Preface, pp. i.–iii. (R. Cont.) ; Text, pp. *1*–84.
   Note.—This edition, a reissue of *Hours of Idleness*, Newark,
1807, was bound in a paper wrapper with ornamental border,
uniform with "*English Bards, and Scotch Reviewers*—price
sixpence."

XII.

Fugitive Pieces/ and/ Reminiscences/ of/ Lord Byron:/ Containing an entire new Edition of/ The Hebrew Melodies,/
With the Addition of/ Several never before Published ;/
The whole illustrated with/ Critical, Historical, Theatrical,
Political, and Theological/ Remarks, Notes, Anecdotes,
Interesting Conversations,/ And Observations, made by
that Illustrious Poet ;/ Together with his Lordship's Autograph ;/ also some/ Original Poetry, Letters and Recol-
lections/ of/ Lady Caroline Lamb./ By I. Nathan,/ Author
of an Essay on the History and Theory of Music,/ The
Hebrew Melodies, etc., etc./ "Pascitur in vivis Livor,
post Fata quiescit :"/ "Tune (*sic*) suus, ex merito, quem-
que tuetur Honos." Ovid./ London :/ Printed for
Whittaker, Treacher, and Co./ Ave Maria Lane./ 1829./
                               [8°

Collation—
   Pp. xxxvi. + 196. The Imprint (*Plummer and Brewis,
Printers, Love Lane, Eastcheap.*) is at the foot of p. 191.
   Note.—The Fugitive Pieces include the two selections from
Parisina included in *Hebrew Melodies* No. i., and three "original
pieces of Lord Byron, which have never before appeared in
print ;" viz. "I speak not—I trace not," etc., "In the valley of
waters," and "They say that hope is happiness."

Poems.

Poems./ By Lord Byron./ Second Edition./ London :/
Printed for John Murray, Albemarle-Street ;/ By W.
Bulmer and Co. Cleveland-Row, St James's,/ 1816./ [8°

Collation—
   Half-title, one leaf, pp. i., ii. ; Title, one leaf, iii., iv. ; Advt.,
pp. v., vi. ; Cont., pp. vii., viii. ; Text, pp. *9*-39 + Notes,

p. [40]. The Imprint (*London : Printed by W. Bulmer and Co./ Cleveland-row, St. James's./*) is at the foot of p. [40].

Contents—

To —— (" When all around," etc.) . . . . . p. 9	Ode (" We do not curse," etc.) . . . . . p. 25
Bright be the place . p. 13	From the French . p. 31
When we two parted p. 14	On the Star, etc.. . p. 34
Stanzas for Music (" There's not a joy," etc.) . . . p. 16	Napoleon's Farewell p. 37
Stanzas for Music (" There be none," etc.) . . . p. 19	To Samuel Rogers, Esq. p. 39
	Notes . . . . . p. 40
Fare Thee Well . . p. 21	

Note.—The motto from Coleridge's *Christabel* (" Alas ! they had been friends in youth ") (14 lines) is on p. 20.

Poems on His Domestic Circumstances.

I.

Poems/ on His/ Domestic/ Circumstances./ I. Fare Thee Well !/ II. A Sketch From Private Life./ By Lord Byron./ With the/ Star of the Legion of Honour,/ And other Poems./ London :/ Printed for W. Hone, 55, Fleet Street./ 1816./ Price One Shilling./   [8°

Collation—

Title, one leaf, pp. 3, 4 ; Text, pp. 5-31 + Note (" The first two Poems were last produced.—The other/ five follow in the order wherein they were written./ April, 1816.), p. [32]. The Imprint (*Hay and Turner, Printers, Newcastle Street, Strand.*) is at the foot of p. [40].

Contents—

Fare Thee Well . . p. 5	Fare Well to France p. 20
A Sketch, etc. . . p. 9	Madame Lavalette . p. 22
Ode (" Oh, shame to thee," etc.). . . . . . . p. 15	Waterloo . . . . p. 24
	On the Star, etc.. . p. 29

Note.—The Half-title is missing in the Museum copy. The Note prefixed to " Waterloo " in the *Morning Chronicle* (March 15, 1816) is reprinted, together with the heading, " Said to be done into English Verse by R. S * * * * * *, P.L. P.R. Master of the Royal Spanish Inqn.—etc., etc., etc."

II.

Poems/ on His/ Domestic Circumstances,/ etc./ With The/ Star of the Legion of Honour,/ And Four Other Poems./ Second Edition./ London :/ Printed for W. Hone, 55, Fleet Street,/ And Sold by J. M. Richardson, No. 23, Cornhill ;/ J. Blacklock, Royal Exchange ; G. Hebert,

36,/ Poultry ; Simpkin and Marshall,/ Stationers'/ Court ;
W. Reynolds, 137, Oxford Street ; and by/ All other
Booksellers./　1816./　　　　　　　　　　　　　　[8°

Collation—
　　Gen. Half-title (New/ Poems,/ By/ Lord Byron./) (R. *Hay &*
Turner, Printers, Newcastle-Street, Strand.), pp. **1, 2** ; Title, one
leaf, pp. **3, 4** ; Text, pp. **5–31**. The Note and Imprint, as above,
are on p. [32].

III.

Poems,/ etc./　By Lord Byron./　With the/ Star of the
Legion of Honour,/ etc., etc./　Sixth Edition./　Containing
Eight Poems./　London :/ Printed for W. Hone, 55, Fleet
Street,/ etc., etc.　1816./　　　　　　　　　　　　[8°

Collation—
　　Title (Imprint as above), pp. **1, 2** ; Text, pp. **3–31**. The Note
(altered to " The other Six follow," etc.) and the Imprint, as
above, are on p. [32].
　　Note.—The additional poem is the *Adieu to Malta* on pp. **12–
14**. The lines *Fare Thee Well*, which are printed in the First
and Second Editions in stanzas, are in the Sixth Edition printed
continuously.

IV.

Poems,/ etc./　By Lord Byron./　With His/ Memoirs and
Portrait./　Eighth Edition./　Containing/ Nine Poems./
Fare Thee Well !/　A Sketch From Private Life./　On
the Star of " The Legion of Honour."/　Adieu to Malta./
The/ Curse of Minerva./　Waterloo./　And Three Others./
London :/　Printed for W. Hone, 55, Fleet Street,/ etc./
1816./　　　　　　　　　　　　　　　　　　　　[8°

Collation—
　　Title (R. Imprint as above), pp. **1, 2** ; Memoirs, etc., pp. **3–6** ;
Text, pp. **7–32**.
　　Note.—The additional poem is the mutilated version of *The
Curse of Minerva* (**111** lines). The Front. is a lithograph of
" Lord Byron," after F. Sieurac.

V.

Poems/ etc./　By Lord Byron,/ etc./　Fifteenth Edition./
Containing/ Nine Poems,/ etc./　London :/ Printed for
W. Hone, 55, Fleet Street,/ etc./　1816./　　　　　　[8°

Collation—
　　Title (R. Imprint as above), pp. **1, 2** ; Memoirs, etc., pp. **3–8**
+ Text, pp. **3–40**.

Note.—The Text of the Fifteenth Edition is identical with the
Text of the Sixth Edition (pp. 3-[32]), including Note and
Imprint on p. [32]. *The Curse of Minerva* is on pp. 33-40. The
Imprint, as above, is repeated on the foot of p. 40.

VI.

Lord Byron's/ Poems,/ on His Own/ Domestic Circumstances./   Fare Thee Well./   Dublin :/   Printed by W.
Espy, 59, Dame-Street./   1816./   [8?

Collation—

Half-title (Poems, etc./   Entered at Stationers'-Hall./), one
leaf, pp. 1, 2 ; Title, one leaf, pp. 3, 4 ; Preface, pp. 5, 6 ; Text,
pp. 7-15.

Note.—The edition contains *Fare Thee Well*, and *A Sketch*, etc.,
without the other poems published by Hone.

VII.

Poems/ on His/ Domestic Circumstances,/ etc. etc./ By/
Lord Byron./   Second Edition./

1. Fare Thee Well/	12. To the Lily of France./
2. A Sketch from Private Life/	13. Ode to the Island of St Helena./
3. On the Star of " The Legion of Honour "/	14. To ——./
4. Ode/	15. Bright be the Place to thy Soul !/
5. Waterloo/	16. Stanzas for Music./
6. Madame Lavalette/	17. To ——./
7. Farewell to France/	18. Stanzas for Music./
8. Adieu to Malta/	19. To ——./
9. The Curse of Minerva/	20. On Reading Lord Byron's Farewell to England./
10. Farewell to England/	
11. To my Daughter, etc/	

To which is Prefixed,/ Memoirs of His Life./   Bristol :/
Printed for W. Sheppard, Exchange ;/ And may be had
of all the Booksellers./   1816./   [12?

Collation—

Title, one leaf, pp. i., ii. ; Memoirs, etc., pp. iii.-vi. ; On
Reading Lord Byron's Farewell to England, pp. i.-iii. (R. Cont.) ;
Text, pp. *1-50*. The Imprint (*Mary Bryan, Printer, (51) Corn-
Street, Bristol.*) is at the foot of p. 50.

Note.—This edition contains the nine poems published by Hone
(1816), four forgeries, six of the *Poems* published by Murray in
1816, and, with a separate pagination, the lines *On Reading Lord
Byron's Farewell to England* (" —— Still my bosom's indig-
nation ").

VIII.

Poems on His Domestic Circumstances, etc.   Boston.   1816.
                                                                [24°
[Catalogue of the Boston Athenæum Library.]

IX.

Poems,/ etc./ By Lord Byron,/ etc./ Twenty-Third Edition./
Containing/ Nine Poems,/ etc./ London :/ Printed for
W. Hone,/ 55, Fleet Street, and 67, Old Bailey,/ (*Three
Doors from Ludgate Hill*,)/ And Sold By J. M. Richard-
son,/ etc./ 1817./   [8°

Collation—
   Pp. 32.

X.

Poems,/ on His/ Domestic Circumstances,/ By/ The Right
Honourable/ Lord Byron :/ To which are added,/ Several
Choice Pieces from His Lordship's Works./ " Lord
BIRON.—By heaven I do love ; and it hath taught me/
to rhyme, and to be melancholy ; and here is part of my
rhyme,/ and here my melancholy."/ SHAKESPEARE'S
LOVE'S LABOUR LOST./ London :/ Printed for J. Limbird,
355, Strand, (East End/ of Exeter 'Change),/ By W. Sears,
45, Gutter Lane, Cheapside./ 1823./   [12°

Collation—
   Pp. vi. + 48.   The Imprint (*Printed by W. Sears, 45, Gutter
Lane, Cheapside, London.*) is at the foot of p. 48.
   Note.—The collection contains twenty-four poems, including
the forgeries, *To my Daughter*, etc. ; *Farewell to England ; Ode
(" Oh, shame to thee," etc.) ;* and *Madame Lavalette.*

XI.

Miscellaneous Poems,/ Including those on His/ Domestic
Circumstances./ By Lord Byron./ To which are prefixed/
Memoirs of the Author, and a Tribute/ To his Memory/
By Sir Walter Scott./ London :/ Printed for John
Bumpus, 85, Newgate Street ;/ And R. Griffin, & Co.,
Glasgow./ 1824./

Collation—
   Pp. xx. + 21-72.   The Imprint (*Printed by A. Hancock, Middle
Row Place, Holborn.*) is at the foot of p. 72.
   Note.—The collection numbers twenty-five poems, including
the forgeries, *Ode* (" Oh, shame to thee," etc.); *Madame Lavalette ;
Farewell to England ; To my Daughter*, etc. ; *Ode to—S!. Helena ;*

To the Lily of France; The Enigma [H.]; and three (genuine) stanzas from the lines, "Well, thou art happy," here entitled *Song to Inez;* and the lines *To Jessy.*

XII.

Miscellaneous Poems/ on His Domestic and Other/ Circumstances./ By Lord Byron./ London :/ Printed By and for William Cole./ 10 Newgate-Street./ 1825./ [12°

Collation—

Pp. 54. The Imprint (*Printed by William Cole, 10, Newgate Street.*) is at the foot of p. 54.

Note.—The edition contains twenty-nine pieces, viz. the twenty-five poems published by John Bumpus in 1824 (No. xl.), together with *The Isles of Greece; Were my Bosom,* etc. ; *Herod's Lament,* etc. ; and *Lord Byron's Latest Verses* ("On this day I complete my thirty-sixth year").

Hints from Horace.

Note.—Two sets of proofs of a portion of *Hints from Horace,* formerly the property of R. C. Dallas, are preserved in the British Museum (*Eg.* 2029). Proof A consists of 100 lines of the English translation (lines 173–272) ; Proof B, pp. [87]–128, consists of 272 lines of the English translation (lines 1–272) and (on opposite pages) 188 lines of the original Latin. These proof-sheets, which must have followed proofs of the Fifth Edition of *English Bards, etc.,* are preceded by a Half-title, *Hints from Horace* (Gothic characters), and by the following subsidiary title :—

Hints from Horace :/ Being a/ Partial Imitation, in English Verse, of the Epistle,/ "Ad Pisones de Arte Poetica ;"/ And intended as a Sequel to/ English Bards and Scotch Reviewers./ [Gothic characters.] "Ergo fungar vice Cotis, acutum/ Reddere quæ ferrum valet, exsors ipsa secandi."/ Hor. De Arte Poet. 304–5./ "Rhymes are difficult things ; they are stubborn things, sir."/ Fielding's Amelia, Vol. III./ Book and Chap. V./ Athens, Franciscan Convent,/ March 12, 1811./

The publication of *Hints from Horace* had been entrusted by Dallas to Cawthorn in July-August, 1811. It may be gathered from various sources (*Letters,* 1898, ii. 24, 54, 56) that Byron was at work on the proofs as late as September 4 ; that by October 11 he had resolved to defer the publication of the *Hints ;* and that, accordingly on October 13, 1811, "they stood still." It was not, however, till after the appearance of *Childe Harold's, etc.* (May-June, 1812) that Byron determined to suppress the already printed Fifth Edition of *English Bards,* and at the same time to abandon the publication of his two other Satires. At this time, says Dallas (*Recollections of the Life of Lord Byron,* 1898, p. 241), "the *Hints from Horace* was far advanced." In his *Recollections, etc.* (pp. 104–113), he gives, by way of a "fair specimen," 156 "lines of the still-unpublished poem ; and, as these extracts are taken from the first 211 lines, and his text corresponds with proof B (see *Poetical Works*, 1898, i. 390, variants ii., iii.), it may be inferred that Dallas transcribed them from his fragmentary proof-sheets, and that the press was stopped at line 272. In 1830, in his *Notices of the Life of Lord Byron* (vol. i. pp. 263–269), Moore printed 165 lines of the "Paraphrase ;" but his selections are drawn from lines 1–458, and it is evident that he had access to an original MS. (*MS. M.*), which is now in Mr. Murray's possession. The full text, which follows the same MS., was first published in vol. v. pp. 273–327 of the six-volume edition of 1831 (*vide ante*, No. xliii. of "Collected Editions").

The Irish Avatar.

Byron wrote the *Irish Avatar* at Ravenna, September 16, 1821. On the 17th he sent a copy of the verses to Moore, then resident at Paris ; and on September 20 he desired Moore to get "twenty copies of the whole carefully and privately printed off." A copy is in the possession of Mr. H. Buxton Forman, C.B., and I am indebted to his kindness for the following description : "The pamphlet consists of four 8vo leaves, viz. half-title ('The Irish Avatar,' in bold capitals, with blank verse), pp. [1], [2] + Text, pp. 3–8. The poem begins on the third page with a dropped head, 'The Irish Avatar' again, and the first four verses. Pp. 4–7 contain six verses each, and p. 8 the remaining four, making up thirty-two in all. The date at the end of p. 8 is 'September 16, 1821.' There is no title-page proper ; a headline, 'The Irish Avatar,' occurs on pp. 4–8, which pages are numbered in Arabic figures in the outside corners, and the thirty-two stanzas are also numbered in Arabic figures. The poem is printed on a half-sheet of a peculiar fine-ribbed paper." Twenty stanzas of *The Irish Avatar* were printed by Medwin in *Conversations of Lord Byron*, 1824, pp. 216–220, and in a second edition, 1824, pp. 332–338. In a "new edition" of the *Conversations, etc.*, 1824, pp. 264–270, the entire poem, numbering thirty-two stanzas, was published for the first time in England (see *Athenæum*, July 27, 1901). *The Irish Avatar* was first published by Murray in 1831 (*Works*, vi. 419–425).

The Island.

I.

The Island,/ or/ Christian and His Comrades./ By the/ Right Hon. Lord Byron./ London, 1823 :/ Printed for John Hunt,/ 22, Old Bond Street./   [8?

Collation—

Half-title (R. *London :| Printed by C. H. Reynell, Broad-Street, Golden-Square*), pp. 1, 2 ; Title, one leaf, pp. 3, 4 ; Author's

Advt., p. 6; Text, pp. 7–79 + Appendix, pp. 81–94. The Imprint, as above, is at the foot of p. 94.

Note.—A Second and a Third Edition, identical with the First, were published by John Hunt in 1823. *The Island* forms part (pp. 193–244) of a collection of Miscellaneous Poems, *Hebrew Melodies, The Deformed Transformed*, etc., printed and published by W. Dugdale, 23, Russell Court, Drury Lane, in 1825.

II.

The Island ;/ or/ Christian and His Comrades./ By The Right Hon. Lord Byron./ Paris :/ Published by A. and W. Galignani,/ At the French, English, Italian, German, and Spanish Library,/ N⁰. 18, Rue Vivienne./ 1823./
[12⁰

Collation—

Half-title (R. *Paris: Printed by A. Belin*), one leaf; Title, one leaf; Second Half-title, pp. 1, 2; Author's Advt., pp. 3, 4; Text + App., pp. 5–95.

III.

The Island, or Christian and His Comrades. New York. 1823. [12⁰
[Cat. of Books in Bates Hall of Pub. Library of Boston.]

Translations of The Island.

German.

Die Insel, ober Christian u. seine Kameraden. Aus d. Engl. (v. F. L. Breuer). Mit gegenübersteh. Originaltext. Leipzig, Brockhaus. 1827. [8⁰
[Kayser, 1834.]

Italian.

L' Isola, poema di lord Byron, traduzione di Morrone. Napoli, tipographia di De Muro, 1840. [8⁰
[*Bibliographia Italiana*, Oct., 1840.]

Polish.

Wyspa czyli Chrystyan i jego towarzysze...Przekład Adama Pajgerta. pp. 62. *druk. "Czasu": Kraków*, 1859. [8⁰.

Swedish.

Ön/ Eller/ Christian och Hans Stallbröder./ Af/ Lord
Byron./ Öfversättning. [Af/ Talis Qualis.] Stockholm,/
J. L. Brudins Förlag./ [1856.]   [8°

Collation—
   Pp. 88.
   Note.—No. 8 of " Byron's Poetiska Berättelser."

The Lament of Tasso.

I.

The/ Lament of Tasso./ By Lord Byron./ London :/ John
Murray, Albemarle-Street./ 1817./   [8°

Collation—
   Title, one leaf, pp. 3, 4 ; Note (on MSS., etc.), pp. 5, 6 ;
Text, pp. 7–19 + p. [20], Advt. of Poems.   The Imprint (*T.
Davison, Lombard-Street,/ Whitefriars, London./*) is at the foot of
p. [20].
   Note.—The Half-title (? missing) is not in the Museum copy.

II.

The/ Lament of Tasso./ By Lord Byron./ Second Edition./
London :/ John Murray, Albemarle-Street./ 1817./ [8°

Collation—
   Title, one leaf, pp. 3, 4 ; Advt., pp. 5, 6 ; Text, pp. 7–18.

III.

The/ Lament of Tasso,/ etc./ Third Edition,/ etc./ 1817./
                                               [8°

Collation—
   Vide supra, No. i.

IV.

The/ Lament of Tasso,/ etc./ Fourth Edition,/ etc./ 1817./
                                              [8°

Collation—
   Half-title (The Lament,/ etc./ Fourth Edition./ 1*s*. 6*d*./)
(R. *T. Davison, Lombard-Street, Whitefriars, London.*), pp. 1, 2,
etc. *Vide supra*, No. i.
   Note.—The Imprint (*T. Davison, Lombard-Street,/ White-
friars, London./*) is at the foot of p. [20]. Twelve pp. of " Books
Printed for John Murray," dated " August, 1817," are bound up
with the Fourth Edition.

V.

The Lament,/ etc./   Sixth Edition./   1818./   [8?

Collation—
Vide supra, No. iv.
Note.—Four pp. of Advts., dated "Albemarle-Street, London, January, 1818," are bound up with the Sixth Edition.

Translations of The Lament of Tasso.
Italian.
I.

Lamento/ del/ Tasso/ di Lord Byron/   Recato in italiano/ Da Michele Leoni/   Pisa/   Presso Niccolò Capurro/ co' caratteri di F. Didot/   1818/   [4?

Collation—
Pp. ix. + *1–27* + Nota dell' Autore, p. [28].
Note.—The Front. is "Tasso in the Hospital of Sant' Anna," drawn by C. Meritoni, and engraved by Lasinio Figlio.   The Italian translation is printed on opposite pages to the English Text.

II.

La/ Magion del Terrore/ . . . La Fantasia e il Disinganno/ ed altri metrici componimenti/ di Gaetano Polidori/ colle sue traduzioni/   Del Lamento del Tasso/ di Lord Byron/ . . . Londra 1843./   Impresso da J. Wilson e W. Ward nella pri-/vata stamperia dell' autore al numero 15 di/ Park Village East, Regent's Park./   [16?

Collation—
Pp. 112–133.

III.

Guglielmo Godio/   Il Lamento di Tasso/   Versione da Byron/   [Six other pieces.]   Torino/   Tipografia di Vincenzo Bona/   Via Ospedale, 3 e Lagrange, 7/   1873./   [8?

Collation—
Pp. 21 + 23–47, *Estri Lontani*, etc.

Lara.
I.

Lara,/ A Tale./   Jacqueline,/ A Tale./   London :/   Printed for J. Murray, Albemarle-Street,/ *By T. Davison, White-friars./*   1814./   [8?

Collation—
　Half-title (Poems), one leaf ; Title, one leaf ; Advt. ; Cont.
(R. Note. Canto I., page 3, line 1, *The Serfs*, etc.) ; Second
Half-title ; Text, pp. *3*–128 (*Lara*, pp. 1–93 ; *Jacqueline*, pp.
95–128) + "Books Printed for John Murray," etc., pp. [129]–
[132]. The Imprint (*T. Davison, Lombard-street,| Whitefriars,
London.|*) is at the foot of p. [132].
　Note.—This edition was issued in blue-paper boards with green
back, the title-label being Lara| Jacqueline| 7*s*. 6*d*.| The
pages measure 170 × 105.

II.

Lara,/　A　Tale./　By Lord Byron./　Fourth　Edition./
London :/　Printed　for John Murray, Albemarle-Street./
1814./　　　　　　　　　　　　　　　　　　　　　　[8°

Collation—
　Half-title (Lara) ; Imprint (*T. Davison, Lombard Street,| Fleet-
street.*), one leaf ; Title, one leaf ; Second Half-title ; Text, pp.
3–70. The Imprint (*T. Davison, Lombard-street,| Whitefriars,
London.|*) is in the centre of p. [72]. In other copies the Text
ends at p. 70, and a note on Section xxiv., Canto II. pp. 71–74,
concludes the volume. The Imprint is not repeated.

III.

Lara.　Boston.　1814.　　　　　　　　　　　　　　[12°

　Collation—
　　Pp. iv. + 8–98.

IV.

Lara.　New York.　1814.　　　　　　　　　　　　　[24°

　Collation—
　　Pp. 136.

V.

Lara,/ A Tale./　By Lord Byron./　Fifth Edition./　London :/
John Murray, Albemarle-Street./　1817./　　　　　　　[8°

Collation—
　Half-title (R. *T. Davison, Lombard - street, Whitefriars,
London.*) ; Title, one leaf ; Text, pp. 1–74 + Advt. of "Poems
By the Right Hon. Lord Byron " (R. *T. Davison, Lombard-street,|
Whitefriars, London.|*), pp. [75], [76].
　Note.—The additional pages (pp. 71–74) contain a note on
"The event in section 24, Canto 2d, suggested by the death, or
rather burial, of the Duke of Gandia."
　Note.—"Lara./　A Tale./　By Lord Byron."/ forms part (pp.

135–174) of a volume "Printed for Thomas Wilson, Oxford
Street. 1825. 12º" The Imprint (*Printed by W. Dugdale*, etc.)
is at the foot of p. 174.

VI.

Lara,/ a Tale by/ Lord Byron :/ Illustrated by C. B. Birch,/
Art-Union of London./ MDCCCLXXIX./   [fol.

Collation—
    Text, pp. *1*–12. The Imprint (*Harrison and Sons, Printers in
Ordinary to Her Majesty, S. Martin's Lane.*) is at the foot of
p. 12. The Text is followed by twenty plates.

Translations of Lara.

Bohemian.

Lara . . . Přeložil Č. Ibla. [In "Poesie Světová."] *v Praze,*
  1885.   [8º

German.

Lara. Übers. v. W. Schäffer u. A Strodtmann.   1886.
Leipzig, Bibl. Institut.   [16º

Collation—
    Pp. 91.
    Note.—No. 88 of "Meyer's Volksbücher."

Italian.

I.

Il Lara/ di Lord Byron/ Tradotto dal signor/ Girolamo
Cº Bazoldo,/ Maggiore di S. M. Britannica re d'Annover./
con giunta/ di tre altre traduzioni dall' inglese, una dal
tedesco,/ e tre canzoni dell' autore./ [Title-vignette,
Cupid with harp.] Parigi./ Dai Torchi di Pillet Maggiore,/
In via des Grands-Augustins, Nº 7./ 1828./   [24º

Collation—
    Pp. *1*–83 + *Il Pensieroso*, etc., pp. 85–138 + Indice, p. [139].
    Note.—This edition was issued in green-paper covers.

II.

Lara. Traduzione di Andrea Maffei, Milano, Hoepli, 1882.
                                    [64º
                   [Pagliaini, 1901.]

Polish.

Lara, poemat w 2 pieśniach, przekład Jul. Korsaka. pp. 70
druk. J. Zawadzkiego: Wilno, 1833.　　　　　　　　[8°.

Servian.

Лара лорда Бајрона. Србски од Ац. Поповића. **pp. 72.**
К. Хинц: у Новом-Саду, 1860. **12°.**

Spanish.

Lara, novela española. Por lord Byron, traducida al castellano, Paris. 1828.　　　　　　　　　　　　　　　　　[18°
　　　　　　　[*B. de la France*, May 17, 1828.]

Swedish.

Lara/ Af/ Lord Byron./　Stockholm,/ Tryckt Hos Joh.
Beckman./　1869./　　　　　　　　　　　　　　　[8°
　Collation—
　　Pp. 5–64.
　　Note.—" Öfversättning Af Talis Qualis "—a pseudonym of
Carl Wilhelm August Strandberg.

Manfred.

I.

Manfred,/ A/ Dramatic Poem./ By Lord Byron./ London :/
John Murray, Albemarle-Street./　1817./　　　　　　[8°
　Collation—
　　Half-title (Manfred) (R. *T. Davison, Lombard-Street, White-
friars, London*), pp. 1, 2 ; Title, one leaf, pp. 3, 4 ; Dramatis
Personæ, pp. 5, 6 ; Text, pp. 7–75 ; Notes, pp. [79]–80. The
Imprint (*T. Davison, Lombard-Street,| Whitefriars, London.|*) is
at the foot of p. 80.
　　Note.—The First Edition was issued with another title-page
(B) : Manfred,/ A/ Dramatic Poem./ " There are more things
in heaven and earth, Horatio,/ " Than are dreamt of in your
philosophy."/ By Lord Byron./ London :/ John Murray,
Albemarle-Street./　1817./　8°
　　There is no half-title in the Museum copy of this alternative
First Edition.

II.

Manfred,/ etc./　Second Edition,/ etc./　1817./　　　　[8°

Note.—The Second Edition is identical with the alternative form (B) of the First Edition. There is no Imprint on p. 80. An Advt. of "Poems by the Right Hon. Lord Byron" is on p. [82].

III.

Manfred,/ A/ Dramatic Poem./ "There are more things in heaven and earth, Horatio,/ Than are dreamt of in your philosophy."/   By Lord Byron./   Philadelphia :/ Published by M. Thomas./   J. Maxwell, Printer./   1817./
[12°

Collation—
Pp. 72.
Note.—*Manfred* was also published at New York in 1817, 24°, pp. 70.

IV.

Manfred./ A Dramatic Poem./ By Lord Byron./ "There are more things," etc. [Motto, two lines]./   London :/ Printed and Published by W. Dugdale,/ *23, Russell Court, Drury Lane.*/   1824./
[12°
Collation—
Pp. 55 + "Notes to Manfred," p. [56]. The Imprint (*Printed by W. Dugdale, Russell Court, Drury Lane, London*) is at the foot of p. [56].
Note.—Manfred./ A Dramatic Poem./ By Lord Byron./ forms part (pp. 175–[216]) of a volume Printed for Thomas Wilson, Oxford Street./ 1825. 12° The Imprint (*Printed by W. Dugdale,* etc.), as above, is at the foot of p. [216].

V.

Manfred,/ A/ Dramatic Poem./   "There are more things in heaven and earth,/ Horatio,/ "Than are dreamt of in your philosophy."/   By Lord Byron./   Brussels :/ Printed at the British Press./
[8°
Collation—
Title, one leaf, pp. 3, 4 ; Dramatis Personæ, pp. 5, 6 ; Text, pp. 7–72 ; Notes, pp. [73], 74 ; Observations, pp. [75]–81.

VI.

Manfred./   A Choral Tragedy,/ In Three Acts,/ By/ Lord Byron./   Thomas Hailes Lacy,/ 89, Strand, London./ [1863.]
[12°
Collation—
Pp. 1–41 + "Costumes," p. [42]. The Imprint (*Printed by Thomas Scott, Warwick Court, Holborn.*) is at the foot of p. 41.

Note.—Vol. 60 of Lacy's "Acting Edition Plays." Pp. 2–6 contain the playbill of Manfred "As Performed at the Theatre Royal, Drury Lane (under the Management of Messrs. Edmund Falconer and F. B. Chatterton), on Saturday, October 10th, 1863."

VII.

Manfred./ Lord Byron./ [Title-vignette, "Hear me, hear me—Astarte."] New and Complete Edition.—Price one Penny./ London. J. Dicks, 313 Strand ; all Booksellers./ [1883, etc.]   [8°

Collation—
Pp. 161–173.
Note.—No. 59 of "Dicks' Standard Plays."

Translations of Manfred.
Bohemian.

Manfred . . . Přelozil Jos. V. Frič. *Praze*, 1882.

Danish.

I.

Manfred,/ af/ Lord Byron./ Oversat/ af/ P. F. Wulff./ There are more things, etc. [Motto, two lines.]/ Hamlet./ Kjøbenhavn, 1820./ Forlagt af Universitets-Boghandler Brummer./ Trykt i der Poppske Bogtrykkerie./ [12°

Collation—
Pp. 107 + Rettelse, p. [108].

II.

Manfred./ Et Dramatisk Digt/ af/ Byron./ Oversat/ af/ Edvard Lembcke./ Kjøbenhavn 1843./ I Commission hos C. A. Reikel./ Trykt hos Bianco Luno./   [8°

Collation—
Pp. 109.

Dutch.

I.

Manfred./ Een Dramatisch Gedicht/ Naar/ Lord Byron,/ Door/ Johan Rudolph Steinmetz./ Amsterdam,/ H. J. Van Kesteren./ 1857./   [8°

Collation—
Pp. xv. + 59 + "Aanteekenigen," pp. [60]–[63] + "Verbeteringen," p. [64].

II.

Byron's/ Manfred./ Een Dramatisch Gedicht./ Metrische Vertaling./ (Toegewijd AAN Mr C. Vosmaer)/ Van/ W. Gosler./ Heusden.—H. Wuijster./ 1882./ [8?

Collation—
Pp. vii. + 78.
Note.—The Front. is a photograph of "Ernst Possart in de rol van Manfred" (Verg: *Illustrirte Zeitung* van 12 Nov. 1881).

French.

I.

Manfred/ Poëme dramatique/ Par/ Lord Byron,/ Traduit/ Par madame la comtesse de Lalaing/ Née comtesse de Maldeghem./ Horatio, il est dans le ciel et sur la terre/ plus de choses que n'en peut concevoir/ votre philosophie./ Hamlet./ Seconde édition./ Bruxelles./ Imprimerie de J. Stienon,/ Faubourg de Louvain, 19./ 1852/ [8?

Collation—
Pp. 61 + "Notes," p. [63].

II.

Manfred/ Poème dramatique de Byron/ Adaptation nouvelle, en vers/ de/ Émile Moreau/ Paris/ Paul Ollendorff, éditeur/ 28 *bis*, rue de Richelieu, 28 *bis*/ 1887/ Tous droits réservés/ [8?

Collation—
Pp. vii. + 28. The Imprint (*Paris.—Typ. G. Chameroi, 19, Rue des Saints Pères—20832*) is at the foot of p. 28.

III.

Lord Byron/ Manfred/ Poème dramatique en 3 actes/ Traduction en vers/ Par/ C. Trébla/ Toulouse/ Édouard Privat, éditeur, rue des Tourneurs/ 1888/ [8?

Collation—
Pp. xiii. + 15–89 + Errata, p. [91]. The Imprint (*Montauban, Imp. et Lith. Ed. Forestiè, rue du Vieux-Palais, 23*) is in the centre of p. [90].

German.

I.

Manfred./ A Tragedy/ By/ Lord Byron./ Leipzig :/ F. A. Brockhaus./ 1819./ [8?
Manfred./ Trauerspiel von Lord Byron./ Teutsch/ von/ Adolf Wagner./ Leipzig :/ F. A. Brockhaus./ 1819./

Collation—

English Title, as above, p. 2 ; German Title, as above, pp. 3, 4 ; Half-title (R. Dramatis Personæ), pp. 5, 6 ; *Personen*, p. 7 ; English and German Texts, pp. 8–209 ; Anmerkungen, pp. 211–239. The Imprint (*Druck und papier von Friedrich Vieweg/ In Braunschweig/*) is in the centre of p. 240.

Note.—I am indebted to the kindness of Mr. Leonard L. Mackall, of Berlin, for the substance of the following note on this work :—

" Pages 213–233 of the Anmerkungen " are devoted to an essay on the play as a whole. This essay is evidently the " Appendix to an English Work," to which Byron refers in the letter accompanying the suppressed Dedication to *Marino Faliero*. " In the Appendix to an English Work, lately translated into German, and published at Leipzig, a judgment of yours upon English poetry is quoted as follows : ' That in English poetry great genius, universal power, a feeling of profundity, with sufficient tenderness and force are to be found, but that altogether these do not constitute poets,' " etc., etc. (see *Poetical Works*, 1901, v. 340, 341, and *Letters*, 1900, v. 100–103). The originals of the Dedication and Letters were conveyed to Goethe by John Murray the third, in 1830 (? 1831) (see *Goethe-Jahrbuch*, 1899, xx. pp. 31–35, where the " Dedication " is printed in full for the first time), and are preserved at Weimar in the " red portfolio " (cf. *Eckermann*, March 26, 1826), in which Goethe kept all his papers connected with Byron. The " judgments " quoted by Byron through " an Italian abstract " from Wagner's Appendix (pp. 217–218) there read *inaccurately* as follows : " In der Englischen Poesie," sagt Goethe, " man findet durchaus einen grossen, tüchtigen, weltgeübten Verstand, ein tiefes, zartes, Gemüth, ein vortreffliches Wollen, ein leidenschaftliches Wirken . . . das alles zuzammengenommen macht noch keinen Poeten . . . nach dieser Ansicht zeigen die meisten Englischen Gedichte einen düstern Ueberdruss des Lebens." These sentences, which should be read in the light of the context, will be found in Goethe's *Dichtung und Wahrheit*, Th. iii. Buch. 13 (1814, now *Wirke*, Weimar ed. xxviii. 213, 214), the book (*Aus meinem Leben, Dichtung und Wahrheit*), which is held up to ridicule in the *Edinburgh Review*, June, 1816, vol. xxvi. pp. 304–317.

II.

Manfred, übersetzt von Thdr. Armin, Göttingen, Kübler, 1836.   [8?

[Kayser, 1841.]

III.

yron's Manfred./ Einleitung, Uebersetzung und/ Anmerkungen./ Ein Beitrag/ zur Kritik der gegenwärtigen deutschen dramatischen/ Kunst und Poesie./ von/

Posgarn./ [*i.e.* G. F. W. Suckow] Breslau,/ im Verlage
bei Josef Mar und Komp./ 1839./ [8º

Collation—
  Pp. 212.

IV.

Manfred, Ein dramat. Gedicht übers. v. O. S. Seeman.
  Berlin, Weidle, 1843. [8º
                    [Kayser, 1848.]

V.

Lord Byron's/ Manfred./ Deutsch/ von/ Hermann von
Kösen./ " Mehr Dinge giebt's im Himmel und auf Erden/
Als eure Weisheit sich wohl träumen lässt."/ (Hamlet.)/
Leipzig,/ Voigt & Günther./ 1858./ [16º

Collation—
  Half-title, Title, and "Zueignung," 8 pp. ; Text, pp. *1–86.*
The Imprint (*Druck von Giesecke & Devrient*) is at the foot of
p. 86.

VI.

Byron's/ Manfred./ Erklärt und übersetzt/ von/ L. Freytag./
Berlin./ Verlag von Gebrüder Pætel./ 1872./ [16º

Collation—
  Pp. 158. The Imprint (*Druck von G. Bernstein in Berlin*) is
at the foot of p. 158.

VII.

Manfred, dramat. Gedicht v. Lord Byron. Frei übers. v.
  Adf. Seubert. [16º
                    [Kayser, 1877.]

Collation—
  Pp. 47.
  Note.—No. 586 of the Universal=Bibliothek, Leipzig, 1871–76.

VIII.

Manfred./ Dramatische Dichtung in drei Abtheilungen/
von/ Lord Byron./ Musik von Robert Schumann./ Jeder
Nachdruck dieses Textbuches, auch von Seiten der Theater-
directionen für/ ihre Aufführungen, ist verboten./ Leipzig,/
Druck und Verlag von Breitkopf und Härtel./ [8º

Collation—
  Pp. 36.
  Note.—No. 66 of Serie III., Breitkopf und Härtel's *Textbiblio-
thek*, 1879–90.

IX.

Manfred. Ein dramatisches Gedicht. Freie Uebersetzung
von Thierry Preyer. Frankfurt, Neumann, 1883. [4°
                                        [Kayser, 1883.]

Collation—
    Pp. 59.

Hungarian.

I.

Byron Lord'/ Élete 's Munkái./ Irta/ Petrichevich Horváth
Lázár./ Második Rész./ Pesten./ Nyomtatta Landerer
és Heckenast./ 1842./   [8°

Collation—
    Pp. xi. + 134 + Jegyzések Manfredhez, pp. [135], [136] +
Sajtó-hibák, p. [137].

II.

Manfred./ Drámai Költemény 3 Felvonásban./ Irta :/
Lord Byron György./ Angolból forditotta :/ D.ᵣ Kludik
Imre./ Byron és a Világfájdalom./ Irta: D.ᵣ Kludik
Imre./ Ára: 40 kr./ Második Kiadás./ Szolnok, 1884./
Nyomatott Bakos Istvánnál./   [8°

Collation—
    Manfred, pp. 1-65 + Byron és a Világfájdalom, pp. 69-112.

III.

Manfred/ Lord Byron Drámai Költeménye/ Forditotta/
Ábrányi Emil./ Budapest 1891/ Singer és Wolfner
Könyvkereskedése./   [8°

Collation—
    Pp. 98.

Italian.

I.

Manfredo. Traduzione di Marcello Mazzoni. Milano, P.
M. Visaj. 1832.   [8°
        [Library of Congress, Washington, 1880.]

Collation—
    Pp. 91.

II.

Tragedie/ di/ Silvio Pellico/ Francesca da Rimini/ [etc., five lines] Manfredo,/ Poema drammatico di Lord Byron,/ (versione in prosa)./ Firenze./ Felice le Monnier./ 1859./ [8?

Collation—
    Manfredo, etc., pp. 437–473.

III.

Manfredo : poema drammatico. Traduzione di Andrea Maffei. Firenze, Le Monnier, 1870. [16?
                                                        [Pagliaini, 1901.]
Collation—
    Pp. xi. + 100.

Polish.

I.

Manfred, poemat dramatyczny, przekład Edm. Stan. Bojanowskiego. *W. G. Korn: Wrocław,* 1835. [12°.

II.

Manfred, poemat...Przekład wolny na wiersz polski przez Michała Chodźkę...Z 4 obrazkami, wyrysował Kossak, *etc.* pp. 89. *w drukarni L. Martinet: Paryż,* [1859]. [8°. *[Published also by Schmidt at Halle.]*

Romaic.

Ο Μαμφρεδ/ Δραματικον Ποιημα/ του/ Λορδου Βυρωνος./ Μεταφρασις/ Επτικου Γκρην./ ὁ οὐρανὸς, 'Ορᾶτι', ἔχει πλείονα κ' ἡ γῆ/ παρ' ὅσα οἱ φιλόσοφοι φαντάζεσθε!/ Shakspere./ Εν Πατραις/ τυπογραφειον και βιβλιοπωλειον/ Ευσταθιου Π. Χριστοδουλου./ Παρὰ τὴν ὁδὸν Έρμοῦ./ 1864./ [8?
Collation—
    Pp. 79 + Παροραματα, p. [80].

Roumanian.

Stoenescu (Th. M.) Teatru . . . Manfred, dupe Lord Byron. *Editura " Revistei Literare:" Bucuresci,* 1896. [8?
Collation—
    Manfred, pp. 173–228.

VOL. VII.   2 N

Russian.

I.

Манфредъ. Драматическая поэма въ трехъ дѣйствіяхъ.
...Переводъ М. Вронченко.

II.

Манфредъ...Переводъ А. Бородина. [" Пантеонъ,"
1841. No. 2.]

III.

Манфредъ...Перев. Е. Зарина. [" Библіотека для
Чтенія." *С.-Петербургъ*, 1858, No. 8.]

IV.

Манфредъ. . . . Переводъ Д. Минаева. [" Русское
Слово," 1863. No. 4.]

Spanish.

I.

Manfredo, drama en tres actos. Por lord Byron. Imp.
de Decourchant à Paris. A Paris, rue du Temple, n. 69.
1829.　　　　　　　　　　　　　　　　　　　　　　[18º
　　　　　　[*Bibl. de la France*, October 17, 1829.]

II.

Manfredo,/ Poema dramático/ de/ Lord Byron./ Traducido en verso directamente del inglés al castellano/ Por/
D. José Alcalá Galiano/ y Fernandez de las Peñas./
Madrid :/ Imprenta de A. Vicente, Preciados, 74./ 1861./
　　　　　　　　　　　　　　　　　　　　　　　[8º

Collation—
　Pp. xiii. + 85.

III.

Lord Byron./ „Manfredo/ y/ Oscar de Alva/ Version castel-
lana/ de Ángel R. Chaves./ Madrid,/ Imprenta de
Eduardo Martinez,/ Calle del príncipe, número, 25./
1876./　　　　　　　　　　　　　　　　　　　　[8º

Collation—
　Pp. xix. + Manfredo, *1*–54 + Oscar de Alva, pp. 55-78 +
Indice, p. [79].

Marino Faliero.

I.

Marino Faliero,/ Doge of Venice./ An Historical Tragedy,/ In Five Acts./ With Notes./ The Prophecy of Dante,/ A Poem./ By Lord Byron./ London: John Murray, Albemarle-Street./ 1821./ [8º

Collation—
Half-title (R. *London :/ Printed by Thomas Davison, White-friars*), pp. i., ii. ; Title, one leaf, pp. iii., iv. ; Cont., pp. v., vi. ; Half-title, with Motto ("*Dux* inquieti turbidus Adriæ."/ Horace./), pp. vii., viii. ; Preface, pp. ix.–xxi. ; Text, pp. *1*–261. The Imprint, as above, is in the centre of p. [262].

Contents—

Marino Faliero . . p. 1	Prophecy of Dante . p. 209
Notes . . . . . p. 169	Notes . . . . . p. 257
Appendix. . . . p. 173	

II.

Marino Faliero, etc./ Second Edition, etc./ 1821./ [8º

Collation—
Vide supra, No. i. Note that in some copies of the First Edition lines 500–507, act v. sc. 1, do not appear. In the Second Edition and in other copies of the First Edition they have been inserted. (See *Poetical Works,* 1901, iv. 447.)

Note.—Another edition (pp. xxi. + 261), in small octavo, was issued by John Murray in 1823.

III.

Marino Faliero, Doge of Venice. 179 pp. Philadelphia, M. Carey and Sons. 1821. [8º
[Library of Congress, Washington, 1880.]

IV.

Marino Faliero, doge of Venice, an historical tragedy in five acts, with notes. By the right hon. lord Byron. Impr. de Belin à Paris—A Paris chez Galignani. [12º
[*Bibl. de la France,* June 29, 1821.]

V.

Marino Faliero,/ Doge of Venice :/ An Historical Tragedy,/ In Five Acts./ By/ Lord Byron./ " Dux inquieti turbidus Adriæ."—Horace./ London :/ John Murray, Albemarle Street./ Sold also by/ Tilt and Bogue, Fleet Street :/

Edinburgh, Oliver and Boyd : Dublin, John Cumming./
1842./   [12º

Collation—
   Title (R. *London :| Printed by H. Spottiswoode,| New-Street-
Square.|*) ; Text, pp. 3-162. The Imprint, as above, is at the
foot of p. 162.

VI.

Marino Faliero./ By/ Lord Byron./ [Title-Vignette, "The
Gory Head rolls down the Giant's steps!"/ New and
Complete Edition.—Price one Penny./ London J. Dicks
313 Strand ; All Booksellers./ [1883, etc.]   [8º

Collation—
   Pp. 461–492.
   Note.—No. 153 of "Dicks' Standard Plays."

Translations of Marino Faliero.

German.

I.

Marino Faliero/ Doge von Venedig./ Geschichtliche
Tragödie/ von/ Lord Byron./ Freie Übersetzung/ von/
Thierry Preyer./ Frankfurt am Main./ Alfred Neu-
mann'sche Buchhandlung./ 1883./   [4º

Collation—
   Title, one leaf ; Personen ; Vorrede, 8 pp. + Text, pp. *1–147.*
The Imprint (*C. Naumann's Druckerei, Frankfurt a. M.*) is in the
centre of p. [148].

II.

Lord Byron's/ Marino Faliero./ Für das herzoglich Sachsen-
Meiningen'sche Hoftheater/ übersetzt und bearbeitet/
von A. Fitger./ Oldenburg./ Schulzesche Hof-Buch-
handlung und Hof-Buchdruckerei./ (A. Schwartz.)/ [8º

Collation—
   Title (R. *Alle Rechte Vorbehalten*) ; Vorwort (R. "Personen") ;
Text, pp. *1–84.*

Mazeppa.

I.

Mazeppa,/ A Poem./ By Lord Byron./ London :/ John
Murray, Albemarle-Street./ 1819./   [8º

Collation—

Half-title (R. *London :/ Printed by Thomas Davison, White-friars.*) ; Title, one leaf ; Half-title (Mazeppa), pp. 1, 2 ; Advt. (quotation from Voltaire, *Hist. de Charles XII.*, pp. 196, 216), pp. 3, 4 ; Text, pp. 5-69. The Imprint, as above, is in the centre of p. [70] + " Lord Byron's Poems," etc., p. 71.

Contents—

Mazeppa . . . . p. 5	A Fragment (Augustus Dar-	
Ode (" Oh Venice ! Venice !"	vell) . . . . . . p. 57	
etc.) . . . . . . p. 47		

II.

Mazeppa, A Poem./ By Lord Byron./ Second Edition./ Paris :/ Published by Galignani,/ At the French, English, Italian, German, and Spanish/ Library, N⁰ 18, Rue Vivienne./ 1819./ [12⁰

Collation—

Half-title (R. *Printed by A. Belin*), pp. 1, 2 ; Title, one leaf, pp. 3, 4 ; Second Half-title, pp. 5, 6 ; Advt., pp. 7, 8 ; Text, pp. 9-69.

Contents—

Mazeppa . . . . p. 9	A Fragment . . . p. 57
Ode (" Oh Venice !" etc.)	
p. 47	

III.

Mazeppa, a poem [with fragments]. Boston. 1819. [24⁰ [Cat. of Books in Bates Hall of Pub. Lib. of Boston, 1866.]

Collation—
Pp. 56.

IV.

Mazeppa, a Poem. Paris, Galignani, 1822. [12⁰ [Quérard, 1827.]

V.

Mazeppa,/ A Poem./ By Lord Byron./ London :/ Printed and Published by W. Dugdale,/ *52 Russell Court, Drury Lane*, 1824./ [12⁰

Collation—
Pp. ii. + 5-35. The Imprint (*Printed by W. Dugdale, Russell Court, Drury Lane, London.*) is at the foot of p. 35.

VI.

Mazeppa a Poem. Mit Worterklärung u. einer Lebenskizze
des Dichters, von H. M. Melford. Braunschweig, Vieweg.
1834.   [12°

[Kayser, 1841.]

VII.

Mazeppa,/ or the/ Wild Horse/ of the/ Ukraine,/ A Poem,
by/ Lord Byron./   London :/ T. Goode, 30, Aylesbury-
st.,/ Clerkenwell./ [1854?]   [32°

Collation—
    Pp. 48.
    Note.—The Front. (lithograph of Lord Byron) is on p. 1. The
Title is printed on the wrapper (black glazed paper) in gold
letters.   The volume measures 60 × 40.

Translations of Mazeppa.
Danish.

Mazeppa./ AF/ Lord Byron./   Ofversättning. [Af Talis
Qualis.]   Stockholm,/ Alb. Bonniers Förlag./ [1853.]
                                                             [8°
Part of "Byron's Poetiska Berättelser."

German.
I.

Mazeppa. Ein Gedicht. Aus d. Engl. treu übertragen v.
Th. Hell. Nebst beigedr. Urschrift. Leipzig, Hinrichs.
1820.   [8°

[Kayser, 1834.]

II.

Mazeppa, übers. im Versmass des Originals v. Dᴿ jur.
Everhard Brauns. Herausg. von Dᴿ jur. Engelbrecht,
Göttingen, Kübler. 1836.   [8°

[Kayser, 1841.]

III.

Nachgelassenes/ von/ Ferdinand Freiligrath./ Mazeppa,/
nach Lord Byron./   der Eggesterstein,/ Erzählung./
Stuttgart./   G. J. Göschen'sche Verlagshandlung./ 1883./
                                                             [8°
Collation—
    Pp. viii. + 88.

Hungarian.

Byron Lord'/ Élete 's munkái./ Irta/ Petrichevich Horváth Lázár./ Harmadik Rész./ Pesten./ Nyomtatta Landerer és Heckenast. 1842./ [8?

Collation—
Title, one leaf; Half-title, one leaf; Dedication; Figyelmezletés (Advt.); Second Half-title; Text (Mazeppa), pp. 1–[80] + Oda, etc., pp. [81]–154 + Sajtó-hibák, p. [155].

Italian.

I.

Il Mazeppa. Versione di Ant. Arioti. Palermo, Lo Bianco. 1847. [16?
[Pagliaini, 1901.]

II.

Mazeppa./ Traduzione/ da/ Georgio Byron./ Di/ I. Virzì./ Palermo,/ Luigi Pedone Lauriel/ Editore/ 1876./ [8?
Collation—
Pp. 63.

III.

Mazeppa. Traduzione di Andrea Maffei. Milano, Hoepli. 1886. [64?
[Pagliaini, 1901.]

Polish.

I.

Mazepa, poemat. Przekład wolny na wiersz polski przez Michała Chodźkę. pp. 39.
Schmidt: w Hali, 1860. [8°.

II.

(Together with Lamartine's *Death of Jonathan.*)

Mazepa, poemat, przekład wolny na wiersze polskie przez Michała Chodźkę, wydanie ozdobione rycinami, *etc.* pp. 66. *Księg. polska: Paryż* [1860]. [8°.

Russian.

I.

Выборъ изъ сочиненій лорда Байрона.　М. Каченовскаго.　1821.

Collation—
　Mazepa, pp. 69-107.
　Note.—In Prose.

II.

Мазепа.　Изъ сочиненій лорда Байрона.　А. Воейкова
"Новости литературы," 1824.　кн. x.　pp. 9-33.

　Note.—In Prose.

III.

Мазепа...пер. Д. Михайловскаго.　["Современникъ,"
1858.　No. 5.]

IV.

Мазепа...Перев. И. Гогніева.　["Драматическій Сбор-
никъ."　*С.-Петербург*, 1860, кн. 4.]

Spanish.

Mazeppa, novela, por L. B. traducida al castellano.　Paris,
　1830.　　　　　　　　　　　　　　　　　　　　　　　　[18°
　　　　　　　　　　　　　　　[*Moniteur*, etc., 1845.]

Monody, etc.

I.

Monody/ On the Death of/ The Right Honourable/ R. B.
Sheridan,/ Written at the Request of a Friend,/ To be
spoke at/ Drury Lane Theatre./　London : Printed for
John Murray, Albemarle Street./　1816./　　　　　[8°

Collation—
　Half-title (Monody./　[Price One Shilling.]/　Entered at
Stationers' Hall) (R. *London : Printed by C. Roworth, Bell-yard,
Temple-bar.*), pp. 1, 2 ; Title, one leaf, pp. 3, 4 ; Text, pp. 5-11
+ pp. [13]-[15], Advts. of Books published by John Murray. The
Imprint, as above, is at the foot of p. [15].

II.

Monody/ on the Death of/ The Right Honourable/ R. B.
Sheridan./　Spoken at/ Drury Lane Theatre./　By Lord

Byron./   New Edition./   London :/   Printed for John
Murray, Albemarle-Street./   1817./   [8°

Collation—
    Half-title as above (R. *T. Davison, Lombard-street, Whitefriars,
London.*), pp. 1, 2 ; Title, one leaf, pp. 3, 4 ; Text, pp. 5–11 +
List of the Poems, etc., p. [12].   The Imprint (*T. Davison,
Lombard-Street,| Whitefriars, London.|*) is at the foot of p. [12].

III.

Monody,/ etc./   New Edition,/ etc./   1818./   [8°

Collation—
    Half-title (R. *London :| Printed by T. Davison, Whitefriars.*),
pp. 1, 2 ; Title, one leaf, pp. 3, 4 ; Text, pp. 5–11 + "Lord
Byron's Poems," etc., p. [12].   The Imprint, as above, is at the
foot of p. [12].
    Note.—Four pp. of Advts., dated "Albemarle-Street, London,
May, 1818," are bound up with this edition.

An Ode to the Framers of the Frame Bill.

A Political/ Ode/   By/ Lord Byron/   Hitherto Unknown
as His Production./   London/ John Pearson 46 Pall
Mall./   1880./   [8°

Collation—
    Half-title (R. [One hundred copies privately printed.]), pp. 1,
2 ; Title, one leaf, pp. 3, 4 ; Note, pp. 5, 6 ; [Copy of Lord
Byron's Letter . . . March 1, 1812], pp. 7, 8 ; Text, pp. [9], [10],
11.

Ode From the French.
Translation.
French.

Traduction de l'Ode/ de/ Lord Byron,/ Sur/ La bataille de
Waterloo./   Par Aristide Guilbert./   Londres :/ Hunt et
Clark,/ 38, Tavistock Street./   MDCCCXXVI./   [8°

Collation—
    Pp. vii. + 9–28.   The Imprint (*De l'Imprimerie de Thomas
Davison,| 10, Duke Street, Smithfield, London.|*) is at the foot of
p. 28.

Contents—

| Preface | . . . . . p. v. | Notes | . . . . . p. 17 |
| Ode | . . . . . p. 9 | | |

Ode to Napoleon Buonaparte.

I.

Ode/ To/ Napoleon Buonaparte./ " Expende Annibalem :—
quot libras in duce summo/ Invenies? "——/ Juvenal,
Sat. X./ The Second Edition./ London :/ Printed for
John Murray, Albemarle-Street,/ By W. Bulmer and Co.
Cleveland-Row,/ S: James'./ 1814./   [8º

Collation—
   Half-title (Ode, etc./ Entered at Stationers' Hall./), pp. 1, 2 ;
Title, one leaf, pp. 3, 4 ; Note from Gibbon's *Decl. and Fall*
(vol. 6, p. 220), pp. 5, 6 ; Text (xv. stanzas), pp. 7-14 + Advt.
of books " By the Right Hon. Lord Byron," p. [15]. The Imprint
(*Printed by W. Bulmer and Co./ Cleveland-Row, S: James's./*) is
at the foot of p. [15].
   Note.—The First Edition of the *Ode* is in the Rowfant Library
Catalogue, 1886, p. 145.

II.

An Ode to Napoleon Bonaparte.   From the 3d Lond. ed.
   Philadelphia, E. Earle.   1814.   [8º
            [Catalogue of Library of Congress, 1880.]

Collation—
   Pp. 11.
   Note.—The *Ode to Napoleon Buonaparte* was also published at
Boston, 1814, 8º, pp. 13 ; and at New York, 1814, 8º, pp. 13.

III.

Ode to Napoleon Buonaparte.   Sixth Edition.   London.
   1814.   [8º
            [Cat. of Manchester Free Library, 1864.]

Collation—
   Pp. 17.

IV.

Ode to Napoleon Buonaparte.   Ninth Edition.   London,
   M.   1814.   [8º
      [Library of the University, St. Andrews, N.B.]
   Collation—
   Pp. 17.

V.

Ode/ To/ Napoleon Buonaparte./ By Lord Byron./ etc./
   Twelfth Edition./   London :/ Printed for John Murray,
   Albemarle-Street./   1816./   [8º

Collation—
Half-title (Ode, etc.) (R. *T. Davison, Lombard-street,| White-friars, London.|*), pp. **1, 2** ; Title, one leaf, pp. 3, 4 ; Note, pp. 5, 6 ; Second Half-title, pp. 7, 8 ; Text (xvi. stanzas), pp. 9–17 + Advt. of books " By the Right Hon. Lord Byron," p. [**19**]. The Imprint, as above, is at the foot of p. [19].

VI.

Ode,/ etc./ Thirteenth Edition./ London :/ John Murray, Albemarle-Street./ 1818./ [8⁰

Collation—
Vide supra, No. i.

Translation of the Ode to Napoleon Buonaparte.
Spanish.

Odas a Napoleon. Por Lord Byron. Imp. de Decourchant, à Paris. 1829. A Paris, rue du Temple, n. 69. [18⁰
[*Bibl. de la France*, October 17, 1829.]

Parisina.

[For First Edition of *Parisina, vide infra, The Siege of Corinth*, No. i.]

Translations.
Danish.

Parisina./ Af/ Lord Byron./ Öfversättning. [Af Talis Qualis.] Stockholm, J. W. Brudins Förlag. [1854.] [8⁰

Collation—
Pp. 36. No. 4 of " Byron's Poetiska Berättelser."

French.

Adolphe Krafft/ Parisina/ Poème/ de Lord Byron/ et fragment de/ Nicolas de Ferrare/ Drame/ Tiré des documents historiques/ Avec commentaires et notices./ Paris/ Ernest Leroux, éditeur/ 28, rue Bonaparte, 28/ 1900 Tous droits réservés./ [8⁰

Collation—
Pp. xiv. + 55 + Errata, p. [57] + Table des Matières, p. [59].
Note.—The Text of *Parisina* is on pp. 3–26.

German.

Gedichte/ von/ Jacob Vinc. Cirkel./ Mit übersetzungen/ von W. Scott's Feld von Waterloo und Byrons/ Parisina etc./ Münster,/ in Commission der Coppenrathschen Buch= und Kunsthandlung./ 1825./   [8°

Collation—
     Pp. **159**. The Imprint (*Münster, gedruckt mit Coppenrathschen Schriften*) is on p. [**160**].
     Note.—The Text of *Parisina, etc.*, is on pp. **127–156**.

Italian.

I.

Parisina/ Poema/ di/ Lord Byron/ Traduzione italiana in versi./ Milano/ Da Placido Maria Visaj/ Stampatore-Librajo nei Tre Re/ 1821./   [8°

Collation—
     Pp. **27**.

II.

Parisina : poema tradotto da Andrea Maffei. Milano, Gnocchi. **1853**.   [16°
                                        [Pagliaini, **1901**.]

Collation—
     Pp. **40**.

III.

Parisina. Traduzione di Carlo Dall' Oro. Mantova, Negretti. **1854**.   [8°
                                        [Pagliaini, **1901**.]

IV.

Parisina, Traduzione in versi sciolti di Paolo Pappalardo. Palermo. **1855**.   [8°
                                        [Pagliaini, **1901**.]

V.

Parisina. Traduzione di Ant. Canepa. Genova, Artisti tip. **1864**.   [16°
                                        [Pagliaini, **1901**.]

Collation—
     Pp. **24**.

Russian.

Паризина...Переводъ В. Вердеревскаго. *С.-Петербургъ,* 1827.

Spanish.

Parisina, novela. Por L. B. Imp. de Decourchant, à Paris.
1830. [18°
[*Bibl. de la France,* October 17, 1829.]

The Prisoner of Chillon.

I.

The/ Prisoner of Chillon,/ And/ Other Poems./ By Lord
Byron./ London :/ Printed for John Murray, Albemarle-
Street./ 1816./ [8°

Collation—
Half-title (The/ Prisoner of Chillon,/ etc./) (R. Advt. of Third
Canto of Childe Harold, and Imprint, *T. Davison, Lombard-
street,/ Whitefriars, London./*), one leaf ; Title, one leaf ; Cont. ;
Text, pp. *1–60.*

Contents—

Sonnet on Chillon	. p. 1	Churchill's Grave	. p. 32
The Prisoner of Chillon	p. 3	The Dream . .	. p. 35
Poems—		The Incantation .	. p. 46
Sonnet	. p. 23	Prometheus . .	. p. 50
Stanzas to —— .	. p. 24	Notes	. p. 55
Darkness . . .	. p. 27		

Note.—On p. 3 the Text is headed "The Prisoner of Chillon.
A Fable."

II.

The/ Prisoner of Chillon./ A Poem/ By Lord Byron./
Lausanne./ Hignou & Company. Book-sellers./ 1818./
[8°

Collation—
Title, one leaf, pp. **1, 2** ; Text, pp. *3–29.*
Note.—The Front. is a lithograph of " Chillon." The seven
poems are not included in this edition.

III.

The/ Prisoner/ of/ Chillon,/ By Lord Byron,/ London :/
Printed by W. Chubb, Fetter Lane./ 1824./ [12°

Collation—
Pp. 35. The Imprint (*W. P. Chubb, Printer, Fetter Lane,
London.*) is at the foot of p. 35.

IV.

The/ Prisoner of Chillon,/ By Lord Byron./ [n.d. ? 1825.]
[12°

Collation—
Pp. *1*-18.
Note.—This edition, which is without a separate Title-page and
bears no Imprint, is bound up with *The Bride of Abydos*, etc.,
Printed for Thomas Wilson, Oxford Street.   1825.

V.

The/ Prisoner/ of/ Chillon./   By Lord Byron./   Geneva./
Published by Barbezat and Delarue,/ Booksellers, 177,
Rue du Rhône./   1830/   [16?

Collation—
Half-title (R. *Printed by Barbezat and Dalarue.*), pp. 1, 2 ;
Title, one leaf, pp. 3, 4 ; Sonnet on Chillon, pp. 5, 6 ; Text, pp.
7–32.
Note.—The volume with the above title is bound in pink
paper cover with title-vignette (helmet, spear, and wreath of bay-
leaves), and dated M.DCCC·XVIII.

VI.

The/ Prisoner of Chillon/   By/ Lord Byron/   Le prisonnier
de Chillon/   Par/ Lord Byron/ précédé d'une/ Notice
historique sur le château de Chillon/   Par/ D. Mar-
tignier/   Lausanne/ Librairie Martignier et Chavannes/
1857/   [8?

Collation—
Half-title (R. *Lausanne.—Printed by Corbaz and Rouiller sen.*),
pp. 1, 2 ; Title, one leaf, pp. 3, 4 ; Notice, etc., pp. 5–7 ; Hist.
de Chillon, pp. 8–21 ; Text and Notes, pp. 25–46.   The seven
poems are not included in this edition.

VII.

The/ Prisoner/ of/ Chillon
Poem/ By/ Lord Byron./   Illuminated by/ W. & G. Audsley./
Architects./   1865./   [4?

Collation—
Illuminated Half-title ; Title ; 17 pp. of Text with illuminated
borders, etc. + p. 18 (Chromo-lithographed/ By/ W. R. Tymms./
Printed & Published by/ Day & Son,/ [Limited],/ London)./

VIII.

Byron's/ Prisoner of Chillon./   With Notes for Teachers
and Scholars./   London :/ T. J. Allman, 463, Oxford
Street./   [1874.]   [16?

Collation—
Pp. 32.
Note.—No. 8 of "Allman's English Classics for Elementary
Schools."

IX.

Byron's/ Prisoner of Chillon./ With Life, Notes,/ Grammatical & Miscellaneous Questions,/ etc., etc./ By R. S. Davies,/ Head Master of Holy Trinity Schools, Hull./ Hull : A. Brown, Scholastic Publisher./ London : Simpkin, Marshall, & Co./ Leeds : Arnold ; Bean & Son./ Darlington : The Education Depôt./ Price Twopence./ [1877.] [12º

Collation—
  Pp. 24.
  Note.—Part of " Brown's Series of English Classics."

X.

The/ Prisoner of Chillon./ By/ Lord Byron./ With Prefatory and Explanatory Notes./ [Monogram, with Motto, *Lucem Libris Disseminamus.*] London : Blackie & Son, 49 & 50 Old Bailey, E.C./ Glasgow, Edinburgh, and Dublin./ 1879./ [16º

Collation—
  Pp. 32.
  Note.—Part of " Blackie's School Classics."

XI.

Byron's/ Prisoner of Chillon :/ With Life and Notes./ For Pupil Teachers and the Upper Standards in/ Schools./ Manchester : J. B. Ledsham, 31, Corporation Street ;/ London : Simpkin, Marshall & Co./ [1879.] [16º

Collation—
  Pp. 35.
  Note.—Part of the " World School Series."

XII.

The/ Prisoner of Chillon/ By/ Lord Byron/ And Part of/ The 3rd Canto of Child [*sic*] Harold/ With a Short Description of the Castle/ And a Notice of the Chief Historical Events/ and Legends connected with its History/ Selected from authentic sources by an English resident./ Fourth Edition/ Vevey/ Loertscher & Son, Editors/ 1880/ [8º

Collation—
  Pp. 59. The Text of *The Prisoner of Chillon* is on pp. 43-53.

XIII.

The Prisoner of Chillon. A Fable. Erklärt v. F. Fischer. Berlin, Weidmann. 1884. [8º

[Kayser, 1887.]

XIV.

The Prisoner of Chillon, with introduction and explanatory notes by Th. C. Cann, Firenze, Bencini, 1885.   [16?
                                         [Pagliaini, 1901.]

XV.

Byron's Prisoner of Chillon and Part of Mazeppa. With Life and Notes. London and Edinburgh. 1894.
                                         [Kölbing, p. 257.]

   Note.—Part of " Chambers' Reprints of English Classics."

XVI.

The Prisoner of Chillon, by Lord Byron. Special Subject. London. Stewart & Co., The Holborn Viaduct Steps, E.C. Edinburgh and Glasgow : Menzies & Co.
                                         [Kölbing, p. 257.]

XVII.

The/ Prisoner of Chillon/ By/ Lord Byron/ With Notes/ Explanatory, Analytical, and Grammatical/ Embracing/ Figures of Speech, and Metre/ By the/ Rev. Henry Evans, D.D./ Commissioner of National Education/ Dublin/ Blackie & Son, Limited, 89 Talbot Street/ London and Glasgow/ 1896/   [16?

Collation—
   Pp. 36.
   Note.—Part of " English Classics for Intermediate Schools and Colleges."

XVIII.

Byron./ The Prisoner of Chillon./ A Fable./ With Life, Introduction, Notes, etc./ Dublin :/ Fallon & Co., 16 Lower Sackville Street./ [Copyright. All Rights Reserved.] [1896.]   [16?

Collation—
   Pp. 36.
   Note.—Part of " School and College Series. Edited by Rev. T. A. Finlay, M.A., F.R.U.I. Price Sixpence, Net."

XIX.

The/ Prisoner of Chillon/ And/ Other Poems/ By/ Lord Byron/ In kritischen Texten/ Mit/ Einleitung und

Anmerkungen/ Herausgegeben/ von Eugen Kölbing/ Weimar/ Verlag von Emil Felber/ 1896/ [8°

Collation—
Pp. ix. + 450.

Translations of The Prisoner of Chillon.
Dutch.

De Gevangene van Chillon; in : Gedichten van K. L. Lede-ganck' met eene Levensschets des Dichters door J. F. J. Heremans. Gent, 1856.

[Kölbing, p. 265.]

French.
I.

Le Prisonnier de Chillon, Poème de Lord Byron librement traduit en vers blancs, précédé d'une notice historique et descriptive du château de Chillon. Vevey. G. Blanchoud, libraire-éditeur.

[Kölbing, p. 264.]

II.

Bonnivard/ A/ Chillon/ *Souviens-toi du temps d'autrefois./* (Deut. xxxii. 7.)/ Drame historique/ En un acte et trois tableaux/ Suivi d'une notice historique et du poème de lord Byron, intitulé : Le Prisonnier de Chillon/ Par un Huguenot/ Genève/ Imprimerie Wyss et Duchêne, rue Verdaine/ 1892/ [8°

Collation—
Pp. 96. There is a prose translation of *The Prisoner of Chillon,* pp. 74–85.
Note.—The Front. is a lithograph of " Chillon."

German.
I.

Lord Byron's Gefangener von Chillon (am Genfer See). Aus dem Englischen metrisch übertragen von G. Kreyenberg. Lausanne, 1861.

[Kölbing, p. 261.]

II.

Der/ Gefangene von Chillon./ Dichtung/ von/ Lord Byron./ In deutscher Uebersetzung mit historischer Einleitung/

von/ M. von der Marwitz./ Vevey & Lausanne,/ Richard
Lesser./ [1865.]   [8°

Collation—
  Pp. xi. + 16.
  Note.—The Front. is a "Photog. de R. Lesser & Cie.,
Vevey," of four female figures supporting a mirror reflecting the
dungeon of Chillon.

III.

Der Gefangene von Chillon. Eine Fabel von Georg Gordon
Lord Byron. Wortgreteu nach H. R. Mecklenburgs
Gründsatzen in deutsche Prosa übersetzt und eingehend
erläutert von Dᵣ phil. R. T.   Berlin, 1886.
                                    [Kölbing, p. 262.]

IV.

Der/ Gefangene von Chillon./ Von/ Lord Byron./ Uebersetzt von J. G. Hagmann./ Sᵗ Gallen & Leipzig/ Verlag
von Busch & Co./ [1892.]   [16°

Collation—
  Pp. 29.
  Note.—The Front. is a lithograph of "Chillon."

Italian.

I.

Il prigionero di Chillon, poema romantico trad. in prosa
italiana. In *Indicatore Livornese*, N. 44, del 11 Gennaio
del 1830.
  [*Saggio di Bibliografie*, Milano, Levino Robecchi, 1887.]

II.

Il prigionero di Chillon : Traduzione di Andrea Maffei,
Milano, Gnocchi, 1853.   [16°
                                    [Pagliaini, 1901.]

Russian.

Шильонскій Узникъ, поэма лорда Байрона. Переводъ
съ англійскаго В. Ж[уковскаго]. pp. i.–viii. 1-24.
С.-Петербургъ, 1822. 8°.

Collation—
  Pp. i.–viii. + 1-24.

Spanish.

El preso de Chillon, novela. Por lord Byron, traduccion castellana. Imp. de Decourchant, à Paris. 1829. [18°.
[*Bibl. de la France*, Oct. 17, 1829.]

Swedish.

Fangen PA Chillon,/ En Dikt/ Af/ Lord Byron./ Öfversätt-ning./ [Af/ Talis Qualis.]/ Stockholm,/ Albert Bonniers Förlag./ [1853, etc.] [8°.

Collation—
  Pp. 30.
  Note.—No. 3 of " Byron's Poetiska Berättelser."

The Prophecy of Dante.

Note.—*The Prophecy of Dante* was first published in the same volume with *Marino Faliero*, 1821. See No. i. (p. 275).

I.

The Prophecy of Dante. Philadelphia. 1821. [12°.
Collation—
  Pp. 48.

II.

The Prophecy of Dante. Paris, Galignani, 1821. [12°.
[Quérard, 1827.]

III.

The/ Prophecy of Dante./ A Poem./ By Lord Byron./ " 'Tis the sunset of life gives me mystical lore,/ " And coming events cast their shadows before."/ Campbell./ London :/ Printed and Published by W. Dugdale,/ 23, Russell Court, Drury Lane./ 1825./ [12°.

Collation—
  Pp. vi. + 7-32. The Imprint (*W. Dugdale, Printer, 23, Russell Court, Drury Lane.*) is at the foot of p. 32.

IV.

The/ Prophecy of Dante./ (Cantos I., II.)/ By/ Lord Byron./ With Critical and Explanatory Notes,/ By L. W. Potts,/ Lecturer on History at the Birkbeck Institute, London./ London :/ Blackie & Son, 49 & 50 Old Bailey, E.C./ Glasgow, Edinburgh, and Dublin./ 1879./ [16°.

Collation—
    Pp. 32. The Imprint (*Glasgow : W. G. Blackie and Co.,
Printers, Villafield.*) is at the foot of p. 32.
    Note.—Part of "Blackie's School Manuals."

Translations of The Prophecy of Dante.

French.

Oeuvres/ de Dante Alighieri./ La Divine Comédie,/ Traduction A. Brizeux./   La Vie Nouvelle,/ Traduction E. J.
Delécluze./   Paris,/   Charpentier, libraire-éditeur./   29,
rue de Seine./   1842./   [8°

Collation—
    Pp. lxxxviii. + 403 + "Table," p. [404].
    Note.—The translation of La Prophétie du Dante (par M.
Benjamin Laroche) (see "Avis de L'Éditeur," p. i.) is on pp.
385–403.

Italian.

I.

Profezia di Dante Alighieri, scritta da lord Byron, e tradotta
dell' inglese.   Impr. de Clò, à Paris.   Paris, chez Barrois
aîné, 1821.   [8°
                [*Bibl. de la France,* October 26, 1821.]

II.

La/ Profezia di Dante./   Di/ Lord Byron./   Tradotta in
terza rima/ da/ L. Da Ponte./   Nuova-Jorca : Publicata
da R. E. W. A. Bartow, 250 Pearl-St./   *Gray & Bunce,
Stampatori./*   1821./   [12°

Collation—
    Pp. 72.
    Note.—The Italian is printed over against the English.   There
is a double Dedication (pp. 3–7), "A Madamgella Giulia
Livingston," and "A Lord Byron."

III.

La Profezia di Dante : poema, reso in versi italiani da Giov.
Giovio, Milano, Bernardoni, 1856.   [8°
                                        [Pagliaini, 1901.]

IV.

La Profezia di Dante : poema accommodato all' indole del
verso italiano da Melchiorre Missirini, publicato da Fr.
Longhena, Milano Guglielmini, 1858.   [8°
                                        [Pagliaini, 1901.]

Spanish.

La Profecia del Dante./ Poema escrito y dedicado/ à la/ Condesa Guiccioli/ En 1819,/ Por lord Byron,/ al visitar en Ravena la tumba de aquel./ Traducido del Frances/ Por/ Antonio Maria Vizcayno,/ y dedicado a su bien amigo/ El Sr. Lic. D. Jose Agustin de Escudero./ Magistrado del supremo tribunal de guerra y marina./ Mexico : 1850./ Imprenta de J. M. Lara, calle de la Palma núm. 4./ [8º

Collation—
Title, etc., 6 pp. + Text, pp. **28**.

Sardanapalus.

I.

Sardanapalus,/ A Tragedy./ The Two Foscari,/ A Tragedy./ Cain,/ A Mystery./ By Lord Byron./ London :/ John Murray, Albemarle-Street./ 1821./ [8º

Collation—
Pp. viii. + 439. Half-title (R. *London : Printed by Thomas Davison, Whitefriars.*), pp. i., ii. ; Title, one leaf, pp. iii., iv. ; Cont., pp. v., vi. ; Preface, pp. vii., viii. ; Text, pp. *1*-439. The Imprint, as above, is on p. [440].

Contents—

Sardanapalus, A Tragedy p. 1	Appendix . . . . p. 305
Notes . . . . . p. 171	Cain, A Mystery . p. 331
The Two Foscari, A Tragedy p. 175	

II.

Sardanapalus, a Tragedy; The Two Foscari, a Tragedy; Cain, a Mystery. Boston. 1822. [16º

Collation—
Pp. 309.

III.

Sardanapalus :/ A Tragedy./ By/ Lord Byron./ London :/ John Murray, Albemarle Street./ 1829./ [8º

Collation—
Title, one leaf, pp. **1, 2** ; Half-title, one leaf, pp. **3, 4** ; Dedication, pp. **5, 6** ; Author's Note, pp. **7, 8** ; Dramatis Personæ, *n.p.* ; Text, pp. *9*-134.
Note.—The Dedication to "The illustrious Goëthe," which was omitted from the edition of **1821** (No. i.), is inserted.

IV.

Sardanapalus: A Tragedy by Lord George Gordon Byron.
Arnsberg, Ritter. 1849.   [16°
                                    [Kayser, 1854.]

Note.—Part of "Sammlung Englischer Schauspiele der neuesten
Zeit."

V.

Sardanapalus,/ King of Assyria./ A Tragedy./ In Five
Acts./ By/ Lord Byron./ Adapted for Representation
by/ Charles Kean./ Thomas Hailes Lacy,/ Wellington
Street, Strand,/ London./ [1853.]   [12°

Collation—
   Pp. 56.
   Note.—No. 155 of "Lacy's Acting Edition of Plays."

VI.

Lord Byron's/ Historical Tragedy/ of/ Sardanapalus./
Arranged for Representation,/ In Three [*sic*] Acts,/ By
Charles Calvert./ Manchester: John Heywood, 141 and
143, Deansgate./ [1877?]   [8°

Collation—
   Pp. vii. + 56.
   Note.—A list of "Opinions of the Press" (see *Poetical Works*,
1901, v. 9) is printed on p. 56 and on the inner leaf of the paper
cover.

VII.

Sardanapalus./ By/ Lord Byron./ [Title-vignette, "Myrrha,
Embrace me: yet once more—yet once more."] New
and Complete Edition.—Price One Penny./ London:
J. Dicks, 313, Strand: All Booksellers./ [1883, etc.]
                                                    [12°

Collation—
   Pp. 495-524.
   Note.—No. 50 of "Dicks' Standard Plays."

Translations of Sardanapalus.

Bohemian.

Sardanapal...Přeložil František Krsek. ("Sborník světové
poesie." svaz. 3.) pp. 204. *Otto: v Praze*, 1891. [8°.

French.

Sardanapale,/ Tragédie,/ Imitée de Lord Byron,/ par L. Alvin,/ Et représentée pour la première fois sur le Théatre Royal/ de Bruxelles, Le 11 Janvier 1834./ Bruxelles,/ Gambier, libraire, rue des Éperonniers N°. 16./ et chez tous les libraires de royaume./ 1834./   [8°

Collation—
  Pp. xviii. + 122.

German.

I.

Sardanapal. Trauerspiel in fünf Akten. Aus dem Engl. übers. von Emma Herz. Posen, Merzbach. 1854. [16°
                         [Kayser, 1860.]

Collation—
  Pp. 214.

II.

Sardanapal./   Trauerspiel in fünf Aufzügen/ von/ Lord Byron./   Bühnenbearbeitung/ Nach der Uebersetzung von Adolf Böttger/ mit einem/ " Vorspiel "/ von/ Max Zerbst./ Jena 1888./   Friedr. Mauke's Verlag./   (A. Schenk.)/ [1888.]   [8°

Collation—
  Pp. 117.

III.

Lord Byron's/ Sardanapal/   Eine Tragödie/ frei übertragen und für die Bühne bearbeitet/ von/ Josef Kainz/ Berlin W/   F. Fontane & Co./   1897/   [8°

Collation—
  Pp. 214.

Italian.

Sardanapalo/ Tragedia in 5 atti/ di/ G. Byron/   Milano/ Edoardo Sonzogno, editore/ 14.—Via Pasquirolo.—14./ 1884./   [8°

Collation—
  Pp. 91.
  Note.—No. 77 of the " Biblioteca Universale."

Polish.

Sardanapal, tragedya, przekład Fryderyka Krauzégo.
    pp. 132.   *wyd. red. " Biblioteki Warszawskiéj" :*
Warszawa, 1872.   [8°.

Romaic.

Σαρδαναπαλος,/ Τραγῳδια του Λορδου Βυρῳνος/ Μεταφρασθεῖσα ἐκ
    τοῦ Ἀγγλικοῦ,/ ο/ υιος της Δουλης/ και/ Ευγενια/ υπο/ Χρηστου Α.
    Παρμενιδου./ Εν Αθηναις,/ εκ του τυπογραφειου Ερμου./ (κατὰ τὴν
    ὁδὸν Περικλέους, ἐν τῇ οἰκίᾳ Ν. Μυκονίου.)/ 1865./   [8°.

Collation—
    Pp. η΄. + 400 + Πιναξ των Περιεχομενων, p. [401].
    Note.—The translation of *Sardanapalus* is on pp. 1–150 ; the
translation of *The Dream* (Το Ἐνυπνιον. Εκ των του Βυρῳνος), on
pp. 171–184.

Russian.

I.

Сарданапалъ...Переводъ Е. Зорина.
    С.-Петербургъ, 1860. 8°.

II.

Сарданапалъ...пер. О. Н. Чюминой. ["Артистъ,"
    1890, кн. 9 и 10.]

Swedish.

Sardanapalus./   Sorgespel I Fem Akter/ Af/ Byron./   Förs-
venskadt och För Scenen Behandladt/ Af/ Nils Arfvidsson./
Första gängen uppfördt à Kongl. Stora Theatern den 17
Nov. 1864./ Stockholm, 1864./ P. A. Norstedt & Söner,/
Kongl. Boktryckare./   [8°.
Collation—
    Pp. 154 + Rättelser, p. [155].

The Siege of Corinth.

I.

The/ Siege of Corinth./ A Poem./ Parisina./ A Poem./
London :/ Printed for John Murray, Albemarle-Street./
1816./   [8°.

Collation—
Half-title (R. *T. Davison, Lombard-street,| Whitefriars, London.*) ; Title, one leaf ; Second Half-title, with Motto ("Guns," etc.), pp. 1, 2 ; Dedication, pp. 3, 4 ; Advt., pp. 5, 6 ; Text, pp. 7–89 + Notes, p. [91] (R. Imprint as above).
Note.—The Siege of Corinth is on pp. 7–57 ; *Parisina,* pp. 59–[91].
Note.—A Second and a Third Edition were issued in 1816. The Museum copy of the First Edition is without the Half-title.

II.

The/ Siege of Corinth :/ A Poem./ Parisina :/ A Poem./ By Lord Byron./ New-York :/ Printed and Published by Van Winkle & Wiley,/ No. 3 Wall-Street./ 1816./
[12°

Collation—
Pp. 94.

III.

The/ Siege of Corinth./ A Poem./ By Lord Byron./ "Guns, Trumpets, Blunderbusses, Drums, and Thunder."/ London :/ Printed and Published by W. Dugdale,/ *23, Russell Court, Drury Lane./* 1824./ [12°

Collation—
Pp. 44. The Imprint (*Printed by W. Dugdale ; Russell-Court, Drury Lane.*) is at the foot of p. 44.

IV.

The Siege of Corinth. Für den Schul. u. Privatgebrauch abgedr. nach der Pariser Ausg. (1835, Galignani.) Lüneburg, Engel. 1854. [8°
[Kayser, 1860.]

Collation—
Pp. 51.

V.

Lines from the Poets/ With Notes/ For use in Elementary and Secondary Schools/ Adapted to the requirements of the New Code and the/ Oxford and Cambridge Local Examinations/ No. 4/ Byron's 'Siege of Corinth'/ London/ National Society's Depository/ Broad Sanctuary, Westminster/ 1879/ [16°

Collation—
Pp. 62.

VI.

Byron's/ Siege of Corinth./ Mit/ Einleitung und Anmer-
kungen/ Herausgegeben/ von/ Eugen Kölbing./ Berlin./
Verlag von Emil Felber./ 1893./   [8°

Collation—
Pp. lx. + 155. The Imprint (*Druck von G. Uschmann in
Weimar.*) is at the foot of p. 155.

VII.

The Siege of Corinth. Mit Anmerkgn. zum Schulgebrauch
hrsg. v. K. Bandow.   [12°
[Kayser, 1891.]

Note.—Part of "English Authors." Bielefeld, Velhagen &
Klasing. 1885–1890.

Translations of The Siege of Corinth.

Dutch.

Het/ Beleg van Corinthe,/ Uit Het Engelsch van/ Lord
Byron./ Door/ Mr I. Van Lennep./ [Title-vignette,
phantom appearing to Alp.] Te Amsterdam bij/ P.
Meijer Warnars./ 1831./   [8°

Collation—
Pp. 59. The Imprint (*Gedrukt Bij C. A. Spin.*) is at the foot
of p. 59.

French.

Le Siége de Corinthe, par lord Byron ; traduit de l'anglais
par Ch. Mancel. Impr. de Guiraudet, à Paris. A Paris,
chez Delaunay ; chez Pillet aîné. 1820.   [12°
[*Bibl. de la France,* September 16, 1820.]

German.

I.

Die Belagerung von Korinth. [Deutsch. v.] A. Wollheim.
Hamburg. Lübbers & Schubert. (?) 1817.   [12°
[*Centralblatt,* 1890, vii. 472.]

II.

Die Belagerung von Korinth. Mit gegenübergedrucktem
Originaltext. Leipzig, Brockhaus. 1820.   [8°
[*Centralblatt,* 1900, vii. 458.]

Note.—*Britische Dichterproben,* ii. 1.

III.

Die Belagerung von Korinth. [Deutsch. v.] G. E. Schumann. Hamburg, Nestler & Melle. 1827. [8°
[*Centralblatt*, 1890, vii. 471.]

Italian.

L'Assedio di Corinto, di Giorgio lord Byron, Versione di Vincenzo Padovan. Venezia, coi tipi del Gondoliere, 1838. [8°
[*Bibliografia Italiana*, March, 1838.]

Spanish.

El Sitio/ de/ Corinto./ Por/ Lord Byron./ Traducido del Francés Al Castellano./ [Title-vignette, Athene with owl.] Paris, Libreria americana,/ Calle del Temple, N°. 9./ 1828./ [16°
Collation—
    Pp. 85.

Swedish.

Belägringen Af Korinth./ Af/ Lord Byron./ Öfversättning./ [Af/ Talis Qualis./ Stockholm,/ Albert Bonniers Förlag./] [1854.] [8°
Collation—
    Pp. 60.
    Note.—No. 2 of " Byron's Poetiska Berättelser."

The Two Foscari.

I.

[*Note.*—For the First Edition of *The Two Foscari*, *vide ante*, *Sardanapalus*, No. i.]
The Two Foscari. New York. 1822. [24°
Collation—
    Pp. 114.

II.

The Two Foscari, an historical tragedy. By the right hon. lord Byron. Impr. de Belin, à Paris. A Paris chez Galignani, 1822. [12°
[*Bibl. de la France*, March 9, 1822.]

III.

The Two Foscari./ By/ Lord Byron./ [Title-vignette,
Death of Jacopo Foscari—"Touch it not, Dungeon Mis-
creants!——"] New and Complete Edition.—Price One
Penny./ London : J. Dicks, 313, Strand. All Booksellers./
[1883, etc.]   [8°

Collation—
   Pp. 525–546.
   Note.—No. 73 of "Dicks' Standard Plays."

Translations of The Two Foscari.

Russian.

Двое Фоскари...пер. Е. Зарина. ["Библіотека для
Чтенія," 1861. No. 11.]

Spanish.

Los dos Fóscaris. Drama histórico en cinco actos y en
verso por D. Manuel Cañete, representado en el teatro de
la Cruz, a beneficio de D. Juan Lombia, en el mes de
noviembre de 1846.

Collation—
   Pp. 24.
   Note.—Part of "Biblioteca Dramatica,"/ etc./ Madrid, 1846./
Imprenta de Don Vicente de Lalama, Editor,/ Calle del Duque
de Alba, n. 13./ 4°

The Vision of Judgment.

Note.—For the First Edition of *The Vision of Judgment,* see
The Liberal, 1822, No. I., pp. 3–39.

I.

Vision of Judgment. Paris, Galignani, 1822.   [12°
                                     [Quérard, 1827.]

II.

The/ Two Visions ;/ or,/ Byron v. Southey./ Containing/
The Vision of Judgment,/ By Dr. Southey, L.L.D./ Poet-
Laureate and Esquire ; Republican and Royalist :/ Also
Another/ Vision of Judgment,/ By Lord Byron./ London :
Printed and Published by W. Dugdale, 19, Tower/ Street,
Seven Dials./ 1822./

Collation—
   Pp. 72.
   Note.—The Text of Lord Byron's *Vision of Judgment* is on pp.
35–72.

The Waltz.

I.

Waltz :/ An Apostrophic Hymn./ By/ Horace Hornem, Esq./ "Qualis in Eurotæ ripis, aut per juga Cynthi/ Exercet DIANA choros."—Ovid./ London : Printed by S. Gosnell, Little Queen Street, Holborn,/ For Sherwood, Neely, and Jones, Paternoster Row./ 1813./ (*Price Three Shillings*.)/ [4º

Collation—

Title, one leaf, pp. [1], [2] ; To the Publisher, pp. 3–6; Text, pp. 7–27. The Imprint (*S. Gosnell, Printer, Little Queen Street, London.*) is at the foot of p. 27.

Note.—The pages of the Text measure 280 × 220.

II.

Waltz :/ An/ Apostrophic Hymn./ By/ Horace Hornem, Esq./ (*The Author of Don Juan.*)/ Qualis in Eurotæ ripis, aut per juga Cynthi/ Exercet DIANA choros./ Virgil./ Such on *Eurotas'* banks, or Cynthia's height,/ *Diana* seems ; and so she charms the sight,/ When in the dance the graceful goddess leads/ The Quire of Nymphs, and overtops their heads./ Dryden's Virgil./ London :/ Benbow, Printer and Publisher, Castle Street,/ Leicester Square./ 1821./ [12º

Collation—

Pp. v. + (Text) 7–36.

Contents—

To the Publisher . . p. iii.	Lines . . . to Mr. Hobhouse
The Waltz. . . . p. 7	[attrib. to Lord Byron] p. 30
Notes . . . . . p. 19	On the Star of "The Legion
To Jessy [attrib. to Lord	of Honour " . . . . p. 31
Byron]. . . . . p. 27	Adieu to Malta . . p. 34
"My Boat is on the shore"	
[attrib. to Lord Byron] p. 29	

Note.—The two last poems are not attributed to **Lord Byron.**

Werner.

I.

Werner,/ A Tragedy./ By Lord Byron./ London :/ John Murray, Albemarle-Street./ 1823./ [8º

Collation—
    Half-title (R. *London :| Printed by Thomas Davison, White-friars.*), pp. i., ii. ; Title, one leaf, pp. iii., iv. ; Dedication, one leaf ("To/ The Illustrious Goëthe,/ By One of His Humblest Admirers,/ This Tragedy is dedicated./"), pp. v., vi. ; Preface, pp. vii., viii. ; Text, pp. *1*–188. The Imprint, as above, is at the foot of p. 188.

II.

Werner, a Tragedy.   Paris, Galignani.   1823.   [12°
                                        [Quérard, 1827.]

III.

Werner./   A Tragedy/ In Five Acts./   By Lord Byron./ With the Stage Business, Casts of Characters,/ Costumes, Relative Positions, etc./   New York :/ M. Douglas, 11 Spruce Street./   And for Sale by all Booksellers./   1848./
                                                          [8°

Collation—
    Pp. v. + *6*–75.
    Note.—No. lxviii. of "Modern Standard Drama."   Edited by John W. S. Hows.

IV.

The/ British Drama./   Illustrated./   Vol. III./   London :/ Published by John Dicks, 313, Strand./   1865./   [8°
    Note.—The Text of "Werner./   A Tragedy, In Five Acts.— By Lord Byron./" is on pp. 767–789.

V.

Werner./   By Lord Byron./   [Title-vignette [*Sieg.*]—"Liar and Fiend!   But you shall not be slain."—[*Act* v. *Scene* 1.]/] New and Complete Edition.—Price One Penny./   London : J. Dicks, 313, Strand ; All Booksellers./ [1883, etc.] [8°
Collation—
    Pp. 767–789.
    Note.—No. 3 of " Dicks' Standard Plays."

VI.

Werner/ or/ The Inheritance/   A Tragedy/ By/ Lord Byron/ London/ George Routledge And Sons/ Broad-way, Ludgate Hill/   Glasgow and New York/   1887/
                                                         [16°

Collation—
    Pp. ix. + *10*–256.   The Imprint (*Ballantyne Press : Edinburgh and London.*) is at the foot of p. 256.

Translations of Werner.

Russian.

I.

Вернеръ...пер. Неизвѣстнаго. С.-Петербургъ, 1829.

II.

Донъ-Жуанъ на островѣ пирата. Перев. Д. Мина. Москва, 1881.

The Liberal.

The/ Liberal./ Verse and Prose From The/ South./ Volume the First./ London, 1822:/ Printed by and for John Hunt,/ 22, Old Bond Street./ [8°

Collation—

Vol. I. : pp. xii. + *3*-399 + Cont., p. [401] (R. "Errata," p. [402]). The Imprint (*London :/ C. H. Reynell, Printer,/ 45, Broad-Street, Golden-Square.*) is at the foot of p. [402].

Vol. II. : [The/ Liberal,/ etc./ Volume The Second./ London, 1823:/ Printed for John Hunt,/ 22, Old Bond Street./], pp. viii. + *1*-377 + Cont. of No. iv., p. [379]. The Imprint (*London :/ Printed by C. H. Reynell, Broad Street, Golden-Square.*) is at the foot of p. [380].

Contents [Lord Byron's contributions]—

Vol. I. : *The Liberal*, No. I. The Vision of Judgment. By Quevedo Redivivus. Suggested by the Composition so entitled by the Author of "Wat Tyler." "A Daniel come to judgment ! yea, a Daniel ! I thank thee, Jew, for teaching me that word." Pp. *3*-39 ; Letter to the Editor of "My Grandmother's Review," pp. 41-50 ; Epigrams on Lord Castlereagh, p. 164.

The Liberal, No. II. Heaven and Earth, A Mystery, Founded on the Following Passage in Genesis, Chap. vi. : "And it came to pass . . . that the sons of God saw the daughters of men that they were fair ; and they took them wives of all which they chose." "And woman wailing for her demon lover."—Coleridge. Part I., etc., pp. 165-206. From the French ("Ægle, beauty and poet," etc.), p. 396 ; Martial.—Lib. 1. Epig. 1 (Translation), p. 398 ; New Duet (" Why how now, saucy Tom ?"), *ibid.*

Vol. II. : *The Liberal*, No. III. *The Blues, A Literary Eclogue,* "Nimium ne crede colori."—VIRGIL. O trust not, ye beautiful creatures, to hue, Though your *hair* were as *red* as your stockings are *blue.* Eclogue the First, etc., pp. *1*-21.

The Liberal, No. IV. Morgante Maggiore di Messer Luigi Pulci, pp. 193-249.

Note.—The text of the original Italian is printed after the English translation.

Dedication of Don Juan.

The following note was attached to the "Dedication" which was prefixed to the First Canto in 1833 (*Works*, 1833, xv. 101) :—

"Note (1). [This 'Dedication' was suppressed in 1819, with Lord Byron's reluctant consent ; but, shortly after his death, its existence became notorious, in consequence of an article in the *Westminster Review*, generally ascribed to Sir John Hobhouse, and for several years the verses have been selling in the streets as a broadside. It could therefore serve no purpose to exclude them on the present occasion.]" See, too, *Poetical Works*, 1903, vi. 3.

I am indebted to the kindness of Mr. H. Buxton Forman, C.B., for the following description of one of these "broadsides," now in his possession :—

"Single sheet foolscap 8vo, consisting of Half-title, 'Dedica-tion/ to/ Don Juan,/' with Imprint on verso ('London :/ printed by C. and W. Reynell, Broad Street,/ Golden Square') ; Title-page, 'Dedication/ to/ Don Juan./ by/ Lord Byron./ London :/ Published by Effingham Wilson,/ Royal Exchange./ 1833./' On the verso of this is a note—

"'[*Why the following Dedication did not appear with the two first published Cantos of the Poem cannot be explained—unless the connection between* Mr. MURRAY *and* Mr. SOUTHEY *sufficiently explains it.*]'

"The first page of the Text (p. 5, but not numbered) contains the dropped head 'Don Juan./ Dedication.' and one stanza. Pp. 6–10 contain two stanzas each, and p. 11 one. The headline 'Don Juan' runs from p. 6 to p. 11, and the stanzas are numbered in Roman capital figures. P. 12 is blank, and is followed by a Half-title, 'Notes,' with a blank verso. The Notes occupy pp. 15 and 16, of which 15 is not numbered, but has a dropped head, 'Notes.' Page 16 is numbered, and has the headline 'Notes.'"

DIADEM HILL (ANNESLEY PARK), WHERE LORD BYRON PARTED FROM MARY CHAWORTH.

[*To face p.* 304.

NOTES.

———❖———

Note (1).—On Genuine and Spurious Issues of "English Bards, and Scotch Reviewers."

Among the first who called attention to the "inextricable tangle" of the several editions of *English Bards, and Scotch Reviewers* was Mr. Leicester Warren, better known as Lord de Tabley, who communicated some notes in 1877 to *Notes and Queries* (Series V. vol. vii. pp. 145, etc.) ; but it was reserved to the late Mr. Dykes Campbell, Mr. Bertram Dobell, and other correspondents to the *Athenæum* (May 5 to July 7, 1894), to point out that the problem was still farther complicated by the existence of spurious issues of at least three out of the five or six distinct editions of the Satire.

All editions, genuine or spurious, claim as their publisher "James Cawthorn, British Library, No. 24 Cockspur Street," but different printers were employed. The First Edition bears the imprint of "T. Collins, Printer, No. 1, Harvey's Buildings, Strand ;" the Second Edition, that of "Deans and Co. Hart Street, Covent Garden ;" the Third Edition, that of "T. Collins," etc. ; the Fourth Edition of 1810, that of "T. Collins," etc. ; the Fourth Edition of 1811 ("James Cawthorn and Sharpe and Hailes"), that of "Cox, Son, and Baylis, Great Queen Street, London." No printer's name was attached to the suppressed Fifth Edition of 1812.

Genuine First Editions have the water-mark, "E. and P. 1804," or "E. and P. 1805," or, possibly, no water-mark at all. A copy of the spurious First Edition, in Mr. Murray's possession, has the water-mark, "S. and C. Wise, 1812." In addition to at least eleven variants in punctuation, the spurious copy prints (p. 5, line 47) "Wizzard" (p. 20 *n.*), "Mædeira," and, in the same note, "Anna d'Afert ;" whereas the genuine copies print correctly "Wizard," "Madeira," and "Anna d'Arfet."

A genuine copy of the Second Edition, which belonged to the late Mr. Dykes Campbell, bears the water-mark "Budgen and Willmot, 1808." On p. 80, line 1007, "Abedeen" is misprinted for "Aberdeen ;" and the same misprint occurs in a copy of the Second Edition in the British Museum. In all probability there was no spurious issue of the Second Edition.

VOL. VII.   2 R

Of the Third Edition (1810), copies bearing the water-mark, " E. & P. 1804," or " G. & R. T.," may be regarded as genuine—rare exceptions among a host of forgeries which either lack a water-mark altogether or bear water-marks of a later period. Mr. Gilbert R. Redgrave, in an article (*The Library*, December 1, 1899, Series II. vol. i. pp. 18–25), notes two distinct and divergent forgeries bearing the water-mark " Pine, and Thomas, 1812." Forgery A prints " myse " for " muse " (line 4), " rove " for " rave " (line 384), etc. ; while forgery B, in a footnote to p. 30, prints " Bowle's' " for " Bowles's," and, at the end of p. 85, " we " for " me," and " farther " for " further." Other copies bear the water-marks, " Allnutt, 1816," " Smith & Allnutt, 1816," " Ivy Mills, 1817," and " I. & R. Ansell, 1818." A copy of a spurious issue of the Third Edition in the British Museum prints " crawl " for " scrawl " (line 47), and " p. 73 " for " p. 85."

It has been surmised, but conclusive proof is not forthcoming, that a so-called Fourth Edition of 1810 (1050 lines), which purports to have been published by James Cawthorn, and bears the imprint, " *Printed by J. Collins, Harvey's Buildings, Strand, London,*" is a spurious issue. It is practically a reprint of the Third Edition ; but in some copies there are misprints not to be found in other piracies— *e.g.* " crouds " for " crowds " (line 269), and " alter " for " altar " (line 285).

Copies of the Fourth Edition of 1810, which may possibly be genuine, bear a water-mark, " G. & R. T.," or are on plain paper. Copies which are manifestly forgeries bear the water-marks, " J. X. 1810 " and " W. Pickering, 1816."

A second Fourth Edition (1052 lines), published by " James Caw-thorn and Sharp & Hailes, 1811," and printed by " Cox, Son, & Baylis," was certainly recognized by Byron as a genuine Fourth Edition, and must have passed through his hands, or been subject to his emendation, before it was sent to press. Copies of this edition bear his MS. emendations of 1811–1812, and marginal notes of 1816. Genuine copies (*e.g.* Leigh Hunt's copy, now in the Forster Collection at the South Kensington Museum) are printed on paper bearing a water-mark, " J. Whatman, 1805." There was, however, another issue of the Fourth Edition of 1811, printed on plain paper. Mr. Redgrave notes certain minute differences between these two issues. In the edition on plain paper there is a hyphen to " Cockspur-Street " on the title-page, and the word " Street " is followed by a comma instead of a semicolon. Again, in the plain-paper copies " Lambe " is spelt with an *e*, and in the water-mark copies the word is correctly spelt " Lamb." In the plain-paper copies the misprint " Postcript " for " Postscript " is repeated, and in the copies bearing a water-mark the word is correctly spelt " Postscript." There are other differences in the advertisements at the end of the volume.

A spurious Fourth Edition in Mr. Murray's possession, which has been enriched with a series of prints of persons and places, bears the water-marks, " 1811," " 1814." Each page has been inserted into a folio sheet bearing the water-mark, " J. Whatman, 1816." A full-sized octavo, in small print (B.M. 11645 P. 15), which purports to be the Fourth Edition of 1811, is probably spurious. It is the survival of a distinct issue from other genuine or spurious copies of the Fourth Edition.

The spurious issues of the Third and Fourth Editions, whether they were printed in Ireland or were secretly thrown upon the market by James Cawthorn after Byron had definitely selected Murray as his publisher, were designed for the general reader and not for the collector. The issue of a spurious First Edition after the improved and enlarged editions of 1809-11 were published, must have been designed for the Byron enthusiast, if not the collector of First Editions.

The Grangerized Fourth Editions prepared by Mr. W. M. Tartt and Mr. Evans in 1819, 1820, and a Third, by John Murray at about the same period, and, more remarkable still, a copy of the Fourth Edition of 1811, prefaced by a specially printed "List of Names mentioned in the *English Bards, and Scotch Reviewers*," interleaved with the additions made in the Fifth Edition (B.M.), point to the existence of a circle of worshippers who were prepared to treat Byron's *Juvenilia* as seriously as the minute critics of the present generation. They seem to have been sufficiently numerous to make piracy, if not forgery, profitable.

Note (2).—CORRESPONDENCE BETWEEN THE FIRST EDITION AS NUMBERED AND THE PRESENT ISSUE AS NUMBERED.

First Edition (696 lines).		*Fifth (Present) Edition* (1070 lines).
1–26	=	103–128
27–246	=	143–362
247–262	=	{ Hobhouse's lines, omitted in Edition 2.
263–372	=	418–528
373–470	=	540–637
471–522	=	707–758
523–526	=	761–764
527–586	=	799–858
587–654	=	881–948
655–667	=	961–972
668–696	=	981–1010

Second, Third, Fourth (a) *Editions* (1050 lines).		*Fifth (Present) Edition* (1070 lines).
1–96	=	1–96
97–521	=	103–527
522–740	=	540–758
741–1050	=	761–1070

Fourth (b) *Edition* (1052 lines).		*Fifth (Present) Edition* (1070 lines).
1–96	=	1–96
97–521	=	103–528
522–1052	=	540–1070

Additions in the Second, Third, and Fourth (a) *Editions.*

[The lines are numbered as in the Second, Third, and Fourth Editions.]

Lines.		Lines.
1- 96	Still must I hear . . . as you read.	96
123-136	Thus saith the Preacher . . . to grovelling Stott.	14
357-411	But if some new-born whim . . . lumbering back again.	55
620-688	Or, hail at once . . . virtue must apply.	69
745-778	When some brisk youth . . . thy pay for coats.	34
839-860	And here let Shee . . . and God-like men.	22
929-940	Yet what avails . . . blazes, and expires.	12
953-960	There Clarke, still . . . libel on mankind.	8
991-1050	Then, hapless Britain, . . . unjustly, none declare	60
		370

696 − 16 (Hobhouse's lines) = 680 + 370 = 1050.

Addition in Fourth Edition (1811).

741-742	Through Crusca's bards . . . columns still.	2

1050 + 2 = 1052.

Additions in the Fifth (*Present*) *Edition.*

97-102	'But hold!' exclaims . . . shine with Pye.	6
528-539	Then, prosper, Jeffrey . . . inspires thy pen.	12
		18

1052 + 18 = 1070.

Emendations of the Text of the Fourth Edition (b) *included in the text of the Fifth and Present Editions.*

Fourth Edition.		Fifth Edition.
Line.		Line.
28	*And men through life her willing slaves obey.*	
	Obeyed by all who nought beside obey.	28
30	*Unfolds her motley store to suit the time.*	
	Bedecks her cap with bells of every clime.	30
32	*When Justice halts, and Right begins to fail.*	
	And weigh their Justice in a golden scale.	32
71	*Fear not to lie, 'twill seem a lucky hit.*	
	Fear not to lie, 'twill seem a *sharper* hit.	71
173	*Low may they sink to merited contempt,*	
174	*And scorn remunerate the mean attempt.*	
	Still for stern Mammon may they toil in vain!	179
	And sadly gaze on Gold they cannot gain.	180
257	*How well the subject suits his noble mind!*	
258	*"A fellow feeling makes us wondrous kind."*	

Fourth Edition.	*Fifth Edition.*
Line.	Line.
So well the subject suits his noble mind,	263
He brays, the Laureate of the long-eared kind.	264

303 *In many marble-covered volumes view*
304 *Hayley, in vain attempting something new :*
305 *Whether he spin his comedies in rhyme,*
306 *Or scrawl, as Wood and Barclay walk, 'gainst time.*

Behold—Ye Tarts !—one moment spare the text !	309
HAYLEY'S last work, and worst—until his next ;	310
Whether he spin poor couplets into plays,	311
Or damn the dead with purgatorial praise.	312

323 *And shows, dissolved in thine own melting tears.*

And shows, still whimpering thro' threescore of years.	329

327 *Whether in sighing winds thou seek'st relief*
328 *Or consolation in a yellow leaf.*

Whether thou sing'st with equal ease and grief,	333
The fall of empires or a yellow leaf.	334

385 *Fresh fish from Helicon ! Who'll buy ? Who'll buy ?*

Fresh fish from Hippocrene ! who'll buy ? who'll buy ?	391

387 *Too much in turtle Bristol's sons delight,*
388 *Too much o'er bowls of Rack prolong the night.*

Your turtle-feeder's verse must needs be flat,	393
Though Bristol bloat him with the verdant fat.	394

502 *First in the ranks illustrious shall be seen.*

First in the oat-fed phalanx shall be seen.	508

511 *As he himself was damned, shall try to damn.*

Damned like the Devil—Devil-like will damn.	517

532 *And grateful to the founder of the feast,*
533 *Declare his landlord can translate, at least.*

And, grateful for the dainties on his plate,	550
Declare his landlord can at least translate.	551

552 *While Kenny's World just suffered to proceed,*
553 *Proclaims the audience very kind indeed.*

While KENNEY'S "World"—ah! where is KENNEY'S wit?—	570
Tires the sad gallery, lulls the listless Pit.	571

563 *Let Comedy resume her throne again.*

Let Comedy assume her throne again.	581

569 *Where GARRICK trod, and KEMBLE lives to tread.*

Where GARRICK trod, and SIDDONS lives to tread.	587

614 *Raise not your scythe, Suppressors of our Vice.*

Whet not your scythe, Suppressors of our Vice.	632

625 *The Arbiter of pleasure and of play.*

Our arbiter of pleasure and of play.	643

661 *And, kinder still, a PAGET for your wife.*

And, kinder still, two PAGETS for your wife.	679

728 *Want your defence, let Pity be your screen.*

Want is your plea, let Pity be your screen.	746

742 *Some stragglers skirmish round their columns still.*

Some stragglers skirmish round the columns still.	760

815 *The spoiler came ; and all thy promise fair*

Fourth Edition.	*Fifth Edition.*
Line.	Line.

816 *Has sought the grave, to sleep for ever there.*
    The Spoiler swept that soaring Lyre away,   834
    Which else had sounded an immortal lay.   835

891 *The native genius with their feeling given.*
    The native genius with their being given.   909

903 *Let* MOORE *be lewd ; let* STRANGFORD *steal from Moore.*
    Let MOORE still sigh ; let STRANGFORD steal from MOORE. 921

922 *For outlawed* SHERWOOD'S *tales of* ROBIN HOOD.
    For SHERWOOD'S outlaw tales of ROBIN HOOD.   940

946 *And even spurns the great Seatonian prize.*
    Even from the tempting ore of Seaton's prize.   964

965 *So sunk in dullness and so lost in shame,*
966 *That* SMYTHE *and* HODGSON *scarce redeem thy fame.*
    So lost to Phœbus, that nor Hodgson's verse   983
    Can make thee better, nor poor Hewson's worse.   984

969 *On her green banks a greener wreath is wove.*
    On her green banks a greener wreath she wove.   987

972 *And modern Britons justly praise their Sires.*
    And modern Britons glory in their Sires.   990

984 *Earth's chief Dictatress, Ocean's mighty Queen.*
    Earth's chief Dictatress, Ocean's lovely Queen.   1002

1005 *But should I back return, no lettered rage*
1006 *Shall drag my common-place book on the stage :*
1007 *Let vain* VALENTIA *rival luckless* CARR,
1008 *And equal him whose work he sought to mar.*
    But should I back return, no tempting press   1023
    Shall drag my Journal from the desk's recess ;   1024
    Let coxcombs, printing as they come from far,   1025
    Snatch his own wreath of Ridicule from Carr.   1026

1016 *I leave topography to classic* GELL.
    I leave topography to rapid GELL.   1034

1018 *To stun mankind with Poesy or Prose.*
    To stun the public ear—at least with Prose.   1036

1049 *Thus much I've dared to do ; how far my lay.*
    Thus much I've dared : if my incondite lay.   1067

Note (3).—THE ANNOTATED COPIES OF THE FOURTH EDITION
OF 1811.

Two annotated copies of the genuine Fourth Edition of *English Bards, etc.* [1811], with MS. corrections in Byron's handwriting, are extant—one in Mr. Murray's possession, and a second in the Forster Library at the South Kensington Museum. The former, which contains the marginal comments marked "B. 1816," has been assumed to have been prepared as a press copy for the Fifth Edition ; but, as the following collation reveals, the latter, which belonged to Leigh Hunt, represents a fuller and later, though not

a final revision.   The half-title bears the inscription, " Byron,
Dec. 31st, 1811.   N—d. A^y [*i.e.* Newstead Abbey] B.

> " *Dum relego—scripsisse pudet—quia plurima cerno—*
> *Me quoque—qui feci—judice digna lini—*B.   J^y 20, 1812."

and the verso the words, " Given me by the author on my birthday,
Oct. 19, 1815.   Leigh Hunt."

                          u
P. 5.   ingen͟ous.   [The misprint is a note of a genuine copy.]

Lines 173, 174.

> ~~Low may they sink to merited contempt,~~
> ~~And scorn remunerate the mean attempt.~~
> Still for stern Mammon may they toil in vain,
> And sadly gaze on Gold they cannot gain.

[This emendation is not given in the Murray copy.]

Lines 257, 258.
                   So
> ~~How~~ well the subject suits his noble mind !
> " ~~A fellow feeling makes us wond'rous kind.~~"
> He brays the Laureat of the long-eared kind !

[The Murray copy, which amends line 258 as above, leaves the
" How " unerased, but the Fifth Edition prints " So."]

Lines 323–328.
> And shows, ~~dissolved in thine own tears.~~
>   still whimpering through threescore years.
> ~~Whether in sighing winds thou seek'st relief,~~
> ~~Or consolation in a yellow leaf.~~
> Whether in equal strains thou vent'st thy grief
> O'er falling Empires or a yellow leaf.

[The Murray copy gives no emendation.   The Fifth Edition
adopts the first correction, but, for the variant in lines 327, 328,
reads—

> Whether thou sing'st with equal ease and grief
> The fall of Empires or a yellow leaf.]

Line 336.   All love thy ~~strain,~~
                                 rhyme

Line 385.   Fresh fish from ~~Helicon~~
                                   Hippocrene

[The Murray copy adds a note : " The Fifth Edition reads
Hippocrene."]

Lines 387, 388.
> ~~Too much in turtle Bristol's sons delight,~~
> ~~Too much o'er bowls of Rack prolong the night.~~
> Your turtle-feeder's verse must needs be flat,
> Though Bristol bloat him with the verdant fat.

[The Murray copy does not contain this emendation, which was adopted in the Fifth Edition.

P. 36 *n*. The Hunt copy gives in MS. the note concerning Moore—"I am informed," etc.—which is printed in the Fifth Edition. There is no similar annotation in the Murray copy.

Line 502. For "ranks illustrious" both annotated copies read "oat-fed phalanx."]

Lines 532, 533.

> And grateful to the founder of the feast,
> Declare his landlord can translate, at least.
> And grateful for the dainties on his plate,
> Declare his landlord can at least translate.

[The amended lines, which appeared in the Fifth Edition, are not in the Murray copy.]

Lines 552, 553.

> While Kenny's World just suffered to proceed,
> Proclaims the audience very kind indeed.
> While Kenny's World—ah where is Kenny's wit?
>   listless
> Tires the sad Gallery—lulls the listening pit.

[The emendation is given in both annotated copies; but the substitution of "listless" for "listening," which is adopted in the Fifth Edition, does not appear in the Murray copy.]

Line 563.

>   Let Comedy resume
>   ass

[The correction is not given in the Murray copy.]

Line 569.

>   ——and Kemble lives to tread.
>   Siddons

[The substitution of "Siddons" for "Kemble," which dates from the Fifth Edition, is not given in the Murray copy.]

Line 728.

>   Want your defence, let Pity be your screen
>   plea
>   Want is your plea, let Pity be your screen.

Lines 815, 816.

> The spoiler came; and all thy promise fair
> Has sought the grave, to sleep for ever there.
> The Spoiler swept that soaring Lyre away,
> Which she had sounded an immortal lay.

[The emendation appears in both the annotated copies.]

L. 903.

>   Let Moore be lewd
>   still sigh

[This emendation does not appear in the Murray copy, but the words [" be lewd "] have been underscored with a pencil, and a **X** placed against them.]

Line 946.

~~And even spurns the great Seatonian prize.~~
Even from the tempting ore of Seaton's prize.

[This emendation is given in both the annotated copies.]

Lines 965, 966.

So sunk in dullness ~~and so lost in shame~~
That ~~SMYTHE and HODGSON scarce redeem thy fame.~~
So sunk in dullness that nor Hodgson's verse
Can make thee better—nor poor Hewson's worse.

[This emendation is not in the Murray copy. The Fifth Edition adopts the further correction, " So lost to Phœbus " for " So sunk in dullness."]

Line 969.   " ~~is~~ wove.
                               she wove.

[This correction is not in the Murray copy.]

Line 972.   —— ~~justly praise~~ their sires.
                   —— glory in their sires.

[This emendation is not given in the Murray copy.
The Leigh Hunt copy gives twenty MS. emendations (besides " Death " for " death," in line 820, and the alteration of "rapid " to "rabid " in the note on Hewson Clarke, line 962) including the note on Moore. The Murray copy gives nine MS. emendations, of which six are identical with those in the Hunt copy. Three emendations are peculiar to the Murray copy—]

(1) Lines 303–306.
        Behold !—ye tarts ! etc. (*vide ante*, p. 309).

(2) Line 614.   " ~~Raise~~ not your scythe.
                       Whet not your scythe.

(3) Line 661.   —— " ~~a Paget~~ for your wife.
                     —— two Pagets for your wife.

APPENDIX TO BIBLIOGRAPHY.

ILLUSTRATIONS OF LORD BYRON'S *POETICAL WORKS.*

Note.—The following catalogue of "illustrations of Lord Byron" has been extracted from pp. 88, 89, 94–96 of "*The Prisoner of Chillon, etc.* Herausgegeben von Eugen Kölbing, Weimar. 1896."

I.

Compositions in outline from Lord Byron's "Manfred" and "Prisoner of Chillon," by Frederick Thrupp, sculptor. London, Pub^d by Ackermann and Co., Strand.

II.

The Pocket Magazine of classic and polite literature. With engravings, illustrative of Lord Byron's Works. Vols. I., II. London : Printed and published by John Arliss. 1818.

III.

Forty illustrations of Lord Byron ; by George Cruikshank. Published by J. Robins and Co., Ivy Lane, Paternoster Row. [June 12, 1824.]

IV.

Six vignettes pour les Œuvres de lord Byron, d'après les tableaux de MM. Alfred et Tony Johannot, gravées par MM. Kœnig, Markl, Maulet, Pourvoyeur, Mauduit. Paris. Furne, libraire-éditeur. 1832.

V.

The Byron Gallery ; a series of historical embellishments to illustrate the poetical works of Lord Byron. London : published by Smith, Elder and Co. 65 Cornhill. 1833.

VI.

Finden's Illustrations of the Life and Works of Lord Byron. With original and selected information on the subjects of the engravings, by W. Brockedon. Vols. I.–III. London: John Murray, Albemarle Street : sold also by Charles Tilt, Fleet Street. 1833–1834.

VII.

Œuvres de Lord Byron, gravures à l'eau-forte, par Réveil, d'après les dessins de A. Colin. Paris. Audot, éditeur du Musée de peinture. 1833.

VIII.

Historical Illustrations of Lord Byron's Works in a series of etchings by Réveil, from original paintings by A. Colin. London, Charles Tilt, 86, Fleet Street. 1834.

IX.

Galerie des dames de Byron. Trente-neuf planches. Paris : Charpentier-éditeur. 1836.

X.

Illustrations of the Works of Lord Byron, consisting of a portrait after Saunders, a vignette title-page after Stothard, engraved by Blanchard, two facsimiles of handwriting of Byron, and twenty etchings on steel by Réveil, from original drawings by A. Colin ; to which are added the select passages in English and French, which form the subject of the engravings. Adapted to all editions. Paris, Baudry, European Library, etc. 1837.

XI.

Les dames de Byron ; or portraits of the principal female characters in Lord Byron's poems. Engraved from original paintings by eminent artists. Under the superintendence of W. and L. Finden. London : Charles Tilt, 86, Fleet Street. 1837.

XII.

Finden's Beauties of Byron ; or, portraits of the principal female characters in Lord Byron's poems. Engraved from original paintings by eminent artists. With extracts illustrating each subject. London : Charles Tilt, Fleet-street, and Thomas Wardle, Philadelphia.

XIII.

Cabinet of Poetry and Romance. Female portraits from the writings of Byron and Scott. With poetical illustrations by Charles Swain. London : David Bogue, 86, Fleet Street. 1845.

XIV.

Illustrations to the Works of Lord Byron. The drawings by Chalon, Leslie, Harding, Herbert, Meadows, Stephanoff, E. Corbould, Fanny Corbaux, Jenkins, and Westall. Engraved under the superintendence of Mr. Charles Heath. A. Fullarton & Co., 106, Newgate Street, London, etc.

XV.

The Byron Gallery of highly finished engravings, illustrating Lord Byron's Works, with selected beauties from his poems. Elucidated by historical and critical notices, together with a sketch of his life, containing important and unpublished matter. By Robert B. McGregor, Esq. New York : published by R. Martin, 46, Anne-street.

CONTENTS OF BIBLIOGRAPHY.

——◆◇◆——

TRANSLATIONS.

Collections of Poems.

Separate Poems and Dramas.

SUMMARY OF BIBLIOGRAPHY.

——◇◆◇——

I. Poetical Works. 2 vols. Philadelphia. 1813.
II. P. Works. 2 v. Boston. 1814.
III. Works. 4 v. London. *Murray*. 1815.
IV. Works. 2 v. London. *M.* 1815.
V. P. Works. 3 v. New York. 1815.
VI. Works. 3 v. Philadelphia. 1816.
VII. Works. 5 v. London. *M.* 1817.
VIII. Poems. 1 v. New York. 1817.
IX. Works. 8 v. London. *M.* 1818–1820.
X. Works. 6 v. Paris. 1818.
XI. Works. 13 v. Leipzig. 1818–1822.
XII. Works. 3 v. London. *M.* 1819.
XIII. Works. 6 v. Paris. 1819.
XIV. Works. 6 v. Zuickau. 1819.
XV. Works. 7 v. Brussels. 1819.
XVI. Works. 4 v. New York. 1820.
XVII. Works. 5 v. London. *M.* 1821.
XVIII. Works. 5 v. Paris. 1821.
XIX. Works. 16 v. Paris. 1822–1824.
XX. Works. 4 v. London. *M.* 1823.
XXI. Works. 12 v. Paris. 1822–1824.
XXII. Works. 12 v. Paris. 1823.
XXIII. Works. 3 v. [vols. v., vi., vii.] London. Knight and
        Lacy. 1824–1825.
XXIV. Works. 8 v. London. *M.* 1825.
XXV. Works. 6 v. [vols. v., vi.] London. *M.* 1825.
XXVI. Complete Works. 7 v. Paris. 1825.
XXVII. Works. 8 v. Philadelphia. 1825.
XXVIII. Works. 8 v. New York. 1825.
XXIX. Works. 32 v. Zuickau. 1825–1827.
XXX. Works. 13 v. Paris. 1826.
XXXI. Works. 1 v. Paris. 1826.
XXXII. Works. 1 v. Frankfort. 1826.
XXXIII. Works. 6 v. London. *M.* 1827.
XXXIV. Works. 4 v. London. *M.* 1828.
XXXV. Works. 1 v. Paris. 1828.

XXXVI. Works. 1 v. Frankfort. 1828.
XXXVII. Works. 6 v. London. *M.* 1829.
XXXVIII. Works. 4 v. London. *M.* 1829.
XXXIX. Poetic Works. 2 v. Philadelphia. 1829.
XL. Works. 1 v. Frankfort. 1829.
XLI. Works. 4 v. London. *M.* 1830.
XLII. Complete Works. 1 v. Paris. 1830.
XLIII. Works. 6 v. London. *M.* 1831.
XLIV. Complete Works. 1 v. Paris. 1831.
XLV. Works. 1 v. Philadelphia. 1831.
XLVI. Works. 14 v. (17 volume edition.) London. *M.*
        1832–1833.
XLVII. Complete Works. 4 v. Paris. 1832.
XLVIII. Works. (Verse and Prose.) 1 v. New York. 1833.
XLIX. Complete Works. 1 v. Paris. 1835.
L. Complete Works. 4 v. Paris. 1835.
LI. Works. 1 v. London. *M.* 1837.
LII. Complete Works. 1 v. Paris. 1837.
LIII. Works. 1 v. London and Leipzig. 1837.
LIV. Complete Works. 7 v. Mannheim. 1837.
LV. Complete Works. 1 v. Paris. 1839.
LVI. P. Works. 8 v. London. *M.* 1839.
LVII. Works. 5 v. Leipzig. 1842.
LVIII. Works. 4 v. Philadelphia. 1843.
LIX. Complete Works. 1 v. Frankfort. 1846.
LX. Works. (Verse and Prose.) 1 v. Hartford. 1847.
LXI. Works. 2 v. Edinburgh. 1850.
LXII. P. Works. 1 v. Philadelphia. 1850.
LXIII. P. Works. 1 v. London. H. G. Bohn. 1851.
LXIV. P. Works. 1 v. Philadelphia. 1851.
LXV. Complete Works. 1 v. Frankfort. 1852.
LXVI. The Illustrated Byron. 1 v. London. H. Vizetelly.
        1854–1855.
LXVII. P. Works. 2 v. Philadelphia. 1853.
LXVIII. P. Works. 1 v. London. C. Daly. 1854.
LXIX. Works. 1 v. Boston. 1854.
LXX. P. Works. 6 v. London. *M.* 1855.
LXXI. P. Works. 1 v. Edinburgh. 1857.
LXXII. P. Works. 1 v. New York. 1857.
LXXIII. P. Works. 1 v. London. *M.* 1857.
LXXIV. P. Works. 1 v. London. *M.* 1859.
LXXV. P. Works. 1 v. Philadelphia. 1859.
LXXVI. P. Works. 1 v. Leipzig. B. Tauchnitz. 1860.
LXXVII. P. Works. 3 v. Leipzig. 1860.
LXXVIII. P. Works. 1 v. Edinburgh. 1861.
LXXIX. P. Works. 10 v. Boston. 1861.
LXXX. P. Works. 1 v. Halifax. 1863.
LXXXI. P. Works. 1 v. Edinburgh. 1868.
LXXXII. P. Works. 1 v. London. F. Warne and Co. 1868.
LXXXIII. P. Works. 1 v. London. J. Dicks. 1869.
LXXXIV. P. Works. 8 v. London. *M.* 1870.

LXXXV. P. Works. 1 v. London. E. Moxon. 1870.
LXXXVI. Complete P. Works. 1 v. London. G. Routledge. 1874.
LXXXVII. P. Works. 1 v. London. Virtue and Co. 1874.
LXXXVIII. P. Works. 1 v. Boston. 1874.
LXXXIX. P. Works. 1 v. London. Ward, Lock, and Co. 1878.
XC. P. Works. 1 v. Boston. 1878.
XCI. P. Works. 1 v. London. Ward, etc. 1880.
XCII. P. Works. 1 v. London. F. Warne. 1881.
XCIII. Complete P. Works. 1 v. London. G. Routledge. 1883.
XCIV. P. Works. 1 v. Edinburgh. 1881.
XCV. P. Works. 12 v. London. Suttaby and Co. 1885.
XCVI. P. Works. 1 v. New York. 1886.
XCVII. P. Works. 1 v. London. W. Scott. 1886.
XCVIII. P. Works. 1 v. London. 1886.
XCIX. Life and Works. 2 v. London, Edinburgh, and Glasgow. 1888.
C. Complete P. Works. 1 v. London. G. Routledge. 1890.
CI. P. Works. 1 v. New York. 1890.
CII. P. Works. 12 v. London. Griffith, Farran, etc. 1891.
CIII. P. Works. 3 v. London. W. Gibbings. 1892.
CIV. Works. 12 v. Philadelphia. 1892.
CV. Dramatic and P. Works. 1 v. Philadelphia. 1898.
CVI. P. Works. 4 v. London. H. Frowde. 1896.
CVII. P. Works. 1 v. London. Bliss, Sands, and Co. 1897.
CVIII. P. Works. 1 v. London. W. P. Nimmo. 1897.
CIX. P. Works. 4 v. Philadelphia. 1897.
CX. P. Works. 1 v. London. G. Henny and Co. *n.d.*
CXI. P. Works. 1 v. New York. *n.d.*
CXII. P. Works. 1 v. New York. *n.d.*
CXIII. P. Works. 1 v. New York. *n.d.*

TRANSLATIONS OF COLLECTED EDITIONS.

French.

I. Œuvres Complètes. 15 tomes. Paris. Ladvocat. 1821.
II. Œuvres C. 13 t. P. Dondey-Dupré. 1830.
III. Œuvres C. 4 t. P. Charpentier. 1836.
IV. Œuvres. 2 t. P. Chapelle. 1842.
V. Œuvres. 3 t. P. Daussin. 1845.
VI. Œuvres C. 1 t. P. Bry aîné. 1856.
VII. Œuvres. 2 t. Alphonse Lemerre. 1891.

German.

I. Lord Byron's Poesien. 31 B. Zwickau. 1821–1828.
II. L. B.'s sämmtliche Werke. 12 B. Frankfurt a. M. 1830.

III. Dichtungen v. L. B. 4 Sammnl. Stuttgart. 1836-1839.
IV. L. B.'s s. W. 1 B. Leipzig. 1839.
V. L. B.'s s. W. 10 B. Pforzheim. 1842.
VI. L. B.'s s. W. 8 B. Berlin. 1865.
VII. Dichtungen v. L. B. 8 B. Hildburghausen. 1865.
VIII. L. B.'s ausgewählte W. 4 B. Leipzig. [1865-1812.]
IX. L. B.'s s. W. 3 B. Leipzig. 1874.
X. L. B.'s W. 6 B. Stuttgart. [1885-1890.]
XI. L. B.'s p. W. 8 B. Stuttgart. 1886.
XII. L. B.'s W. 6 B. Berlin. 1888.
XIII. Byron's s. W. 8 B. 1901.

Modern Greek.

Τα Απαντα του Βυρωνος. 3 v. Εν Αθηναις. 1895.

Italian.

I. Opere complete di Lord Byron. 1 t. Padova. 1842.
II. Opere. 1 t. Napoli. 1853.
III. Opere. 1 t. Napoli. 1857.
IV. Opere. 1 t. Napoli. 1886.

Polish.

I. Poezye Lorda Byrona. Pt. 1. Petersburg. 1857.
II. Poezye L. B. 1 v. Warszawa. 1885.

Russian.

I. Сочиненія Лорда Байрона. 5 т. С.-Петербургъ. 1864-66.
II. Байронъ. С.-Петербургъ. 1876.

Spanish.

Biblioteca Universal. Coleccion de Los Mejores Autores. T. lxiii. Madrid. 1880.

Swedish.

Byron's Poetiska Berättelser. Stockholm. 1854-1856.

SELECTIONS.

I. The Beauties of Byron. London. J. Sudbury. 1823.
II. The Beauties of B. Lⁿ. J. Limbird. 1827.
III. Life and Select Poems. Lⁿ. 1828.
IV. The Beauties of L. B. Philadelphia. 1828.
V. The Beauties of B. Paris. 1829.
VI. Lord B.'s Select Works. 3 v. Frankfort a. M. 1831-1832.
VII. Childe Harold's, etc. ; The Giaour, etc. Paris. 1832.
VIII. L. B.'s Select P. W. Paris and Lyons. 1835.
IX. L. B.'s Select W. London and Berlin. 1837.
X. The Beauties of B. Lⁿ. T. Tegg and Son. 1837.

XI. The Beauties of B.   L^n.   *n.d.*
XII. B.'s Select W.   Paris.   1843.
XIII. A Selection from L. B.'s P. W.   Marienwerder.   1846.
XIV. Select P. W.   L^n.   Adam Scott.   1848.
XV. L. B.'s Select W.   Oldenburg.   1848.
XVI. Selections.   London.   *M.*   1854.
XVII. A Selection.   1 v.   [A. C. Swinburne.]   L^n.   Moxon and
     Co.   1866.
XVIII. Songs by L. B.   L^n.   Virtue and Co.   1872.
XIX. Selections.   London.   *M.*   1874.
XX. *Beautés de B.*   Paris.   1876.
XXI. Favourite Poems.   Boston.   1877.
XXII. Beauties of B.   Stuttgart.   *n.d.*
XXIII. Poetry of B.   (Matthew Arnold.)   L^n.   Macmillan and Co.
      1881.
XXIV. Gems from B.   1 v.   New York.   1886.
XXV. Selections from the Poetry of L. B.   New York.   1900.
XXVI. Poems of Lord Byron.   L^n.   A. and C. Black.   1901.

Translations of Selections.

Armenian.

Lord B.'s Armenian Exercises and Poetry.   Venice.   1886.

French.

I. Choix de Poésies.   2 t.   Genève et Paris.   1820.
II. Les Beautés de L. B.   P.   1838.
III. Écrin poétique de lit. angl.   P.   1841.
IV. Chefs-d'œuvre de L. B.   P.   1847.
V. Rough Hewing of L. B.   In French.   L^n.   J. W. Kolckmann.
   1869.
VI. Chefs-d'œuvre de L. B.   2 t.   P.   1874.

German.

I. Byron's ausgewählte Dichtungen.   Leipzig.   1838.
II. Byron-Anthologie.   Schwerin.   1866.
III. Auswahl aus Byron.   1892.

Italian.

I. Poemi di Lord G. B.   Torino.   1827.
II. Opere scelte.   Milano.   1852.
III. A' Mici Amici.   1873.

MISCELLANEOUS POEMS.

I. An Ode.   On the Star, etc.   New York.   1816.
II. Three Poems.   London.   E. Wilson.   1818.
III. English Bards, etc., etc.   Paris.   1818.
IV. The Works of the R. H. L. B., cont. Eng. Bards, etc.,
    etc.   Philadelphia.   1820.

v. Poems by the R. H. L. B. L^n. Jones and Co. 1825.
vi. The Miscell. Poems. L^n. Benbow. 1825.
vii. Don Juan, Complete ; Eng. Bards, etc., etc. L^n. J. F. Dove. 1827.
viii. Don Juan ; Hours of Idleness, etc. 2 v. L^n. J. F. Dove. 1828.
ix. The Miscell. Works. L^n. Hunt and Clarke. 1830.
x. The Corsair—Lara. Paris. 1830.
xi. The Bride, etc. The Corsair, etc., etc. Paris. 1832.
xii. Manfred—Marino Faliero, etc. Paris. 1832.
xiii. Don Juan—The Age of Bronze, etc. Paris. 1832.
xiv. Miscellanies. 3 v. London. M. 1837.
xv. Tales. 2 v. London. M. 1837.
xvi. Lord Byron's Tales. Halifax. 1845.
xvii. The Giaour—The Bride, etc.—etc. L^n. H. G. Clarke and Co. 1848.
xviii. Miscellanies. 2 v. London. M. 1853.
xix. Tales and Poems. London. M. 1853.
xx. Beppo and Don Juan. 2 v. London. M. 1853.
xxi. Poems by the R^t. Hon. L. B. L^n. T. Nelson and Sons. 1855.
xxii. Tales and Poems. Leipzig. B. 1857.
xxiii. Poems. L^n. G. Routledge. 1859.
xxiv. Eastern Tales. L^n. D. Bogue. 1859.
xxv. Byron's Siege, etc., etc. Madras. 1876.
xxvi. Poems. L^n. G. Routledge. 1880.
xxvii. Poems of L. B. 2 v. L^n. Cassell and Co. 1886.
xxviii. Byron's Prisoner of Chillon and Siege of Corinth. Halle. 1886.
xxix. The Corsair—Lara. Boston. 1893.

TRANSLATIONS OF MISCELLANEOUS POEMS.

Bohemian.

Korsár. Lara. V Praze. 1885.

Danish.

i. Udvalgte Dramatiske Digte. København. 1873.
ii. Byron—Manfred, etc. København. 1889.
iii. Beppo. Dommedagssynet. Af L. B. København. 1891.

Dutch.

i. Navolgingen van L. B. Haarlem. 1848.
ii. Gedichten van L. B. Leiden. 1870.

French.

i. Le Corsaire—Mazeppa. Paris. 1848.
ii. Le Prisonnier, etc.—etc., etc. P. 1862.
iii. Le Corsaire—etc., etc. P. 1868.

IV. Chefs-D'œuvre de L. B.   2 v.   P.   1874.
V. L. B. Les Deux Foscari, etc.   P.   1881.
VI. Le Corsaire.   Lara.   P.   1892.

German.

I. Gefangener von Chillon u. Parisina.   Breslau.   1821.
II. Manfred.   Die Finsterniss.   Berlin.   1835.
III. Der Giaur.   Hebraische Gesänge.   1854.
IV. Kain. Ein Mysterium.   Mazeppa.   Leipzig.   1855.
V. Manfred.   Der Gef. v. Chillon. Heb. Ges.   Münster.   1857.
VI. L. B. Mazeppa, Korsar, u. Beppo.   Leipzig.   1864.
VII. Die Braut v. Ab.   Der Traum.   Hamburg.   1872.
VIII. Der Gefangene v. Chillon.   Mazeppa.   Leipzig.   1871–1876.
IX. Der Gef. v. Chillon.   Parisina.   Halle.   1887.

Hungarian.

Byron Lord' Élete 's Munkái.   Pesten.   1842.

Icelandic.

Bandinginn i Chillon og Dramurinn.   Kaupmannahöfn.   1866.

Italian.

I. Poemi di Lord G. Byron.   2 v.   Lugano.   1832.
II. P. di Giorgio L. B.   Milano.   1834.
III. P. di Giorgio L. B.   2 v.   Milano.   1842.
IV. Poemi e novelle.   Milano.   1882.
V. Opere . . . di G. Casella.   2 v.   Firenze.   1884.
VI. Misteri e canti.   Milano.   1886.
VII. Misteri, novelle e liriche.   Firenze.   1890.

Polish.

I. Poemata i powieści.   Warszawa.   1820.
II. Powieści.   Warszawa.   1831.
III. Paryzyna, Kalmar i Orla.   Wilno.   1834.
IV. Poezye Lorda B.   W. Paryżu.   1835.
V. Tłomaczenia A. E. Odyńca.   W. Lipsku.   1838.
VI. Tłomaczenia A. E. Odyńca.   W. Lipsku.   1841.
VII. Poemata.   Warszawa.   1846.
VIII. Pięć Poematów Lorda Birona.   Leszno.   1853.
IX. Kruzer (Karol) Przekłady, etc.   5 t.   Warszawa.   1876.

Portuguese.

Traducções Poeticas de F. J. Pinheiro Guimarães.   Rio de Janeiro.   1863.

Roumanian.

Din Scrierile Loui L. B.   Boukouresti.   1834.

Spanish.

I. Odas A Napoleon. Paris. 1830.
II. Poemas de L. B. Barcelona. 1876.
III. Cuatro Poemas de L. B. New York. 1877.
IV. D. Juan El Hijo de Doña Inés. Barcelona. 1883.

COLLECTIONS OF DRAMAS.

I. Dramas by Lord Byron. 2 v. London. *M.* 1837.
II. Dramas by Lord Byron. 2 v. London. *M.* 1853.

Translations of Collections of Dramas.

German.

Lord Byron's Dramatische Werke. Hildburghausen. 1870.

Italian.

I. Marino Faliero e I Due Foscari. Savona. 1845.
II. Tragedie di Giorgio Lord Byron. Firenze. 1862.

Spanish.

Poemas dramáticos de Lord Byron. Madrid. 1886.

POEMS, DRAMAS, AND COLLECTIONS OF POEMS.

THE AGE OF BRONZE.

The Age of Bronze. Lⁿ. John Hunt. 1823.

BEPPO.

I. Beppo, A Venetian Story. Second Ed. London. *M.* 1818.
II. Beppo, etc. Fifth Ed. London. *M.* 1818.
III. Beppo. Boston. 1818.
IV. Beppo, etc. P. A. and W. Galignani. 1821.

Translations of Beppo.

Dutch.

Vertalingen en Navolgingen, etc. [Beppo Eine Venetiansche Vertelling, pp. 119–159.] Amsterdam. 1824.

French.

Beppo, Poëme de Byron. Trad. p. S. Clogenson. P. Michel Lévy f. 1865.

Russian.

Беппо.

Spanish.

Beppo, novela veneciana.　P.　1830.

Swedish.

Beppo, En Venetiansk Historia.　Stockholm.　1853, etc.

BRIDE OF ABYDOS.

I. The Bride of Abydos.　A Turkish Tale.　London.　*M.*
　　1813.
II. The Bride, etc.　Second Ed.　London.　*M.*　1813.
III. The Bride, etc.　Fourth Ed.　London.　*M.*　1813.
IV. The Bride, etc.　Sixth Ed.　London.　*M.*　1814.
V. The Bride, etc.　Philadelphia.　1814.
VI. The Bride, etc.　London.　1844.

TRANSLATIONS OF BRIDE OF ABYDOS.

Bohemian.

Nevěsta z Abydu.　V Praze.　1854.

Bulgarian.

Абидонска Невѣста.　Москва.　1850.

Dutch.

De Abydeensche Verloofde.　Amsterdam.　1826.

French.

I. Zuleika et Selim.　P.　Plancher.　1816.
II. La Fiancée d'Abydos.　Gand, Houdin.　1823.

German.

I. Die Braut von Abydos.　Frankfort-a-M.　1819.
II. Die Braut, etc.　London.　1843.
III. Die Braut, etc.　Halle.　1884.

Hungarian.

Az abydoszi ara.　B'pest.　1884.

Italian.

La fidanzata d'Abido.　Milano.　1854.

Polish.

Dziewica z Abydos.　Warszawa.　1818.

Russian.

I. Абидосская Невѣста. 1821.
II. Невѣста Абидосская. С.-Петербургъ. 1826.
    Second edition. С.-Петербургъ. 1831.
III. Абидосская Невѣста. Москва. 1859.

Swedish.

Bruden Från Abydos. Stockholm. 1853, etc.

CAIN.

I. Cain ; A Mystery. London. Benbow. 1822.
II. Cain, etc. Lⁿ. R. Carlile. 1822.
III. Cain, etc. Lⁿ. H. Gray. 1822.
IV. Cain, A Mystery. New York. 1822.
V. Cain, etc. P. A. and W. Galignani. 1822.
VI. Cain, etc. Lⁿ. Benbow. 1824.
VII. Lord Byron's Cain, etc. Lⁿ. William Crofts. 1830.
VIII. Cain, etc. Lⁿ. J. Watson. 1832.
IX. Cain, etc. Breslau. 1840.
X. Cain. J. Dicks. 1883, etc.

TRANSLATIONS OF CAIN.

Bohemian.

Kain. V Praze. 1871.

French.

Caïn, Mystère dramatique. P. Servier. 1823.

German.

I. Cain, ein Mysterium. Berlin. 1831.
II. Cain. Ein Mysterium. Leipzig. 1871-1876.

Hebrew.

קַיִן שִׁיר־חִזָּיוֹן עַל־פִּי כִתְבֵי הַקֹּדֶשׁ מֵאֵת לוֹרְד בַּיְרוֹן תִּרְגֵּם מֵאַנְגְלִית לְעִבְרִית דוד
פרישמן וַוארשא תרי״ס

Hungarian.

I. Kain. Franklin-Társulat. 1895.
II. Kain. B'pest. 1898.

International Language.

Kain. Mistero de Lord Byron. Nurnbergo. 1896.

Italian.

Caino : mistero. Milano. 1852-6.

Polish.

Kain. Lwów. 1868.

Russian.

I. Каинъ. С.-Петербургъ. 1881.
II. Каинъ. Москва. 1883.

CHILDE HAROLD'S PILGRIMAGE.

I. Childe Harold's Pilgrimage. A Romaunt. London. *M.* 1812.
II. Childe Harold's, etc. Second Ed. London. *M.* 1812.
III. Childe Harold's, etc. Third Ed. London. *M.* 1812.
IV. Childe Harold's, etc. Fourth Ed. London. *M.* 1812.
V. Childe Harold's, etc. Fifth Ed. London. *M.* 1812.
VI. Childe Harold's, etc. First Amer. Ed. Philadelphia. 1812.
VII. Childe Harold's, etc. Sixth Ed. London. *M.* 1813.
VIII. Childe Harold's, etc. Seventh Ed. London. *M.* 1814.
IX. Childe Harold's, etc. Eighth Ed. London. *M.* 1814.
X. Childe Harold's, etc. Tenth Ed. London. *M.* 1815.
XI. Childe Harold's, etc. Canto the Third. London. *M.* 1816.
XII. Childe Harold's, etc. Canto the Fourth. London. *M.* 1818.
XIII. Childe Harold's, etc. Canto the Fourth. New York. 1818.
XIV. Childe Harold's, etc. Eleventh Ed. London. *M.* 1819.
XV. Childe Harold's, etc. 2 v. London. *M.* 1819.
XVI. Childe Harold's, etc. 2 v. Leipzig. 1820.
XVII. Childe Harold's, etc. Lⁿ. W. Dugdale. 1825.
XVIII. Childe Harold's, etc. P. A. and W. Galignani. 1825.
XIX. Childe Harold's, etc. London. W. Dugdale. 1826.
XX. Childe Harold's, etc. London. T. Colmer. 1827.
XXI. Childe Harold's, etc. 2 v. Paris. 1827.
XXII. Childe Harold's, etc. London. John Duncombe. 1831.
XXIII. Childe Harold's, etc. Nuremberg and New York. 1831.
XXIV. Childe Harold's, etc. London. *M.* 1837.
XXV. Childe Harold's, etc. Mannheim. 1837.
XXVI. Childe Harold's, etc. London. *M.* 1841.
XXVII. Childe Harold's, etc. London. 1842.
XXVIII. Childe Harold's, etc. London. *M.* 1853.
XXIX. Childe Harold. Hamburg. 1853.
XXX. Childe Harold's, etc. 2 v. Berlin. 1854.
XXXI. Childe Harold's, etc. London. *M.* 1859.
XXXII. Childe Harold's, etc. New Ed. London. *M.* 1860.
XXXIII. Childe Harold's, etc. New Ed. London. *M.* 1860.
XXXIV. Childe Harold's, etc. Leipzig. 1862.
XXXV. Childe Harold's, etc. London. C. Griffin and Co. 1866.
XXXVI. Childe Harold's, etc. Münster. 1867.

XXXVII. Byron's Childe Harold's, etc. L^n. and Edinburgh. 1877.
XXXVIII. Lord Byron's Childe Harold's, etc. P. Lib. Ch. Delagrave. 1882.
XXXIX. Childe Harold's, etc. P. Poussielque f. 1883.
XL. Clarendon Press Series. Childe Harold. Oxford. 1885.
XLI. Childe Harold's, etc. London. Chatto. 1885.
XLII. Lord Byron. Childe Harold's, etc. Berlin. 1885.
XLIII. Cassell's Nat. Lib. Childe Harold's, etc. L^n., P., N. Y., and Melbourne. 1886.
XLIV. Childe Harold's, etc. Boston. 1886.
XLV. Childe Harold's, etc. Philadelphia. 1886.
XLVI. Childe Harold's, etc. Leipzig. 1886.
XLVII. Childe Harold's, etc. Bielefeld. 1885-6.
XLVIII. Childe Harold's, etc. L^n. G. Routledge and Sons. 1888.
XLIX. Childe Harold's, etc. Bielefeld. 1891.
L. Sir J. Lubbock's Hundred Best Books. Childe Harold's, etc. L^n. G. Routledge and Sons. 1892.
LI. Byron's Childe Harold. L^n. G. Bell and Sons. 1893.
LII. Byron. Childe Harold. P. Lib. Hachette et Cie. 1893.
LIII. Childe Harold's, etc. New York. 1894.
LIV. Arnold's Brit. Classics. Childe Harold's, etc. L^n. Edw. Arnold. 1897.
LV. Childe Harold. L^n. J. M. Dent. 1898.
LVI. Childe Harold's, etc. Cantos I., II. L^n. Macmillan and Co. 1899.
LVII. Childe Harold's, etc. Cantos III., IV. L^n. Macmillan and Co. 1899.
LVIII. Childe Harold's, etc. 2 v. New York. 1899.
LIX. Childe Harold's, etc. New York. 1899.
LX. Childe Harold's, etc. New York. 1900.
LXI. Lord Byron. Childe Harold's, etc. Glasgow and Dublin. 1901.
LXII. Lord Byron. Childe Harold's, etc. Glasgow and Dublin. 1901.

TRANSLATIONS OF CHILDE HAROLD'S PILGRIMAGE.

Armenian.

Childe Harold's, etc. Venice. 1872.

Bohemian.

Childe Haroldova pout'. 1890.

Danish.

Junker Harolds Pilgrimsfart. Kjøbenhavn. 1880.

French.

I. Le Pélerinage de C. H. P. Dupont. 1828.
II. Le Pélerinage de C. H. P. Ponthieu. 1828.
III. Le Pélerinage de C. H. P. Lib. de Ch. Blériot. 1861.

IV. C. H. Poëme de L. B. P. E. Dentu. 1862.
V. Le Pélerinage de C. H. Saint-Quentin. 1862.
VI. Childe Harold. P. Amyot. 1870.
VII. Childe Harold. P. Hachette et Cie. 1881.
VIII. Childe Harold's, etc. P. Poussielque f. 1883.
IX. Childe Harold. P. Delalain f. 1892.
X. Childe Harold. P. Belin f. 1892. :

German.

I. Harold, der Verwiesene. Leipzig. 1835.
II. Ritter Harold's Pilgerfahrt. Stuttgart. 1836.
III. Jungherrn Harold's P. Stralsund. 1839.
IV. Erster Gesang des C. H. Ansbach. 1845.
V. Byron's Ritter Harold. Leipzig. 1846.
VI. Childe Harold's P. Frankfurt a. M. 1853.
VII. Harold's P. Köln. 1865.
VIII. Childe Harold's P. Hildburghausen. 1868.
IX. Jung Harold's P. Berlin. 1869.
X. Ritter Harold's P. Leipzig. 1871–1876.
XI. Childe Harold's P. 1893.

Hungarian.

Childe Harold. Genfben. 1857.

Italian.

I. L'Italia, Canto IV. del pellegrinaggio di C. H. 1819.
II. Il pellegrinaggio del Giovine Aroldo. Genova. 1836.
III. L'Italia, Canto di L. B. Milano. 1848.
IV. Il pell. del giov. A. Napoli. 1858.
V. Il pell. del giov. A. Venezia. 1860.
VI. Byron. Pell. D'Aroldo. Milano. 1866.
VII. Italia C. di Gior. Byron. Firenze. 1872.
VIII. Il pell. D'Aroldo. Firenze. 1873.

Polish.

I. Poezye . . . Wędrówki Czaild Harolda. Petersburg. 1857.
II. Pielgrzymka C. H. we Lwowie. 1857.
III. Wędrówki C. H. Prz. F. Krauze. 1865–1871.
IV. Wędrówki Rycerza H. Warszawa. 1895.
V. Wędrówki C. H. Krakow. 1896.

Russian.

I. Чайльдъ-Гарольдъ.
II. Чайльдъ-Гарольдъ.

Swedish.

Childe Harolds Pilgrimsfärd. Stockholm. 1832.

The Corsair.

I. The Corsair, A Tale. London. *M.* 1814.
II. The Corsair, etc. Second Ed. London. *M.* 1814.
III. The Corsair, etc. Third Ed. London. *M.* 1814.
IV. The Corsair, etc. Fourth Ed. L^n. *M.* 1814.
V. The Corsair, etc. Fifth Ed. London. *M.* 1814.
VI. The Corsair, etc. Sixth Ed. London. *M.* 1814.
VII. The Corsair, etc. Seventh Ed. London. *M.* 1814.
VIII. The Corsair, etc. New York. 1814.
IX. The Corsair, etc. Ninth Ed. London. *M.* 1815.
X. The Corsair, etc. Tenth Ed. London. *M.* 1818.
XI. The Corsair, etc. L^n. W. Dugdale. 1825.
XII. The Corsair, etc. L^n. 1844.
XIII. The Corsair, etc. Glasgow. 1867.

Translations of The Corsair.

German.

I. Der Korsar. Berlin. 1816.
II. Der Korsar. Altona. 1820.
III. Der Korsar. Leipzig. 1852.
IV. Der Corsar. Mainz. 1852.
V. Der Korsar. Leipzig. 1871–1876.

Hungarian.

A Kalóz. B'pest. 1892.

Italian.

I. Il Corsaro. Torino. 1819.
II. Il Corsaro. Milano. 1820.
III. Il Corsaro. Milano. 1842.
IV. Il Corsaro. Firenze. 1842.
V. Il Corsaro. Bologna. 1870.
VI. Il Corsaro. V. di C. Rosnati. 1879.

Russian.

Морской разбойникъ. С.-Петербургъ. 1827.

Spanish.

I. El Corsario. Paris. 1827.
II. El Corsario. Valencia. 1832.

Swedish.

Corsaren. Stockholm. 1868.

The Curse of Minerva.

I. The Curse of Minerva. London. [4to.] 1812.
II. The Curse, etc. Philadelphia. [?] 1815.
III. The Curse, etc. P. Galignani. 1818.

THE DEFORMED TRANSFORMED.

I. The Deformed Transformed. London. J. and H. L. Hunt. 1824.
II. The Def. Transf. P. A. and W. Galignani. 1824.
III. The Def. Transf. L^n. J. Dicks. 1883, etc.

TRANSLATION OF THE DEFORMED TRANSFORMED.

Hungarian.

Budapesti Árvizkönyv., etc. Pesten. 1840.

DON JUAN.

Cantos I., II.

I. Don Juan. London. Printed by T. Davison. [4°] 1819.
II. D. Juan. L^n. Pt. by T. Davison. 1819.
III. D. Juan. L^n. J. Onwhyn. 1819.
IV. D. Juan. L^n. Pt. by T. Davison. 1820.
V. D. Juan. L^n. Sherwin and Co. 1820.
VI. D. Juan. L^n. Pt. by T. Davison. 1822.

Cantos III., IV., V.

I. D. Juan. L^n. Pt. by T. Davison. 1821.
II. D. Juan. L^n. Sherwin and Co. 1821.
III. D. Juan. Fifth Ed. L^n. Pt. by T. Davison. 1822.

Cantos I.–V.

I. D. Juan. L^n. W. Benbow. 1822.
II. D. Juan. L^n. Hodgson and Co. 1822.
III. D. Juan. L^n. Peter Griffin. 1823.
IV. D. Juan. L^n. G. Smeeton. 1826.

Cantos VI., VII., VIII.

I. D. Juan. L^n. John Hunt. [8°] 1823.
II. D. Juan. L^n. W. Dugdale. 1823.
III. D. Juan. L^n. John Hunt. [12°] 1823.

Cantos IX., X., XI.

I. D. Juan. L^n. John Hunt. [8°] 1823.
II. D. Juan. L^n. John Hunt. [12°] 1823.

Cantos XII., XIII., XIV.

I. D. Juan. L^n. John Hunt. [8°] 1823.
II. D. Juan. L^n. John Hunt. [12°] 1823.
III. D. Juan. L^n. Pt. for the Booksellers. 1823.
IV. D. Juan. P. A. and W. Galignani. 1824.

Cantos XV., XVI.

I. D. Juan. L^n. John and H. L. Hunt. [8°] 1824.
II. D. Juan. L^n. John and H. L. Hunt. [12°] 1824.
III. D. Juan. L^n. Pt. for the Booksellers. 1824.
IV. D. Juan. L^n. Pt. for John Hunt. 1824.
V. D. Juan. P. A. and W. Galignani. 1824.

Full Text.

I. D. Juan. 2 v. L^n. Pt. for the Booksellers. 1826
II. D. Juan. L^n. W. Clark. 1826.
III. D. Juan. L^n. T. and J. Allman. 1827.
IV. D. Juan. 2 v. L^n. T. Davison. 1828.
V. D. Juan. 2 v. L^n. Pt. for the Booksellers. 1828.
VI. D. Juan. Nuremberg and New York. 1832.
VII. D. Juan. L^n. Scott and Webster. 1833.
VIII. D. Juan. L^n. Pt. for the Booksellers. 1835.
IX. D. Juan. 2 v. London. *M.* 1837.
X. D. Juan. Mannheim. 1838.
XI. D. Juan. L^n. H. G. Bohn. 1849.
XII. D. Juan. L^n. and N. Y. 1874.
XIII. D. Juan. L^n. Chatto and Windus. 1875.
XIV. D. Juan. L^n. G. Routledge and Sons. 1886.

TRANSLATIONS OF DON JUAN.

Danish.

I. D. Juan. Fredericia. 1854.
II. Byron. D. Juan. Kjøbenhavn. 1880.

French.

I. Don Juan. 2 v. P. P. Renouard. 1827.
II. D. Juan. 2 v. P. *Lib. centrale.* 1866.
III. D. Juan. P. DeGorge-Cadot. 1869.
IV. D. Juan. P. Lemerre. 1878.

German.

I. Don Juan. Essen. 1839.
II. Byron's D. Juan. Bremen. 1845.
III. Byron's D. Juan. Leipzig. 1849.
IV. Byron's D. Juan. Hildburghausen. 1867.

Italian.

I. Don Giovanni. Torino. 1853.
II. D. Giovanni. Milano. 1865.
III. Gior. Byron. Aidea Epis. del don Giov. Verona. 1875.
IV. Il D. Juan. Milano. 1876.
V. D. Giovanni. Milano. 1880.

Polish.

 I. Don Żuan. Tarnopol. 1863.
 II. Ustęp z drugiéj pieśni Don Żuana. Kraków. 1877.
III. Don Żuań, pieśń trzecia. Kraków. 1877.
 IV. Don Żuań, pieśń druga, trzecia i czwarta. Tarnopol. 1879.
  V. Don Żuan. Warszawa. 1885.

Roumanian.

Don Juan dela Lord Byron. Bucuresci. 1847.

Russian.

  I. Донъ-Жуанъ. С.-Петербургъ. 1846.
 II. Донъ-Жуанъ. 2 v. С.-Петербургъ. [1847.]
III. Донъ-Жуанъ...Глава первая. Лейпцигъ. 1862.
 IV. Донъ-Жуанъ. С.-Петербургъ. 1866, 67.
  V. Донъ-Жуанъ. 2 v. С.-Петербургъ. 1889.
 VI. Донъ-Жуанъ. 2 т. С.-Петербургъ. 1892.

Servian.

Дон-Жуанъ. 2 свес. Београд. 1888.

Spanish.

 I. Don Juan, novela. Paris. 1829.
II. Don Juan. Madrid. 1876.

Swedish.

 I. Don Juan. Stockholm. 1838.
II. Don Juan. 2 v. Stockholm. 1857.

ENGLISH BARDS, AND SCOTCH REVIEWERS.

   I. The British Bards, A Satire. 1808.
  II. English Bards, and Scotch Reviewers. First Ed. L^n.
      James Cawthorn. 1809.
 III. English B., etc. Second Ed. L^n. J. Cawthorn. 1809.
  IV. English B., etc. Third Ed. L^n. J. Cawthorn. 1810.
   V. English B., etc. Fourth Ed. L^n. J. Cawthorn. 1810.
  VI. English B., etc. Fourth Ed. L^n. J. Cawthorn. 1811.
 VII. English B., etc. Fifth Ed. [L^n. J. Cawthorn.] 1811.
VIII. English B., etc. First Amer. Ed. Philadelphia. 1811.
  IX. English B., etc. Charleston. 1811.
   X. English B., etc. Boston. 1814.
  XI. English B., etc. New York. 1817.
 XII. English B., etc. P. Galignani. 1818.
XIII. English B., etc. Brussels. 1819.
 XIV. English B., etc. Geneva. 1820.
  XV. English B., etc. L^n. Benbow. 1823.
 XVI. English B., etc. Glasgow. J. Starke. 1824.

XVII. English B., etc. Glasgow. M'Intosh and Co. 1825.
XVIII. English B., etc. L^n. W. Dugdale. 1825.
XIX. English B., etc. L^n. T. Kay. 1827.

FARE THEE WELL! AND A SKETCH FROM PRIVATE LIFE.

I. Fare Thee Well. March 18, 1816.
II. Fare Thee Well! April 4, 1816.
III. Fare Thee Well. Second Version. April 7, 1816.
IV. A Sketch from Private Life. March 30, 1816.
V. A Sketch, etc. Another Copy. April 2, 1816.
VI. Fare Thee Well!—A Sketch, etc. L^n. Sherwood, Neely, and Jones. 1816.
VII. Fare Thee Well. Bristol. 1816.
VIII. Fare Thee Well. Edinburgh. 1816.

THE GIAOUR.

I. The Giaour, A Fragment of a Turkish Tale. London. *M.* 1813.
II. The Giaour, etc. A new Ed. London. *M.* 1813.
III. The Giaour, etc. Third Ed. London. *M.* 1813.
IV. The Giaour, etc. Boston. 1813.
V. The Giaour, etc. Fifth Ed. London. *M.* 1813.
VI. The Giaour, etc. Sixth Ed. L^n. *M.* 1813.
VII. The Giaour, etc. Seventh Ed. London. *M.* 1813.
VIII. The Giaour, etc. Ninth Ed. London. *M.* 1814.
IX. The Giaour, etc. Tenth Ed. London. *M.* 1814.
X. The Giaour, etc. Eleventh Ed. London. *M.* 1814.
XI. The Giaour, etc. Twelfth Ed. London. *M.* 1814.
XII. The Giaour, etc. Fourteenth Ed. London. *M.* 1815.
XIII. The Giaour, etc. L^n. W. Dugdale. 1825.
XIV. The Giaour, etc. London. *M.* (Tilt and Bogue, Edinb.) 1842.
XV. The Giaour, etc. London. 1844.

TRANSLATIONS OF THE GIAOUR
French.

Le Giaour. P. J. M. H. Bigeon. 1828.

German.

I. Der Gauer. Berlin. 1819.
II. Der Gjaur. Leipzig. 1820.
III. Der Gjaur. Leipzig. 1871–1876.

Italian.

I. Il Giaurro. Genova e Parigi. 1817.
II. Il Giaurro. Milano. 1884.

Polish.

I. Giaur. Puławy. 1830.
II. Giaur. Paryż. 1834.

Romaic.

I. Ποιηματα Βυρωνος ὁ Γκιαουρ. Ἀθηνῃσι. 1873.
II. Σακελλαριου Βιβλιοθηκη τ. Λαου . . . ὁ Γκιαουρ. Ἐν Ἀθηναις. 1898.

Russian.

I. Джяуръ. 1821.
II. Джяуръ. Москва. 1822.
III. Гяуръ. С.-Петербургъ. 1862.
IV. Гяуръ. С.-Петербургъ. 1873.
V. Гяуръ Байрона. С.-Петербургъ. 1874.

Servian.

Ђаур лорда Бајрона. у Новом-Саду. 1860.

Spanish.

El Giaur ó el infiel. Madrid. 1828.

Swedish.

Giaurn. Stockholm. 1855.

HEAVEN AND EARTH.

I. Heaven and Earth, A Mystery. L^n. Benbow. 1824.
II. Heaven and Earth, etc. P. Galignani. 1823.
III. Heaven and Earth, etc. ? W. Dugdale. 1825.

TRANSLATIONS OF HEAVEN AND EARTH.

French.

Essai sur Le Génie, etc. P. Ladvocat. 1824.

Italian.

Cielo e terra. Milano. 1853.

Russian.

Небо и Земля. т. I.

HEBREW MELODIES.

I. A Selection of Hebrew Melodies. L^n. I. Nathan. 1815.
II. Hebrew Melodies. London. *M.* 1815.

III. Hebrew Melodies. Boston. 1815. 24⁰
IV. Hebrew Melodies. Philadelphia. 1815. 16⁰
V. Hebrew Melodies. Lⁿ. W. Dugdale. 1823.
VI. Hebrew Melodies. Lⁿ. W. Dugdale. 1825.

TRANSLATIONS OF HEBREW MELODIES.

Bohemian.

Hebrejské melodie. V Praze. 1890.

Danish.

Lord Byron : Jødiske Sange. Christiania. 1889.

German.

I. Hebräische Gesänge. Berlin. 1820.
II. Hebr. Gesän. Laibach. 1833.
III. Germanische Melodien. Bonn. 1862.
IV. Lord Byron's Heb. Gesän. Karlsruhe. 1863.
V. Heb. Gesän. Memmingen. 1866.

Hebrew.

Hebrew Melodies of Lord Byron. Leipzig. 1890.

Italian.

I. Melodie Ebraiche. Napoli. 1837.
II. Le Mel. ebree. Ivrea. 1855.

Russian.

Еврейскія мелодіи. С.-Петербургъ. 1860.

Swedish.

Hebreiska Melodier. Helsingfors. 1862.

FUGITIVE PIECES AND MINOR POEMS.

I. Fugitive Pieces. A Facsimile Reprint of the Supp. Ed. of 1806. 1886.
II. Poems on Various Occasions. Newark. 1807.
III. Hours of Idleness. Newark. 1807.
IV. Poems Original and Translated. Newark. 1808.
V. Imitations and Translations. Lⁿ. Longman, etc. 1809.
VI. Hours, etc. P. Galignani. 1819.
VII. Hours, etc. Lⁿ. Sherwin and Co. 1820.
VIII. Hours, etc. Third Ed. P. Galignani. 1820.
IX. Hours, etc. Lⁿ. Benbow. 1822.
X. Hours, etc. P. A. and W. Galignani. 1822.
XI. Hours, etc. Glasgow. 1825.
XII. Fugitive Pieces and Reminiscences of Lord Byron. Lⁿ. Whittaker, Treacher, and Co. 1829.

POEMS.

Poems. Second Ed. London. *M.* 1816.

POEMS ON HIS DOMESTIC CIRCUMSTANCES.

I. Poems on His Domestic Circumstances. London. W. Hone. 1816.
II. Poems, etc. Second Ed. L^n. W. Hone. 1816.
III. Poems, etc. Sixth Ed. L^n. W. Hone. 1816.
IV. Poems, etc. Eighth Ed. L^n. W. Hone. 1816.
V. Poems, etc. Fifteenth Ed. L^n. W. Hone. 1816.
VI. L. B.'s Poems on His Own, etc. Dublin. 1816.
VII. Poems on His Domestic, etc. Second Ed. Bristol. 1816.
VIII. Poems on His Domestic, etc. Boston. 1816.
IX. Poems, etc. Twenty-third Ed. L^n. W. Hone. 1817.
X. Poems, etc. L^n. J. Limbird. 1823.
XI. Miscell. Poems, including those on His Domestic, etc. L^n. John Bumpus. 1824.
XII. Miscell. Poems on His Domestic, etc. L^n. William Cole. 1825.

HINTS FROM HORACE.

THE IRISH AVATAR.

THE ISLAND.

I. The Island, or Christian and His Comrades. L^n. John Hunt. 1823.
II. The Island, etc. P. A. and W. Galignani. 1823.
III. The Island, etc. New York. 1823.

TRANSLATIONS OF THE ISLAND.

German.

Die Insel, etc. Leipzig. 1827.

Italian.

L' Isola. Napoli. 1840.

Polish.

Wyspa czyli Chrystyan i jego towarzysze. Kraków. 1859.

Swedish.

Ön Eller Christian, etc. Stockholm. 1856.

THE LAMENT OF TASSO.

I. The Lament of Tasso. London. *M.* 1817.
II. The Lament, etc. Second Ed. London. *M.* 1817.

III. The Lament, etc. Third Ed. London. *M.* 1817.
IV. The Lament, etc. Fourth Ed. London. *M.* 1817.
V. The Lament, etc. Sixth Ed. London. *M.* 1818.

TRANSLATIONS OF THE LAMENT OF TASSO.

Italian.

I. Lamento del Tasso. Pisa. 1818.
II. La Magion del Terrore. Londra. J. Wilson. 1843.
III. Gugl. Godio. Il Lamento, etc. Torino. 1873.

LARA.

I. Lara, A Tale. Jacqueline, A Tale. London. *M.* 1814.
II. Lara, etc. Fourth Ed. London. *M.* 1814.
III. Lara. Boston. 1814.
IV. Lara. New York. 1814.
V. Lara, etc. Fifth Ed. London. *M.* 1817.
VI. Lara, etc. Art Union of London. 1879.

TRANSLATIONS OF LARA.

Bohemian.

Lara. V Praze. 1885.

German.

Lara. Leipzig. 1886.

Italian.

I. Il Lara di L. B. Parigi. 1828.
II. Lara. Milano. 1882.

Polish.

Lara. Wilno. 1833.

Servian.

Лара лорда Бајрона. у Новом-Саду. 1860.

Spanish.

Lara. Paris. 1828.

Swedish.

Lara. Stockholm. 1869.

MANFRED.

I. Manfred. London. *M.* 1817.
II. Manfred. Second Ed. London. *M.* 1817.
III. Manfred. Philadelphia. J. Maxwell. 1817

IV. Manfred. Lⁿ. W. Dugdale. 1824.
V. Manfred. Brussels. Printed at the British Press. *n.d.*
VI. Manfred. A Choral Tragedy. Lⁿ. T. H. Lacy. 1863.
VII. Manfred. Lⁿ. J. Dicks. 1883, etc.

TRANSLATIONS OF MANFRED.

Bohemian.

Manfred. Praze. 1882.

Danish.

I. Manfred. Kjøbenhavn. 1820.
II. Manfred. Kjøbenhavn. 1843.

Dutch.

I. Manfred. Amsterdam. 1857.
II. Byron's Manfred. Heusden. 1882.

French.

I. Manfred. Bruxelles. 1852.
II. Manfred. P. Paul Ollendorff. 1887.
III. Lord Byron. Manfred. Toulouse. 1888.

German.

I. { Manfred. A Tragedy. Leipzig. 1819.
    { Manfred. Trauerspiel. Teutsch v. A. Wagner. Leipzig.
      1819.
II. Manfred. Göttingen. 1836.
III. Byron's Manfred. Breslau. 1839.
IV. Manfred. Berlin. 1843.
V. Lord Byron's Manfred. Leipzig. 1858.
VI. Byron's Manfred. Berlin. 1872.
VII. Manfred. Leipzig. 1871–1876.
VIII. Manfred. Leipzig. 1879–1890.
IX. Manfred. Frankfurt. 1883.

Hungarian.

I. Byron Lord' Élete 's Munkái. Pesten. 1842.
II. Manfred. Szolnok. 1884.
III. Manfred. Budapest. 1891.

Italian.

I. Manfredo. Milano. 1832.
II. Tragedie di Silvio Pellico. Manfredo. Firenze. 1859.
III. Manfredo. Firenze. 1870.

Polish.

I. Manfred. Wrocław. 1835.
II. Manfred. Paryż. 1859.

Romaic.

Ο Μαμφρεδ. Εν Πατραις. 1864.

Roumanian.

Stoenescu (Th. M.) Teatru . . . Manfred. Bucuresci. 1896.

Russian.

 I. Манфредъ.
 II. Манфредъ.
 III. Манфредъ. С.-Петербургъ. 1858.
 IV. Манфредъ.

Spanish.

 I. Manfredo. P. De Decourchant. 1829.
 II. Manfredo. Madrid. 1861.
 III. Lord Byron. Manfredo. Madrid. 1876.

MARINO FALIERO.

 I. Marino Faliero. L^n. *M.* 1821.
 II. Marino Faliero. Second Ed. L^n. *M.* 1821.
 III. Marino Faliero. Philadelphia. 1821.
 IV. Marino Faliero. P. Galignani. 1821.
 V. Marino Faliero. L^n. *M.* [Tilt and Bogue, Edinb.] 1842.
 VI. Marino Faliero. L^n. J. Dicks. 1883, etc.

TRANSLATIONS OF MARINO FALIERO.

German.

 I. Marino Faliero. Frankfurt am Main. 1883.
 II. Lord Byron's Marino Faliero. Oldenburg. *n.d.*

MAZEPPA.

 I. Mazeppa, A Poem. London. *M.* 1819.
 II. Mazeppa, etc. Second Ed. P. Galignani. 1819.
 III. Mazeppa. Boston. 1819.
 IV. Mazeppa. P. Galignani. 1822.
 V. Mazeppa. L^n. W. Dugdale. 1824.
 VI. Mazeppa. Braunschweig. 1834.
 VII. Mazeppa. L^n. T. Goode. 1854.

TRANSLATIONS OF MAZEPPA.

Danish.

Mazeppa. Stockholm. 1853.

German.

I. Mazeppa. Leipzig. 1820.
II. Mazeppa. Göttingen. 1836.
III. Mazeppa. Stuttgart. 1883.

Hungarian.

Byron Lord' Élete 's munkái. Pesten. 1842.

Italian.

I. Il Mazeppa. Palermo. 1847.
II. Mazeppa. Palermo. 1876.
III. Mazeppa. Milano. 1886.

Polish.

I. Mazepa. W. Hali. 1860.
II. Mazepa. Paryż. 1860.

Russian.

I. Выборъ изъ сочиненій лорда Байрона. 1821.
II. Мазепа.
III. Мазепа.
IV. Мазепа. С.-Петербургъ. 1860.

Spanish.

Mazeppa, novela. Paris. 1830.

MONODY ON THE DEATH OF . . . SHERIDAN.

I. Monody, etc. Lⁿ. *M.* 1816.
II. Monody, etc. New Ed. Lⁿ. *M.* 1817.
III. Monody, etc. New Ed. Lⁿ. *M.* 1818.

AN ODE TO THE FRAMERS OF THE FRAME BILL.

A Political Ode. Lⁿ. J. Pearson. 1880.

ODE FROM THE FRENCH.

TRANSLATION.

French.

Traduction de l'Ode. Londres. 1826.

ODE TO NAPOLEON BUONAPARTE.

I. Ode to Napoleon Buonaparte. London. *M.* 1814.
II. An Ode to N. B. Philadelphia. E. Earle. 1814.

III. Ode to N. B.   Sixth Ed.   London.   *M*. 1814.
IV. Ode to N. B.   Ninth Ed.   London.   *M*. 1814.
V. Ode to N. B.   Twelfth Ed.   London.   *M*. 1816.
VI. Ode to N. B.   Thirteenth Ed.   London.   *M*. 1818.

TRANSLATION OF THE ODE TO NAPOLEON BUONAPARTE.

Spanish.

Odas a Napoleon.   P.   De Decourchant.   1829.

PARISINA.

TRANSLATIONS.

Danish.

Parisina.   Stockholm.   1854.

French.

Parisina.   Adolphe Krafft.   P.   Ernest Leroux.   1900.

German.

Parisina.   Gedichte von J. V. Cirkel.   Münster.   1825.

Italian.

I. Parisina.   Milano.   1821.
II. Parisina.   Milano.   1853.
III. Parisina.   Mantova.   1854.
IV. Parisina.   Palermo.   1855.
V. Parisina.   Genova.   1864.

Russian.

Паризина.   С.-Петербургъ.   1827.

Spanish.

Parisina.   P.   Imp. de Decourchant.   1830.

THE PRISONER OF CHILLON.

I. The Prisoner of Chillon.   London.   *M*. 1816.
II. The P. of Chillon.   Lausanne.   1818.
III. The P. of Chillon.   L^n.   W. Chubb.   1824.
IV. The P. of Chillon.   L^n.   ? 1825.
V. The P. of Chillon.   Geneva.   1830.
VI. The P. of Chillon.   Lausanne.   1857.
VII. The P. of Chillon.   Illuminated.   L^n.   W. & G. Audsley. 1865.
VIII. Byron's P. of Chillon.   L^n.   T. J. Allman.   1874.
IX. Byron's P. of Chillon.   L^n.   Simpkin, Marshall, and Co. 1877.

X. The P. of Chillon. L^n. Blackie and Son. 1879.
XI. Byron's P. of Chillon. L^n. Simpkin, Marshall, and Co. 1879.
XII. The P. of Chillon. Vevey. 1880.
XIII. The P. of Chillon. Berlin. 1884.
XIV. The P. of Chillon. Firenze. 1885.
XV. Byron's P. of Chillon. L^n. and Edinb. 1894.
XVI. The P. of Chillon. L^n. Stewart and Co. *n.d.*
XVII. The P. of Chillon. L^n. and Glasg. Blackie and Son. 1896.
XVIII. Byron. The Prisoner of Chillon. Dublin. 1896.
XIX. The P. of Chillon. Weimar. 1896.

TRANSLATIONS OF THE PRISONER OF CHILLON.

Dutch.

De Gevangene van Chillon. Gent. 1856.

French.

I. Le Prisonnier de Chillon. Vevey. *n.d.*
II. Bonnivard A Chillon. Le P. de Ch. Genève. 1892.

German.

I. Lord Byron's Gefangener von Chillon. Lausanne. 1861.
II. Der Gefangene von Chillon. Vevey and Lausanne. 1865.
III. Der Gefangene von Chillon. Berlin. 1886.
IV. Der Gefangene von Chillon. St Gallen and Leipzig. 1892.

Italian.

I. Il prigionero di Chillon. Milano. 1830.
II. Il prigionero di Chillon. Milano. 1853.

Russian.

Шильонскій Узникъ. С.-Петербургъ. 1822.

Spanish.

El preso de Chillon. Paris. 1829.

Swedish.

Fången På Chillon. Stockholm. 1853.

THE PROPHECY OF DANTE.

I. The Prophecy of Dante. Philadelphia. 1821.
II. The Pr. of Dante. P. Galignani. 1821.
III. The Pr. of Dante. L^n. W. Dugdale. 1825.
IV. The Pr. of Dante. L^n. Blackie and Son. 1879.

TRANSLATIONS OF THE PROPHECY OF DANTE.

French.

Œuvres de Dante Alighieri. La Pr. du Dante. P. Charpentier. 1842.

Italian.

I. Profezia di Dante. P. Barrois. 1821.
II. La Profezia di Dante. Nuova-Jorca. 1821.
III. La Pr. di Dante. Milano. 1856.
IV. La Pr. di Dante. Milano. 1858.

Spanish.

La Profecia del Dante. Mexico. 1850.

SARDANAPALUS.

I. Sardanapalus, . . . The Two Foscari, . . . Cain. London. M. 1821.
II. Sardanapalus, The Two Foscari, Cain. Boston. 1822.
III. Sardanapalus. London. M. 1829.
IV. Sardanapalus. Arnsberg. 1849.
V. Sardanapalus. L^n. T. H. Lacy. 1853.
VI. L. B.'s Hist. Tragedy of Sardanapalus. Manchester. 1877.
VII. Sardanapalus. L^n. J. Dicks. 1883, etc.

TRANSLATIONS OF SARDANAPALUS.

Bohemian.

Sardanapal. V Praze. 1891.

French.

Sardanapale. Bruxelles. 1834.

German.

I. Sardanapal. Posen. 1854.
II. Sardanapal. Jena. 1888.
III. Lord Byron's Sardanapal. Berlin. 1897.

Italian.

Sardanapalo. Milano. 1884.

Polish.

Sardanapal. Warszawa. 1872.

Romaic.

Σαρδαναπαλος. Εν Αθηναις. 1865.

Russian.

I. Сарданапалъ. С.-Петербургъ. 1860.
II. Сарданапалъ.

Swedish.

Sardanapalus. Stockholm. 1864.

THE SIEGE OF CORINTH.

I. The Siege of Corinth. London. *M.* 1816.
II. The Siege, etc. New York. 1816.
II. The Siege, etc. L^n. W. Dugdale. 1824.
IV. The Siege, etc. Lüneburg. 1854.
V. The Siege, etc. L^n. Nat. Soc. Depository. 1879.
VI. Byron's Siege of Corinth. Berlin. 1893.
VII. The Siege, etc. Bielefeld. 1885-1890.

TRANSLATIONS OF THE SIEGE OF CORINTH.

Dutch.

Het Beleg van Corinthe. Amsterdam. 1831.

French.

Le Siége de Corinthe. P. Pillet aîné. 1820.

German.

I. Die Belagerung von Korinth. Hamburg. 1817.
II. Die Belagerung v. K. Leipzig. 1820.
III. Die Belagerung v. K. Hamburg. 1827.

Italian.

L'Assedio di Corinto. Venezia. 1838.

Spanish.

El Sitio de Corinto. P. Lib. Americana. 1828.

Swedish.

Belägringen Af Korinth. Stockholm. 1854.

THE TWO FOSCARI.

I. The Two Foscari. New York. 1822.
II. The Two Foscari. P. Galignani. 1822.
III. The Two Foscari. L^n. J. Dicks, etc. 1883.

TRANSLATIONS OF THE TWO FOSCARI.

Russian.

Двое Фоскари.

Spanish.

Los dos Fóscaris. Biblioteca Dramatica. Madrid. 1846.

THE VISION OF JUDGMENT.

I. Vision of Judgment. P. Galignani. 1822.
II. The Two Visions. L^n. W. Dugdale. 1822.

THE WALTZ.

I. Waltz : An Apostrophic Hymn. L^n. Printed by S. Gosnell. 1813.
II. Waltz, etc. L^n. Benbow. 1821.

WERNER.

I. Werner, A Tragedy. London. *M.* 1823.
II. Werner. P. Galignani. 1823.
III. Werner. New York. 1848.
IV. The British Drama (Werner, Vol. iii. pp. 767–789). L^n. John Dicks. 1865.
V. Werner. L^n. J. Dicks. 1883, etc.
VI. Werner. L^n. George Routledge. 1887.

TRANSLATIONS OF WERNER.

Russian.

I. Вернеръ. С.-Петербургъ. 1829.
II. Донъ-Жуанъ. Москва. 1881.

THE LIBERAL.

The Liberal [Vols. I., II.]. L^n. John Hunt. 1822, 1823.

Dedication of Don Juan. L^n. Effingham Wilson. 1833.

THE PRISON CALLED TASSO'S CELL, IN THE HOSPITAL OF SANT' ANNA, AT FERRARA.

[*To face p.* 348.

INDEX.

The figures in italics refer to the notes only.

———◆———

O

S

VOL. VII.

3 K

INDEX TO FIRST LINES.

————◆◇◆————

(The first line is given of every *Poem*, and of each *Canto* of the longer
Poems: that of the *Plays* is omitted.)

THE END.

PRINTED BY WILLIAM CLOWES AND SONS, LIMITED, LONDON AND BECCLES.